The Best Bed & Breakfast in England, Scotland & Wales

2007–2008

Joanna Mortimer

Sigourney Welles

Jill Darbey

The finest Bed & Breakfast accommodations in the
British Isles
from the Scottish Hebrides to
London's Belgravia
Country Houses, Town Houses, City Apartments, Manor Houses,
Village Cottages, Farmhouses, Castles

The Globe Pequot Press, Guilford, Connecticut, U.S.A.

All editorial photographs appear courtesy of britainonview.

Library of congress catalogue No. 0-7627-3982-7

ISBN 0-7627-4294-1. ISBN 978-0-7627-4294-3

Published in North America by The Globe Pequot Press.

Printed and bound in China. Produced by Phoenix Offset Ltd.

Contents

Foreword

Bed and Breakfast is a great way to travel and a fantastic way to see the fabulous British countryside. Today thousands of people are discovering for themselves that it is possible to combine high quality accommodation with friendly, personal attention at very reasonable prices. The New York Times said about us that "...after an unannounced inspection of rooms booked through The Worldwide Bed & Breakfast Association it is clear that the standards of comfort and cleanliness are exemplary ...at least as good as in a five star hotel and in most cases, better, reflecting the difference between sensitive hosts taking pride in their homes and itinerant hotel staff doing as little as they can get away with..."

Discerning travellers are turning away from the impersonal hotels with the expensive little refrigerators and microwave breakfasts in each room. How much nicer to have a real English breakfast to begin the day, enough to keep you going until evening. Many of our houses will provide dinner too - often the hostess will be a Cordon Bleu cook and the price will be within your budget. We try to provide the best accommodation possible within a wide range of prices, some as little as £25.00 per person per night, whilst others will be up to £100 per person per night. The choice is yours, but you can be certain that each will be the best available in that particular area of the country at that price.

We inspect all the accommodation recommended in this guide. We have our own inspectors who ensure that standards are maintained. And we want to hear from you if you have been disappointed in any way by your accommodation. We encourage everyone to use the recommendations and complaints pages at the back of the book. Let us know your opinion of the accommodation or inform us of any delightful homes you may have come across and would like to recommend for future inclusion. In order to avoid masses of classification signs and symbols we simply say that each establishment has passed our inspection so you can be sure it is very clean, in good condition and properly run. Then we encourage you to read about each home, what they offer and their respective price range, so that you find the one that best suits your expectations. Our hosts in turn offer hospitality in their own unique style, so each home naturally retains its individuality and interest. We have found this to be a very successful recipe which often leads to lasting friendships.

Bed and Breakfast really is a marvellous way to travel, meeting a delightful cross section of fellow travellers with whom to exchange information and maybe an address or two. This is the fun and real pleasure that is part of Bed and Breakfasting. Once you've tried it you will be a dedicated Best Bed and Breakfaster.

How to use this guide

To get the full benefits of staying at our Bed & Breakfast homes it is important to appreciate how they differ from hotels, so both hosts & guests know what to expect.

Arrival & Departure

These times are more important to a family than to hotel desk clerks, so your time of arrival (E.T.A.) is vital information when making a reservation either with the home directly or with one of our agencies. This becomes even more important to your reception if you intend travelling overnight & will be arriving in the early morning. So please have this information & your flight number ready when you book your rooms. At most B & Bs the *usual check-in time is 6 P.M. & you will be expected to check out by 10 A.M.* on the morning of departure. These arrangements do vary from home to home. The secret to an enjoyable visit is to let your hosts know as much about your plans as possible & they will do their best to meet your requirements Further details you should let your hosts know when planning your trip are; Do you prefer to be in a non-smoking home? Do you suffer from any allergies? Can you make it up a flight of stairs? Any special dietary requirements? Do you prefer an ensuite bathroom? Do you prefer a shower instead of a bath? The ages of any children travelling. Will you be staying for dinner? In all these cases let your host know what you need & the details can be arranged before you arrive.

Prices

The prices quoted throughout the guide are per double room per night based on two persons sharing. Single occupancy usually attracts a supplement. Prices will increase during busy seasons. Always confirm the prevailing rate when making a reservation.

Rooms

Rooms are described as follows:
Single:1 bed (often quite small).
Double:1 large bed (sometimes King or Queen size)
Twin: 2 separate single beds.
Four-poster: a King or Queen size bed with a canopy above supported by four corner posts.
Bathrooms and toilets are described as:
Shared: these facilities are shared with some other guests or perhaps the hosts.
Private: for your use only, however they may occasionally be in an adjacent room.
En-suite: private facilities within your bedroom suite.

Key

The following symbols are used throughout this guide.

⊖ = smoking is not allowed

🔔 = evening meals are provided

🐾 = children are welcome

🐾 = pets are welcome

How to make a reservation

Making a Reservation

Once you have chosen where you want to stay, have all the following information ready & your reservation will go smoothly. Here is a brief check list of questions you will probably be asked
Dates: check in & check out.
Flight number.
Estimated time of arrival at the home?
Type & number of rooms?
Toilet & Bathroom facilities?
Smoking or non-smoking?.
Any allergies?
Special dietary requests?.
Number of children in the party & ages?
Any other preferences?

Reservations Outside London

We encourage you to make use of the information in this guide & on our website

www.bestbandb.co.uk Outside London hosts may require varying amounts of advance payment. Remember, many B & Bs are small, family-run establishments and are not always able to accept payment by credit card. The confirmed prices shall be those prevailing on the dates required. *The rates shown in this guide are sometimes subject to change. You must confirm the rate when booking your accommodation.*

Cancellation

Notice of cancellation must be given as soon as possible & the following notice of cancellation & the following suggested rates shall apply outside London only;
0 ....9 days notice   no   refund
10 ....29 days notice   50% refund
30 ....49 days notice   80% refund

The Discount Offer

This offer is made to people who have bought this year's book & wish to make reservations for Bed & Breakfast in London through our London Reservation Agency. The offer only applies to a minimum stay of three consecutive nights at one of our London homes between the dates of;
January 07. 2007 to April 01. 2007
September 15. 2007 to December 01 2007
Only one discount per booking is allowed. Call the reservation office to make your booking in the normal way & tell the clerk that you have bought the book & wish to have the discount. After a couple of questions the discount will be deducted.

London reservation agency

We offer an outstanding selection of accommodation in London. As with all our accommodation each one has been personally inspected so you can be sure of the highest standards. We offer an immensely wide range of accommodation. We have a type, style and location to suit everyone. From city apartments close to shops, museums and galleries to spacious homes in leafy residential suburbs near the river, parks and restaurants. No matter what your reason for visiting London we can accommodate you. Whether on business or vacation the Best Bed & Breakfast provides great accommodation together with a fast, efficient reservation service. Our helpful staff are always happy to advise you on all your accommodation requirements. We are located in London, we know the city and all our hosts. We know how to provide an enjoyable, affordable, hassle free trip. There are plenty of ways to contact us. To make a reservation simply do one of the following;
e-mail bestbandb@atlas.co.uk
www.bestbandb.co.uk
tel.:+ 44 (0)20 7243 8720
tel.:+ 44 (0)20 7243 8722
fax:+ 44 (0)20 7243 8736

The London Reservation Agency
There is a minimum two night consecutive stay at our London homes. Reservations for London homes can only be made through one of our Worldwide Bed & Breakfast Agencies. They can be contacted by 'phone, fax, e-mail or on-line www.bestbandb.co.uk. All reservations must be confirmed with advance payments which are non-refundable in the event of cancellation. You simply pay the balance due after you arrive at the home. The advance payment can be made with major credit & charge cards or by cheque. Cash is the preferred method of paying the balance & always in pounds sterling.

The advance payments confirm each night of your visit, not just the first one. When arriving at a later date or departing at an earlier date than those confirmed, the guest will be liable to pay only the appropriate proportion of the stated balance that is due. For example, staying three nights out of four booked means paying 3/4 of the stated balance due. The advance payment is non-refundable. A minimum of 2 nights will always apply.

Alterations
If you wish to alter or change a previously confirmed booking through one of the agencies there will be a further fee of £15.00.

Cancellations
All advance payments for London are non-refundable. The Worldwide Bed & Breakfast Agencies reserve the right to alter your accommodation should it be necessary & will inform you of any alteration as soon as possible.

Counties map

Each county has been assigned a page number where a more detailed map can be found. These maps include principal towns, major roads & the location of each Bed & Breakfast establishment.

SCOTLAND 298

1 INVERCLYDE
2 DUNBARTON & CLYDEBANK
3 RENFREWSHIRE
4 EAST RENFREWSHIRE
5 GLASGOW
6 EAST DUNBARTONSHIRE

7 NORTH LANARKSHIRE
8 FALKIRK
9 CLACKMANNAN
10 WEST LOTHIAN
11 EDINBURGH
12 MID LOTHAIN

North Sea

Irish Sea

ENGLAND

WALES 334

1 BRIDGEND
2 RHONDA CYNON TAFF
3 MERTHYR TYDFIL
4 CAERPHILLY
5 BLAENAU GWENT
6 TORFAEN

English Channel

General Information

To help overseas visitors with planning their trip to Britain, we have compiled the next few pages explaining the basic requirements & customs you will find here.

Before you arrive

Documents you will have to obtain before you arrive; Valid passports & visas. Citizens of Commonwealth countries or the U.S.A. do not need visas to enter the U.K. Bring your local Driving Licence.

Medical Insurance.-This is strongly recommended although visitors will be able to receive free emergency treatment. If you have to stay in hospital in the U.K. you will be asked to pay unless you are a citizen of the European Community.

Restrictions on arrival

Immigration procedures can be lengthy & bothersome, be prepared for questions a) where are you staying in the U.K.? b) do you have a round trip ticket c) how long do you intend to stay? d) how much money are you bringing in? e) do you have a credit card?

Do not bring any animals with you as they are often subject to 6 months quarantine & there are severe penalties for bringing in pets without appropriate licences. Do not bring any firearms, prohibited drugs or carry these things for anyone else. If you are in doubt about items in your possession, declare them at Customs.

After you have arrived

You can bring in as much currency as you like. You can change your own currency or travellers cheques at many places at varying rates. Airports tend to be the most expensive places to change money & the 'Bureau de Change" are often closed at nights. Bring enough Sterling to last you at least 2 or 3 days. Banks often charge commission for changing money. Most Cashcard machines (or A.T.M.'s) will dispense local currency using your charge card, if they are affiliated systems, & don't charge commissions to your account. Major credit cards/charge cards are widely accepted & you may only need to carry small amounts of cash for "pocket money".

Driving

Don't forget to drive on the Left... especially the first time you get into a car... at the airport car hire parking lot... or from the front of a railway station... or straight after breakfast... old habits are hard to shake off. If you need to know the rules, get a copy of the Highway Code. You must wear a seat belt & so must any other front seat passenger. The speed limits are clearly shown in most areas - generally 30 mph. in residential areas (48 kph) & 70 mph on motorways (113 kph.). Traffic lights are usually at the side of the road & not hanging overhead. Car hire is relatively expensive in the U.K. & it is often a good idea to arrange this before you arrive. Mileage charges, V.A.T. (Sales Tax) & insurance are usually charged extra & you will need to be over 21 to hire a car in the

General Information

U.K. Petrol (gas) is also relatively expensive & you may find petrol stations hard to find or closed at night in rural areas... so fill up often. Driving in London is not a recommended experience for newcomers & parking is also a very expensive.

Buses & Coaches

If you are not driving & only want to travel 5-10 miles there are good bus services within most towns & cities, however, rural routes have seriously declined over the last few years. There are regular & fast coach services between the major towns which are very popular - so book ahead to be sure of a seat.

Trains

There is an extensive railway system throughout the U.K. which serves the major towns on a fast & frequent basis. These services can be expensive unless you book in advance & like most railway systems are subject to delays.

Tubes (Subways)

London is the only city with an extensive subway system although some other towns do have "Metro" trains of linked under & overground systems. The "tube" is a very popular means of getting around London, but it can get very crowded & unpleasant at "rush hours". It is often the preferred way to get into London from Heathrow Airport in the early morning, when there are long delays on the roads that hold up both buses & taxis. The "tube" in London is operated by London Transport which also operates the London bus service ... the famous red buses. Most newsagents sell tickets which allow you to travel all over London on tubes, buses & trains at very good rates, called Oystercards... a transfer system.

Telephones

When calling the U.K. from abroad always drop the 0 from the area code. In the U.K. the only free calls are the emergency services - 999. You may use your calling card to call home or call collect, ask the operator to "reverse charge" the call. The internet can now be accessed from some public phone booths. Phonecards are becoming more popular as the number of boxes that only accept these cards increases. Cards can be bought at Post Offices & many newsagents & shops.

Doctors/Chemists

All local police stations have lists of chemists & doctors.

Voltage

The standard voltage throughout the country is 240v AC.50Hz. If you bring small electrical appliances with you, a converter will be required.

Tipping

Is not obligatory but if you wish to tip for service it is generally between 10%-15%.

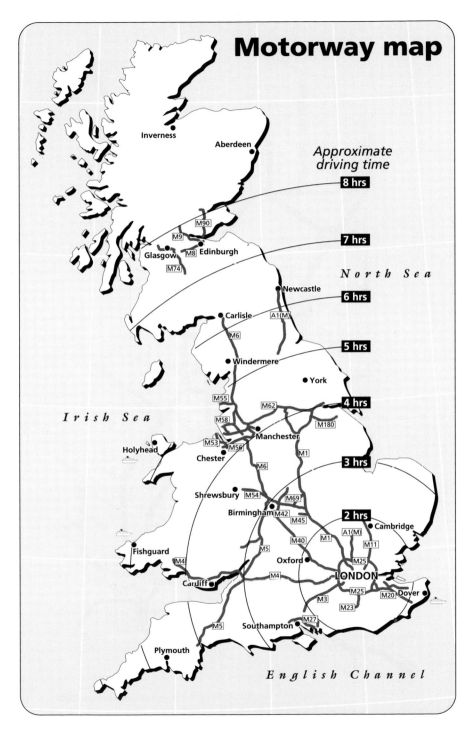

Motorway map

Approximate driving time

8 hrs
7 hrs
6 hrs
5 hrs
4 hrs
3 hrs
2 hrs

Inverness

Aberdeen

North Sea

M90

M9

M8 Edinburgh

Glasgow

M74

Newcastle

A1(M)

Carlisle

M6

Windermere

York

Irish Sea

M55

M62

M58

M180

M53

M56 Manchester

Holyhead

Chester

M1

M6

Shrewsbury

M54

M69

Birmingham M42

M45

M5

M40

M1

A1(M) Cambridge

M11

Fishguard

M4

Oxford

M25

LONDON

Cardiff

M4

M25

M3

M20 Dover

M23

Southampton M27

M5

Plymouth

English Channel

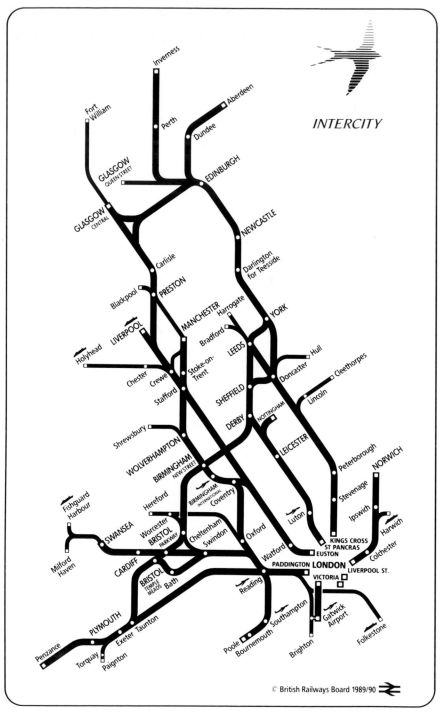

INTERCITY

© British Railways Board 1989/90

TLB/90/1008

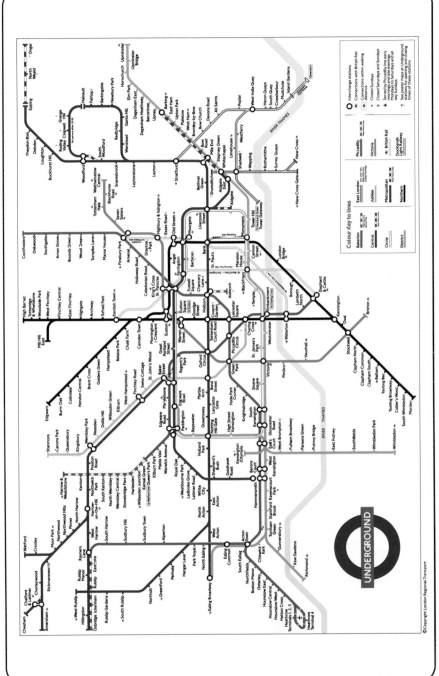

London

London is totally unique. A busy, vibrant city, offering a mix of the traditional & the cutting edge. Here diversity & difference is everyday life.

This is the city for world-class art, exhibitions, beautiful landmark buildings & parks, gourmet cuisine, designer fashions, award-winning theatre productions and more.

Many of the museums are free to enter and all have thousands of exhibits. The British Museum displays enormous collections of antiquities from prehistoric to the bronze & iron ages to the 20th century. The British Library houses the Magna Carta & Shakespeare's first folio amongst others. For budding scientists The Science Museum provides the opportunity to try over 2000 interactive exhibits; it is largest museum of its kind in the world. The National Gallery houses one of the greatest collections of European painting in the world. Tate Modern is Britain's national museum of modern art. It not only has wonderful pieces by artists like Matisse and Picasso but also shows contemporary works & installations. The wonderful Victoria & Albert Museum is home to 3000 years worth of artefacts from many of the world's richest cultures.

For a panoramic view of London, visit the London Eye, which is situated across the river from the Houses of Parliament. On a fine day you can see over 30 of London's landmark buildings.

There are plenty of open spaces to enjoy in London too. From Regents Park, designed in 1811 by John Nash, & home to an open-air theatre with productions from May to Sept. & London Zoo to Hyde Park with its Serpentine Gallery, boating lakes & Speaker's Corner.

If shopping is your passion, then look no further as London has over 30,000 shops ranging from the affordable to designer fashions, all set to tempt you. Oxford Street has over 300 stores, while Bond Street is home to many upmarket jewellers & fashion houses.

Covent Garden, in the heart of theatreland, has an eclectic mix of small speciality stores, designer craft markets, cafes & restaurants.

London

Galleries

Barbican Art Gallery - Silk Street EC2
A changing programme of major photography, fine art and design exhibitions.

Bayswater Road Artists - Bayswater Road W2
Almost a mile long with hundreds of artists and craftsmen selling their own original work. Open every Sunday throughout the year, rain or shine.

Dali Universe - County Hall South Bank SE1
Over 500 works by the surrealist master Salvador Dali, the exhibition features the Lobster Telephone, Mae West Lips Sofa and the original canvas in the Hitchcock film, 'Spellbound'.

Estorick Collection - 39A Canonbury Square N1
Collection of paintings and sculpture by 20thC Italian artists. Futurist works by Balla, Boccioni, Carra, Russolo and Severini. The collection also includes figurative art and sculpture created between 1890 and 1950 by artists such as Modigliani, Marino Marini, Giorgio Morandi and Giorgio de Chirico.

Guildhall Art Gallery - Guildhall Yard EC2
Collection of 17th, 18th, 19th and 20thC. works of art. Fine architecture and a sumptuous setting for an important and varied collection of paintings, located in the heart of the City. Works by Constable, Landseer, Rossetti, Tissot and Millais.

Hayward Gallery - South Bank Centre SE1
Shows four exhibitions of international stature annually. The Gallery specialises in the works of modern masters and the most exciting names in contemporary art. Western European painting from about 1250-1900. Includes work by Botticelli, Leonardo da Vinci, Rembrandt, Gainsborough, Turner, Renoir, Cezanne and Van Gogh.

National Portrait Gallery - St Martin's Place WC2
Portraits in all mediums, depict famous and infamous British men and women from the Tudors to the present day.

Queen's Gallery - Buckingham Palace SW1
Works of art from the Royal Collection. In addition to the Treasures of the Royal Collection.

Queen's House - Romney Road SE1
The first classical-style house in England, by Inigo Jones. Paintings include Canaletto.

Royal Academy of Arts - Piccadilly W1
One of the finest galleries in London with a changing programme of exhibitions.

The Saatchi Gallery - Chelsea SW3
(Opening Summer 2007) An innovative forum for contemporary art, presenting work by largely unseen young artists or by established international artists whose work has been rarely if ever exhibited in the UK.

Tate Britain - Millbank SW1
The national gallery of British art from 1500 to the present day. Tate holds the greatest collection of British art in the world including works by Constable, Gainsborough, Gilbert and George, Hockney, Hodgkin, Hogarth, Moore, Rossetti and Turner and many, many more.

Tate Modern - Bankside SE1
International modern and contemporary art, including major works by Matisse, Picasso and Rothko and contemporary work by artists such as Matthew Barney, Chris Ofili and Gerhard Richter.

London

Museums

Bank of England Museum - Bartholomew Lane EC2

Museum housed within the Bank of England traces the history of the Bank from its foundation by Royal Charter in 1694 to its role today as the nation's central bank. Gold bars dating from ancient times, coins, a unique collection of banknotes.

Ben Uri Gallery - 108a Boundary Road NW8

The London Jewish Museum of Art was founded in 1915, it is Europe's only dedicated Jewish museum of art.

British Museum - Great Russell Street WC1

Founded in 1753 by Act of Parliament, from the collections of Sir Hans Sloane, One of the great museums of the world, showing the works of man from prehistoric to modern times with collections drawn from the whole world. Famous objects include the Rosetta Stone, sculptures from the Parthenon, the Sutton Hoo and Mildenhall treasures and the Portland Vase.

Florence Nightingale Museum - SE1

Florence Nightingale is famous around the world for her influence on modern nursing.

Handel House Museum - 25 Brook Street W1

Handel House Museum was home to George Frideric Handel from 1723 until his death in 1759. It was here that Handel composed 'Messiah', 'Zadok the Priest' and 'Music for the Royal Fireworks'.

Museum of the Garden-Lambeth Palace Rd SE1

Houses a unique collection, telling the story of the history of gardening and the work of celebrated gardeners. Special focus is given to the Tradescant family, gardeners to Charles I and Charles II.

Museum of London - 150 London Wall EC2

Discover over 2000 years of the capital's history from prehistoric to modern times. Highlights include the Roman gallery, reconstructed Victorian walk including shops, Newgate prison, the Great Fire Experience and a display of Elizabethan jewellery.

National Maritime Museum-Romney Rd SE10

This national museum explains Britain's worldwide influence through its explorers, traders, migrants and naval power.

Natural History Museum - Cromwell Rd SW7

Hundreds of exciting, interactive exhibits. Highlights include 'Dinosaurs', the ultimate dinosaur exhibition; 'Creepy-Crawlies', 'Human Biology', an exhibition about ourselves; 'Ecology' and 'Mammals', with its unforgettable blue whale. 'The Power Within', offering an 'earthquake experience'.

Victoria and Albert Museum-Cromwell Rd SW7

Ceramics, furniture, fashion, glass, jewellery, metalwork, photographs, sculpture, textiles and paintings. Where else but the V&A, the greatest museum of art and design, home to 3000 years of artefacts from many of the world's richest cultures. National collection of paintings by Constable, the largest collection of Italian Renaissance sculpture outside Italy and the stunning British Galleries, illustrating the history of Britain through the country's art and design.

Home No. 01
Best Bed & Breakfast
PO Box 31655   London W11 4WR
Tel: +44 (0)20-7243-8720   Fax: +44 (0)20-7243-8736

Nearest Tube: Putney Bridge
This is an attractive Victorian terraced house, situated in a quiet residential street in Fulham, yet only 3 mins' walk from the station. Offering 1 spacious double-bedded room with an en-suite bathroom & a twin-bedded room with a private bathroom. Each room is comfortable, tastefully furnished & has a colour T.V. & hairdryer. Breakfast is served in the very pleasant dining room. There are many good restaurants & shops within a short walking distance. An excellent location from which to explore London with good transport links. Parking by arrangement (separate charge). Children by arrangement.

bestbandb@atlas.co.uk
www.bestbandb.co.uk
64.00 - £80.00

Home No. 14
Best Bed & Breakfast
PO Box 31655   London W11 4WR
Tel: +44 (0)20-7243-8720   Fax: +44 (0)20-7243-8736

Nearest Tube: Marble Arch
Situated in the heart of central London, yet in a surprisingly quiet location, this modern townhouse is the perfect place from which to explore this vibrant city. The charming host offers 3 spacious & attractively furnished double, twin-bedded or family rooms (1 King-size), each with T.V. & tea/coffee & en-suite facilities. Close by are a myriad of cafes, bars & restaurants to suit all tastes & budgets. Meander through Hyde Park, browse in exclusive Mayfair boutiques or visit a host of attractions; all are within easy reach from this comfortable home. Easy access to Paddington station for the Heathrow Express.

bestbandb@atlas.co.uk
www.bestbandb.co.uk
£74.00 - £110.00

see p.18

Home No. 08
Best Bed & Breakfast
PO Box 31655   London W11 4WR
Tel: +44 (0)20-7243-8720   Fax: +44 (0)20-7243-8736

Nearest Tube: Maida Vale
An attractive Victorian maisonette very well situated only 3 mins' walk from the tube. Offering 1 spacious & comfortably furnished twin-bedded room with T.V., tea/coffee-making facilities & an en-suite shower room. Breakfast is served in the pleasant dining area looking out onto the pretty garden. Good local pubs & restaurants. An excellent location providing easy access to many attractions; with a direct tube link to Piccadilly Circus & the Embankment. Also, Paddington Station for the Heathrow Express to the airport.

bestbandb@atlas.co.uk
www.bestbandb.co.uk
£70.00 - £88.00

Home No. 17
Best Bed & Breakfast
PO Box 31655   London W11 4WR
Tel: +44 (0)20-7243-8720   Fax: +44 (0)20-7243-8736

Nearest Tube: Richmond
Situated in an excellent 17th-century terrace, this is an outstanding home, elegantly furnished throughout with antiques. 3 guest rooms: 1 double 4-poster, 1 twin-bedded room & a triple with a 4-poster & a single bed. Each has a super private bathroom. 2 of the bedrooms have French doors leading onto an Italiante garden, the triple room commands views of the Thames. Historic Richmond with its wealth of shops & riverside restaurants are a few mins walk. Easy access to central London. Waterloo 12 mins by train. Heathrow Airport 20 mins by taxi.

bestbandb@atlas.co.uk
www.bestbandb.co.uk
£90.00 - £160.00

Home 17

London

Tel: +44 (0)20-7243-8720 Fax: +44 (0)20-7243-8736

email:bestbandb@atlas.co.uk www.bestbandb.co.uk

see p.20

Home No. 18
Best Bed & Breakfast
PO Box 31655   London W11 4WR
Tel: +44 (0)20-7243-8720   Fax: +44 (0)20-7243-8736

Nearest Tube: High St. Kensington
A beautiful house, furnished with many interesting paintings & situated in the heart of Kensington. The charming host offers 1 light & airy, twin-bedded room with a good private bathroom. There is also another, equally attractive twin-bedded room, across the hall, which is ideal for a third or fourth member of the party. Each bedroom is well-furnished & a colour T.V. is available. Only a short walk from the High Street with its many shops & restaurants & within easy reach of Kensington Palace & gardens, Knightsbridge & the museums at South Kensington. Children by over 5 years. Parking by arrangement (separate fee.)

bestbandb@atlas.co.uk
www.bestbandb.co.uk
£70.00 - £90.00

Home No. 39
Best Bed & Breakfast
PO Box 31655   London W11 4WR
Tel: +44 (0)20-7243-8720   Fax: +44 (0)20-7243-8736

Nearest Tube: Earls Court
A superb home situated in Kensington, which has been designer decorated & furnished to the highest standard with antiques throughout. The accommodation includes 2 double & 1 twin bedded room. Each beautiful bedroom is large & airy with a lovely bathroom en-suite, T.V. & tea/coffee facilities. An elegant dining room. A delightful garden where breakfast can be served if the weather is good. Guests have their own private entrance. A good location only 10 mins. to Harrods by tube. Parking by arrangement (separate fee.) Children over 12 years. Easy access to Heathrow Airport by tube.

bestbandb@atlas.co.uk
www.bestbandb.co.uk
£98.00 - £130.00

Home No. 31
Best Bed & Breakfast
PO Box 31655   London W11 4WR
Tel: +44 (0)20-7243-8720   Fax: +44 (0)20-7243-8736

Nearest Tube: Parsons Green
A charming Victorian terraced house, situated only 12 minutes from many excellent shops & restaurants in Fulham. The welcoming host has elegantly furnished this property throughout. Accommodation is in 1 attractive double-bedded room. It is very comfortable & has a good private bathroom. There is also a cosy single room for a third member of the party. A Continental breakfast is served. Situated only a short walk from the station & transport links, this is an excellent base from which to explore London. Children over 12 years.

bestbandb@atlas.co.uk
www.bestbandb.co.uk
£60.00 - £80.00

Home No. 44
Best Bed & Breakfast
PO BOX 31655   London W11 4WR
Tel: +44 (0)20-7243-8720   Fax: +44 (0)20-7243-8736

Nearest Tube: Richmond
Situated in the heart of delightful Richmond this really is the perfect location for a relaxing break in London. The charming host, who is an interior designer has refurbished this Victorian home & offers 1 gorgeous double-bedded room which has a superb private bathroom adjacent. Delicious Continental breakfasts are served in the lovely kitchen/diner which overlooks a pretty plantsmans garden. Richmond abounds with fashionable shops & restaurants. Within easy reach of several stately homes. Transport facilities are excellent & Waterloo is 15 mins by train.

bestbandb@atlas.co.uk
www.bestbandb.co.uk
£74.00 - £90.00

Home 39

London

Tel: +44 (0)20-7243-8720 Fax: +44 (0)20-7243-8736

email:bestbandb@atlas.co.uk   www.bestbandb.co.uk

Home No. 48
Best Bed & Breakfast
PO Box 31655   London W11 4WR
Tel: +44 (0)20-7243-8720   Fax: +44 (0)20-7243-8736

Nearest Tube: Parsons Green
This is a beautifully decorated, very stylish late Victorian house, situated in Parsons Green & only 20 mins. from Harrods by tube. The accommodation includes 2 superior twin-bedded rooms & 1 single room, all are en-suite & have colour T.V. & tea/coffee-making facilities. Each room is furnished to the highest standards of comfort. A country house breakfast is served. After visiting London's many attractions, relax in the guest lounge in the evening. A selection of good restaurants within a short walking distance, ask for your hosts recommendations. Children are welcome by arrangement.

bestbandb@atlas.co.uk
www.bestbandb.co.uk
£85.00 - £100.00

Home No. 52
Best Bed & Breakfast
PO Box 31655 London W11 4WR
Tel: +44 (0)20-7243-8720   Fax: +44 (0)20-7243-8736

Nearest Tube: South Kensington
Located in Chelsea, in a quiet residential street yet, only a short walk from a host of fashionable shops & restaurants. A charming Victorian terraced house which has been attractively decorated throughout with many interesting prints & artifacts. The friendly hosts offer 1 spacious double-bedded room & an equally comfortable twin-bedded room. Each room has an excellent en-suite shower room, T.V. & tea/coffee-making facilities. A delightful family home with easy access to the museums at South Kensington, Knightsbridge & Harrods. Plus excllent local bus routes to Oxford Street & Trafalgar Square.

bestbandb@atlas.co.uk
www.bestbandb.co.uk
£68.00 - £88.00

Home No. 51
Best Bed & Breakfast
PO Box 31655   London W11 4WR
Tel: +44 (0)20-7243-8720   Fax: +44 (0)20-7243-8736

Nearest Tube: Holland Park
Set in a quiet, secluded street, this is a unique modern mews house with an original Victorian brick kiln attached. Situated only short walk from fashionable restaurants, antique shops, world famous Portobello Antiques Market & Holland Park. Beauitfully furnished throughout by the host who is an interior designer. 1 delightful & spacious en-suite double room, well-appointed with dressing room, T.V. etc. Also, a single room with adjacent private shower room. Continental breakfast. A charming home, centrally situated with easy access to many of London's attractions.

bestbandb@atlas.co.uk
www.bestbandb.co.uk
£78.00 - £96.00

Home No. 60
Best Bed & Breakfast
PO Box 31655   London W11 4WR
Tel: +44 (0)20-7243-8720   Fax: +44 (0)20-7243-8736

Nearest Tube: High St. Ken.
This is a beautifully appointed home with literary connections, which is located in a quiet cul-de-sac, close to Kensington Palace & Hyde Park.   A lift will take you to the 2nd floor accommodation. In what was once the family home of author Virginia Wolf, the charming host now offers a delightful, spacious double room with brass bed, en-suite shower, T.V. & tea/coffee-making facilities. A delicious full English breakfast is also served.   Knightsbridge, Kensington High Street, Hyde Park, the Royal Albert Hall, shops & restaurants are all just a short walk from here.

bestbandb@atlas.co.uk
www.bestbandb.co.uk
£74.00 - £90.00

Home No. 63
Best Bed & Breakfast
PO Box 31655   London W11 4WR
Tel: +44 (0)20-7243-8720   Fax: +44 (0)20-7243-8736

Nearest Tube: Sloane Square
An attractive 2-storey penthouse apartment with prize-winning roof garden, situated in the heart of fashionable Chelsea & only minutes from the River Thames & the trendy shops & restaurants of the King's Road. The delightful host, who is an artist, is always happy to offer guests recommendations on what to see & do. There is 1 very comfortable double-bedded room with an en-suite bath/shower room, T.V. etc. A large Continental breakfast is served in the attractive dining room which is adorned with many of the hosts interesting pictures. A great base for your stay in London.

bestbandb@atlas.co.uk
www.bestbandb.co.uk
£70.00 - £90.00

Home No. 65
Best Bed & Breakfast
PO Box 31655   London W11 4WR
Tel: +44 (0)20-7243-8720   Fax: +44 (0)20-7243-8736

Nearest Tube: Baker Street
An elegant Georgian townhouse, situated only a 2 min. walk from Baker Street in the heart of central London, only moments from Regent's Park & Mayfair. It is beautifully furnished throughout & there are many French antiques. A selection of charming guest rooms including double, single & triple rooms. Each bedroom is spacious, attractively decorated, & completely unique & has an en-suite/private bathroom, T.V. & 'phone. An elegant lounge in which guests may relax where tea/coffee is available. A large Continental breakfast is served. A delightful home in a marvellous location only minutes from the West End.

bestbandb@atlas.co.uk
www.bestbandb.co.uk
£114.00 - £130.00

Home No. 64
Best Bed & Breakfast
PO Box 31655   London W11 4WR
Tel: +44 (0)20-7243-8720   Fax: +44 (0)20-7243-8736

Nearest Tube: Camden Town
A unique timber & glass house (designed by the host who is an architect), set in a quiet residential street, yet only a short walk from the station, the bustling market & many shops & restaurants. The delightful hosts offer 1 attractive double-bedded room with T.V. & tea/coffee-making facilities & an equally attractive single room for a third member of the party. Each room is light & airy, comfortable & modern in design. An excellent private bathroom. Breakfast is served in the lovely open-plan kitchen/dining area which overlooks the pretty garden.

bestbandb@atlas.co.uk
www.bestbandb.co.uk
£80.00 - £120.00

Home No. 66
Best Bed & Breakfast
Box 31655   London W11 4WR
Tel: +44 (0)20-7243-8720   Fax: +44 (0)20-7243-8736

Nearest Tube: Earls Court
A spacious apartment located at garden level offering contemporary accommodation in 1 double bedded room with en-suite facilities, T.V. , fridge & 'phone. The friendly host (a fashion designer) has tastefully furnished & pleasantly decorated this apartment with many interesting paintings. Guests may relax in the garden which is accessible from their room. Situated only a few minutes walk from the underground station, this home is within easy reach of museums, galleries, restaurants, shops & theatres. Easy access to Heathrow Airport by tube.

bestbandb@atlas.co.uk
www.bestbandb.co.uk
£70.00 - £90.00

Home 77

London

Tel: +44 (0)20-7243-8720 Fax: +44 (0)20-7243-8736

email:bestbandb@atlas.co.uk www.bestbandb.co.uk

Home No. 76
Best Bed & Breakfast
PO Box 31655   London W11 4WR
Tel: +44 (0)20-7243-8720   Fax: +44 (0)20-7243-8736

Nearest Tube: Earls Court
A lovely Victorian terraced house, situated just a short walk from the tube. The friendly host offers 1 king-size double or twin-bedded room with very large en-suite bath & separate shower & 1 king-size double with adjacent private bath & shower. Each room has a colour T.V., hairdryer & clock/radio & has been beautifully decorated & furnished by this most helpful host. A full English breakfast is served. Very close to all the best places for shopping, museums, sight-seeing & within walking distance of many excellent restaurants. Children over 8 by arrangement. Excellent transport links to Heathrow & Gatwick Airports.

bestbandb@atlas.co.uk
www.bestbandb.co.uk
£68.00 - £84.00

Home No. 83
Best Bed & Breakfast
PO Box 31655   London W11 4WR
Tel: +44 (0)20-7243-8720   Fax: +44 (0)20-7243-8736

Nearest Tube: Stamford Brook
This is a spacious Edwardian house set in a quiet street only 4 mins' walk from the station. The charming hosts offer 1 spacious & beautifully decorated Queen-size double-bedded room with Victorian-style brass bedstead, fridge, T.V./video, trouser press, tea/coffee-making facilities, an excellent bathroom en-suite & a double sofa-bed (useful for families.) Breakfast is served in the conservatory overlooking the garden. Only 7 mins' walk from the River Thames with its variety of riverside pubs, serving good food in the evening. Easy access to central London & Heathrow Airport. Children over 8 years.

bestbandb@atlas.co.uk
www.bestbandb.co.uk
£70.00 - 90.00

see p.23

Home No. 77
Best Bed & Breakfast
PO Box 31655   London W11 4WR
Tel: +44 (0)20-7243-8720   Fax: +44 (0)20-7243-8736

Nearest Station: Clapham Jt.(B.R.)
A large Edwardian house built for Earl Spencer backing onto a private park. Breakfast may be served in the dining room or large conservatory overlooking the garden. There is 1 double en-suite room, 1 family room en-suite, 1 twin bedded room with private facilities, also, 1 double room with shared bathroom. Plenty of car parking space. There are two cats & a friendly dog. The hosts are well-travelled & very charming. Smoking permitted on the ground floor. Only 10 mins into central London by train.

bestbandb@atlas.co.uk
www.bestbandb.co.uk
£70.00 - £90.00

Home No. 85
Best Bed & Breakfast
PO Box 31655   London W11 4WR
Tel: +44 (0)20-7243-8720   Fax: +44 (0)20-7243-8736

Nearest Tube: Fulham Broadway
Situated in the heart of Fulham, this is a delightful 3 storey Victorian house conveniently located only 3 mins' walk from the tube. The very friendly hosts offer 1 double-bedded room with an en-suite bathroom & another double-bedded room with a shower room en-suite. Each bedroom is beautifully decorated & very comfortable. T.V. & tea/coffee facilities are available. There are many famous bars, bistros & restaurants in Fulham Broadway. Heathrow Airport & Londons' many attractions are easily accessible by tube.

bestbandb@atlas.co.uk
www.bestbandb.co.uk
£70.00 - £86.00

Bedfordshire, Berkshire, Hertfordshire & Essex

Bedfordshire

The county of Bedfordshire is an area of great natural beauty from the Dunstable Downs in the south to the great River Ouse in the north, along with many country parks & historic houses & gardens.

Two famous wildlife parks are to be found, at Woburn &Whipsnade. The Woburn Wild Animal Kingdom is Britain's largest drive-through safari park, with entrance to an exciting leisure park all included in one admission ticket.

Whipsnade Zoo came into existence in the 1930's as a country retreat for the animals of London Zoo, but is now very much a zoo in its own right & renowned for conservation work.

Woburn Abbey, home of the Dukes of Bedford for three centuries, is often described as one of England's finest showplaces. Rebuilt in the 18th century the Abbey houses an important art collection & is surrounded by a magnificent 3,000 acre deer park.

John Bunyan drew on many local Bedfordshire features when writing the Pilgrims Progress.

Berkshire

Berkshire is a compact county but one of great variety & beauty.

In the East is Windsor where the largest inhabited castle in the world stands in its majestic hilltop setting. Nine centuries of English monarchy have lived here, & it is home to the present Queen. The surrounding parkland, enormous yards, vast interior & splendour of the State Apartments make a trip to Windsor Castle an unforgettable experience.

To the West are the gently rolling Berkshire Downs where many a champion racehorse has been trained.

To the north of the county, the River Thames dominates the landscape - offering an opportunity for a river-bank stroll & a leisurely drink at one of the many country pubs.

In the south is the Kennet & Avon Canal, a peaceful waterway with horse-drawn barges.

Historically, Berkshire has occupied an important place due to its strategic

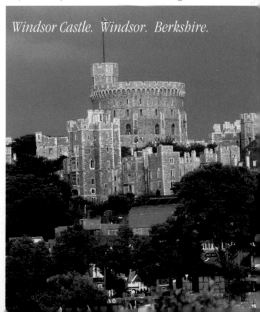

Windsor Castle. Windsor. Berkshire.

Bedfordshire, Berkshire, Hertfordshire & Essex

position commanding roads to & from Oxford & the north & Bath & the west.

Roundheads & Cavaliers clashed twice near Newbury during the 17th century English Civil Wars. Their battles are colourfully recreated by historic societies like the Sealed Knot.

The Tudor period brought great wealth from wool-weaving. Merchants built wonderful houses & some built churches but curiously, there is no cathedral in Berkshire.

Hertfordshire

Old & new exist side by side in Hertfordshire. This attractive county includes historic sites, like the unique Roman theatre in St. Albans, as well as new additions to the landscape such as England's first Garden City at Letchworth.

The countryside varies from the chalk hills & rolling downlands of the Chilterns to rivers, lakes, canals & pretty villages. The county remains largely rural despite many large towns & cities. The Grand Union Canal, built at the end of the 18th century to link the Midlands to London, passes through some glorious scenery, particularly at Cassiobury Park in Watford.

Verulamium was a newly-built town of the Roman Empire. It was the first name of Alban, himself a Roman, who became the first Christian to be martyred for his faith in England. The great Abbey church was built by the Normans around his original church, & it was re-established under the Rule of St. Benedict & named St. Albans some 600 years after his death.

Essex

Essex is a county of commerce, busy roads & busier towns, container ports & motorways, yet it is also a landscape of mudflats & marshes, of meadows & leafy lanes, villages & duckponds. Half timbered buildings & thatched & clapboard cottages stand among rolling hills topped by orange brick windmills.

The coast on the east, now the haunt of wildfowl, sea-birds, sailors & fishermen has seen the arrival of Saxons, Romans, Danes, Vikings & Normans. The names of their settlements remain - Wivenhoe, Layer-de-la-Haye, Colchester & Saffron Walden - the original Saxon name was Walden, but the Saffron was added when the crocus used for dyes & flavouring was grown here in the 15th century.

The seaside resorts of Southend & Clacton are bright & cheery, much-loved by families for safe beaches and all round traditional seaside entertainment. Harbours here are great favourites with anglers & yachtsmen.

Inland lie the watermeadows & windmills, willows & cool green water which shaped the life & work of John Constable, one of the greatest landscape painters. Scenes are instantly recognizable today as you walk to Dedham along the banks of the River Stour.

Bedfordshire, Berkshire, Hertfordshire & Essex

Bedfordshire Gazeteer

Area of outstanding natural beauty.
Dunstable Downs, Ivinghoe Beacon.

Historic Houses

Woburn Abbey
House & gardens, extensive art collection, deer park, antiques centre.

Other things to see & do

Bedford Butterfly Park
Set in 10 acres of wild flower hay meadows. A global conservation park.
The Glenn Miller Museum - Bedford
Old Warden
The village houses a collection of working vintage planes. Flying displays each month from April to October.
Shuttleworth Collection
A unique collection of historic aircraft spanning 100 years of flight
Woburn Safari Park - Woburn
Famous for it free roaming lions.
Whipsnade Zoo - Whipsnade

Berkshire Gazeteer

Areas of outstanding natural beauty.
North West Downs.

Historic Houses & Castles

Windsor Castle - Royal Residence at Windsor
State apartments, house, historic treasures. The Cloisters, Windsor Chapel, Medieval house.
Basildon Park - Nr. Pangbourne
Overlooking the Thames. 18th century Bath stone building, massive portico & linked pavilions. Painted ceiling in Octagon Room, gilded pier glasses. Garden & wooded walks.
Cliveden - Nr. Taplow
Once the home of Nancy Astor.

Churches

Lambourn (St. Michael & All Saints)
Norman with 15th century chapel. 16th century brasses, glass & tombs.

Padworth (St. John the Baptist)
12th century Norman with plastered exterior, remains of wall paintings, 18th century monuments.
Warfield (St. Michael & All Angels)
14th century decorated style. 15th century wood screen & loft.

Museums

Newbury Museum - Newbury
Natural History & Archaeology
Paleolithic to Saxon & Medieval times.
Household Cavalry Museum - Windsor

Other things to see & do

Racing - at Newbury, Ascot & Windsor
Highlight of the racing year is the Royal Meeting at Ascot each June, attended by the Queen & other members of the Royal Family.
Antiques - Hungerford
A famous centre for antiques.

Hertfordshire Gazeteer

Areas of outstanding natural beauty.
Parts of the Chilterns.

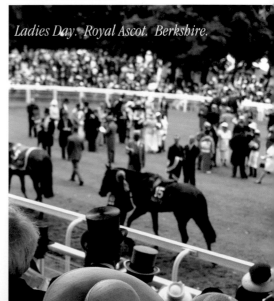

Ladies Day. Royal Ascot. Berkshire.

Bedfordshire, Berkshire, Hertfordshire & Essex

Historic Houses & Castles

Hatfield House - Hatfield
Home of the Marquess of Salisbury. Jacobean House & Tudor Palace - childhood home of Queen Elizabeth I.

Knebworth House - Knebworth
Family home of the Lyttons. 16th century house transformed into Victorian High Gothic. Furniture, portraits. Formal gardens & unique Gertrude Jekyll herb garden.

Shaw's Corner - Ayot St. Lawrence
Home of George Bernard Shaw.

Cathedrals & Churches

St. Albans Cathedral - St. Albans
9th century foundation, murals, painted roof over choir, 15th century reredos, stone rood screen.

Stanstead St. Abbots (St. James)
12th century nave, 13th century chancel, 15th century tower & porch, 16th century North chapel, 18th century box pews & 3-decker pulpit.

Watford (St. Mary)

Essex Gazeteer

Areas of outstanding natural beauty. Dedham Vale, Epping Forest.

Houses & Castles

Audley End House - Saffron Walden
1603 - Jacobean mansion on site of Benedictine Abbey. State rooms & Hall.

Castle House - Dedham
Home of the late Sir A. Munnings. President R.A. Paintings & other works.

Hedingham Castle - Castle Hedingham
Norman keep & Tudor bridge.

Layer Marney Tower - Nr. Colchester
1520 Tudor brick house. 8 storey gate tower. Formal yew hedges & lawns.

St. Osyth's Priory - St. Osyth
Was Augustinian Abbey for 400 years until dissolution in 1537, 13th-18th century buildings. 13th century chapel. Wonderful gatehouse containing works of art including ceramics & Chinese Jade.

Spains Hall - Finchingfield
Elizabethan Manor incorporating parts of earlier timber structure. Paintings, furniture & tapestries.

Cathedrals & Churches

Brightlingsea (All Saints)
15th century tower - some medieval painting fragments. Brasses.

Castle Hedingham (St. Nicholas)
12th century doorways, 14th century rood screen, 15th century stalls, 16th century hammer beams, altar tomb.

Copford (St. Michael & All Angels)
12th century wall paints. Continuous vaulted nave & chancel

Finchingfield (St. John the Baptist)
Norman workmanship. 16th century tomb -18th centuary tower & cupola.

Layer Marney (St. Mary)
Tudor brickwork, Renaissance monuments, medieval screens, wall paintings.

Little Maplestead (St. John the Baptist)
14th century, one of the five round churches in England, having hexagonal nave, circular aisle, 14th century arcade.

Newport (St. Mary the Virgin)
13th century. Interesting 13th century altar (portable) with top which becomes reredos when opened. 15th century chancel screen. Pre-Reformation Lectern. Some old glass.

Museums & Galleries

Dutch Cottage Museum - Canvey Island
17th century thatched cottage of octagonal Dutch design. Exhibition of models of shipping used on the Thames through the ages.

Ingatestone Hall - Ingatestone
Norman Keep now exhibiting archeological materi from Essex & especially Roman Colchester.

Southchurch Hall - Southend-on-Sea
14th century moated & timber framed manor house - Tudor wing, furnished as medieval manor.

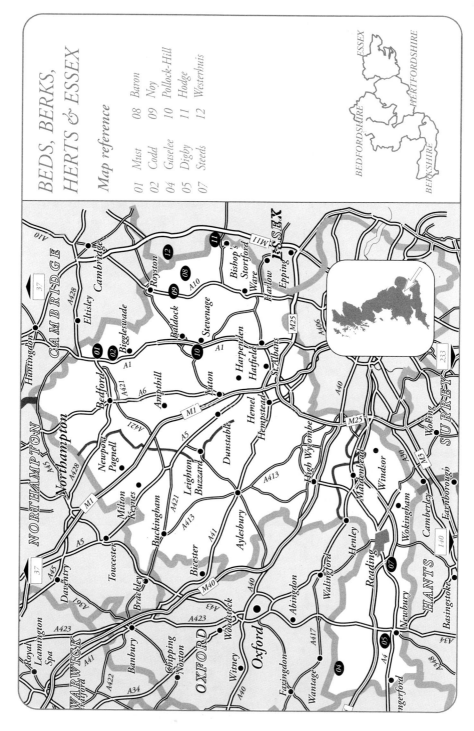

BEDS, BERKS, HERTS & ESSEX

Map reference

01	Must	08	Baron
02	Codd	09	Noy
04	Gaselee	10	Pollock-Hill
05	Digby	11	Hodge
07	Steeds	12	Westerhuis

Janet Must
Church Farm 41 High Street Roxton Bedford MK44 3EB
Bedfordshire
Tel: (01234) 870234   Fax 01234 870234

Near Rd: A.1, A.421
Church Farm is a Grade II listed, 17th-century part-timber framed house. It is a perfect base for those wanting somewhere a little special & a comfortable place to stay. Accommodation is in 3 attractive & delightful bedrooms (all en-suite), each with a colour T.V. & tea/coffee-making facilities. (In the twin room, there is the 'Coat of Arms' of the Stuart Kings.) A delicious breakfast is served in the attractive beamed 17th-century dining room. There are a number of walks around the village & countryside, & good local inns for evening meals. Church Farm is a charming home; a haven from a hectic world.

churchfarm@amserve.net
www.bestbandb.co.uk   £60.00 - £65.00
Open: all year   Map ref no. 01

Judy & Nick Gaselee
Saxon Cottage Upper Lambourn Hungerford
RG17 8QN Berkshire
Tel: (01488) 71503   Fax 01488 71585

Near Rd: M.4 J.14, B.4000
Saxon Cottage is in the famous racehorse training village of Upper Lambourn & is very close to the gallops. It is the delightful home of Nick & Judy Gaselee; Nick has recently retired from training horses & is happy to take guests to see the gallops in the mornings. 2 very comfortable bedrooms (1 double & 1 twin) with private facilities. Also, another twin room, which is suitable for children. Dinner is by arrangement & includes fresh vegetables from the garden, when in season. A variety of local pubs & restaurants, also serve excellent food. 6 miles from Hungerford & within easy reach of Bath & Oxford.

judy.gaselee@virgin.net   www.SmoothHound.co.uk/
hotels/saxon-cottage.html   £60.00 - £60.00
Open: all year (excl.xmas & new year) Map ref no. 04

Mrs Margaret Codd
Highfield Farm   Tempsford Road   Sandy SG19 2AQ
Bedfordshire
Tel: (01767) 682332   Fax 01767 692503

Near Rd: A.1, A.421
A tranquil & very welcoming house with comfort, warmth & a friendly atmosphere in a lovely setting on an arable farm. There are 9 attractive bedrooms, 8 en-suite, including 4 ground-floor rooms in tastefully converted stables. Highfield Farm is set back off the A.1, giving peaceful seclusion & yet easy access to London, Cambridge, Bedford, the Shuttleworth Collection, the R.S.P.B. & the east-coast ports. Ample parking. (Dogs by arrangement.) Single supplement. Most guests return to this lovely home.

margaret@highfield-farm.co.uk
www.highfield-farm.co.uk   £70.00 - £75.00
Open: all year   Map ref no. 02

Mrs Charlotte Digby
Rookwood Farmhouse   Stockcross   Newbury
RG20 8JX   Berkshire
Tel: (01488) 608676   FAX 01488 657961

Near Rd: A.4, A.34, M.4
This charming & comfortable former farmhouse combines ease of access with rural views & a large garden. The attractive guest bedrooms are in a newly converted coach house which is traditionally furnished & yet affords all modern facilities. In winter, there is a welcoming log fire in the guests' sitting room, while in summer, breakfast is served in the conservatory overlooking the swimming pool. Within easy reach of Henley & Windsor by car. Rookwood Farmhouse is an ideal base for a relaxing break.

enquiries@rookwoodfarmhouse.co.uk
www.rookwoodfarmhouse.co.uk   £70.00 - £70.00
Open: all year   Map ref no. 05

Mrs Jane Steeds
Highwoods Hermits Hill Burghfield Common
Reading RG7 3BG   Berkshire
Tel: (0118) 9832320   Fax 0118 9831070

Near Rd: A.4, M.4
A friendly, relaxing atmosphere at this fine Victorian country house set in 4 acres of attractive garden & grounds (with tennis court) & unspoilt, far-reaching views. Offering spacious, attractive & comfortable bedrooms with period furniture. 1 double with en-suite bathroom & 2 further bedrooms with bathroom & power shower. There is ample secure parking. Also, a gallery specialising in English watercolours & prints. Good pubs nearby. An excellent location providing access to London, Heathrow Airport, Windsor, Oxford & Bath.

jane.steeds@btinternet.com   www.bestbandb.co.uk
£60.00 - £70.00 Open: all year (excl. xmas & new year)
Map ref no. 07

Mrs Jacqueline Noy
Chipping Hall Farm   Chipping Buntingford SG9 0PH
Hertfordshire
Tel: (01763) 271514   Fax 01763 272833

Near Rd: A. 10
Chipping Hall is an attractive Georgian farmhouse set on a family-run arable farm. Offering 2 attractive guest rooms in the main house, which share a bathroom. Also, in an annexe overlooking the garden, The Old Dairy, offers comfortable accommodation with en-suite facilities. In the attractive walled garden, there is an outdoor heated pool for use in the summer. Chipping Hall Farm is a charming home within easy reach of Duxford Imperial War Museum, Audley End, Cambridge, & Stansted & Luton Airports. Evening meals by prior arrangement.

stay@chippinghall.co.uk www.chippinghall.co.uk
£57.50 - £80.00 Open: all year (excl. xmas)
Map ref no. 09

see p.32

Helen Baron
Brick House Farm   Great Hormead
Buntingford SG9 0PB   Hertfordshire
Tel: (01763) 289356

Near Rd: B.1038
The farmhouse is situated on the outskirts of the picturesque village of Gt Hormead in an idyllic location and yet within a short drive of the A10. Guests can expect a warm welcome at this peaceful & secluded home. The attractive rooms with their en-suite facilities have delightful views over rolling farmland. All rooms have TV/videos, welcome tray & hairdryers. Tennis court & heated outdoor swimming pool available for guests' use at selected times. Ample parking. Many guests return.

helen@brickhousefarm.net www.brickhousefarm.net
£60.00 - £75.00 Open: all year
Map ref no. 08

Samantha Pollock-Hill
Homewood Park Lane   Old Knebworth
Stevenage SG3 6PP   Hertfordshire
Tel: (01438) 812105   Fax 01438 812572

Near Rd: A.1 M
Homewood is a classic blend of comfort & style: an Edwardian country house which is also a well-equipped family home. It has been used as a location for period drama by the B.B.C., & is often sought out by admirers of its designer, the distinguished architect Edwin Lutyens. You will be treated as a member of the family, or your privacy will be respected - whichever you prefer. 2 bedrooms, with en-suite/private bathroom. Also a family suite. Dogs & evening meals (min. 4 persons) by prior arrangement.

bookings@homewood-bb.co.ukwww.homewood-bb.co.uk
£70.00 - £90.00 Open: all year (excl. xmas)
Map ref no. 10

Homewood

Park Lane Old Knebworth Stevenage SG3 6PP

Tel:(01438) 812105 Fax 01438 812572 email:bookings@homewood-bb.co.uk www.homewood-bb.co.uk

John & Angela Hodge
The Cottage 71 Birchanger Lane Birchanger
Bishop's Stortford CM23 5QA Essex
Tel: (01279) 812349 Fax 01279 815045

Near Rd: A.120, M.11
Situated with a quiet village, The Cottage is a charming 17th-century listed house offering 15 comfortable en-suite bedrooms, all with colour T.V. & tea/coffee-making facilities. Oak-panelled reception rooms with log burners & a conservatory/dining room looking onto mature gardens. The Cottage is a very convenient base for trips to Cambridge, London & East Anglia, & it is within easy reach of Stansted Airport & Bishops Stortford. Private parking available. A delightful home, & an ideal location for a relaxing short break.

bookings@thecottagebirchanger.co.uk
www.thecottagebirchanger.co.uk £75.00 - £80.00
Open: all year (excl.xmas & new year) Map ref no. 11

Mrs Tineke Westerhuis
Rockells Farm Duddenhoe End Saffron Walden
CB11 4UY Essex
Tel: (01763) 838053 Fax 01763 838053

Near Rd: A.11
Rockells is an arable farm, which is situated in a beautiful corner of Essex. The Georgian house has a large garden with a 3-acre lake for coarse fishing All of the 3 attractive & comfortable bedrooms have en-suite facilities. 1 room is situated on the ground floor. On the farm are several footpaths. There are many beautiful villages in the area. Rockells Farm is also within easy reach of Audley End House, Duxford Air Museum & Cambridge. London is approx. 1 hour by car or train. Stansted Airport is approx. 30 mins by car. A charming home.

evert.westerhuis@tiscali.co.uk www.rockellsfarm.co.uk
£50.00 - £60.00 Open: all year
Map ref no. 12

Cambridgeshire & Northamptonshire

Cambridgeshire

A county very different from any other, this is flat, mysterious, low-lying Fenland crisscrossed by a network of waterways both natural & man-made.

The Fens were once waterlogged, misty marshes but today the rich black peat is drained and grows carrots, sugar beet, celery and the best asparagus in the world.

Drive north across the Fens & slowly you become aware of a great presence dominating the horizon. Ely cathedral, the "ship of the Fens", sails closer. The cathedral is a masterpiece with its graceful form & delicate tracery towers. Begun before the Domesday Book was written, it took the work of a full century before it was ready to have the timbered roof raised up. Norman stonemasons worked with great skill & the majestic nave is glorious in its simplicity. Their work was crowned by the addition of the Octagon in the 14th century. Despite the ravages of the Reformation, the lovely Lady Chapel survives as one of the finest examples of decorated architecture in Britain with its exquisitely fine stone carving.

To the south, the Fens give way to rolling chalk hills & fields of barley, wheat & rye, & Cambridge. Punts gliding through the broad river, between smooth, lawned banks, under willow trees, past college buildings as extravagant as wedding cakes. The names of the colleges resound through the ages - Peterhouse, Corpus Christi, Kings, Queens, Trinity, Emmanuel. This is city of learning & progress, & a city of great tradition.

Northamptonshire

Northamptonshire has many features to attract & interest the visitor, from the town of Brackley in the south with its charming buildings of mellow stone, to ancient Rockingham Forest in the north. There are lovely churches and splendid historic houses as well as many waterways. Horse-racing at Towcester & motor-racing at Silverstone draws the crowds, but there are quieter pleasures in visits to Canons Ashby, or to Sulgrave Manor, home of George Washington's ancestors.

In the pleasantly wooded Rockingham Forest area are numerous delightful villages, one of which is Ashton with its many traditional thatched cottages,

Kings College Chapel. Cambridge

Cambridgeshire & Northamptonshire

Cambridgeshire Gazeteer
Areas of outstanding natural beauty.
The Nene Valley.

Historic Houses & Castles

Anglesy Abbey - Nr. Cambridge
Origins in the reign of Henry I. Was redesigned into Elizabethan Manor by Fokes family. Houses the Fairhaven collection of Art treasures - stands in 100 acres of Ground.

Hinchingbrooke House - Huntingdon
13th century nunnery converted mid-16th century into Tudor house. Later additions in 17th & 19th centuries.

King's School - Ely
12th & 14th centuries - original stonework & vaulting in the undercroft, original timbering 14th century gateway & monastic barn.

Kimbolton Castle - Kimbolton
Tudor Manor house - has associations with Katherine of Aragon. Remodelled by Vanbrugh 1700's - gatehouse by Robert Adam.

Longthorpe Tower - Nr. Peterborough
13th & 14th century fortification - rare wall paintings.

Peckover House - Wisbech
18th century domestic architecture - charming Victorian garden.

University of Cambridge Colleges

Peterhouse	1284
Clare	1326
Pembroke	1347
Gonville & Caius	1348
Trinity Hall	1350
Corpus Christi	1352
King's	1441
Queen's	1448
St. Catherine's	1473
Jesus	1496
Christ's	1505
St. John's	1511
Magadalene	1542
Trinity	1546
Emmanuel	1584
Sidney Sussex	1596
Downing	1800

Wimpole Hall - Nr. Cambridge
18th & 19th century - beautiful staterooms - aristocratic house.

Cathedrals & Churches

Alconbury (St. Peter & St. Paul)
13th century chancel & 15th century roof. Broach spire.

Babraham (St. Peter)
13th century tower - 17th century monument.

Ely Cathedral
Rich arcading - west front incomplete. Remarkable interior with Octagon - unique in Gothic architecture.

Great Paxton (Holy Trinity)
12th century.

Harlton (Blessed Virgin Mary)
Perpendicular - decorated transition. 17th century monuments.

Hildersham (Holy Trinity)
13th century - effigies, brasses & glass.

Lanwade (St. Nicholas)
15th century - medieval fittings.

Peterborough Cathedral
Great Norman church fine example - little altered. Painted wooden roof to nave remarkable west front Galilee Porch & spires later additions.

Ramsey (St. Thomas of Canterbury)
12th century arcades - perpendicular nave. Late Norman chancel with Angevin vault.

St. Neots (St. Mary)
15th century.

Sutton (St. Andrew)
14th century.

Trumpington (St. Mary & St. Nicholas)
14th century. Framed brass of 1289 of Sir Roger de Trumpington.

Westley Waterless (St. Mary the Less)
Decorated. 14th century brass of Sir John & Lady Creke.

Wimpole (St. Andrew)

Cambridgeshire & Northamptonshire

14th century. Rebuilt 1749 - splendid heraldic glass.

Yaxley (St. Peter)
15th century chancel screen, wall paintings, fine steeple.

Museums & Galleries

Cromwell Museum - Huntingdon
Exhibiting portraits, documents, etc. of the Cromwellian period.

Fitzwilliam Museum - Cambridge
Gallery of masters, old & modern, ceramics, applied arts, prints & drawing, medieval manuscripts, music & art library.

Scott Polar Research Institute - Cambridge
Relics of expeditions & the equipment used. Current scientific work in Arctic & Antarctic.

University Archives - Cambridge
13th century manuscripts, Charters, Statutes, Royal letters & mandates. Wide variety of records of the University.

University Museum of Archaeology & Anthropology - Cambridge
Collections illustrative of Stone Age in Europe, Africa & Asia. Britain prehistoric to medieval times. Prehistoric America. Ethnographic material from South-east Asia, Africa & America.

University Museum of Classical Archaeology - Cambridge

Northamptonshire Gazeteer

Historic Houses & Castles

Althorp - Nr. Northampton
Family home of the Princess of Wales, with fine pictures & porcelain.

Boughton House - Nr. Kettering
Furniture, tapestries & pictures in late 17th century building modelled on Versailles, in beautiful parkland.

Canons Ashby House - Nr. Daventry
Small 16th century manor house with gardens & church.

Deene Park - Nr. Corby
Family home for over 4 centuries, surrounded by park, extensive gardens & lake.

Holdenby House - Nr. Northampton
Gardens include part of Elizabethan garden, with original entrance arches, terraces & ponds. Falconry centre. Rare breeds.

Kirby Hall - Nr. Corby
Large Elizabethan mansion with fine gardens.

Lamport Hall - Nr. Northampton
17th & 18th century house with paintings, furniture & china. One of the first garden rockeries in Britain. Programme of concerts & other special events.

Rockingham Castle - Nr. Market Harborough
Norman gateway & walls surrounding mainly Elizabethan house , with some pictures & Rockingham china.

Rushton Triangular Lodge - Nr. Kettering
Symbolic of the Trinity, with 3 sides, 3 floors, trefoil windows.

Sulgrave Manor - Nr. Banbury
Early English Manor, home of George Washington's ancestors.

Museums

Abington Museum - Northampton
Domestic & social life collections in former manor house.

Museum of Leathercraft - Northampton
History of leather use, with Queen Victoria's saddle, & Samuel Pepys' wallet.

Waterways Museum - Stoke Bruerne   Nr. Towcester
200 years of canal & waterway life, displayed beside the Grand Union Canal.

Cathedrals & Churches

Brixworth Church - Nr. Northampton
One of the finest Anglo-Saxon churches in the country, mostly 7th century.

Earls Barton Church - Nr. Northampton
Fine Anglo-Saxon tower & Norman arch & arcading.

Church of the Holy Sepulchre - Northampton
Largest & best preserved of four remaining round churches in England, dating from 1100.

CAMBRIDGESHIRE & NORTHAMPTONSHIRE

Map reference

01 Hindley
02 Nix
03 Farndale
04 Roper
05 Wood
06 Clarke

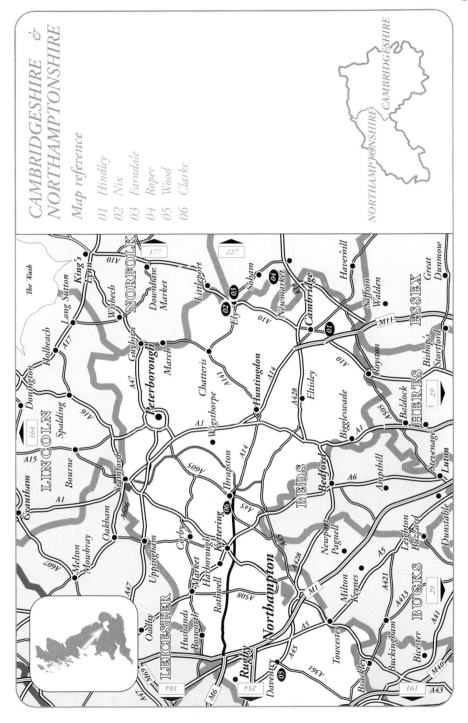

Olga & David Hindley
Purlins   12 High Street   Little Shelford   Cambridge
CB2 5ES   Cambridgeshire
Tel/Fax: (01223) 842643   Mobile 07785 790204

Near Rd: A.10
Purlins is a lovely, individually designed family home, with 2 acres of parkland, situated in a quiet, pretty village on the Cam, just 4 miles south of Cambridge. An ideal centre for Colleges, Audley End House, the Imperial War Museum & bird watching. The accommodation includes 3 well-appointed double bedrooms (2 ground-floor), all with en-suite bathrooms, colour T.V. & tea/coffee-making facilities. Varied breakfasts are served (special diets by arrangement).   There are good restaurants nearby. Children over 8 years are welcome. Single supplement.

dgallh@ndirect.co.uk www.bestbandb.co.uk
£66.00 - £71.00   Open: apr - oct
Map ref no. 01

Jenny & Robin Farndale
Cathedral House 17 St Mary's Street   Ely CB7 4ER
Cambridgeshire
Tel: (01353) 662124

Near Rd: A.10
Although established 10 years ago, Cathedral House remains one of Ely's best kept secrets. Situated within the shadow of Ely's magnificent cathedral, this Grade II listed house, whilst retaining many original features offers well-appointed spacious accommodation in 2 very attractive double suites & a twin en-suite. All of the rooms overlook the tranquil walled garden abundant with mature shrubs & foliage. Breakfast is served at the family table where you can meet fellow guests & enjoy convivial conversation. Children over 12 years are welcome.

farndale@cathedralhouse.co.uk
www.cathedralhouse.co.uk £75.00 - £90.00
Open: all year   Map ref no. 03

Mrs Hilary Nix
Hill House Farm 9 Main Street   Coveney Ely CB6 2DJ
Cambridgeshire
Tel: (01353) 778369   Fax 01353 778369

Near Rd: A.142, A.10
A warm welcome awaits you at this spacious Victorian farmhouse, situated in the quiet village of Coveney, 3 miles from the cathedral city of Ely. Open views of the surrounding countryside & easy access to Cambridge, Newmarket & Huntingdon.   Ideal for touring Cambridgeshire, Norfolk & Suffolk. Wicken Fen & Welney wildfowl refuge nearby. 1 twin & 2 double en-suite rooms, 1 ground floor. All have their own entrance & T.V. etc. A lounge & garden for guests' use. Single supplement.

info@hillhousefarm-ely.co.uk
www.hillhousefarm-ely.co.uk   £56.00 - £60.00
Open: all year (excl. xmas)   Map ref no. 02

Jan & Malcolm Roper
Queensberry 196 Carter Street   Fordham CB7 5JU
Cambridgeshire
Tel: (01638) 720916   Fax 01638 720233

Near Rd: A.14, A.142, A.10
A delightful Georgian home, as featured in many T.V. travel programmes, set in large grounds with croquet lawn & parking.   Ideally situated for touring East Anglia, Cambridge, Duxford, Ely Cathedral, Newmarket, Bury St. Edmunds, & National Trust & English Heritage properties. Equine tours can be arranged. 2 attractive bedrooms, 1 en-suite & 1 with a private bathroom. Fordham is the 1st village off the A.14 on the Newmarket to Ely A.142 road. Good local eateries. Children & dogs by arrangement.

queensberry@queensberry196.demon.co.uk
www.bestbandb.co.uk £60.00 - £60.00
Open: all year   Map ref no. 04

Clive & Eileen Wood
The Old Coach House   Lower Catesby   Daventry
NN11 6LF   Northamptonshire
Tel: (01327) 310390Fax 01327 312220

Near Rd: A.425, A.361

A Victorian former coach house which has been elegantly converted into a large family home with a superb garden. The West Terrace has a commanding view of the open countryside, as seen from the double rooms, whilst the twin room overlooks the lake.   The property adjoins the site of a former priory founded in 1175 & is on the Jurassic Way. Silverstone, Stoneleigh, Rugby & Birmingham Airport are within a 45 min. drive. Offering spacious & comfortable accommodation, The Old Coach House is a special place to stay. Children over 8 years welcome.

coachhouse@lowercatesby.co.uk
www.lowercatesby.co.uk   £80.00 - £100.00
Open: all year (excl.xmas & new year) Map ref no. 05

Mrs Audrey Clarke
Dairy Farm   12 St. Andrews Lane Cranford St. Andrew
Kettering NN14 4AQ   Northamptonshire
Tel: (01536) 330273

Near Rd: A.14

Situated in an idyllic Northamptonshire village, Dairy Farm is a charming 17th-century farmhouse, featuring oak beams & inglenook fireplaces. There are comfortable bedrooms, all with en-suite/private bathroom. Families are very well catered for. There is a delightful garden, containing an ancient circular dovecote & a charming summer house, for guests to enjoy in a relaxed & friendly atmosphere. Delicious meals are served, using farmhouse produce (if ordered in advance). Dogs by arrangement. Dairy Farm is the perfect spot for a relaxing short break.

www.bestbandb.co.uk
£64.00 - £76.00 Open: all year
Map ref no. 06

Cheshire & Lancashire

Cheshire

Cheshire is located between the Peak District & the mountains of North Wales & is easily accessible from three major motorways. It has much to attract long visits but is also an ideal stopping-off point for travellers to the Lake District & Scotland, or to North Wales or Ireland. There is good access eastwards to York & the east coast & to the south to Stratford-upon-Avon & to London.

Cheshire can boast seven magnificent stately homes, the most visited zoo outside London, four of Europe's largest garden centres & many popular venues which feature distinctive Cheshire themes such as silk, salt, cheese, antiques & country crafts.

The Cheshire plain with Chester, its fine county town, & its pretty villages, rises up to Alderley Edge in the east from where there are panoramic views, & then climbs dramatically to meet the heights of the Peaks.

To the west is the coastline of the Wirral Peninsula with miles of sandy beaches & dunes &, of course, Liverpool.

The countryside shelters very beautiful houses. Little Moreton Hall near Congleton, is one of the most perfect imaginable. It is a black & white "magpie" house, not one of its walls is perpendicular, yet it has withstood time & weather for nearly four centuries, standing on the waterside gazing at its own reflection.

Tatton Hall is large & imposing & is splendidly furnished with many fine objects on display. The park & gardens are a delight & especially renowned for the azaleas & rhododendrons. In complete contrast is the enormous radio telescope at Jodrell Bank where visitors can be introduced to planetary astronomy in the planetarium.

Chester is a joy; a walk through its streets is like walking through living history. The old city is encircled by city walls enclosing arcaded streets with handsome black & white galleried buildings. There are many excellent shops along these "Rows". Chester Cathedral is a fine building of monastic foundation with a peaceful cloister & outstanding wood carving in the choir stalls. Boat rides can be taken along the River Dee which flows through the city.

Manchester has first rate shopping, restaurants, sporting facilities, theatres & many museums ranging from an excellent costume museum to the fascinating Museum of Science & Industry.

Liverpool grew from a tiny fishing village on the northern shores of the Mersey River, receiving its charter from King John in 1207. Commercial & slave trading with the West Indies led to massive expansion in the 17th & 18th centuries. The Liverpool of today owes much to the introduction of the steam ship in the mid 1900s, which enabled thousands of Irish to emigrate during the potato famine in Ireland.

Cheshire & Lancashire

Lancashire

Lancashire can prove a surprisingly beautiful county. Despite its industrial history of cotton production, there is magnificent scenery & there are many fine towns & villages. Connections with the Crown & the clashes of the Houses of Lancaster & York have left a rich heritage of buildings with a variety of architecture. There are old stone cottages & farmhouses, as well as manor houses from many centuries.

For lovers of the countryside, Lancashire has the sweeping hills of Bowland, the lovely Ribble Valley, the moors of Rossendale & one mountain, mysterious Pendle Hill.

The Royal Forest of Bowland is a forest without trees, which has provided rich hunting grounds over the centuries. An old windswept pass runs over the heights of Salter Fell & High Cross Fell from Slaidburn, where the Inn, the "Hark to Bounty", was named after the noisiest hound in the squire's pack & used to be the courtroom where strict forest laws were enforced.

Further south, the Trough of Bowland provides an easier route through the hills, & here is the beautiful village of Abbeystead in Wynesdale where monks once farmed the land. The church has stained glass windows portraying shepherds & their flocks & there are pegs in the porch for the shepherds' crooks.

Below the dramatic hills of Bowland, the green valley of the Ribble climbs from Preston to the Yorkshire Dales. Hangridge Fell, where the tales of witches are almost as numerous as those of Pendle Hill, lies at the beginning of the valley.

Pendle Hill can be reached from the pretty village of Downham which has Tudor, Jacobean & Georgian houses, village stocks & an old inn. Old Pendle rises abruptly to 1831 feet & is a strange land formation. It is shrouded in legend & stories of witchcraft.

Between Pendle Hill & the moors of Rossendale are the textile towns of Nelson, Colne, Burnley, Accrington & Blackburn. The textile industry was well established in Tudor times & the towns grew up as markets for the trading of the cloth woven in the Piece Halls.

The beautiful Downham countryside. Lancashire.

Cheshire & Lancashire

Cheshire Gazeteer

Area of outstanding natural beauty
Part of the Peaks National Park.

Addington Hall - Macclesfield
15th century Elizabethan Black & White half
timbered house.

Bishop Lloyd's House - Chester
17th century half-timbered house (restored).
Fine carvings. Has associations with Yale
University & New Haven, USA.

Chorley Old Hall - Alderley Edge
14th century hall with 16th century Elizabethan
wing.

Forfold Hall - Nantwich
17th century Jacobean country house, with
fine panelling.

Gawsworth Hall - Macclesfield
Fine Tudor half-timbered Manor House. Tilting
ground. Pictures, furniture, sculptures, etc.

Lyme Park - Disley
Elizabethan with Palladian exterior by Leoni.
Gibbons carvings. Beautiful park with herd of
red deer.

Peover Hall - Over Peover, Knutsford
16th century- stables of Tudor period; has the
famous magpie ceiling.

Tatton Park - Knutsford
Beautifully decorated & furnished Georgian
House with a fine collection of glass, china &
paintings including Van Dyke & Canaletto.
Landscaping by Humphrey Repton.

Little Moreton Hall - Nr. Congleton
15th century timbered, moated house with 16th
century wall-paintings.

Cathedrals & Churches

Acton (St. Mary)
13th century with stone seating around walls.
17th century effigies.

Bunbury (St. Boniface)
14th century collegiate church - alabaster effigy.

Congleton (St. Peter)
18th century - box pews, brass candelabrum,
18th century glass.

Chester Cathedral - Chester
Subjected to restoration by Victorians - 14th
century choir stalls.

Malpas (St. Oswalds)
15th century - fine screens, some old stalls, two
family chapels.

Mobberley (St. Wilfred)
Medieval - 15th century rood screen, wall
paintings, very old glass.

Shotwick (St. Michael)
Twin nave - box pews, 14th century quatre - foil
lights, 3 deck pulpit.

Winwick (St. Oswald)
14th century - splendid roof. Pugin chancel.

Wrenbury (St. Margaret)
16th century - west gallery, monuments &
hatchments. Box pews.

Liverpool Cathedral -
The Anglican Cathedral was completed in 1980
after 76 years of work. It is of massive
proportions, the largest in the U.K. with much
delicate detailed work.

Museums & Galleries

Grosvenor Museum - Chester
Art, folk history, natural history, Roman
antiquities including a special display of
information about the Roman army.

Chester Heritage Centre - Chester
Interesting exhibition of the architectural heritage
of Chester.

Cheshire Military Museum - Chester
The three local Regiments are commemorated
in this museum.

King Charles Tower - Chester
Chester at the time of the Civil War illustrated
by dioramas.

Museum & Art Gallery - Warrington
Anthropology, geology, ethnology, botany &
natural history. Pottery, porcelain, glass,
collection of early English watercolours.

**West Park Museum & Art Gallery -
Macclesfield**
Sketches by Landseer & Tunnicliffe.

Cheshire & Lancashire

Lancashire Gazeteer

Areas of outstanding natural beauty.
The Forest of Bowland, Parts of Arnside & Silverdale.

Historic Houses & Castles

Rufford Old Hall - Rufford
15th century screen in half-timbered hall of note. Collection of relics of Lancashire life.

Chingle Hall - Nr. Preston
13th century - small manor house with moat. Rose gardens. Haunted!

Astley Hall - Chorley
Elizabethan house reconstructed in 17th century. Houses pictures, tapestries, pottery & furniture.

Gawthorpe Hall - Padiham
17th century manor house with 19th century restoration. Moulded ceilings & some fine panelling. A collection of lace & embroidery.

Bramall Hall - Bramall
Fine example of half-timbered (black & white) manor house built in 14th century & added to in Elizabethan times.

Lancaster Castle - Lancaster
Largest of English castles - dates back to Norman era.

Astley Hall - Chorley
16th century half-timbered grouped around central court. Rebuilt in the Jacobean manner with long gallery. Unique furniture.

Hoghton Tower - Nr. Preston
16th century - fortified hill-top mansion - magnificent banquet hall. Dramatic building - walled gardens & rose gardens.

Thurnham Hall - Lancaster
13th century origins. 16th century additions & 19th century facade. Beautiful plasterwork of Elizabethan period. Jacobean staircase.

Cathedrals & Churches

Lancaster (St. Mary)
15th century with 18th century tower. Restored chapel - fine stalls.

Whalley (St. Mary)
13th century with 15th century tower, clerestory & aisle windows. Fine wood carving of 15th century canopied stalls.

Halsall (St. Cuthbert)
14th century chancel, 15th century perpendicular spire. 14th century tomb. Original doors, brasses & effigies. 19th century restoration.

Tarleton (St. Mary)
18th century, part 19th century.

Great Mitton (All Hallows)
15th century rood screen, 16th century font cover, 17th century pulpit.

Museums & Galleries

Blackburn Museum - Blackburn
Collections of local history, archeology, ceramics, geology & natural history. Fine collection of coins & medieval illuminated manuscripts & early printed books.

Bury Museum & Art Gallery - Bury
Houses fine Victorian oil & watercolours. Turner, Constable, Landseer & de Wint.

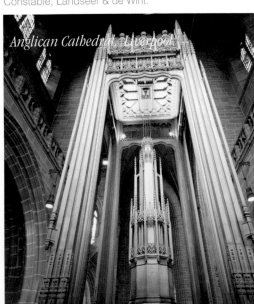

Anglican Cathedral, Liverpool.

CHESHIRE & LANCASHIRE

Map reference

01 Hill   03 Ahooie   05 Taylor   07 M. Smith
02 Ikin   04 Ritchie   06 Rothwell   08 J. Smith

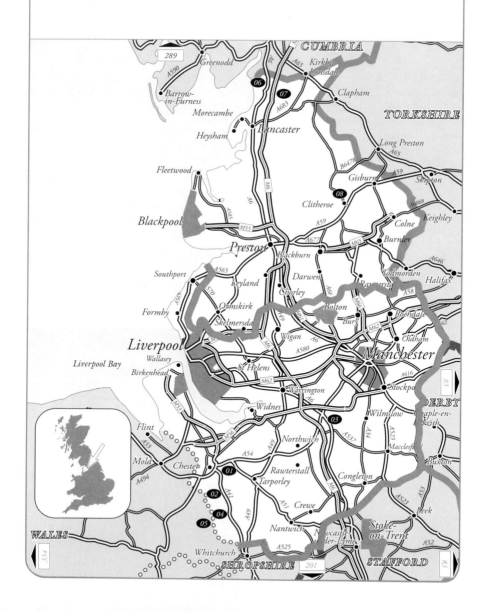

Nigel & Clare Hill
Cotton Farmhouse   Cotton Edmunds   Chester
CH3 7PG   Cheshire
Tel: (01244) 336616   Fax 01244 336616

Near Rd: A.51, A.41
Cotton Farmhouse is surrounded by farmland where Nigel & Clare run a herd of beef cows & their calves & a flock of 300 geese. Wonderfully peaceful but under 4 miles from Chester, it is an ideal base to discover the beautiful city with its Roman origins & unique medieval "rows". All of the bedrooms are large, comfortable & attractively furnished with good attention to detail. Colour T.V., tea/coffee-making facilities, radio & en-suite bathroom for every room. Children over 10 years are. Cotton Farmhouse is a stylish home, which is perfect for exploring Cheshire.

info@cottonfarm.co.uk www.cottonfarm.co.uk
£62.00 - £62.00 Open: all year
Map ref no. 01

Mr & Mrs Abooie
Longview Hotel & Restaurant 51 & 55 Manchester Road
Knutsford WA16 0LX Cheshire
Tel: (01565) 632119   Fax 01565 652402

Near Rd: A.50
Set in this pleasant Cheshire market town overlooking the common is this lovely, friendly hotel, furnished with many antiques that reflect the elegance of this Victorian building. Great care has been taken to retain its character, while also providing all required comforts for the discerning traveller. The accimmodation includes 26 en-suite bedrooms, which are prettily decorated, giving them that cared-for feeling which is echoed throughout the hotel. Excellent meals are served. You are assured of a warm friendly welcome as soon as you step into reception.

enquiries@longviewhotel.com www.longviewhotel.com
£72.50 - £137.50 Open: all year (excl.xmas & new year)
Map ref no. 03

Mrs Ann Ikin
Golborne Manor Platts Lane Chester CH3 9AN
Cheshire
Tel: (01829) 770310   Fax 01829 770370

Near Rd: A.41
Golborne Manor is an elegant 19th-century country residence with glorious views, renovated to a high standard & set in 3 1/2 acres of gardens & grounds. Beautifully decorated with spacious en-suite bedrooms. Farmhouse breakfasts. Evening meals (available Mon-Fri) by arrangement. Piano & croquet set available for guests' use. Large car park. Easy access for motorways. 10 mins' drive south from Chester on the A.41, turning right a few yards after Van Centre (on the left). Single supplement.

info@golbornemanor.co.uk www.golbornemanor.co.uk
£60.00 - £85.00 Open: all year
Map ref no. 02

Neil & Kathie Ritchie
Tilston Lodge Tilston   Malpas SY14 7DR
Cheshire
Tel: (01829) 250223   Fax 01829 250223

Near Rd: A.41
A warm welcome awaits you at this glorious Victorian country house set in 16 acres of landscaped garden & pasture. Originally built as a gentleman's Hunting Lodge, Tilston Lodge is now an elegant home, providing luxurious accommodation. Bedrooms are spacious & traditionally furnished with antiques to complement the original features of the house. Each room is en-suite & is generously equipped to ensure guests have a comfortable stay. Ideal for touring in Cheshire, Shropshire & north Wales.

www.bestbandb.co.uk
£78.00 - £80.00 Open: all year
Map ref no. 04

Worthenbury Manor

Worthenbury Wrexham LL13 0AW

Tel:(01948)770342

email:enquiries@worthenburymanor.co.uk www.worthenburymanor.co.uk

see p.46

Ian Taylor
Worthenbury Manor   The Manor   Wrexham   LL13 0AW
Cheshire
Tel: (01948) 770342

Near Rd: A.525, A.41
Surrounded by rolling Cheshire Plains, Welsh Marches & National Trust properties, Worthenbury Manor makes the ideal setting for a relaxing break. In this fully restored Grade II listed building with oak panelling & 4-poster beds, you can indulge yourself with dinner, prepared by a qualified chef using fresh local produce. This is guaranteed to be an experience you will want to repeat again & again. Worthenbury Manor is an elegant home, situated 2 miles from Bangor on Dee & 4 miles from Malpas. Children over 10 years welcome. Animals by arrangement.

enquiries@worthenburymanor.co.uk
www.worthenburymanor.co.uk   £60.00 - £80.00
Open: feb - nov   Map ref no. 05

Roy & Melanie Smith
Capernwray House   Capernwray   Carnforth   LA6 1AE
Lancashire
Tel: (01524) 732363

Near Rd: A.6
Capernwray House is a tastefully furnished country home set in rolling countryside with panoramic views. Offering 3 attractive bedrooms, each with en-suite facilities, tea/coffee, hairdryer, colour T.V., etc. A comfortable residents' lounge with T.V., books, magazines & games. Conveniently situated & within easy reach of the Lake District, Yorkshire Dales, the coast, Lancaster & RSPB Leighton Moss. Ideal stop-over en-route North/South. Evening meals by arrangement, although there are many traditional pubs & inns close by. Children over 10 years..

thesmiths@capernwrayhouse.com
www.capernwrayhouse.com   £55.00 - £55.00
Open: all year (excl.xmas & new year)   Map ref no. 07

see p.48

Mrs Sally-Ann Rothwell
The Bower   3 Yealand Road   Yealand Conyers
Carnforth   LA5 9SF   Lancashire
Tel: (01524) 734585   Fax 01524 734585

Near Rd: A.6
A beautiful, small Georgian country house, set in an Area of Outstanding Natural Beauty. There are superb walks right from the door, including to Leighton Moss RSPB reserve. The accommodation includes 2 lovely bedrooms, 1 with a double & single bed & en-suite bathroom, & 1 with king-size double bed & private bathroom. The Bower is perfect for exploring the Lake District & Yorkshire Dales. 5 mins' from M.6. Very peaceful location, & ideal for stop-overs to or from Scotland. Children over 12.

info@thebower.co.uk   www.thebower.co.uk
£68.00 - £88.00   Open: all year
Map ref no. 06

Jean Smith
Peter Barn Country House   Cross Lane   Waddington
Clitheroe   BB7 3JH   Lancashire
Tel: (01200) 428585

Near Rd: A.59
Nestling on the edge of the Forest of Bowland, & surrounded by a beautiful garden with stream & ponds, is the award-winning Peter Barn. Superb accommodation, oak beams & log fires in the 1st-floor sitting room with panoramic views of the glorious Ribble Valley. All 3 bedrooms are most attractive, & each has an en-suite or private bathroom & tea/coffee-making facilities. The home-made marmalade is delicious. Good walking & exploring - Browsholme Hall, Whalley Abbey ... or just relaxing. Children over 12.

jean@peterbarn.co.uk   www.bestbandb.co.uk
£56.00 - £58.00   Open: all year (excl.xmas & new year)
Map ref no. 08

The Bower

3 Yealand Road Yealand Conyers Carnforth LA5 9SF

Tel:(01524) 734585 Fax 01524 734585 email:info@thebower.co.uk www.thebower.co.uk

Cornwall

Cornwall

Cornwall is an ancient Celtic land, a narrow granite peninsula with a magnificent coastline of over 300 miles & wild stretches of moorland.

The north coast, washed by Atlantic breakers, has firm golden sands & soaring cliffs. The magnificent beaches at Bude offer excellent surfing & a few miles to the south you can visit the picturesque harbour at Boscastle & the cliff-top castle at Tintagel with its legends of King Arthur. Newquay, with its beaches stretching for over seven miles, sheltered coves & modern hotels & shops, is the premier resort on Cornwall's Atlantic coast. St. Ives, another surfing resort, has great charm which has attracted artists for so long & is an ideal place from which to explore the Land's End peninsula.

The south coast is a complete contrast with wooded estuaries, sheltered coves, little fishing ports, & popular resorts. Penzance, with its warmth & vivid colours, is an all-the-year-round resort & has wonderful views across the bay to St. Michael's Mount. Here are excellent facilities for sailing & deep-sea fishing, as there are at Falmouth & Fowey with their superb harbours. Mevagissey, Polperro & Looe are fine examples of traditional Cornish fishing villages.

In the far west of Cornwall, you can hear about a fascinating legend: the lost land of Lyonesse - a whole country that was drowned by the sea. The legend goes that the waters cover a rich & fertile country, which had 140 parish churches. The Anglo-Saxon Chronicle records two great storms within a hundred years, which drowned many towns & innumerate people. Submerged forests are known to lie around these coasts - & in Mount's Bay beech trees have been found with the nuts still hanging on the branches, so suddenly were they swamped.

Today, St Michael's Mount & the Isles of Scilly are said to be all that remains of the vanished land. St. Michael's Mount, with its tiny fishing village & dramatic castle, can be visited on foot at low tide or by boat at high water. The Isles of Scilly, 28 miles beyond Land's End, have five inhabited islands, including Tresco with its sub-tropical gardens. Trips to the many uninhabited islands are a delight.

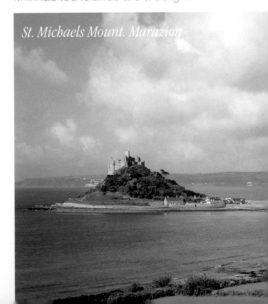

St. Michaels Mount, Marazion

Cornwall

Cornwall Gazeteer

Areas of outstanding natural beauty.
Almost the entire county.

Historic Houses & Castles

Anthony House - Torpoint
18th century - beautiful & quite unspoiled Queen
Anne house with excellent panelling & fine
period furnishings.

Cotehele House - Calstock
15th & 16th century house, still contains the
original furniture, tapestry, armour.

Ebbingford Manor - Bude
12th century Cornish manor house, with
walled garden.

Godolphin House - Helston
Tudor - 17th century colonnaded front.

Lanhydrock - Bodmin
17th century - splendid plaster ceilings, picture
gallery with family portraits 17th/20th centuries.

Mount Edgcumbe House - Plymouth
Tudor style mansion - restored after destruction
in 1949. Hepplewhite furniture & portrait by
Joshua Reynolds.

St. Michael's Mount - Penzance
Medieval castle & 17th century with 18th & 19th
century additions.

Pencarrow House & Gardens - Bodmin
18th century Georgian Mansion - collection of
paintings, china & furniture - mile long drive
through fine woodlands & gardens.

Old Post Office - Tintagel
14th century manor house in miniature - large
hall used as Post Office for a period, hence
the name.

Trewithen - Probus Nr. Truro
Early Georgian house with lovely gardens.

Trerice - St. Newlyn East
16th century Elizabethan house, small with
elaborate facade. Excellent fireplaces, plaster
ceilings, miniature gallery & minstrels' gallery.

Cathedral & Churches

Altarnun (St. Nonna)
15th century, Norman font, 16th century bench
ends, fine rood screen.

Bisland (St. Protus & St. Hyacinth)
15th century granite tower - carved wagon
roofs, slate floor. Georgian wine - glass pulpit,
fine screen.

Kilkhampton (St. James)
16th century with fine Norman doorway, arcades
& wagon roofs.

Laneast (St. Michael or St. Sedwell)
13th century, 15th century enlargement, 16th
century pulpit, some painted glass.

Lanteglos-by-Fowley (St. Willow)
14th century, refashioned 15th century, 13th
century font, 15th century brasses & altar tomb,
16th century bench ends.

Launcells (St. Andrew)
Interior unrestored - old plaster & ancient roofs
remaining, fine Norman font with 17th century
cover, box pews, pulpit, reredos, 3 sided
alter rails.

Probus (St. Probus & St. Gren)
16th century tower, splendid arcades, three
great East windows.

St. Keverne (St. Keverne)
Fine tower & spire. Wall painting in 15th
century interior.

St. Neot (St. Neot)
Decorated tower - 16th century exterior,
buttressed & double-aisled. Many windows of
medieval glass renewed in 19th century.

Museums & Galleries

Museum of Witchcraft - Boscastle
Relating to witches, implements & customs.

Military Museum - Bodmin
History of Duke of Cornwall's Light Infantry.

Public Library & Museum - Cambourne
Collections of mineralogy, archaeology, local
antiquities & history.

Cornish Museum - East Looe
Collection of relics relating to witchcraft customs
& superstitions. Folk life & culture of district.

Helston Borough Museum - Helston

Folk life & culture of area around Lizard.

Museum of Nautical Art - Penzance
Exhibition of salvaged gold & silver treasure from underwater wreck of 1700's.

Museum of Smuggling - Polperro
Activities of smugglers, past & present.

Penlee House Museum - Penlee, Penzance
Archaeology & local history & tin mining exhibits.

Barbara Hepworth Museum - St. Ives
Sculpture, letters, documents, photographs, etc., exhibited in house where Barbara Hepworth lived.

Old Mariners Church - St. Ives
St. Ives Society of Artists hold exhibitions here.

County Museum & Art Gallery - Truro
Ceramics, art, local history & antiquities, & Cornish mineralogy.

Historic Monuments

Cromwell's Castle - Tresco - Scilly Isles
17th century castle.

King Charles' Fort - Tresco - Scilly Isles
16th century fort.

Old Blockhouse - Tresco - Scilly Isles
16th century coastal battery.

Harry's Wall - St. Mary's - Scilly Isles
Tudor Coastal battery.

Pendennis Castle - Falmouth
Fort from time of Henry VII.

Restormel Castle - Lostwithiel
13th century ruins.

St. Mawes Castle - St. Mawes
16th century fortified castle.

Tintagel Castle - Tintagel
Medieval ruin on wild coast, King Arthur's legendary castle.

Things to see & do

Camel trail - Padstow to Bodmin
12 miles of recreation path along scenic route, suitable for walkers, cyclists & horse-riders.

Dobwalls Theme Park - Nr. Liskeard

Cornish Cyder Farm - Penhallow
Friendly and informative guided tours taking you through the ancient process of cyder making. The press house and bottlery producing traditional farm house cyders and Cornish Country fruit wines.

Flambards Experience - Helston
Award winning Flambards Victorian Village – a life-size re-creation of a lamp-lit village with more than 50 shops, traders and homes showing life in Victorian England.

Geevor Tin Mine - Pendeen
A unique collection of mining artefacts and memorabilia, mineral displays, photographs of the mine and miners at work and an incredible 3D model of the coastal mine workings. The surface buildings contain magnificent machinery such as the winders and compressors. The mill enables visitors to see where the ore was processed to produce the tin concentrate that Geevor sold. An underground tour with takes visitors into the fascinating long-abandoned 18th century Wheal Mexico mine, re–discovered in 1995.

Jamaica Inn - Launceston
Made famous by Daphne du Maurier's novel of the same name, Jamaica Inn, set high amongst the wild yet beautiful landscape of Bodmin Moor, visit the Daphne du Maurier room. Full of memorabilia including her famous Sheraton writing desk. Then experience the fascinating Daphne du Maurier's Smugglers at Jamaica Inn – a spectacular theatrical presentation of her most famous novel, Jamaica Inn, told in tableaux, sound and light.

Seal sanctuary - Gweek Nr. Helston
Seals, exhibition hall, nature walk, aquarium, beal hospital, donkey paddock.

Padstow tropical bird gardens - Padstow

Mynack Theatre - Porthcurno
An amphitheatre carved out of the granite cliff overlooking the Atlantic.

Tresco Abbey Gardens - Tresco
Collection of sub-tropical flora.

Trethorne Leisure Farm - Launceston
Visitors are encouraged to feed & stroke the animals.

CORNWALL

Map reference

01	Nicholls	16	Wilson
02	Bennett	17	Tuckett
03	Halliday	18	Studley
04	T. Tremayne	20	Epperson
05	Otway-R.	21	Nancarrow
06	Sleep	22	Martin
07	Griffin	23	Taylor
08	Castle	24	Heasman
09	Rowe	25	Johnson
10	Ffitch	26	Holt
11	Henly	27	Morgan
12	Mackenzie	28	Barstow
13	Woodley	29	Sylvester
14	Taylor	30	A. Tremayne
15	Abbey	31	Bloor

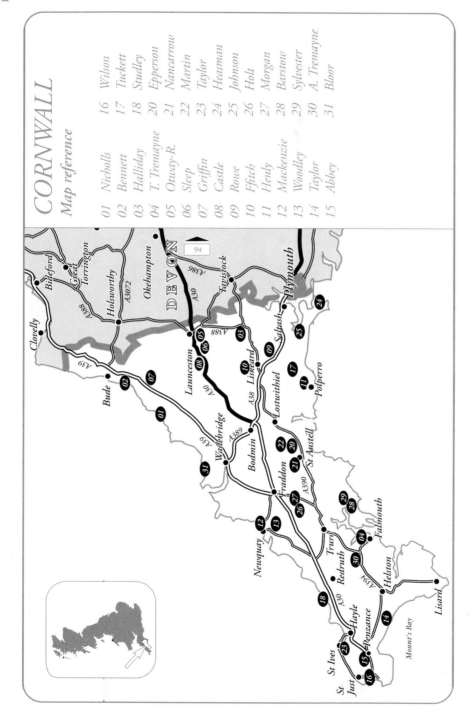

Steve & Cheryl Nicholls
Trerosewill Farm Paradise Boscastle PL35 0BL
Cornwall
Tel: (01840) 250727   Fax 01840 250545

Near Rd: A.39
Trerosewill offers luxurious award-winning accommodation overlooking the picturesque fishing village of Boscastle. All bedrooms are en-suite & equipped to the highest standard & include a King-size 4-poster bed with en-suite corner bath Jacuzzi. There are unsurpassed panoramic sea views of Lundy Island & the beautiful North Cornish coast. An extensive breakfast menu including home-made preserves & bread. Kennelling available by arrangement. Farm Trail & badger watching. Children over 7 years welcome. A warm traditional Cornish welcome awaits you at this delightful home.

enquiries@trerosewill.co.uk   www.trerosewill.co.uk
£62.00 - £85.00   Open: mid feb - mid nov
Map ref no. 01

Mrs Lavinia Halliday
Browda   Linkinborne Callington PL17 7NB
Cornwall
Tel: (01579) 362235

Near Rd: A.388
This 250-acre organic farm is sited in a wonderfully quiet & unspoilt river valley & centres around the large, comfortable Grade II listed 17th-century farmhouse. The atmosphere is informal & friendly, the emphasis on quality & simplicity. Bedrooms (1 double en-suite, 1 double with private facilities & 1 single) are traditionally furnished & all overlook the gardens. Eat breakfast outside (weather permitting) & afterwards explore the woods, fields & lakes. No T.V. (2 couples maximum plus 1 if all the same party.) Children over 10. Excellent local pub offers evening meals, with a seasonal menu incorporating fresh local produce.

www.bestbandb.co.uk
£68.00 - £68.00   Open: all year
Map ref no. 03

Mrs Sylvia Bennett
The Lodge   Crackington Haven Bude EX23 0JW
Cornwall
Tel: (01840) 230347Fax 01840 230347

Near Rd: A.39
The Lodge is set in its own extensive gardens with far-reaching rural views. It is approached by a long sweeping drive with ample space for parking. There is a delightful guest lounge with T.V. where tea & coffee are available, & an attractive double room with en-suite facilities. A full English breakfast is served in the dining room, which has stunning views across the valley. The peace & tranquillity of The Lodge offers an excellent base from which to explore the delights of Cornwall.

jim.sylvia@ukonline.co.uk   www.bestbandb.co.uk
£50.00 - £60.00   Open: all year
Map ref no. 02

T. P. Tremayne
The Home' Country House Hotel Penjerrick
Budock Water Falmouth TR11 5EE   Cornwall
Tel: (01326) 250427   Fax 01326 250143

Near Rd: A.39
A quiet & charming country house, with views over Maenporth & Falmouth Bay. Accommodation is in 18 comfortable rooms, 16 with a private/en-suite bath/shower. All have tea/coffee-making facilities. A colour-T.V. lounge & bar are available, & guests may relax in the beautiful sheltered garden. A golf course & boating facilities nearby. A friendly host, who prepares delicious meals using local produce. Special diets provided for by arrangement. Children over 10. Animals by arrangement.

www.bestbandb.co.uk
£70.00 - £80.00   Open: apr - oct
Map ref no. 04

Jos & Mary-Anne Otway-Ruthven
Hornacott   South Petherwin   Launceston PL15 7LH
Cornwall
Tel: (01566) 782461   Fax 01566 782461

Near Rd: B.3254
Hornacott nestles in the River Inny Valley with sloping gardens & a stream surrounded by fields. Offering a spacious suite of rooms in a wing of the house, with a private sitting room, bedroom & en-suite bathroom & an additional single room for an accompanying family member/friend. Guests really enjoy the space, comfort & privacy amidst peaceful surroundings & the visitors book is a testament to happy guests, many of whom return again. Evening meals & animals by prior arrangement. A delightful home from which to explore Cornwall & its many attractions.

otwayruthven@btinternet.com www.hornacott.co.uk
£76.00 - £76.00   Open: all year (excl. xmas)
Map ref no. 05

Mrs Valerie Griffin
Wheatley Farm   Maxworthy   Launceston PL15 8LY
Cornwall
Tel: (01566) 781232

Near Rd: A.39
Superb accommodation in a lovely character Victorian farmhouse awaits you at Wheatley Farm. Peaceful location, perfect for a relaxing holiday, which brings guests back time & time again. It is an excellent base for exploring Cornwall & Devon, within easy reach of the Eden Project & also near the coast. There is a luxury indoor heated swimming pool, plus sauna & spa. Home-made food, using local produce - including superb dinners. Wheatley Farm is a lovely welcoming place to stay at any time of year. Children over 5 years.

BB@wheatley-farm.co.uk   www.wheatley-farm.co.uk
£58.00 - £66.00   Open: feb - oct
Map ref no. 07

Mrs Barbara Sleep
Trevadlock Farm   Trevadlock   Launceston PL15 7PW
Cornwall
Tel: (01566) 782239   Fax 01566 782239

Near Rd: A.30
Superb accommodation on a working farm in the heart of the countryside. Delicious breakfasts are served, using fresh local produce, just perfect for a relaxing holiday. Ideally placed for touring Cornwall & Devon north & south coasts, Eden, Heligan & National Trust properties. A.30 - 1 1/2 miles. Well-appointed comfortable furnished bedrooms with hospitality trays, T.V. & hairdryers & central heating; so enjoy a special break at any time of year. London 4 hrs. Children over 5 years. Please visit the web site for more information.

trevadlock@farming.co.uk   www.trevadlock.co.uk
£55.00 - £60.00   Open: all year
Map ref no. 06

John & Marcia Castle
Trekenner Court Pipers Pool Launceston PL15 8QG
Cornwall
Tel: (01566) 880118

Near Rd: A.395
Trekenner Court is in a tranquil spot with glorious views over Bodmin Moor. Set in 4 acres, it's built around a Mediterranean-style courtyard with Oleanders & geraniums. In good weather you can breakfast outside by the fountain with fresh orange juice, local bacon, sausages & eggs from the family's hens. Dinner by arrangement. En-suite bedrooms & guest sitting-room. Many pubs & restaurants nearby. The glorious surfing beaches of North Cornwall are 20 mins, golf 5 mins, Eden 45 mins, gardens & numerous National Trust properties. Stabling available.

trekennercourt@hotmail.co.uk
£60.00 - £60.00   Open: all year
Map ref no. 08

Stephanie Rowe
Tregondale Farm Menheniot Liskeard PL14 3RG
Cornwall
Tel: (01579) 342407 Fax 01579 342407

Near Rd: A.390, A.38
The Rowe family make your stay special. There is a wealth of charm & period features in this manor house with original walled garden. Peaceful, lovely countryside. 3 pretty en-suite bedrooms with T.V. & tea/coffee. Log fires. Home local produce a speciality. Tennis court. Woodland Farm Trail 200 acre mixed farm, an abundance of wildlife & flowers, award-winning pedigree south Devon cattle & lambs in spring. Near many National Trust properties, Heligan Garden & Eden Project. Looe 6 miles. Just come & discover the beauty of Cornwall. Children over 5.

tregondale@btconnect.com www.tregondalefarm.co.uk
£54.00 - £70.00 Open: all year
Map ref no. 09

Mr Ffitch
Redgate Smithy Redgate St. Clear Liskeard PL14 6RU
Cornwall
Tel: (01579) 321578

Near Rd: A.30, A.38
Redgate Smithy is a 200 year old converted Smithy, situated above the beautiful Golitha Falls, on the River Fowey, on the southern edge of Bodmin Moor. Close to Siblyback Lake, and to the Cornish Mining Heritage at Minions. Birds & wildlife abound on & around the moor. Good walking, riding & fishing facilities locally. A lovely woodland garden for guests' use. Comfortable beamed, cottage style bedrooms, with TV etc. Home-cooked breakfasts, using local produce, freshly prepared on the range. Good local pubs & restaurants for dinner. Children over 12.

enquiries@redgatesmithy.co.uk
www.redgatesmithy.co.uk **£60.00 - £60.00**
Open: all year (excl.xmas & new year) *Map ref no. 10*

Mrs Jean Henly
Bucklawren St. Martins Looe PL13 1NZ
Cornwall
Tel: (01503) 240738 Fax 01503 240481

Near Rd: B.3253
An elegant 19th century farmhouse set on a working farm, with spectacular views over Looe Bay. The peaceful location (set in the countryside but only 3 miles from Looe) offers excellent accommodation with large, individually decorated & furnished ensuite bedrooms some with sea views. Enjoy a traditional farmhouse breakfast of fresh local produce in the dining room. While other meals can be taken at The Granary Restaurant within a nearby converted barn. An ideal base for the Eden Project, the Lost Gardens of Heligan & Monkey Sanctuary. Golf, riding & water sports all available close by.

bucklawren@btopenworld.com www.bucklawren.com
£54.00 - £61.00 Open: mar - nov
Map ref no. 11

Barry & Annie Rosier
Allhays Country Style Bed & Breakfast Porthallow
Talland Bay Looe PL13 2JB Cornwall
Tel: (01503) 273188

Near Rd: A.387
Allhays is a spacious family house built in the late 1930s, set in its own peaceful gardens with breathtaking views over the wild & romantic remoteness of Talland Bay. Ideal for walking the coastal path. Many National Trust properties are nearby, as well as the Lost Gardens of Heligan & the Eden Project. Very comfortable & attractive accommodation. Ample car parking. Extensive breakfasts with home-baked breads, free range & organic produce are served. Peace & quiet prevails. Children over 9 years. An ideal base for exploring Cornwall.

info@allhays.co.uk www.allhays.co.uk
£70.00 - £90.00 Open: all year (excl. dec)
Map ref no.

Trenance Lodge Hotel

83 Trenance Road Newquay TR7 2HW

Tel:(01637) 876702 Fax 01637 878772

email:info@trenance-lodge.co.uk   www.trenance-lodge.co.uk

see p.56

Mac & Jennie Mackenzie
Trenance Lodge Hotel   83 Trenance Road
Newquay TR7 2HW   Cornwall
Tel: (01637) 876702   Fax 01637 878772

Near Rd: A.3092
Trenance Lodge is an attractive house standing in its own grounds, overlooking the lakes & gardens of Trenance Valley, leading to the Gannel Estuary. The restaurant has an excellent reputation for serving the finest fresh local food in elegant surroundings. Adjoining the restaurant is a spacious bar lounge, where guests can relax & plan their excursions. Accommodation is in 5 comfortable & tastefully furnished bedrooms, en-suite, with colour T.V., radio & tea/coffee-making facilities. This is an excellent base for touring Cornwall, with a warm welcome assured.

info@trenance-lodge.co.uk   www.trenance-lodge.co.uk
£60.00 - £70.00   Open: all year
Map ref no. 12

see p.58

Christine & Charles Taylor
Ednovean Farm Ednovean Lane Perranuthnoe
Nr. Penzance TR20 9LZ   Cornwall
Tel: (01736) 711883   Fax 01736 710480

Near Rd: A.394
A small farm nestling above the peaceful village of Perranuthnoe, with glorious views towards St. Michael's Mount & Mounts Bay. A stunning 17th-century barn, which has been lovingly renovated, with elegant, tastefully furnished country-style en-suite bedrooms, some with private terraces or sumptuous 4-poster beds. All rooms with little luxuries to spoil you. After a delicious breakfast, stroll to the village, cliff-top walks, secluded coves or just enjoy the view. An elegant home. Ednovean Farm is the perfect spot for a relaxing break.

info@ednoveanfarm.co.uk   www.ednoveanfarm.co.uk
£80.00 - £100.00   Open: all year (excl. xmas)
Map ref no. 14

Kathy Woodley
Degembris Farmhouse St. Newlyn East
Newquay TR8 5HY   Cornwall
Tel: (01872) 510555   Fax 01872 510230

Near Rd: A.3058
The original manor house of Degembris was built in the 16th century & is now used as a barn. The present-day house, surrounded by attractive gardens, was built a mere 200 years ago, & its slate-hung exterior blends well with the rolling countryside. There are 5 bedrooms, 3 en-suite, each decorated in a co-ordinating theme, with dried flowers & stripped pine enhancing the country atmosphere. Hearty breakfasts are served. Centrally situated in superb countryside, yet close to the sea, Degembris Farmhouse is the perfect holiday base.

kathy@degembris.co.uk   www.degembris.co.uk
£60.00 - £64.00   Open: all year (excl. xmas)
Map ref no. 13

The Abbey Hotel
Abbey Street Penzance TR18 4AR
Cornwall
Tel: (01736) 366906   Fax 01736 351163

Near Rd: A.30
Set high above the historic harbour in Penzance & overlooking the world famous Mount's Bay, beckons a small gem of a hotel. Housed in one of Penzance's most important listed buildings dating from the mid 1600s, The Abbey, with its walled garden, courtyard & period features, allows you to discover true comfort, the fruits of a very thoughtful kitchen & service so good you hardly notice it. Bedrooms are luxuriously furnished in a distinctive & individual style & many rooms have far reaching views overlooking the bay & St. Michael's Mount beyond.

hotel@theabbeyonline.co.uk
www.theabbeyonline.co.uk   £120.00 - £190.00
Open: all year   Map ref no. 15

Ednovean Farm

Ednovean Lane Perranuthnoe Nr. Penzance TR20 9LZ

Tel:(01736) 711883 Fax 01736 710480

email:info@ednoveanfarm.co.uk www.ednoveanfarm.co.uk

Trenderway Farm

Pelynt Polperro PL13 2LY

Tel:(01503) 272214 Mobile 07817 273442

email:enquiries@trenderwayfarmholidays.co.uk   www.trenderwayfarmholidays.co.uk

Dennis & Linda Wilson
Boscean Country Hotel   Bosweddon Road   St. Just
Penzance TR19 7QP   Cornwall
Tel: (01736) 788748   Fax 01736 788748

Near Rd: A.3071
Set in 3 acres of private walled gardens in an Area of
Outstanding Natural Beauty on the heritage coast. The
Boscean Country Hotel is an ideal base from which to
explore west Cornwall. Built in 1912, this Edwardian country
house has a magnificent oak panelled entrance hall,
lounge, dining room & staircase from which there are
stunning sea views. The accommodation includes 12 en-
suite bedrooms with all amenities. Log fires when
appropriate. Licensed bar. Evening meals are available.
Children over 7.

boscean@aol.com   www.bosceancountryhotel.co.uk
£50.00 - £56.00   Open: all year
Map ref no. 16

The Studley Family
Aviary Court Mary's Well   Illogan
Redruth TR16 4QZ   Cornwall
Tel: (01209) 842256   Fax 01209 843744

Near Rd: A.30
Couples return each year to this charming 300-year-old
country house set in 2 acres of secluded, well-kept gardens
with tennis court. An ideal touring location - coast 5 mins'
away & St. Ives Tate, Heligan, Eden Project, St. Michael's
Mount & Maritime Museum all within easy reach. 6 well-
equipped bedrooms with en-suite, tea/coffee-making
facilities, biscuits, mineral water, fresh fruit, phone & view
of the gardens. The restaurant serves delicious food (prior
arrangement advisable) with a selection of wine. Children
over 3 yrs welcome.

info@aviarycourthotel.co.uk
www.aviarycourthotel.co.uk £76.00 - £78.00
Open: all year   Map ref no. 18

see p.59

Lynne & Anthony Tuckett
Trenderway Farm   Pelynt   Polperro PL13 2LY
Cornwall
Tel: (01503) 272214 Mobile 07817 273442

Near Rd: A.387
At Trenderway you will find an oasis of peace & pure luxury
from uniquely designed rooms, to the gourmet breakfast
of local produce, fresh from the farmhouse Aga. A refuge
from boisterous families & noisy groups. Trenderway offers
couples a perfect Cornish haven in stunning 5 star rated
accommodation. Enjoy the therapeutic calm of walks
around the lakes that beam with wildlife. In the evening,
dine at numerous delectable restaurants & inns in the ports
of Polperro, Looe & Fowey.

enquiries@trenderwayfarmholidays.co.uk
www.trenderwayfarmholidays.co.uk £70.00 - £90.00
Open: all year (excl. xmas)   Map ref no. 17

see p.61

Jane & Steve Epperson
Anchorage House Nettles Corner Boscundle
Tregrehan Mills   St. Austell PL25 3RH   Cornwall
Tel: (01726) 814071   Fax 01726 813462

Near Rd: A.390
Anchorage House is a national award-winning, luxury guest
lodge that has the feel of a small, private hotel offering
candlelit suppers, Spa treatments, heated pool & gym.
Located in the centre of Cornwall & only 5 mins from the
Eden Project & Carlyon Bay beach & golf, guests are
treated to large, comfy beds, sparkling clean guest rooms,
luxurious bathrooms with huge tubs & separate power
showers. Breakfast is divine & suppers in the Glass Room
magical. Jane & Steve are generous hosts & you'll feel
wonderfully spoilt. Everything is immaculate & luxurious.

info@anchoragehouse.co.uk
www.anchoragehouse.co.uk £110.00 - £140.00
Open: mar - nov   Map ref no. 20

Anchorage House

Nettles Corner Boscundle Tregrehan Mills St. Austell PL25 3RH

Tel:(01726) 814071 Fax 01726 813462

email:info@anchoragehouse.co.uk www.anchoragehouse.co.uk

Judith Nancarrow
Poltarrow Farm   St. Mewan   St. Austell PL26 7DR
Cornwall
Tel: (01726) 67111   Fax 01726 67111

Near Rd: A.390
Tucked away in its' own grounds, the charming farmhouse
at Poltarrow has just 5 en-suite bedrooms. Each room is
decorated & furnished to a high standard to ensure your
comfort.   Ideally situated for both the Eden Project &
Heligan Gardens - all of Cornwall is easily reached from
this delightful home. Treat yourself to a farmhouse
breakfast of local produce served in the conservatory &
take advantage of the indoor swimming pool & sports hall.
In the evening, relax in front of a log fire in the comfortable
sitting room Your hosts look forward to meeting you.
Children over 5 years welcome.

enquire@poltarrow.co.uk   www.poltarrow.co.uk
£66.00 - £70.00   Open: all year (excl.xmas & new year)
Map ref no. 21

Suzanne & Chris Taylor
The Woodside Hotel   The Belyars   St. Ives TR26 2DA
Cornwall
Tel: (01736) 795681

Near Rd: A.3074
St Ives hotels are rarely set in more peaceful locations than
that of The Woodside Hotel - yet it is still within five minutes
walk of the town centre. You can enjoy magnificent views
of the harbour & the beautiful coastline from most
bedrooms, all public rooms, the gardens & pool-side
terrace. The heated outdoor swimming pool is open May
to September. The attractive en-suite bedrooms are
comfortable & amenities include T.V., hairdryer & hot drinks
tray. A spacious lounge with games area & a residents
bar are available for relaxation. A wonderful location from
which to explore St Ives & Cornwall's myriad of delights.

info@woodside-hotel.co.uk   www.woodside-hotel.co.uk
£72.00 - £108.00   Open: all year (excl. xmas)
Map ref no. 23

see p.63

Keith Martin
Nanscawen Manor House   Prideaux Road
St. Blazey PL24 2SR   Cornwall
Tel: (01726) 814488

Near Rd: A.390
A beautiful 15th-century manor house with an elegant,
stately Georgian wing, set in 5 acres of grounds with
stunning views across a romantic valley. Keith & Fiona
offer you a relaxed welcome & friendly hospitality. Enjoy
the heated outdoor swimming pool. The luxurious
bedrooms are all en-suite, & beautifully decorated to the
highest standards, with spa baths. Keith's delicious
breakfasts are a treat to the eye & the palette. Ideal for
visiting Heligan Gardens, Fowey, Lanhydrock & the Eden
Project (2 miles.) Children over 12.

keith@nanscawen.com   www.nanscawen.com
£96.00 - £120.00   Open: all year
Map ref no. 22

Ann Heasman
Cliff House Devonport Hill Kingsand
Torpoint PL10 1NJ   Cornwall
Tel: (01752) 823110   Fax 01752 822595

Near Rd: A.374
Cliff House is a Grade II listed, 17th-century building,
converted from 2 cottages into 1 house around 150 years
ago. Although modernised to include en-suite facilities, it
still retains many of its original features. A drawing room,
with wonderful views, log fires, T.V. etc. is available for
guests' use. It has a large balcony through French windows
overlooking Plymouth Sound, Cawsand Bay & the village.
Ann is an enthusiastic wholefood cook, & meals (by
arrangement) include home-made soups, mousses &
freshly baked bread.

cbkingsand@aol.com   www.cliffhouse-kingsand.co.uk
£55.00 - £75.00   Open: all year
Map ref no. 24

Nanscawen Manor House

Prideaux Road St. Blazey PL24 2SR

Tel:(01726) 814488

email:keith@nanscawen.com www.nanscawen.com

Carol & Tony Johnson
Sheviock Barton   Sheviock   Torpoint PL11 3EH
Cornwall
Tel: (01503) 230793   Mobile 07775 688403

Near Rd: A.374
Sheviock Barton is situated in the centre of the small unspoilt village of Sheviock, directly opposite the 13th-century church.   The 300-year-old house has been sympathetically restored & offers 3 guest bedrooms (1 family & 2 doubles), each with T.V. & en-suite facilities. Also, a guest sitting room in which to relax plus a games room. Enjoy a full cooked breakfast served in the large farmhouse kitchen with 4-oven Aga. Set on the Rame Peninsula, there are many beaches within easy reach & lovely fishing villages, country houses & gardens to visit.   The Eden Project is 35 mins' by car.

thebarton@sheviock.freeserve.co.uk
www.sheviockbarton.co.uk £60.00 - £60.00
Open: all year (excl.xmas & new year) Map ref no. 25

Patrick Morgan & Vivienne Kelly
Bissick Old Mill   LadockTruro TR2 4PG
Cornwall
Tel: (01726) 882557

Near Rd: B.3275
Bissick Old Mill, formerly a working corn mill, is conveniently situated in the village of Ladock (10 mins' drive from Truro), & provides exceptional standards of comfort, cuisine & hospitality.   Low ceilings, beams, stone walls & an impressive fireplace all contribute to its character.   The breakfast menu offers a range of hot dishes, which are freshly prepared using local & home made produce & provides a memorable aspect to your stay.   Centrally situated, Bissick Old Mill is an ideal base from which to visit all areas of Cornwall, whether it be on business or purely for pleasure.

enquiries@bissickoldmill.plus.com
www.bissickoldmill.co.uk £60.00 - £75.00
Open: all year   Map ref no. 27

Mrs Barabara Holt
Oxturn House   Ladock   Truro TR2 4NQ
Cornwall
Tel: (01726) 884348   Fax 01726 884248

Near Rd: A.30
Barbara & Ian's main priority is your comfort & care at Oxturn House. The bedrooms are spacious & prettily decorated with lovely rural views & include 2 super king-size doubles/twins with all amenities. Guests are welcome to relax in the elegant drawing room, the large garden or on the terrace.   A local pub (2 mins' walk) serves good food & other restaurants are just a short drive. Truro is 10 mins' by car & there is easy access to the Eden Project, Heligan Gardens & both coasts. Only 5 miles to the A.30 & the rest of Cornwall. Children over 12.

oxturnhouse@hotmail.com www.oxturnhouse.co.uk
£52.00 - £60.00 Open: feb - nov
Map ref no. 26

Oliver & Rosemary Barstow
Crugsillick Manor Ruan High Lanes   Truro TR2 5LJ
Cornwall
Tel: (01872) 501214   Fax 01872 501874

Near Rd: A.3078
A hidden treasure of the Roseland Peninsula, one of Cornwall's loveliest areas - meandering lanes, unspoilt fishing villages & sheltered coves.   Find Crugsillick, a beautiful Grade II listed Queen Anne manor house, offering peace & comfort.   Stroll down the smugglers' path below the house to glorious beaches & spectacular coastline, visit historic houses, famous gardens, the Eden Project & Falmouth's new Maritime Museum - returning to dine, if you wish, on freshly caught seafood & home-grown vegetables. Children over 12. Animals by arrangement.

barstow@adtel.co.uk   www.adtel.co.uk
£86.00 - £114.00   Open: all year
Map ref no. 28

Graham & Annabelle Sylvester
Polsue Manor   Ruanbighlanes   Truro   TR2 5LU
Cornwall
Tel: (01872) 501270

Near Rd: B.3078. A.390
Graham & Annabelle Sylvester moved to Polsue Manor 7 years ago. It is very much a family-run B & B. While staying here you are well-placed for the Eden Project, Lost Gardens of Heligan, Trewithen & many of the outstanding National Trust gardens. A footpath leads to a wide, safe, sandy beach. This really is the ideal place for a relaxing break. En-suite bathrooms, comfortable & attractively decorated bedrooms, a well-proportioned sitting room in which to relax, a dining room where delicious breakfasts are served and a warm welcome await you at Polsue Manor.

www.polsuemanor.co.uk
£80.00 - £80.00   Open: all year
Map ref no. 29

Michael & Jo Bloor
Porteath Barn   St. Minver   Wadebridge   PL27 6RA
Cornwall   Tel: (01208) 863605
Fax 01208 863954   Mobile 0771 2591725

Near Rd: A.39
Porteath Barn is a beautifully converted 'H' shaped barn offering attractive & tastefully furnished guest accommodation in 1 wing on the ground floor. Situated in a secluded valley of 8 acres with a track leading down to the coast path & beach at low tide. An easy drive to the fabulous Eden Project & many famous Cornish gardens. There are many good eating houses from pubs to Michelin-starred restaurants within just a few miles. Rock is a 10-min. drive for watersports & a ferry to Padstow. Children over 12 years welcome.

mbloor@ukonline.co.uk   www.bestbandb.co.uk
£60.00 - £70.00   Open: all year
Map ref no. 31

Ann Tremayne
Apple Tree Cottage   Laity Moor   Ponsanooth
Truro   TR3 7HR   Cornwall
Tel: (01872) 865047

Near Rd: A.39
Apple Tree Cottage, set amid rolling countryside with delightful gardens & river, is furnished with country antiques & has a warm, welcoming atmosphere. The large lounge has a log fire, & traditional farmhouse breakfasts, cooked on the Aga, are taken in the sunlit dining room. The attractive bedrooms have pine double beds, tea/coffee-making facilities, washbasins & lovely views. Several National Trust gardens & the famous Trebah Gardens on the Helford River are only 15 mins' away. Children over 10 years. Animals by arrangement.

appletreecottage@talk21.com
www.cornwall-online.co.uk   £56.00 - £60.00
Open: all year (excl. xmas)   Map ref no. 30

Cumbria

Cumbria

The Lake District National Park is deservedly famous for its magnificent scenery. Here, England's highest mountains & rugged fells surround shimmering lakes & green valleys. But there is more to Cumbria than the beauty of the Lake District. It also has a splendid coastline, easily accessible from the main lakeland centres, as well as a border region where the Pennines, the backbone of England, reach their highest point, towering over the Eden valley.

Formation of the dramatic Lakeland scenery began in the Caledonian period when earth movements raised & folded ancient rocks, submerging them under seas & covering them with limestone. During the ice age great glaciers ground

Ullswater. Cumbria.

out the lake beds & dales of todays landscape. The craggy outcrops of the Borrowdale Volcanics with Skiddaw at 3054 feet, to the gentle dales, the open moorlands & the lakes themselves. Each lake is distinctive, some with steep mountain sides sliding straight to the water's edge, others more open with sloping wooded hillsides. Elterwater, the enchanting "lake of swans" is surrounded by reed & willows at the foot of Langdale. The charm of Ullswater inspired Wordsworth's famous poem "Daffodils".

The changeable weather of the mountainous region can produce a sudden transformation in the character of a tranquil lake, raising choppy waves across the darkened surface to break along the shoreline. It is all part of the fascination of Lakeland.

Fell walking is the best way to appreciate the full beauty of the area. There are gentle walks along the dales, & the tops of the ridges are accessible to walkers with suitable footwear & an eye to the weather. Ponytrekking is another popular way to explore the countryside.

Fairs & festivals flourish in Lakeland. The famous Appleby Horse Fair, held in June is the largest fair of its kind in the world & attracts a huge gypsy gathering. Traditional agriculture shows, sheep dog trials & local sporting events abound. The Grasmere Sports, held each August include gruelling fell races, Cumberland wrestling, hound trails & pole-leaping.

Cumbria

Cumbria Gazeteer
Area of outstanding natural beauty.
The Lake District National Park.

House & Castles
Carlisle Castle - Carlisle
12th century. Massive Norman keep - half-moon battery - ramparts, portcullis & gatehouse.
Brough Castle - Kirby Stephen
13th century - on site of Roman Station between York & Carlisle.
Dacre Castle - Penrith
14th century - massive pele tower.
Sizergh Castle - Kendal
14th century - pele tower - 15th century great hall. English & French furniture, silver & china - Jacobean relics. 18th century gardens.
Belle Island - Boweness-on-Windermere
18th century - interior by Adams Brothers, portraits by Romney.
Swarthmoor Hall - Ulverston
Elizabethan house, mullioned windows, oak staircase, panelled rooms. Home of George Fox - birthplace of Quakerism - belongs to Society of Friends.
Lorton Hall - Cockermouth
15th century pele tower, priest holes, oak panelling, Jacobean furniture.
Muncaster Castle - Ravenglass
14th century with 15th & 19th century additions - site of Roman tower.
Rusland Hall - Ulveston
Georgian mansion with period panelling, sculpture, furniture, paintings.
Levens Hall - Kendal
Elizabethan - very fine panelling & plasterwork - famous topiary garden.
Hill Top - Sawrey
17th century farmhouse home of Beatrix Potter - contains her furniture, china & some of original drawings for her children's books.
Dove Cottage - Grasmere
William Wordsworth's cottage - still contains his furnishing & his personal effects as in his lifetime.

Brantwood - Coniston
The Coniston home of John Ruskin, said to be the most beautifully situated house in the Lake District. Exhibition, gardens, bookshops & tearooms.

Cathedrals & Churches
Carlisle Cathedral - Carlisle
1130. 15th century choir stalls with painted backs - carved misericords, 16th century screen, painted roof.
Cartmel Priory (St. Mary Virgin)
15th century stalls, 17th century screen, large east window, curious central tower.
Lanercost Priory (St. Mary Magdalene)
12th century - Augustinian - north aisle now forms Parish church.
Greystoke (St. Andrew)
14th/15th century. 19th century misericords. Lovely glass in chancel.
Brougham (St. Wilfred)
15th century carved altarpiece.
Furness Abbey
12th century monastery beautiful setting.
Shap Abbey
12th century with 16th century tower.

Museums & Galleries
Abbot Hall - Kendal
18th century, Georgian house with period furniture, porcelain, silver, pictures, etc. Also contains modern galleries with contemporary paintings, sculptures & ceramics. Changing exhibitions on show.
Carlisle Museum & Art Gallery - Carlisle

Things to see & do
Keswick Sheep Dog Demonstrations - Keswick
With hundreds of sheep grazing on miles of rugged fell, the dogs help gather the animals. A unique opportunity to meet and watch the dogs in training as they show their ability to handle sheep - and ducks - guided by whistles, commands and instinct! Every Wednesday at 4.00 pm, May to September.

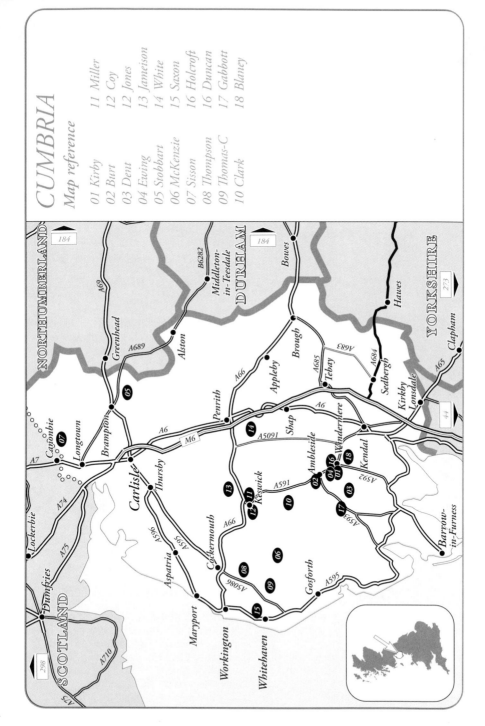

CUMBRIA

Map reference

01 Kirby	11 Miller
02 Burt	12 Coy
03 Dent	12 Jones
04 Ewing	13 Jameison
05 Stobbart	14 White
06 McKenzie	15 Saxon
07 Sisson	16 Holcroft
08 Thompson	16 Duncan
09 Thomas-C	17 Gabbott
10 Clark	18 Blaney

Robert & Helen Kirby
Buckle Yeat Nr.Sawrey   Hawkshead
Ambleside LA22 0LF   Cumbria
Tel: (015394) 36446

Near Rd: A.591
Buckle Yeat is famous for its connections with Beatrix Potter.
Although over 200 years old, it has been sympathetically
& tastefully refurbished throughout. There is a large lounge
with log fire & an attractive dining room which also serves
morning coffee & afternoon teas. The accommodation
includes 6 comfortable en-suite bedrooms. There are many
good local pubs & restaurants which offer excellent meals.
Buckle Yeat is in an ideal position for touring Lakeland,
with walks, fishing & birdwatching all nearby; perfect for a
relaxing break away from it all. Animals by arrangement.
A warm welcome awaits you.

info@buckle-yeat.co.uk   www.buckle-yeat.co.uk
£66.00 - £70.00   Open: all year
Map ref no. 01

Judy & Graham Dent
The Garth Country House Nr. Sawrey Hawkshead
Nr. Ambleside LA22 0JZ Cumbria
Tel: (015394) 36346

Near Rd: B.5285
The Garth is a comfortable Victorian country house,
carefully restored, in Near Sawrey, one of the prettiest,
unspoiled villages in the South Lakes. The house sits in 2
acres of garden, overlooking Grizedale & across Esthwaite
to the Langdales & Coniston. It is beautifully furnished &
decorated throughout & guests are encouraged to relax in
the lounge, with welcoming log fire on cooler evenings,
where there are books, games & even a piano for your
use. The en-suite bedrooms offer every comfort with T.V.,
CD player & more. Many places to eat locally. Near Sawrey
is within easy reach of the very best of Lakeland.

enquiries@thegarthcountryhouse.co.uk
www.thegarthcountryhouse.co.uk £70.00 - £95.00
Open: all year (excl. xmas)   Map ref No. 03

Ian & Helen Burt
The Old Vicarage Vicarage Road   Ambleside LA22 9DH
Cumbria
Tel: (015394) 33364

Near Rd: A.591
The Old Vicarage is a charming detached Victorian house,
set in its own peaceful wooded grounds, overlooking
Rothay Park. A perfect base from which to explore the
fells or to go boating on the lakes. There are 10 bedrooms
with en-suite facilities, each room is furnished to a high
standard & has T.V./DVD player etc. Some rooms with 4-
poster or king-size beds & others with spa baths. Guests
are welcome to enjoy the indoor heated pool, sauna & hot
tub or you can relax in the attractive sun lounge or tranquil
garden. Walking, fishing, riding, golf & watersports nearby.

the.old.vicarage@kencomp.net
www.oldvicarageambleside.co.uk £63.75 - £110.00
Open: all year   Map ref no. 02

Mr & Mrs C A Ewing
Beechwood   Beresford Road Bowness-on-Windermere
LA23 2JG   Cumbria
Tel: (015394) 43403

Near Rd: A.591
Beechwood is superbly situated in Bowness-on-
Windermere, set back from the road overlooking the quiet
Rose Gardens. Bedrooms are individually decorated to a
very high standard & many have king-size beds & a small
sofa. All rooms have T.V./video & cd player. A
complimentary video library is available & there is also an
elegantly refurbished lounge in which to relax. Beechwood
is a 5 min. stroll to the Lake & Esplanade, with many shops
& restaurants close by.

enquiries@beechwoodlakes.co.uk
www.beechwoodlakes.co.uk £60.00 - £110.00
Open: all year   Map ref no. 04

Wood House

Buttermere CA13 9XA

Tel:(017687) 70208 Fax 017687 70241

email:woodhouse.guest@virgin.net www.wdhse.co.uk

see p.73

Sheila Stobbart
Hullerbank   Talkin   Brampton CA8 1LB
Cumbria
Tel: (016977) 46668   Fax 016977 46668

Near Rd: A.69
Attractive pink-washed Georgian style farmhouse dated 1635-1751 standing in its own grounds, near the picturesque village of Talkin, 2 1/2 miles from Brampton. Superb walking country & central for Hadrian's Wall, the Lake District & the Borders. A friendly, relaxed atmosphere awaits. 3 bedrooms with private facilities, tea/coffee trays & colour T.V. & a comfortable sitting room with small inglenook fireplace & separate dining room where excellent breakfasts are served.   2 inns with restaurant facilities nearby. Children over 12 years.

info@hullerbank.freeserve.co.uk
www.hullerbankbnb.co.uk   £56.00 - £58.00
Open: feb - dec   Map ref no. 05

Mr & Mrs Sisson
Bessiestown Catlowdy Penton Longtown
Carlisle CA6 5QP Cumbria
Tel: (01228) 577219   Fax 01228 577019

Near Rd: B.6318
A multi-award-winning country guest house, overlooking the Scottish borders, where a friendly, relaxing atmosphere is assured. 6 recently refurbished, en-suite rooms with radio, T.V. & tea/coffee-making facilities.   Delightfully decorated public rooms & conservatory. Also, ground-floor accommodation in extremely comfortable courtyard cottages. 1 room with facilities for the disabled. Delicious home-cooking. Residential drinks licence. Guests may use the indoor heated swimming pool.   A good stop-off to/from Scotland & N. Ireland.

info@bessiestown.co.uk   www.bessiestown.co.uk
£70.00 - £75.00 Open: all year (excl. xmas day)
Map ref no. 07

see p.70

Michael & Judy McKenzie
Wood House Buttermere CA13 9XA
Cumbria
Tel: (017687) 70208   Fax 017687 70241

Near Rd: A.66
The view overlooking Wood House was chosen by J.M.W. Turner RA for his famous painting of Buttermere in 1798. A visitor describing the interior has written, "The furnishings & decor are serene & beautiful though completely unpretentious."   The splendid en-suite bedrooms have spellbinding views over the lake. BBC Good Food Magazine - "Excellent dinners & breakfasts are served in the elegant dining room." Good walks. Local activities include boating & fishing. Red Squirrels live in the grounds. Wood House is an outstanding home.

woodhouse.guest@virgin.net   www.wdhse.co.uk
£80.00 - £90.00 Open: feb - nov
Map ref no. 06

see p.72

Hazel Thompson
New House Farm Lorton Nr.Cockermouth CA13 9UU
Cumbria   Tel: (01900) 85404
Fax 01900 85478   Mobile 07841 159818

Near Rd: B.5289
Set superbly in the Lorton/Buttermere Valley, this unique award-winning 17th-century Grade II listed house is full of elegant antiques & original features such as flagged floors, oak beams &.stone fireplaces, where log fires crackle on colder days. There are 5 luxurious bedrooms, all en-suite, 2 with oak 4-posters & all with uninterrupted views of the surrounding mountains. Great food. Welcoming hosts. Children over 6. Animals by arrangement. Walker's recommendation: 'After a long day's walk, relax in the hot tub in the garden with a bottle of wine under the stars!'

hazel@newhouse-farm.co.uk
www.newhouse-farm.co.uk   £134.00 - £138.00
Open: all year   Map ref no. 08

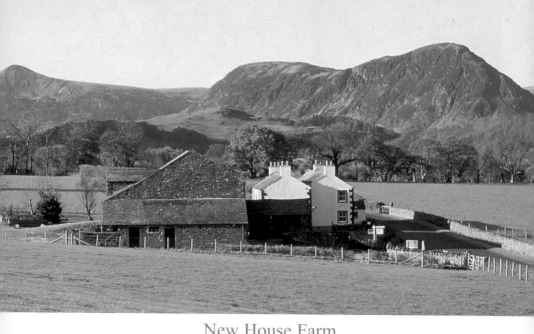

New House Farm

Lorton Nr. Cockermouth CA13 9UU

Tel (01900) 85404 Fax 01900 85478 Mobile 07841 159818

email:hazel@newhouse-farm.co.uk www.newhouse-farm.co.uk

Bessiestown

Catlowdy Longtown Carlisle CA6 5QP

Tel:(01228) 577219 Fax 01228 577019

email:info@bessiestown.co.uk www.bessiestown.co.uk

Greystones Hotel

Ambleside Road Keswick CA12 4DP

Tel:(017687) 73108

email:greystones@keslakes.freeserve.co.uk www.greystones.tv

see p.76

Malcolm Thomas-Chapman
The Shepherds Arms Hotel Ennerdale Bridge CA23 3AR
Cumbria
Tel: (01946) 961249

Near Rd: A.5086
The Shepherds Arms Hotel is situated on Wainwright's world famous Coast to Coast walk. Offering tastefully furnished accommodation in 3 twin & 3 double rooms all en-suite. Also 1 double & 1 twin room with private bathroom. Family rooms are also available. Bedrooms are non-smoking & are well-equipped with tea/coffee facilities etc. Breakfast is served in the Georgian panelled dining room, where evening meals are sometimes available & are complemented by a selection of fine wines. The Shepherds Arms Bar is open to the public; specialities include real ales & a full bar menu with locally sourced produce.

shepherdsarms@btconnect.com
www.shepherdsarmshotel.co.uk £75.00 - £75.00
Open: all year Map ref no. 09

Duncan & Jane Miller
The Grange Country House Manor Brow Keswick
CA12 4BA Cumbria
Tel: 017687 72500

Near Rd: A.591
Grange Country House is situated in its own grounds, with excellent parking, overlooking Keswick-on-Derwentwater & the beautiful surrounding mountains. Lovely bedrooms with those extra touches together with comfort, care, quality furnishings & relaxed hospitality make this award-winning home a perfect holiday base. The exceptional breakfast menu will give you an ideal start to your day in Lakeland. The Grange is somewhere special for lovers of the countryside. Lounge licence. Proprietors recommended restaurant/pub list for evening meals.

info@grangekeswick.com www.grangekeswick.com
£72.00 - £92.00 Open: mar - nov
Map ref no. 11

see p.74

Martin & Angela Clark
Banerigg Guest House Lake Road Grasmere LA22 9PW
Cumbria
Tel: (015394) 35204

Near Rd: A.591
Banerigg House is delightfully situated overlooking Grasmere lake & the local hills. All 6 bedrooms have modern amenities & most have lake views. A spacious lounge with log fire plus plenty of books, maps & walking guides for you to use. A delicious & plentiful breakfast is served in the dining room overlooking the lake. The house is ideally located for fell walking, sailing & canoeing. Angela & Martin have been offering their unique hospitality at Banerigg for over 26 years & are always on hand to help you plan your walk, or find a special place to eat.

banerigg2001@hotmail.com
www.baneriggguesthouse.co.uk £64.00 - £70.00
Open: all year (excl. xmas) Map ref no. 10

Robert & Janet Jones
Greystones Hotel Ambleside Road Keswick CA12 4DP
Cumbria
Tel: (017687) 73108

Near Rd: A.591
Greystones enjoys an enviable position overlooking the grounds of St. John's Church, & has excellent fell views. It is just a short walk to the market square & Lake Derwentwater. The accommodation includes 8 delightful en-suite rooms, each with T.V., tea/coffee-making facilities & a folder of suggested walks & tours. Private parking is available. Greystones is an excellent base for a relaxing break & is ideal for exploring the lakes & the surrounding area. Children over 9 years welcome.

greystones@keslakes.freeserve.co.uk www.greystones.tv
£50.00 - £62.00 Open: jan - nov
Map ref no. 12

The Grange Country House

Manor Brow Keswick CA12 4BA

Tel:017687 72500

email:info@grangekeswick.com www.grangekeswick.com

Alan & Angela Jameison
Scales Farm Country Guest House   Scales   Threlkeld
Keswick CA12 4SY   Cumbria
Tel: (017687) 79660   Fax 017687 79510

Near Rd: A.66
Stunning open views & a warm friendly welcome await you at Scales Farm, a traditional 17th-century fells farmhouse sensitively modernised to provide accommodation of the highest standard. All of the bedrooms are tastefully furnished, en-suite, centrally heated, with tea/coffee-making facilities, colour T.V. & fridges. A separate entrance from the private car park allows guests direct access to the rooms & the traditional lounge. There is a Lakeland Inn/Restaurant next door, which serves appetising meals. Scales Farm is a lovely base for touring or walking in this magnificent region.

scales@scalesfarm.com www.scalesfarm.com
£56.00 - £64.00 Open: all year (excl. xmas)
Map ref no. 13

Mrs Lesley White
Beckfoot Country House Helton   Nr.Penrith CA10 2QB
Cumbria
Tel: (01931) 713241   Fax 01931 713391

Near Rd: A.66, A.6
A fine old residence featuring a half-panelled hall, staircase & attractive panelled dining room. Set in 3 acres of grounds in the delightful Lake District, it is a quiet, peaceful retreat for a holiday base, & is within easy reach of the many pleasure spots in the area. The accommodation includes 7 tastefully furnished bedrooms, all with private shower/bathroom & tea/coffee-making facilities & a comfortable ground-floor annexe twin-bedded room. A dining room, drawing & reading room in which to relax. Beckfoot Country House is a delightful base for a touring holiday in Cumbria. Animals by arrangement.

info@beckfoot.co.uk www.beckfoot.co.uk
£70.00 - £98.00 Open: mar - nov
Map ref no. 14

Roger & Irene Coy
Lairbeck Hotel   Vicarage Hill   Keswick CA12 5QB
Cumbria
Tel: (017687) 73373   Fax 017687 73144

Near Rd: A.66
Featured on television's 'Wish You Were Here?' holiday programme, Lairbeck Hotel is only 10 mins' walk from Keswick town centre, in a secluded location with superb mountain views. Here you can treat yourself to traditional, award-winning dining & hospitality in a friendly informal atmosphere & relax in front of cosy log fires. All of the 14 comfortable bedrooms are en-suite & individually decorated. Single & ground-floor rooms, plus a 4-poster room is available. Spacious parking facilities. Children over 5 years welcome.

bbb@lairbeckhotel-keswick.co.uk
www.lairbeckhotel-keswick.co.uk   £84.00 - £96.00
Open: mid mar - dec   Map ref no. 11

Jane & David Saxon
Moresby Hall Moresby   Whitehaven CA28 6PJ
Cumbria
Tel: (01946) 696317   Fax 01946 694385

Near Rd: A.595
Grade I listed Moresby Hall dates from around 1250, although the front facade dates from approx. 1620. Enjoy genuine hospitality in this charming country house, which offers 4 beautifully appointed guest rooms, including the De Ashby Suite with 4-poster bed & hydro-massage power shower/steam room en-suite. Evening meals are freshly prepared by Jane & served in the elegant dining room. Situated close to the impressive Georgian harbour of Whitehaven, Moresby hall is also convenient for visiting the Lakes, Cockermouth & Keswick. Children over 8.

jane@moresbyhall.co.uk www.moresbyhall.co.uk
£100.00 - £140.00 Open: all year
Map ref no. 15

Brian & Frances Holcroft
Lynwood Guest House   Broad Street
Windermere LA23 2AB Cumbria
Tel: (015394) 42550   Fax 015394 42550

Near Rd: A.592
A Victorian Lakeland stone house built in 1865, offering 5 centrally heated comfortablke bedrooms, each with en-suite bathrooms, all with modern amenities including colour T.V. & tea/coffee-making facilities. Guests may relax in the T.V. lounge which is available throughout the day. Centrally located, only 150 yards from village shops & restaurants, & only 5 mins' from the bus & railway station. The host is a Lakeland tour guide, & is happy to assist in planning your stay. Children over 5 years are welcome. An excellent base from which to explore Lakeland.

enquires@lynwood-guest-house.co.uk
www.lynwood-guest-house.co.uk £50.00 - £60.00
Open: all year   Map ref no. 16

Robert & Janz Duncan
Blenheim Lodge Brantfell Road
Bowness-on-Windermere Windermere LA23 3AE
Cumbria   Tel: (015394) 43440

Near Rd: A.5074, A.591
Peaceful, friendly guest house, ideally situated in an elevated position, nestled against woodlands & boasting panoramic views of Lake Windermere. Situated next to the Dalesway - half-minutes walk to a welcome drink & hot bath! Single, double, family & twin bedrooms with en-suite/private facilities & a lounge with fireplace. Healthy breakfast options include fresh local produce & home-baked croissants. Bowness centre & Lake Windermere are 5 minutes walk. Parking. Free country club membership & WAADA fishing permits.

enquiries@blenheim-lodge.com
www.blenheim-lodge.com £70.00 - £116.00
Open: all year   Map ref no. 16

Catherine Gabbott
The Coach House Lake Road   Windermere LA23 2EQ
Cumbria
Tel: (015394) 44494

Near Rd: A.591
The property was originally a Victorian Coach House, but now the interior is more chic and minimalist, achieved through the bold use of bright colours and contemporary furnishings. The modern decor continues in the en-suite bedrooms including one pretty room in fuchsia pink, and another in duck egg blue. Stylish iron beds and a host of extra amenities, coupled with freshly prepared breakfasts with locally sourced produce ensure a comfortable and relaxed experience.

enquiries@lakedistrictbandb.com
www.lakedistrictbandb.com £58.00 - £80.00
Open: all year   Map ref no. 17

see p.79

Tony & Liz Blaney
Fairfield Garden Guest House Brantfell Road
Bowness-on-Windermere   Windermere LA23 3AE
Cumbria   Tel: (015394) 46565

Near Rd: A.591
Fairfield is a small friendly, family-run B & B in a 200-year-old house, set in its own grounds with a large beautiful garden & terrace. Close to the waterfront & with its own car park, 200 metres from the shops, pubs/restaurants & waterfront of Bowness. Fairfield is an ideal base for exploring the area. 10 en-suite bedrooms with modern facilities. Bar & free internet access are available. Generous breakfasts are a speciality. Dinner is available during the low season only. Animals by arrangement.

info@the-fairfield.co.ukw ww.the-fairfield.co.uk
£58.00 - £94.00 Open: all year (excl. xmas)
Map ref no. 18

Fairfield Garden Guest House

Brantfell Road Bowness-on-Windermere Windermere LA23 3AE

Tel:(01539) 46565 email:info@the-fairfield.co.uk www.the-fairfield.co.uk

Derbyshire & Staffordshire

Derbyshire

A county with everything but the sea, this was Lord Byron's opinion of Derbyshire, & the special beauty of the Peak District was recognised by its designation as Britain's first National Park.

Purple heather moors surround craggy limestone outcrops & green hills drop to sheltered meadows or to deep gorges & tumbling rivers.

Derbyshire's lovely dales have delightful names too - Dove Dale, Monk's Dale, Raven's Dale, Water-cum-Jolly-Dale, & they are perfect for walking. The more adventurous can take up the challenge of the Pennine Way, a 270 mile pathway from Edale to the Scottish border.

The grit rock faces offer good climbing,

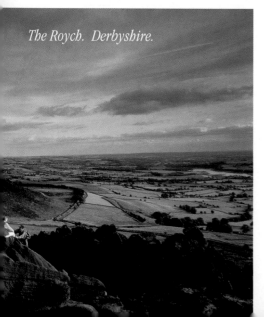

The Roych. Derbyshire.

particularly at High Tor above the River Derwent, & underground there are extensive & spectacular caverns. There are show caves at the Heights of Abraham, which you reach by cable-car, & at Castleton, source of the rare Blue John mineral, & at Pole's Cavern in Buxton where there are remarkable stalactites & stalagmites.

Buxton's splendid Crescent reflects the town's spa heritage, & the Opera House is host to an International Festival each summer.

The waters at Matlock too were prized for their curative properties & a great Hydro was built there in the last century, to give treatment to the hundreds of people who came to "take the waters".

Bakewell is a lovely small town with a fascinating market, some fine buildings & the genuine Bakewell Pudding, (known elsewhere as Bakewell tart).

Well-dressing is a custom carried on throughout the summer in the villages & towns. It is a thanksgiving for the water, that predates the arrival of Christianity in Britain. Flower-petals, leaves, moss & bark are pressed in intricate designs into frames of wet clay & erected over the wells, where they stay damp & fresh for days.

The mining of lead & the prosperity of the farms brought great wealth to the landowning families who were able to employ the finest architects & craftsmen.

Derbyshire & Staffordshire

Staffordshire

Staffordshire is a contrast of town & county. Miles of moorland & dramatic landscapes lie to the north of the country, & to the south is the Vale of Trent & the greenery of Cannock Chase. But the name of Staffordshire invokes that of the Potteries, the area around Stoke-on-Trent where the world-renowned ceramics are made.

The factories that produce the Royal Doulton, Minton, Spode & Coalport china will arrange tours for visitors, & there is a purpose-built visitor centre at Barlaston displaying the famous Wedgwood tradition.

The Gladstone Pottery Museum is set in a huge Victorian potbank, & the award-winning City museum in Stoke-on-Trent has a remarkable ceramics collection.

There is lovely scenery to be found where the moorlands of Staffordshire meet the crags & valleys of the Peak District National Park. From the wild & windy valleys of The Roaches (from the French 'roche') you can look across the county to Cheshire & Wales. Drivers can take high moorland roads that are marked out as scenic routes.

The Staffordshire Way, completed in 1983, was the first of the paths to be created and spans the length of the County for 148 kilometres from Mow Cop in the north to Kinver Edge in the south. Starting among rugged gritstone hills on the edge of the

Peak District National Park, the Staffordshire Way turns south towards Rudyard Lake and Leek beyond.

The valleys of the Dove & Manifold are beautiful limestone dales & ideal for walking or for cycling. Sir Izzak Walton, author of "The Compleat Angler" drew his inspiration, & his trout, from the waters here.

The valley of the River Churnet is both pretty & peaceful, being largely inaccessible to cars. The Caldon Canal, with its colourful narrowboats, follows the course of the river & there are canal-side pubs, picnic areas, boat rides & woodland trails to enjoy. The river runs through the grounds of mock-Gothic Alton Towers, now a leisure park.

The Vale of Trent is largely rural with small market towns, villages, river & canals.

Cannock Chase covers 20 square miles of heath & woodland & is the home of the largest herd of fallow deer in England. Shugborough Hall stands in the Chase. The ancestral home of Lord Lichfeld, it also houses the Stafforshire County Museum & a farm for rare breeds including the famous Tamworth Pig.

Burton-on-Trent is known as the home of the British brewery industry & there are two museums in the town devoted to the history of beer. Lichfield is a small & picturesque city with a cathedral which dates from the 12th century.

Derbyshire & Staffordshire

Derbyshire Gazeteer

Areas of outstanding natural beauty.
Peak National Park. The Dales.

Houses & Castles

Chatsworth - Bakewell
17th century, built for 1st. Duke of Devonshire.
Furniture, paintings & drawings, books, etc.
Fine gardens & parklands.
Haddon Hall - Bakewell
Medieval manor house - complete. Terraced
rose gardens.
Hardwick Hall - Nr. Chesterfield
16th century - said to be more glass than wall.
Fine furniture, tapestries & furnishings.Herb garden.
Kedlestone Hall - Derby
18th century - built on site of 12th century Manor
house. Work of Robert Adam - has world
famous marble hall. Old Master paintings. 11th
century church nearby.
Melbourne Hall - Nr. Derby
12th century origins - restored by Sir John Coke.
Fine collection of pictures & a variety of works of
art. Magnificent gardens & famous wrought
iron pagoda.
Sudbury Hall - Sudbury
Has fine examples of work of the greatest
craftsmen of the period-Grinling Gibbons, Pierce
and Laguerre.
Winster Market House - Nr. Matlock
17th century stone built market house.

Cathedrals & Churches

Chesterfield (St. Mary & All Saints)
13th & 14th centuries. 4 chapels, polygonal
apse, medieval screens, Jacobean pulpit.
Derby (All Saints)
Perpendicular tower - classical style - 17th
century plate, 18th century screen.
Melbourne (St. Michael & St. Mary)
Norman with two west towers & crossing tower.
Splendid plate, 18th century screen.
Normbury (St. Mary & St. Barloke)
14th century - perpendicular tower.

Staffordshire Gazeteer

Houses & Castles

Ancient High House - Stafford
16th century - largest timber-framed town house
in England.
Shugborough - Nr. Stafford
Ancestral home of the Earl of Lichfield. Mansion
house, paintings, silver, ceramics, furniture.
County Museum. Rare Breeds Farm.
Moseley Old Hall - Nr. Wolverhampton
Elizabethan house formerly half-timbered.
Stafford Castle
Large & well-preserved Norman castle in
grounds with castle trail.
Tamworth Castle
Norman motte & bailey castle with later
additions. Museum.

Cathedrals & Churches

Croxden Abbey
12th century foundation Cistercian abbey. Ruins
of 13th century church.
Ingestre (St. Mary the Virgin)
A rare Wren church built in1676.
Lichfield Cathedral
Unique triple-spired 12th century cathedral.
Tamworth (St. Editha's)
Founded 963, rebuilt 14th century. Unusual
double spiral staircase.
Tutbury (St. Mary's)
Norman church with impressive West front.

Museums & Galleries

City Museum & Art Gallery - Stoke-on-Trent
Modern award-winning museum. Ceramics,
decorative arts, etc.
Dr. Johnson Birthplace Museum - Lichfield
The story of his life and achievements is told
through pictures, furniture, manuscripts and
personal items.
Izaak Walton Cottage & Museum - Shallowfield
Museum dedicated to the Author, containing
many historical exhibits.

DERBYSHIRE & STAFFORDSHIRE

Map reference

01 Mayes
02 Chambers
03 Foster
04 Moffett
05 Hull-Bailey

06 Mairs
07 Lewis
08 Taylor
09 Sutcliffe
10 Ball

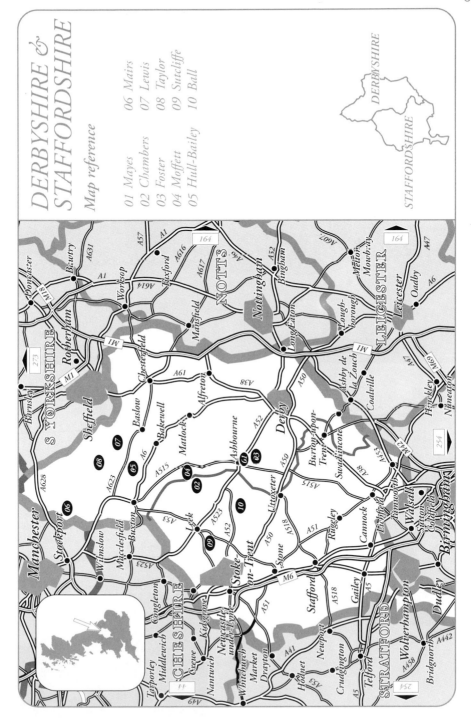

Biggin Hall

Biggin-by-Hartington Buxton SK17 0DH

Tel:(01298) 84451 Fax 01298 84681

email:enquiries@bigginhall.co.uk www.bigginhall.co.uk

Paula & Alan Coker Mayes
Omnia Somnia The Coach House The Firs Ashbourne
DE6 1HF Derbyshire
Tel: (01335) 300145

Near Rd: A.52
Omnia Somnia - Everything is a dream - and you may think you are dreaming when you stay at Ashbourne's award-winning guest accommodation. The house itself snuggles into a hillside & the double en-suite rooms have unique character, from a picture gallery & 2 person bath in Oriens, to the hideaway bedroom of Occidens & the sumptuous 4-poster of Meridies. Fine detail is everywhere with quality furnishings & effects to delight the senses. Bedrooms are located on the ground floor, while the lounge & dining room is upstairs as is access to the garden. The hospitality & food are second to none.

alan@omniasomnia.co.uk www.omniasomnia.co.uk
£95.00 - £100.00 Open: all year
Map ref no. 01

Mrs Sylvia Foster
Shirley Hall Hall Lane Shirley Ashbourne DE6 3AS
Derbyshire
Tel: (01335) 360346 Fax 01335 360346

Near Rd: A.52
Shirley Hall is a lovely, peaceful old farmhouse, just to the south of Ashbourne, close to the village of Shirley. In the centre of rolling pastureland enjoy the tranquillity of this part-moated, timbered farmhouse, surrounded by a large lawned garden. There are 3 attractive bedrooms with en-suite bathrooms, colour T.V. & tea/coffee-making facilities. The delicious full English breakfast with home-made bread & preserves is renowned. The local village pub is excellent for evening meals. Coarse-fishing is available on the farm & woodland walks are nearby.

sylviafoster@shirleyhallfarm.com
www.shirleyhallfarm.com £60.00 - £66.00
Open: all year Map ref no. 03

see p.84

Naomi Chambers & Nick Lourie
Stanshope Hall Stanshope Ashbourne DE6 2AD
Derbyshire
Tel: (01335) 310278

Near Rd: A.515
Stanshope Hall, with its informal feel but with every comfort, stands in splendid isolation among the dry stone walls of the southern Peak District. Walks from the door lead to verdant Dovedale or the undiscovered seclusion of the Manifold Valley. The most attractive en-suite bedrooms have hand-painted walls & frescos in the bathrooms. Excellent candle-lit dinners (by arrangement) are prepared using uncomplicated but imaginative recipes with fresh local & garden produce.

naomi@stanshope.demon.co.uk www.stanshope.net
£80.00 - £90.00 Open: all year (excl. xmas)
Map ref no. 02

James Moffett
Biggin Hall Biggin-by-Hartington Buxton SK17 0DH
Derbyshire
Tel: (01298) 84451 Fax 01298 84681

Near Rd: A.515
A delightful 17th-century old hall, Grade II* listed, completely restored & keeping all the character of its origins, with massive oak beams. 19 comfortable rooms, all charmingly furnished, 1 with a 4-poster bed, all with en-suite facilities & modern amenities. Guests have the choice of 2 sitting rooms, 1 with a log fire, 1 with colour T.V. & library, & there is a lovely garden. The house is beautifully furnished, with many antiques. Children 12 & over are welcome. Animals by arrangement.

enquiries@bigginhall.co.uk www.bigginhall.co.uk
£75.00 - £130.00 Open: all year
Map ref no. 04

Cressbrook Hall

Cressbrook Buxton SK17 8SY

Tel:(01298)871289 Fax 01298 871845 email:stay@cressbrookhall.co.uk www.cressbrookhall.co.uk

see p.86

see p.88

Mrs B Hull-Bailey
Cressbrook Hall   Cressbrook   Buxton SK17 8SY
Derbyshire
Tel: (01298)871289   Fax 01298 871845

Near Rd: A.6
Cressbrook Hall, built 170 years ago, is an imposing & memorable country residence stunningly situated on the edge of the steep limestone gorge carved by the River Wye close to Monsal Dale. Surrounded by beautiful formal gardens & private rural grounds, Cressbrook Hall is memorable for its fine architecture & lovely interiors. Elegant en-suite B & B rooms are complemented by an exquisite period dining room; & the recently restored Orangery makes a most spectacular venue for wedding receptions, family reunions etc. Self-catering cottages. (Dinner by arrangement for groups of 12 or more.)

stay@cressbrookhall.co.uk   www.cressbrookhall.co.uk
£95.00 - £115.00   Open: all year
Map ref no. 05

David & Meirlys Lewis
Delf View House Church Street Eyam
Hope Valley S32 5QH Derbyshire
Tel: (01433) 631533   Fax 01433 631972

Near Rd: A.623
Beautiful & tranquil accommodation in an elegant listed Georgian country house in historic Eyam village in the magnificent Peak National Park. Guests are warmly welcomed in the drawing room, which is delightfully furnished with antiques, pictures & books. The 3 superb bedrooms, 1 en-suite, include a Sheraton 4-poster & 18th-century French twin beds. Sumptuous breakfasts served in the oak-beamed dining room. There are restaurants nearby, 1 within 3 mins' walk. Delf View Houyse is ideal for visiting Chatsworth, Haddon & Eyam Hall. Children over 12 years welcome.

lewis@delfview.co.uk   www.delfview.co.uk
£76.00 - £92.00 Open: all year
Map ref no. 07

Mrs J Mairs
Woodlands   Woodseats Lane   Charlesworth
Glossop SK13 5DP   Derbyshire
Tel: (01457) 866568

Near Rd: A. 626
Woodlands is a delightful Victorian guest house with licensed tea rooms, which is situated in the village of Charlesworth in Derbyshire's magnificent Peak District. 3 bedrooms (all with en-suite/private facilities) have been furnished with great attention to detail. The decor is light & airy, linens are crisp & fresh & each bathroom gleams. Breakfast is a feast & is taken in the fabulous conservatory with views over the garden & beyond. 3 local pubs offer evening meals. Chatsworth House, Lyme Park, Buxton & Manchester within easy reach. Children over 12.

mairs@lineone.net   www.woodlandshighpeak.co.uk
£55.00 - £65.00   Open: all year
Map ref no. 06

see p.89

Philip & Vivienne Taylor
Underleigh House   OffEdale Road   Hope
Hope Valley S33 6RF Derbyshire
Tel: (01433) 621372   Fax 01433 621324

Near Rd: A.6187
Set in an idyllic & peaceful location amidst glorious scenery, this extended cottage & barn conversion (dating from 1873) is the perfect base for exploring the Peak District. Underleigh is in the heart of magnificent walking country. Each of the 6 en-suite rooms is furnished to a high standard with many thoughtful extras included. Delicious award-winning breakfasts in the flagstoned dining hall feature local & home-made specialities. After a day in the Peak Park, relax in the beamed lounge (with a log fire when chilly) or on the terrace surrounded by flowers. Children over 12.

underleigh.house@btconnect.com
www.underleighhouse.co.uk   £70.00 - £90.00
Open: all year (excl.xmas & new year)   Map ref no. 08

Delf View House

Church Street Eyam S32 5QH

Tel:(01433) 631533 Fax 01433 631972

email:lewis@delfviewhouse.co.uk www.delfviewhouse.co.uk

Underleigh House

off Edale Road Hope Valley S33 6RF

Tel:(01433) 621372 Fax 01433 621324 email:underleigh.house@btconnect.com www.underleighhouse.co.uk

Mrs Elaine Sutcliffe
Choir Cottage & Choir House   Ostlers Lane   Cheddleton
Nr. Leek   ST13 7HS   Staffordshire
Tel: (01538) 360561   Mobile 07719 617078

Near Rd: A.520
Chior Cottage, a 17th-century stone cottage, was once a
resting place for ostlers. It now provides beautifully
appointed bedrooms, with full en-suite facilities, central
heating, colour T.V., tea/coffee tray & 'phone. The Pine
Room & Rose Room have 4-poster beds, & 1 room is
suitable as a family suite. All rooms are very comfortable.
Set in a quiet location but convenient for exploring the Peak
District, potteries & Alton Towers. Excellent food & careful
attention to detail are assured.

enquiries@choircottage.co.uk   www.choircottage.co.uk
£60.00 - £70.00   Open: all year
Map ref no. 09

C. M. Ball
Manor House Farm   Prestwood   Denstone
Uttoxeter ST14 5DD   Staffordshire
Tel: (01889) 590415   Fax 01335 342198

Near Rd: A.50
A beautiful Grade II listed farmhouse, set amid rolling hills
& rivers. Accommodation is in 3 attractive bedrooms, all
with 4-poster beds & an en-suite bathroom. (1 room can
be used as a twin.) The house is tastefully furnished
throughout with antiques & retains many traditional features
including an oak-panelled breakfast room. Guests are
welcome to relax in the extensive gardens with grass tennis
court & Victorian summer house. Ideal for visiting Alton
Towers, the Peak District or the potteries.

cm_ball@yahoo.co.uk   www.4posteraccom.com
£52.00 - £58.00   Open: all year
Map ref no. 10

Devon

Devon

Here is a county of tremendous variety. Two glorious & contrasting coastlines with miles of sandy beaches, sheltered coves & rugged cliffs. There are friendly resorts & quiet villages of cob & thatch, two historic cities, & a host of country towns & tiny hamlets as well as the wild open spaces of two national parks.

From the grandeur of Hartland Point east to Foreland Point where Exmoor reaches the sea, the north Devon coast is incomparable. At Westward Ho!, Croyde & Woolacombe the rolling surf washes the golden beaches & out to sea stands beautiful Lundy Island, ideal for bird watching, climbing & walking. The tiny village of Clovelly with its cobbled street tumbles down the cliffside to the sea. Ilfracombe is a friendly resort town & the twin towns of Lynton & Lynmouth are joined by a cliff railway.

The south coast is a colourful mixture of soaring red sandstone cliffs dropping to sheltered sandy coves & the palm trees of the English Riviera. This is one of England's great holiday coasts with a string of popular resorts; Seaton, Sidmouth, Budleigh Salterton, Exmouth, Dawlish, Teignmouth & the trio of Torquay, Paignton & Brixham that make up Torbay. To the south, beyond Berry Head are Dartmouth, rich in navy tradition, & Salcombe, a premiere sailing centre in the deep inlet of the Kingsbridge estuary. Plymouth is a happy blend of holiday resort, tourist centre, historic & modern city, & the meeting-point for the wonderful old sailing vessels for the Tall Ships Race.

Inland the magnificent wilderness of Dartmoor National Park offers miles of sweeping moorland, granite tors, clear streams & wooded valleys, ancient stone circles & clapper bridges. The tors, as the Dartmoor peaks, are called are easily climbed & the views from the tops are superb. Widecombe-in-the-Moor, with its imposing church tower, & much photographed Buckland-in-the-Moor are only two of Dartmoor's lovely villages.

The Exmoor National Park straddles the Devon/Somerset border. It is a land of wild heather moorland above deep wooded valleys & sparkling streams. The home to herds of red deer & soaring buzzards.

Buckland in the Moor. Devon.

Devon

Gazeteer

Areas of outstanding natural beauty.
North, South, East Devon.

Houses & Castles

Arlington Court - Barnstaple
Regency house, collection of shell, pewter &
model ships.

Bickleigh Castle - Nr. Tiverton
Thatched Jacobean wing. Great Hall &
armoury. Early Norman chapel, gardens
& moat.

Buckland Abbey - Nr. Plymouth
13th century Cistercian monastery - 16th century
alterations. Home of Drake - contains his relics
& folk gallery.

Bradley Manor - Newton Abbot
15th century Manor house with perpendicular
chapel.

Cadhay - Ottery St. Mary
16th century Elizabethan Manor house.

Castle Drogo - Nr.Chagford
Designed by Lutyens - built of granite, standing
over 900 feet above the gorge of the Teign river.

Chambercombe Manor - Illfracombe
14th-15th century Manor house.

Castle Hill - Nr. Barnstaple
18th century Palladian mansion - fine furniture of
period, pictures, porcelain & tapestries.

Hayes Barton - Nr. Otterton
16th century plaster & thatch house. Birthplace
of Walter Raleigh.

Oldway - Paignton
19th century house having rooms designed to
be replicas of rooms at the Palace of Versailles.

Powederham Castle - Nr. Exeter
14th century medieval castle much damaged in
Civil War. Altered in 18th & 19th centuries. Fine
music room by Wyatt.

Saltram House - Plymouth
Some remnants of Tudor house built into
George II house, with two rooms by Robert
Adam. Excellent plasterwork & woodwork.

Shute Barton - Nr. Axminster
14th century battlemented Manor house with
Tudor & Elizabethan additions.

Tiverton Castle - Nr. Tiverton
Fortress of Henry I. Chapel of St. Francis.
Gallery of Joan of Arc.

Torre Abbey Mansion - Torquay
Abbey ruins, tithe barn. Mansion house with
paintings & furniture.

Cathedrals & Churches

Atherington (St. Mary)
Perpendicular style - medieval effigies & glass,
original rood loft. Fine screens, 15th century
bench ends.

Ashton (St. John the Baptist)
15th century - medieval screens, glass & wall
paintings. Elizabethan pulpit with canopy, 17th
century altar railing.

Bere Ferrers (St. Andrew)
14th century rebuilding - 14th century glass,
16th century benches, Norman font.

Bridford (St. Thomas a Becket)
Perpendicular style - medieval glass &
woodwork. Excellent rood screen c.1530.

Cullompton (St. Andrew)
15th century perpendicular - Jacobean west
gallery - fan tracery in roof, exterior carvings.

Exeter Cathedral
13th century decorated - Norman towers.
Interior tierceron ribbed vault (Gothic) carved
corbels & bosses, moulded piers & arches.
Original pulpitum c.1320. Choir stalls with
earliest misericords in England c.1260.

Haccombe (St. Blaize)
13th century effigies, 14th century glass, 17th
century brasses, 19th century screen, pulpit &
reredos.

Kentisbeare (St. Mary)
Perpendicular style - checkered tower. 16th
century rood screen.

Ottery St. Mary (St. Mary)
13th century, 14th century clock, fan vaulted
roof, tomb with canopy, minstrel's gallery, gilded
wooded eagle. 18th century pulpit.

Parracombe (St. Petrock)
Unrestored Georgian - 16th century benches, mostly perpendicular, early English chancel.

Sutcombe (St. Andrew)
15th century - some part Norman. 16th century bench ends, restored rood screen, medieval glass & floor tiles.

Swimbrige (St. James)
14th century tower & spire - medieval stone pulpit, 15th century rood screen, font cover of Renaissance period.

Tawstock (St. Peter)
14th century, Italian plasterwork ceiling, medieval glass, Renaissance memorial pew, Bath monument.

Buckfast·Abbey
Living Benedictine monastery, built on medieval foundation. Famous for works of art in church, modern stained glass, tonic wine & bee-keeping.

Museums & Galleries

Bideford Museum - Bideford
Geology, maps, prints, shipwright's tools, North Devon pottery.

Burton Art Gallery - Bideford
Hubert Coop collection of paintings etc.

Butterwalk Museum - Dartmouth
17th century row of half timbered buildings, nautical museum. 140 model ships.

Newcomen Engine House - Nr. Butterwalk Museum
Original Newcomen atmospheric/pressure steam engine c.1725.

Royal Albert Memorial Museum Art Gallery - Exeter
Collections of English watercolours, paintings, glass & ceramics, local silver & natural history.

Rougemont House Museum - Exeter
Collections of archaeology & local history. Costume & lace collection.

Guildhall - Exeter
Medieval structure with Tudor frontage - City regalia & silver.

Exeter Maritime Museum - Exeter
Largest collection in the world of working boats, afloat, ashore & under cover.

The Steam & Countryside Museum - Exmouth
Very large working layout - hundreds of exhibits. Including Victorian farmhouse farmyard pets for children.

Alcott Farm Museum - Shebbear
A unique collections of agricultural implements & photographs, etc.

The Elizabethan House - Totnes
Period costumes & furnishings, tools, toys, domestic articles, etc.

The Elizabethan House - Plymouth
16th century house with period furnishings.

City Museum & Art Gallery - Plymouth
Collections of pictures & porcelain, English & Italian drawing. Reynolds' family portraits, early printed books, ship models.

Cookworthy Museum - Kingsbridge
Story of china clay. Local history, shipbuilding tools, rural life.

Honiton & Allhallows Public Museum - Honiton
Collection of Honiton lace, implements etc. Complete Devon Kitchen.

Lyn & Exmoor Museum - Lynton
Life & history of Exmoor.

Torquay & Natural History Society Museum - Torquay
Collection illustrating Kent's Cavern & other caves - natural history & folkculture.

Historic Monuments

Okehampton Castle - Okehampton
11th -14th century chapel, keep & hall.

Totnes Castle - Totnes
13th - 14th century ruins of Castle.

Blackbury Castle - Southleigh
Hill fort - well preserved.

Dartmouth Castle - Dartmouth
15th century castle - coastal defence.

Lydford Castle - Lydford

DEVON
Map reference

01 Payne
02 Laugharne
03 Pirrie
04 Chapple
05 Daniel
06 Todd
07 Whitby
08 Renshaw
09 Witting
10 Gardner
10 M. Wright
11 Hyde
12 Wroe
13 North
14 Jennings
15 Orchard
16 Pile
17 Merchant
18 Oakey
19 Bell

20 Gregson
21 Cuming
22 Pardoe
23 Turner
24 Keane
25 Napier-Bell
26 Scharenguivel
27 Sampson
28 Rowlatt
29 Cunningham
30 D. Wright
31 Grimley
32 Brown
33 Pugsley
34 Strong
35 French
36 Worth
37 Bidwell
38 Tucker

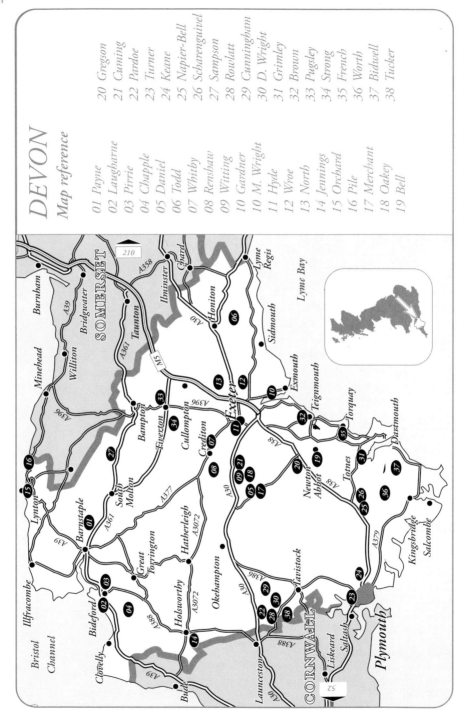

Jackie & Antony Payne
Huxtable Farm   West Buckland   Barnstaple EX32 0SR
Devon
Tel: (01598) 760254   Fax 01598 760254

Near Rd: A.361
Huxtable Farm is a medieval farmhouse (with en-suite facilities, beams & low doorways!) set on a secluded sheep farm with abundant wildlife & panoramic views. Delicious home-cooked candlelit dinners of farm/local produce are serfved with a complimentary glass of home-made wine (BYO too!) Evening meals are by prior arrangement. Log fires, tennis court, sauna, games room & Devon wildlife trail. Off the beaten track, the farm is ideally situated for exploring Exmoor & North Devon coast. A Devon cream tea welcome awaits you!

info@huxtablefarm.co.uk   www.huxtablefarm.co.uk
£64.00 - £68.00   Open: feb - nov
Map ref no. 01

Lynn Pirrie
The Pines at Eastleigh   Eastleigh Bideford EX39 4PA
Devon
Tel: (01271) 860561

Near Rd: A.39
A Georgian country house set in 7 acres with magnificent views over the Torridge estuary to Lundy Island. Selected by the AA as "one of Britain's Best in 2006". Log fires, king-size beds, garden room bar with library, maps & a warm welcome await guests. Breakfasts use home-produced ingredients: fruit from the garden, home-made yoghurt & prize-winning local meats. Special diets can be catered for. Ground-floor rooms are available. All rooms are en-suite, some with feature bathrooms. All have T.V., tea/coffee-making facilities, 'phone etc. Children over 9.

pirrie@thepinesateastleigh.co.uk
www.thepinesateastleigh.co.uk   £35.00 - £90.00
Open: all year   Map ref no. 03

Andrew & Heather Laugharne
The Mount   Northdown Road   Bideford EX39 3LP
Devon
Tel: (01237) 473748

Near Rd: A.39
The Mount is a small, interesting Georgian house which is full of character & charm. It is set in a pretty garden with large handsome trees. A peaceful haven yet only 5 mins' walk from the town centre with its quay, narrow streets & medieval bridge. The 8 attractive bedrooms are tastefully furnished & have en-suite facilities & colour T.V. (1 ground-floor room.) Breakfasts are delicious. The Mount is conveniently situated for Exmoor, Dartmoor, Clovelly, Lundy & the beautiful North Devon coastline with its many sandy beaches & rugged cliffs.

andrew@themountbideford.fsnet.co.uk
www.themount1.cjb.net   £60.00 - £70.00
Open: all year (excl. xmas)   Map ref no. 02

Iris & Brian Chapple
Meadow Park Buckland Brewer   Bideford EX39 5NY
Devon
Tel: (01237) 451511

Near Rd: A.39
Offering a warm welcome & traditional farmhouse fare combined with panoramic views over its own farmland to the distant hills of Dartmoor & Exmoor your stay at Meadow Park is sure to be memorable. The ground floor bedrooms are tastefully furnished & provide en-suite facilities, tea/coffee & T.V. A full English breakfast is offered with options for the smaller appetite. Good food is served at the local 13th century thatched inn. An ideal location for the North Devon/Cornwall coast, RHS Rosemoor Gardens, Tarka Trail & world famous Clovelly with its cobbled street & harbour.

iris.chapple@meadow-park.co.uk
www.meadow-park.co.uk   £48.00 - £60.00
Open: all year (excl. xmas)   Map ref no. 04

Tim Daniel
Parford Well   Sandy Park   Chagford TQ13 8JW
Devon
Tel: (01647) 433353

Near Rd: A.382
This attractive house is a restful & friendly home. Good quality & style are combined in the attractive, comfortable bedrooms, which together with the guests' sitting room overlook the well-tended pretty walled garden & surrounding meadows. Delicious breakfasts are served. There are wonderful walks on the doorstep both in the wooded valley of the River Teign & on the open moor. There is also a charming thatched Inn, just around the corner. Children over 8 years are welcome. Parford Well is the perfect place to relax & unwind.

tim@parfordwell.co.uk   www.parfordwell.co.uk
£65.00 - £80.00   Open: all year
Map ref no. 05

Sylvia & Peter Whitby
2 Taw Vale Terrace Station Road Crediton EX17 3BU
Devon
Tel: (01363) 777879   Fax 01363 777879

Near Rd: A.377
A spacious Grade II listed Georgian style residence & grounds on the edge of Crediton. An attractive family home with a warm welcome for up to 6 guests. The High Street is but a 10-minute stroll for a variety of good eating establishments, friendly local shops & leisure facilities. The property is situated within easy reach of Exeter, Dartmoor, Exmoor & both coasts. An ideal spot for a relaxing break, it is ideally positioned for touring the West Country by car or public transport.

www.bestbandb.co.uk
£50.00 - £50.00   Open: all year
Map ref no. 07

Maggie Todd
Smallicombe Farm   Northleigh Colyton EX24 6BU
Devon
Tel: (01404) 831310   Fax 01404 831431

Near Rd: A.35, A.30
Relax & enjoy an idyllic rural setting yet be close to the coast. Smallicombe nestles in 70 acres of ancient pasture & woodland. The ground-floor 'Garden Suite' (wheelchair accessible) of sitting room, bedroom & bathroom together with the 2 upstairs en-suite bedrooms overlook an unspoilt valley landscape. The sitting room offers a warm welcome with its huge inglenook. Treat yourself to a scrumptious farmhouse breakfast including award-winning sausages from your hosts prize-winning Rare Breed Berkshire pigs.

maggie_todd@yahoo.com   www.smallicombe.com
£56.00 - £65.00   Open: all year
Map ref no. 06

Simon & Melisa Renshaw
The New Inn   Coleford Crediton EX17 5BZ
Devon
Tel: 01363 84242 Fax 01363 85044

Near Rd: A.377
The New Inn is a 13th-century thatched inn nestling in a quiet valley by the side of a brook. Accommodation in this attractive property includes 5 (non-smoking) en-suite bedrooms with 'phone, T.V. & tea/coffee-making facilities. There is also an extensive menu, using fresh local produce whenever possible. Local amenities include several golf courses, fishing, horse riding & sport & leisure facilities. Easy access to Dartmoor, Exmoor & the north & south Devon coasts.

enquiries@thenewinncoleford.co.uk
www.thenewinncoleford.co.uk   £55.00 - £85.00
Open: all year   Map ref no. 08

Debra & Paul Witting
Easton Court Easton Cross Chagford
Dartmoor TQ13 8JL Devon
Tel: (01647) 433469 Fax 01647 433654

Near Rd: A.382

Home of 'Brideshead Revisited', Easton Court is a charming Tudor country house, set in 4 acres of grounds within the Dartmoor National Park. The Edwardian wing houses 5 tastefully furnished en-suite guest rooms, all well-equipped & all with stunning views towards the Teign Valley Gorge. The light & airy, comfortable guest lounge/breakfast room & access to the delightful gardens completes this luxury accommodation. Easton Court is an ideal base for touring Dartmoor & the West Country. Children over 10 years are welcome.

stay@easton.co.uk   www.easton.co.uk
£64.00 - £72.00   Open: all year
Map ref no. 09

Mark Wright & Paul Da-Costa-Greaves
The Galley Restaurant & Spa with Cabins   41 Fore Street
Topsham   Exeter EX3 0HU   Devon
Tel: 0845 6026862

Near Rd: A.30

Discovering the secret is just the beginning with celebrity & Masterchef of Great Britain Paul Da-Costa-Greaves, who also happens to be a spiritual healer & alternative therapist & runs his kitchen under the guidance of Zen. Luxury accommodation offering stylish bedrooms & bathrooms, private outdoor jacuzzi, spa treatments & hot tub. Amazing food in the award-winning fish & seafood restaurant with panoramic river views & a touch of olde worlde charm. Children over 12 years are welcome. This really is what dreams are made of...

fish@galleyrestaurant.co.uk
www.galleyrestaurant.co.uk   £150.00 - £250.00
Open: all year   Map ref no. 10

Marlene & Richard Gardner
Reka Dom   43 The Strand   Topsham   Exeter EX3 0AY
Devon
Tel: (01392) 873385   Fax 01392 873385

Near Rd: A.38

Reka Dom is a 17th-century Heritage Merchant's House in the historic town of Topsham, with panoramic estuary, sea & countryside views. Offering 3 suites with private facilities. Each room is tastefully furnished with T.V./video/DVD, tea/coffee, fruit & confectionery. Reka Dom is renowned for its hospitality & offers a wide choice at breakfast, with organic produce where possible. Dinner by arrangement. Reiki Healing, massage & beauty therapies are available in the calm of this unique setting. Dogs by arrangement.

beautifulhouse@hotmail.com   www.rekadom.co.uk
£70.00 - £78.00   Open: all year
Map ref no. 10

Rick & Sue Hyde
Raffles   11 Blackall Road Exeter EX4 4HD
Devon
Tel: (01392) 270200   Fax 01392 270200

Near Rd: A.30

Raffles is a large Victorian house, very central & close to the University, retaining many original architectural features. The owners have applied their experience in the antique trade to enhance decorations & furnishings. This is a very friendly house with personal service. Organic food is our preference & breakfasts are hearty. Off-street parking is available. An ideal base for exploring Devon. For further information & photographs, visit our web site or telephone for a copy of our brochure.

raffleshtl@btinternet.com www.raffles-exeter.co.uk
£64.00 - £66.00   Open: all year
Map ref no. 11

Mr & Mrs JB Wroe
Lower Marsh Farm   Marsh Green Exeter EX5 2EX
Devon
Tel: (01404) 822432

Near Rd: A.30
Gracious, comfortable accommodation in a lovely 16th century Grade II listed farmhouse, in its own extensive gardens, lawns & paddocks, with orchard, pond & stream. The house retains many fascinating period features & is charmingly furnished with antiques. Guest bedrooms are attractive, light & airy with firm, good quality beds & central heating throughout. Log fires in the guest sitting room & breakfast room in winter. Home made or local breakfast produce. Very convenient for A.30, M.5, Exeter, the east Devon & Jurassic coast, Exeter International Airport & West Point or as a stopover on the way to Cornwall. Parking.

lowermarshfarm@eclipse.co.uk
www.lowermarshdevon.co.uk   £60.00 - £66.00
Open: jan - mid dec Map ref no. 12

see p.99

Mrs Pat Jennings
Leworthy Farmhouse Lower Leworthy   Nr. Pyworthy
Holsworthy EX22 6SJ Devon
Tel: (01409) 259469

Near Rd: A.388
A charming Georgian farmhouse nestling in an unspoilt backwater with lawns, meadow & a fishing lake. The inviting guest rooms are beautifully furnished with antiques or pine & have en-suite/private facilities, T.V., fresh flowers & an abundant hospitality tray. A peaceful lounge in which to relax with chiming clocks & sparkling Victoriana china. A traditional farmhouse breakfast with free-range eggs is served or kippers, prunes, porridge etc. Good walking, cycling & fishing nearby & only 20 mins' from the spectacular north Cornish coast. Leworthy is a warm & friendly peaceful haven.

leworthyfarmhouse@yahoo.co.uk
www.leworthyfarmhouse.co.uk £60.00 - £65.00
Open: all year Map ref no. 14

John & Ros North
Heath Gardens   Broadclyst   Exeter EX5 3HL
Devon
Tel: (01392) 462311

Near Rd: B.3181
Located on the outskirts of the village of Broadclyst, 5 miles from the cathedral city of Exeter; this delightful 17th-century listed artisan's cottage enjoys views over open countryside. It is ideally suited for visiting east & mid Devon, Dartmoor & the beautiful South Hams. 5 mins drive to the National Trust's Killerton House or a little further afield Knightshayes Court. 3 en-suite bedrooms (1 is located on the ground floor.) Hospitality trays offer a selection of beverages, fresh milk & home made cake.   4 pubs & a restaurant within walking distance or a short drive.

info@heathgardens.co.uk www.heathgardens.co.uk
£50.00 - £50.00 Open: all year (excl. xmas)
Map ref no. 13

Karen & Mike Orchard
Highcliffe House Sinai Hill Lynton EX35 6AR
Devon
Tel: (01598) 752235   Fax 01598 753815

Near Rd: A.39
Highcliffe House is an elegant Victorian house set in an acre of hillside c.600ft above sea level overlooking the beautiful Exmoor coastline to Wales. With 6 exceptionally appointed & tastefully furnished bedrooms, all en-suite, your hosts offer a haven of tranquility for a short break or walking holiday in the very best of luxury guest accommodation. With wonderful freshly prepared breakfasts to set you up for the day & fine dining at weekends, a warm welcome awaits you.

info@highcliffehouse.co.uk www.highcliffehouse.co.uk
£76.00 - £96.00 Open: feb - nov
Map ref no. 15

Leworthy Farmhouse

Lower Leworthy Pyworthy (Nr.)Holsworthy EX22 6SJ

Tel:(01409) 259469

email:leworthyfarmhouse@yahoo.co.uk www.leworthyfarmhouse.co.uk

Susan Pile
Coombe Farm　Countisbury　Lynton EX35 6NF
Devon
Tel: (01598) 741236

Near Rd: A.39
Coombe Farm is a 365-acre, hill-sheep farm, with an early-17th-century farmhouse set betwixt Lynmouth & the legendary Doone Valley. The coast path runs through the farm at Desolate. All within the spectacular Exmoor National Park. The tastefully furnished en-suite bedrooms include 1 double, 1 twin & 2 family rooms. All have hot-drink facilities, shaver points, & bath & hand towels. Central heating. There is a lounge with woodburner fire & colour T.V. in which you can relax after spending the day exploring this delightful county.

coombefarm@freeuk.com　www.brendonvalley.co.uk/
coombe_farm.htm.　£49.00 - £58.00
Open: mar - nov Map ref no. 16

Gill & David Oakey
Great Doccombe Farm　Doccombe　Moretonhampstead
TQ13 8SS　Devon
Tel: (01647) 440694

Near Rd: A.30
Great Doccombe Farm is situated in the pretty hamlet of Doccombe, within the Dartmoor National Park, on the B.3212 from Exeter. This is an ideal base for walking in the Teign Valley & nearby moors, with golf, riding & fishing nearby. This lovely 16th-century granite farmhouse is surrounded by gardens & fields. The attractive & tastefully furnished bedrooms (1 ground-floor) are all en-suite, & have shower, T.V. & tea/coffee-making facilities. A traditional English breakfast is served. Great Doccombe Farm is a perfect place to relax.

david.oakey3@btopenworld.com
www.greatdoccombefarm.co.uk　£48.00 - £50.00
Open: all year　Map ref no. 18

Trudie Merchant
Great Sloncombe Farm　Moretonhampstead TQ13 8QF
Devon
Tel: (01647) 440595　Fax 01647 440595

Near Rd: A.382
Great Sloncombe Farm is a listed, granite-&-cob-built, 13th-century farmhouse. Set in a peaceful Dartmoor valley, the rambling house has a magical atmosphere, & is furnished with oak & pine, antique china & interesting old photographs. The 3 warm, comfortable & pleasant bedrooms are all en-suite, with every facility included. Delicious breakfasts, with home-made bread are served. Children over 8 yrs by arrangement. A charming home for a relaxing short break.

bmerchant@sloncombe.freeserve.co.uk
www.greatsloncombefarm.co.uk　£60.00 - £66.00
Open: ALL YEAR Map ref no. 17

Nigel Bell
Sampsons Farm Hotel Restaurant　Preston
Newton Abbot TQ12 3PP Devon
Tel: (01626) 354913　Fax 01626 332673

Near Rd: A.38, A.380
Sampsons is a welcoming thatched farmhouse, set in its own grounds in a tiny, sleepy village & yet it is only 5 mins from the A.38 & A.380. There are a wealth of oak beams, log fires, history & tranquillity & a renowned restaurant serving delicious country produce. Pretty en-suite rooms are available in the barn conversions around the courtyard., some with private patios & a luxurious spacious suite. Also, charming en-suite rooms in the farmhouse. Lovely river & meadow walks on the doorstep. Parking. Children 10+.

nigel@sampsonsfarm.com　www.sampsonsfarm.com
£50.00 - £85.00　Open: ALL YEAR
Map ref no. 19

Penpark Country House B & B
Bickington Newton Abbot TQ12 6LH
Tel:(01626) 821314 email:maddy@penpark.co.uk www.penpark.co.uk

see p.101

Mrs Madeleine Gregson
Penpark Country House B & B   Bickington
Newton Abbot TQ12 6LH Devon
Tel: (01626) 821314

Near Rd: A.38
Situated within the Dartmoor National Park with magnificent
hilltop views. Penpark is an elegant country house designed
by Clough Williams Ellis of Portmeirion fame. There are 5
acres of formal & informal gardens & an all-weather tennis
court. The accommodation includes 3 charming &
comfortable rooms with private facilities. 1 double/twin
with balcony, 1 double room & the garden room, which is
a double/family room with 3 double-glazed doors opening
onto the garden. Breakfasts are a speciality. Penpark is a
perfect base for relaxing & exploring with a wide choice of
very good pubs & restaurants.

maddy@penpark.co.uk   www.penpark.co.uk
£64.00 - £70.00   Open: all year
Map ref no. 20

Alison Pardoe
Stowford House   Lewdown Okehampton EX20 4BZ
Devon
Tel: (01566) 783415

Near Rd: A.30
A warm welcome & fabulous breakfasts await you at this
delightful Georgian country house. Stowford House is
perfectly located for exploring Devon & Cornwall, including
the lovely Tamar Valley, Dartmoor & the coast. The world
renowned Eden Project & several National Trust properties
are nearby. The 3 large & tastefully furnished bedrooms,
the elegant drawing room & garden ensure a relaxing stay
at this beautiful home. The area also offers good walking,
cycling, golf, riding & sailing. There is an excellent pub &
choice of restaurants nearby.

alison@stowfordhouse.com www.stowfordhouse.com
£60.00 - £68.00 Open: all year (excl. xmas)
Map ref no. 22

Mrs Mary Cuming
Great Wooston Farm   Moretonhampstead
Newton Abbot TQ13 8QA   Devon   Tel: (01647) 440367
Mobile 07798 670590   Fax 01647 440367

Near Rd: A.30
Great Wooston Farm was once part of the Manor House
Estate owned by Lord Hambledon. Situated high above
the Teign Valley in the Dartmoor National Park, with views
across the moors. Plenty of walks, golf, fishing & riding
nearby. The farmhouse is surrounded by a delightful
garden of 1/2 an acre, also BBQ & picnic area. 3 pleasant
bedrooms, 2 en-suite, 1 with 4-poster bed, 1 with private
bathroom, with every facility included. Excellent breakfasts
are served. Also, a guests' lounge for your relaxation after
a day exploring the magical Dartmoor. Children over 8.

info@greatwoostonfarm.com
www.greatwoostonfarm.com   £56.00 - £62.00
Open: ALL YEAR Map ref no. 21

John & Daphne Turner
Westways   706 Budshead Road   Crownhill
Plymouth PL6 5DY   Devon
Tel: (01752) 776617   Mobile 0777 8479696

Near Rd: A.38, A.386
Situated approx. 3 1/2 miles from Plymouth city centre,
this attractive detached house offers pleasant
accommodation in 3 well-furnished (non-smoking) rooms,
with tea/coffee-making facilities. Excellent breakfasts are
served in the elegant dining room. Guests may choose to
relax & plan their excursions in the comfortable sitting room
or make use of the small T.V. room. A homely & friendly
base both for visitors wishing to make the most of the many
attractions in the area, & for touring Devon. Children over
12 years welcome.

turner.jd@blueyonder.co.uk   www.bestbandb.co.uk
£50.00 - £60.00 Open: all year
Map ref no. 23

see p.104

Loretta Keane
Homeleigh B & B 5 George Lane Plympton
Plymouth PL7 1LJ   Devon
Tel: (01752) 330478

Near Rd: A.38
A beautiful family run 18th century cottage, located in the medieval sector of Plympton St. Maurice. A charming home with original character beams & inglenook fireplaces. Bedrooms are attractive & include. tea/coffee, I.V., radio & hairdryer. Your hosts will ensure that you are warm, comfortable & well fed with fresh, home-baked ingredients, including delicious Devon Cream Teas. Perfect for a relaxing weekend break or for visitors on business in the area, Homeleigh offers a more personal place to reside rather than the often cold & formal atmosphere of a hotel. An ideal location for Dartmoor & the south coast beaches.

homeleighbandb@blueyonder.co.uk
www.homeleighbandb.co.uk £50.00 - £50.00
Open: all year (excl. xmas & new year)   Map ref no. 24

Faith & John Scharenguivel
Coombe House   North Huish   South Brent TQ10 9NJ
Devon
Tel: (01548) 821277   Fax 01548 821277

Near Rd: A.38
Gracious Georgian residence set in 33 acres in a designated Area of Outstanding Natural Beauty. The accommodation includes 4 tastefully furnished cn suite bedrooms, some with 4-posters, with T.V., radio, hairdryer & tea/coffee tray. An elegant dining room & guest loungewith log fire . Delicious home-cooked food prepared using fresh local produce (by arrangement.) The coast, Dartmoor, Totnes, Salcombe, Plymouth & Exeter are all within easy reach. 4 barn conversions for self-catering in 4 acres of grounds. Children over 12. Also, 4 barn conversions are available for self-catering.

coombehouse@hotmail.com
www.coombehouse.uk.com   £60.00 - £90.00
Open: all year   Map ref no. 26

Mrs Christa Napier-Bell
Brookdale House   North Huish   South Brent TQ10 9NF
Devon
Tel: (01548) 821661

Near Rd: A.38
Brookdale House is a Grade II listed Tudor style house, situated in a peaceful secluded valley with delightful grounds. Offering 3 individually designed bedrooms, with T.V. & tea/coffee-making facilities. Each room is elegantly furnished with antiques in period style. A delicious Aga-cooked breakfast is served using only the finest local ingredients. This is a charming home, perfect for a relaxing break & an excellent base from which to explore Dartmoor or the many coastal attractions. Animals by arrangement.

www.bestbandb.co.uk
£55.00 - £60.00 Open: all year
Map ref no. 25

Theresa Sampson
Kerscott Farm   Ash Mill   South Molton EX36 4QG
Devon
Tel: (01769) 550262   Fax 01769 550910

Near Rd: A.361
Kerscott Farm offers quality accommodation at a sensible price. This peaceful Exmoor working farm & olde worlde farmhouse is mentioned in the Domesday Book (1086). It has an absolutely fascinating interior with many antiques, pictures & china - a rare find. There are beautiful, extensive views. There are 3 pretty & tastefully furnished en-suite bedrooms with colour T.V. & tea/coffee-making facilities. Wholesome country cooking, pure spring water. An ideal base from which to explore glorious Devon.

kerscott.farm@virgin.net   www.devon-bandb.co.uk
£56.00 - £60.00 Open: all year (excl.xmas & new year)
Map ref no. 27

Coombe House

North Huish South Brent TQ10 9NJ

Tel:(01548) 821277 Fax 01548 821277

email:coombehouse@hotmail.com www.coombehouse.uk.com

see p.106

Mrs Maureen Rowlatt
Tor Cottage Chillaton Nr. Tavistock PL16 0JE
Devon
Tel: (01822) 860248   Fax 01822 860126

Near Rd: A.30
Award-winning Tor Cottage has a warm & relaxed atmosphere & nestles in its own private valley. 18 acres of wildlife hillsides. Lovely gardens & a streamside setting. Beautifully appointed en-suite bed/sitting rooms with own log fires & a private terrace & gardens. Sumptuous breakfasts (vegetarian options). Dinner booking service at local restaurants. Heated outdoor pool (summer). Tranquil base adjacent Dartmoor Valley. Tor Cottage is central for touring Devon/Cornwall & coastlines. Easy 45 min. drive to the Eden Project. Special rate autumn/spring breaks are available.

info@torcottage.co.uk   www.torcottage.co.uk
£140.00 - £150.00
 Open: all year (excl.xmas & new year) Map ref no. 28

David & Jill Wright
Quither Mill Chillaton Tavistock PL19 0PZ
Devon
Tel: Tel: (01822) 860160   Fax 01822 860160

Near Rd: A.30
Quither Mill is situated in a sleepy hamlet & is Grade II listed, being of architectural & historical interest. Dating from the 18th century, the mill wheel & workings are intact. Guests enjoy the comfort of the attractive, beautiful beamed en-suite bedrooms & of course, a delicious full English breakfast. David & Jill are proud of their reputation for fine cooking, which is drawn from 20 years in the hotel world. Dinner really is a memorable experience. This is a delightful home for a relaxing break or for those guests who wish to explore Devon & beyond..

quither.mill@virgin.net   www.quithermill.co.uk
£80.00 - £80.00 Open: ALL YEAR
 Map ref no. 30

Victoria Cunningham
Burnville House Brentor   Tavistock PL19 0NE
Devon
Tel: (01822) 820443

Near Rd: A.386
This substantial Georgian house stands in informal gardens amidst beech woods & rhododendrons in the heart of a 250 acre livestock farm within Dartmoor National Park. Large comfortable bedrooms, tastefully furnished with antiques have stunning moorland views & luxurious bathrooms. Delicious food is made with local produce, log fires, the perfect place to relax, unwind & absorb the beauty & tranquillity of Dartmoor. Heated pool, tennis court & clay pigeon shooting are available.

burnvillef@aol.com   www.burnville.co.uk
£60.00 - £75.00 Open: all year
Map ref no. 29

Hilary Tucker
Beera Farmhouse Milton Abbot Tavistock PL19 8PL
Devon
Tel: (01822) 870216   Fax 01822 870216

Near Rd: A.30
Beera is a large, traditional stone built Victorian farmhouse set in an Area of Outstanding Natural Beauty. The farm is a 160-acre beef & sheep farm on the bank of the river Tamar. Guests are welcome to walk on the farm & take in the beautiful scenery. 3 attractive en-suite bedrooms (1 with 4-poster), each with T.V. & tea/coffee-making facilities. Evening meals are provided by arrangement. Ideally situated for touring the West Country & within easy reach of the coast, Dartmoor National Park, National Trust properties & the Eden Project (40 mins.)

hilary.tucker@farming.co.uk   www.beera-farm.co.uk
£60.00 - £80.00
 Open: ALL YEAR (Excl. Xmas & New Year) Map ref no. 38

Tor Cottage

Chillaton Nr. Tavistock PL16 0JE

Tel:(01822) 860248 Fax 01822 860126

email:info@torcottage.co.uk www.torcottage.co.uk

see p.108

Jennifer Richardson Brown
Wytchwood   West Buckeridge   Teignmouth TQ14 8NF
Devon
Tel: (01626) 773482   Mobile 07971 783454

Near Rd: A.381
Award-winning Wytchwood has been the family home of the Richardson Browns for over 40 years acquiring an unrivalled reputation for outstanding hospitality, quality home cooking & stylish accommodation enjoying panoramic views. Interior designed bedrooms with en-suite/private bathrooms fulfil every expectation. Option of a self-contained suite. Indulge in the ultimate Devonshire cream tea, with selection of sponges & cakes taken in the beautiful garden on sunny days. Breakfast on home-made bread & rolls, preserves, orchard honey & garden produce. Ideal for exploring the coast, moors & open countryside.

Wytchwood@onetel.com   www.richardsonbrown.com
£60.00 - £80.00   Open: all year
Map ref no. 32

Phillida & Martin Strong
West Bradley Templeton Tiverton EX16 8BJ
Devon
Tel: (01884) 253220   Fax 01884 259504

Near Rd: B.3137
West Bradley offers total immersion amidst beauty with fields on either side of a long drive, Dartmoor views, bluebells in spring, a sparkling stream & a pretty garden. Total privacy too, in the 18th-century upside down barn on the side of a 17th-century Devon long house. A handmade oak staircase, oak floors, tasteful furnishings, rugs, a large comfortable bed & a good sofabed. Excellent riding & stabling is also available for your own horse. West Bradley is a perfect spot for a relaxing break in this delightful part of Devon. A supplement is payable for single occupancy. A warm welcome awaits you.

martin.strong@btinternet.com   www.bestbandb.co.uk
£58.00 - £70.00   Open: ALL YEAR
Map ref no. 34

Barbara Pugsley
Hornhill Farmhouse   Exeter Hill   Tiverton   EX16 4PL
Devon
Tel: (01884) 253352

Near Rd: A.361
Hornhill, originally a coaching inn, has panoramic views over the beautiful Exe valley. Set in a large garden & surrounded by farmland. The charming hosts offer guests comfort, warmth, delicious home-cooking & a happy atmosphere. The house, furnished with antiques, has 3 attractive bedrooms (1 with a Victorian 4-poster), each with private bathroom, T.V. & tea/coffee facilities. 1 is suitable for the partially disabled. Guests are invited to relax in the elegant drawing room, with plenty of books & a cosy log fire on chilly evenings.

hornhill@tinyworld.co.uk
www.hornhill-farmhouse.co.uk £56.00 - £60.00
Open: all year (excl.xmas & new year) Map ref no. 33

Mike & Wendy French
Fairmount House Hotel Herbert Road Chelston
Torquay TQ2 6RW   Devon
Tel: (01803) 605446   Fax 01803 605446

Near Rd: A.380
Experience somewhere special & feel completely at home in the tranquillity, warmth & informal atmosphere of this small hotel. Offering 8 comfortable en-suite bedrooms, unhurried breakfasts & undisturbed evenings. (2 lower-ground-floor rooms have private doors opening onto the garden.) Renowned for its mild climate, Torquay boasts a profusion of sub-tropical plants & miles of beaches & sheltered coves. Nestling away from the busy seafront, near Cockington Village & Country Park, Fairmount offers quality, comfort & genuine friendly service.

stay@fairmounthousehotel.co.uk
www.fairmounthousehotel.co.uk   £50.00 - £66.00
Open: ALL YEAR Map ref no. 35

Wytchwood

West Buckeridge Teignmouth TQ14 8NF
Tel:(01626) 773482 Mobile 07971 783454
email:Wytchwood@onetel.com www.richardsonbrown.com

Orchard House

Horner Halwell Totnes TQ9 7LB

Tel:(01548) 821448

email:helen@orchard-house-halwell.co.uk www.orchard-house-halwell.co.uk

see p.111

Harry & Carole Grimley
Parliament House   Longcombe Nr. Totnes TQ9 6PR
Devon
Tel: (01803) 840288

Near Rd: A.385
An ancient rambling thatched house where in 1688 William
of Orange is said to have held his first parliament. The
simple, yet attractive interior has many interesting details.
One bedroom has a double Victorian brass bed with a
sunny en-suite shower/bathroom & the other is a super
king/twin with a blue 'toile de Jouy' private bathroom.
Delicious breakfasts made from locally sourced produce
are served in the panelled dining room. The pretty garden
is a delight to relax in after a day spent exploring this
outstandingly beautiful region..

parliamenthouse@btopenworld.com
www.bestbandb.co.uk   £65.00 - £75.00
Open: ALL YEAR Map ref no. 31

Glynis & Peter Bidwell
Lower Norton Farmhouse   East Allington
Totnes TQ9 7RL   Devon
Tel: (01548) 521246

Near Rd: A.381
Only 10 mins' from the sea, perfectly situated for exploring
the ancient south Devon towns of Dartmouth, Totnes &
Kingsbridge. The lovely Georgian farm house nestles in
an outstandingly beautiful valley. You will be treated as
family in a very relaxed atmosphere. Stay all day, sit in the
lounge, on the terrace with a cream tea or visit the many
National Trust houses close by. Superb en-suite rooms
offering every comfort, great breakfasts & wonderful
candlelit dinners in a 400-year-old dining hall - wonderful.
Children over 10 years welcome.

lowernorton@tiscali.co.uk
www.lowernortonfarmhouse.co.uk £60.00 - £70.00
Open: all year   Map ref no. 37

see p.109

Mrs Helen Worth
Orchard House Horner Halwell Totnes TQ9 7LB
Devon
Tel: (01548) 821448

Near Rd: A.381   Surrounded by quiet countryside
in a beautiful valley between Totnes & Kingsbridge,
Orchard House is ideally placed for the nearby South Devon
coastline & Dartmoor. It offers 3 wonderfully furnished en-
suite bedrooms, each with colour T.V., clock/radio, hairdryer
& tea/coffee-making facilities. Also, guests' sitting room
with antiques & log fire. In the spacious dining room
breakfasts are served on a large platter using local produce
& home-made preserves. Large garden & private parking.
Children over 3 years.

helen@orchard-house-halwell.co.uk
www.orchard-house-halwell.co.uk £50.00 - £55.00
Open: MAR - OCT Map ref no. 36

Lower Norton Farmhouse

East Allington Totnes TQ9 7RL

Tel:(01548) 521246

email:lowernorton@tiscali.co.uk www.lowernortonfarmhouse.co.uk

Dorset

Dorset

The unspoilt nature of this gem of a county is emphasised by the designation of virtually all of the coast & much of the inland country as an Area of Outstanding Natural Beauty. Along the coast from Christchurch to Lyme Regis there are a fascinating variety of sandy beaches, towering cliffs & single banks, whilst inland is a rich mixture of downland, lonely heaths, fertile valleys, historic houses & lovely villages of thatch & mellow stone buildings.

Thomas Hardy was born here & took the Dorset countryside as a background for many of his novels. Few writers can have stamped their identity on a county more than Hardy on Dorset, forever to be known as the "Hardy Country". Fortunately most of the area that he so lovingly described remains unchanged, including Egdon Heath & the county town of Dorchester, famous as Casterbridge.

In the midst of the rolling chalk hills which stretch along the Storr Valley lies picturesque Cerne Abbas, with its late mediaeval houses & cottages & the ruins of a Benedictine Abbey. At Godmanstone is the tiny thatched "Smiths Arms" claiming to be the smallest pub in England.

The north of the county is pastoral with lovely views over broad Blackmoor Vale. Here is the ancient hilltop town of Shaftesbury, with cobbled Gold Hill, one of the most photographed streets in the country.

Coastal Dorset is spectacular. Poole harbour is an enormous, almost circular bay, an exciting mixture of 20th century activity, ships of many nations & beautiful building of the 15th, 18th & early 19th centuries.

Westwards lies the popular resort of Swanage, where the sandy beach & sheltered bay are excellent for swimming. From here to Weymouth is a marvellous stretch of coast with scenic wonders like Lulworth Cove & the arch of Durdle Door.

Chesil Beach is an extraordinary bank of graded pebbles, as perilous to shipping today as it was 1,000 years ago. It is separated from the mainland by a sheltered lagoon known as the Fleet.

Durdle Door, Dorset.

Dorset

Dorset Gazeteer
Areas of outstanding natural beauty.
The Entire County.

Houses & Castles

Athelthampton
Medieval house - one of the finest in all England.
Formal gardens.

Barneston Manor - Nr. Church Knowle
13th - 16th century stone built manor house.

Forde Abbey - Nr. Chard
12th century Cistercian monastery - noted
Mortlake tapestries.

Manor House - Sandford Orcas
Mansion of Tudor period, furnished with period
furniture, antiques, silver, china, glass,
paintings.

Hardy's Cottage - Higher Bockampton
Birthplace of Thomas Hardy, author(1840-1928).

Milton Abbey - Nr. Blandford
18th century Georgian house built on original
site of 15th century abbey.

Purse Caundle Manor - Purse Caundle
Medieval Manor - furnished in style of period.

Parnham House - Beaminster
Tudor Manor - some later work by Nash.
Leaded windows & heraldic plasterwork. Home
of John Makepeace & the International School
for Craftsmen in Wood. House & gardens etc.

Sherborne Castle - Sherborne
16th century mansion - continuously occupied
by Digby family.

No. 3 Trinity Street - Weymouth
Tudor cottages now converted into one house,
furnished 17th century.

Smedmore - Kimmeridge
18th century manor.

Wolfeton House - Dorchester
Medieval & Elizabethan Manor. Fine stone
work, great stair. 17th century furniture -
Jacobean ceilings & fireplaces.

Cathedrals & Churches

Bere Regis (St. John the Baptist)
12th century foundation - enlarged in 13th &
15th centuries. Timber roof & nave, fine
arcades.16th century seating.

Blandford (St. Peter & St. Paul)
18th century - ashlar - Georgian design.
Galleries, pulpit, box pews, font & mayoral seat.

Bradford Abbas (St. Mary)
14th century - parapets & pinnacled tower,
panelled roof. 15th century bench ends, stone
rood screen. 17th century pulpit.

Cerne Abbas (St. Mary)
13th century - rebuilt 15th & 16th centuries, 14th
century wall paintings, 15th century tower, stone
screen, pulpit possibly 11th century.

Chalbury (dedication unknown)
13th century origin - 14th century east windows,
timber bellcote. Plastered walls, box pews, 3-
decker pulpit, west gallery.

Christchurch (Christ Church)
Norman nave - ribbed plaster vaulting -
perpendicular spire. Tudor renaissance
Salisbury chantry - screen with Tree of Jesse:
notable misericord seats.

Milton Abbey (Sts. Mary, Michael, Sampson & Branwaleder)
14th century pulpitum & sedilia, 15th century
reredos & canopy, 16th century monument,
Milton effigies 1775.

Sherborne (St. Mary)
Largely Norman but some Saxon remains -
excellent fan vaulting, of nave & choir. 12th &
13th century effigies -15th century painted glass.

Studland (St. Nicholas)
12th century - best Norman church in the
country. 12th century font, 13th century
east windows.

Whitchurch Canonicorum (St. Candida & Holy Cross)
12th & 13th century. 12th century font, relics of
patroness in 13th century shrine, 15th century
painted glass, 15th century tower.

Wimbourne Minster (St. Cuthberga)
12th century central tower & arcade, otherwise
13th-15th century. Former collegiate church.

Dorset

Georgian glass, some Jacobean stalls & screen. Monuments & famed clock of 14th century.

Yetminster (St. Andrew)
13th century chancel - 15th century rebuilt with embattled parapets. 16th century brasses & seating.

Museums & Galleries

Abbey Ruins - Shaftesbury
Relics excavated from Benedictine Nunnery founded by Alfred the Great.

Russell-Cotes Art Gallery & Museum - Bournemouth
17th-20th century oil paintings, watercolours, sculptures, ceramics, miniatures, etc.

Rothesay Museum - Bournemouth
English porcelain, 17th century furniture, collection of early Italian paintings, arms & armour, ethnography, etc.

Bournemouth Natural Science Society's Museum
Archaeology & local natural history.

Brewery Farm Museum - Milton Abbas
Brewing & village bygones from Dorset.

Dorset County Museum - Dorchester
Geology, natural history, pre-history. Thomas Hardy memorabilia

Philpot Museum - Lyme Regis
Old documents & prints, fossils, lace & old fire engine.

Guildhall Museum - Poole
Social & civic life of Poole during 18th & 19th centuries displayed in two-storey Georgian market house.

Scapolen's Court - Poole
14th century house of local merchant exhibiting local & archaeological history of town, also industrial archaeology.

Sherborne Museum - Sherborne
Local history & geology - abbey of AD 705, Sherborne missal AD 1400, 18th century local silk industry.

Gallery 24 - Shaftesbury
Art exhibitions - paintings, pottery, etc.

Red House Museum & Art Gallery - Christchurch
Natural history & antiques of the region. Georgian house with herb garden.

Priest's House Museum - Wimbourne Minster
Tudor building in garden exhibiting local archaeology & history.

Other things to see & do

Abbotsbury Swannery - Abbotsbury
Unique wildlife attraction. The only place in the world where over 600 swans can be visited during the nesting and hatching time (end May-end June). Audiovisual presentation. Ugly duckling trail. Mass feeding 12 noon and 4pm.

Castleton Water Wheel - Sherbourne
The waterwheel was built in 1869 by Stothert and Pitt and rebuilt in 1898 by Edward White. On open days the wheel can be seen working and driving an 1883 pump-set built by Sparrows of Martock. In addition, several stationary engines are on display as well as a wide range of relevant artefacts. The Nether Cerne waterwheel, perhaps the oldest "all iron" wheel in England.

Mangerton Mill - Bridport
17th Century working water mill and Museum of Rural Bygones, set in peaceful rural valley on the river Manger.Trout fishing and riverside walk.

Almshouse Of St John The Baptist & St John The Evangelist - Sherborne
The picturesque Almshouse was built in the 15th Century for "12 poor men and 4 poor women" and is now home to 18 elderly residents. Of particular interest are the remarkable 15th century Triptych; copies of the illuminated Royal Licence and Foundation Deed; an original letter dated 1594 from Sir Walter Raleigh to the Almshouse Master.

Dorset Heavy Horse Centre - Verwood
Meet the magnificent heavy horses, including Shires, Ardennes, Clydesdales, Suffolks & Percherons in the daily working horse shows. Groom the friendly miniature Shetland Ponies & donkeys & help feed some of the other animals.

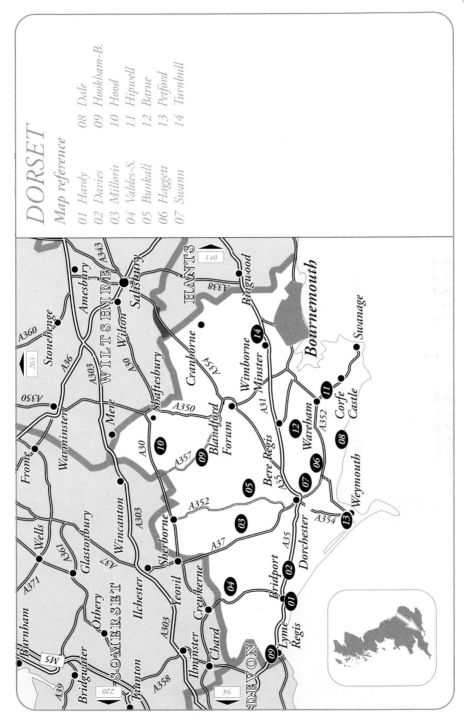

DORSET

Map reference

01 Hardy	08 Dale
02 Davies	09 Hookham-B.
03 Millorit	10 Hood
04 Valdes-S.	11 Hipwell
05 Bunkall	12 Barne
06 Haggett	13 Petford
07 Swann	14 Turnbull

see p.117

Louisa & Alan Hardy
Britmead House 154 West Bay Road
Bridport DT6 4EG Dorset
Tel: (01308) 422941

Near Rd: A.35
A friendly welcome in a relaxed & comfortable atmosphere. Renowned for good food, a high standard of facilities, personal service & attention to detail. Situated between Bridport, the fishing harbour of West Bay, Chesil Beach & the Dorset Coastal Path. The accommodation includes 8 comfortable & individually decorated en-suite bedrooms, 3 of the rooms are on the ground floor, all with T.V., tea/coffee-making facilities & hairdryer. The south-facing lounge & dining room overlook the garden & open countryside beyond. Private parking.

britmead@talk21.com www.britmeadhouse.co.uk
£56.00 - £70.00 Open: ALL YEAR
Map ref no. 01

Anita & Andre Millorit
Brambles Woolcombe Melbury Bubb
Dorchester DT2 0NJ Dorset
Tel: (01935) 83672

Near Rd: A.37
Set in beautiful, tranquil countryside, Brambles is a beautiful thatched cottage offering every comfort, superb views & a very friendly welcome. There is a choice of en-suite twin, double or single rooms, all tastefully furnished & very comfortable & with colour T.V. & tea/coffee-making facilities. A pretty garden available for relaxing in. A delicious full English or Continental breakfast served. Evening meals available by prior arrangement. There are many interesting places to visit & wonderful walks for enthusiasts. A wonderful property from which to explore Dorset.

bramblesbandb@hotmail.co.uk
www.bramblesdorset.co.uk £64.00 - £64.00
Open: all year (excl. xmas) Map ref no. 03

Sydney & Jayne Davies
Innsacre Farmhouse Shipton Gorge Bridport DT6 4LJ
Dorset
Tel: (01308) 456137 Fax 01308 421187

Near Rd: A.35
17th-century farmhouse & barn in a magical & peaceful setting. Hidden midway between Lyme Regis & Dorchester, 3 miles from the sea & National Trust coastal path. South-facing, 10 acres of spinneys, steep hillsides, orchard & lawns in a beautiful setting. A mix of French rustic style, English comfort & a genuine, warm welcome. All rooms en-suite (with T.V. & tea tray). Large, cosy sitting-room, log fires, beams & delicious breakfasts. Private parking. Licensed. Children over 9. Single supplement.

innsacre.farmhouse@btinternet.com
www.innsacre.com £75.00 - £85.00
Open: ALL YEAR (Excl. Xmas & New Year) Map ref no. 02

Mrs Sally Valdes-Scott
Woodwalls House Corscombe Dorchester DT2 0NT
Dorset
Tel: (01935) 891477 Fax 01935 891477

Near Rd: A.356, A.37
Woodwalls is a pretty country house set in 12 acres of its own grounds, surrounded by wild flower meadows, woods & fields, creating a haven of peace & tranquillity. 2 light, airy bedrooms, 1 double en-suite & 1 twin with private bathroom, each with colour T.V. & tea/coffee-making facilities are available for guests. A pretty award-winning pub serving excellent food is within easy reach. Your hosts pride themselves on their breakfasts, which include honey from their own bees & home-made marmalade.

www.bestbandb.co.uk
£70.00 - £70.00 Open: ALL YEAR (Excl. Xmas)
Map ref no. 04

Brambles

Woolcombe Melbury Bubb Dorchester DT2 0NJ

Tel:(01935) 83672 email:bramblesbandb@hotmail.co.uk www.bramblesdorset.co.uk

Mrs Tia Bunkall
Holyleas House   Buckland Newton
Dorchester DT2 7DP   Dorset
Tel: (01300) 345214   Mobile 07968 341887

Near Rd: B.3143

The family labrador will welcome you to this elegant country house set in 1/2 acre of pretty walled gardens. A peaceful village surrounded by rolling hills & good walks yet only 10 miles from Sherborne & Dorchester & 30 mins' from the World Heritage coast. Superb gardens & numerous historic houses close by. Double & twin en-suite rooms with many extra touches & a single with private facilities. Guests' own sitting room with log fire in winter. Sumptuous breakfasts with locally sourced & organic produce served in the dining room. There is a village pub within easy walking distance. Animals by arrangement.

tiabunkall@holyleas.fsnet.co.uk
www.holyleashouse.co.uk   £70.00 - £75.00
Open: all year (excl. xmas)   Map ref no. 05

Rose & Furse Swann
Yoah Cottage West Knighton   Dorchester DT2 8PE
Dorset Tel: (01305) 852087

Near Rd: A.352

Yoah Cottage is a most characterful Grade II listed 17th/18th-century building - old beams, inglenook fireplaces, antiques, old rugs & modern paintings. Its owners are ceramic sculptors. Accommodation is in 2 attractive guest bedrooms, 1 double/twin & 1 twin. Guests occupy the 18th-century end of the cottage with own bathroom & sitting room with log fire. There is a lovely garden in which to relax. Delicious food is served. Only 10 mins' drive from World Heritage coast, 5 mins from Thomas Hardy's birthplace. Evening meals by arrangement. Children over 7 years welcome.

www.bestbandb.co.uk
£50.00 - £65.00   Open: all year (excl.xmas & easter)
Map ref no. 07

Mrs Tessa Tripp & Mrs Doris Haggett
Long Acre   25 Moreton Road   Owermoigne
Dorchester DT2 8HY   Dorset
Tel: (01305) 853806

Near Rd: A.352

A peaceful secluded family home set in an acre of garden, surrounded by fields in the pretty village of Owermoigne, 7 miles south-east of Dorchester. The accommodation includes 2 bedrooms with T.V., tea/coffee-making facilities, 1 twin/double en-suite & 1 double with private shower room. Ideal base to explore unspoilt countryside & World Heritage Coastline. Many places of interest within easy reach, including the popular family attraction Monkey World. There are excellent pubs nearby.

tessa.tripp@homecall.co.uk www.longacre-dorset.co.uk
£50.00 - £60.00   Open: all year (excl.xmas & new year)
Map ref no. 06

Avril & Michael Dale
Gatton House   Main Road   West Lulworth
Lulworth Cove BH20 5RL Dorset
Tel: (01929) 400252   Fax 01929 400252

Near Rd: A.352

Spectacularly positioned, quiet & comfortable, this small hotel is set amongst the Purbeck Hills, yet only a strolling distance from famous Lulworth Cove. The house has a spacious breakfast room, 8 attractive bedrooms (all en-suite) & a lounge with colour T.V.. Outside, the terrace provides a perfect venue for morning coffee or afternoon tea. Gatton House is an ideal location for walking or touring Dorset's beauty spots, & it is within easy reach of Bournemouth, Poole, Swanage, Dorchester & Weymouth.

avril@gattonhouse.co.uk   www.gattonhouse.co.uk
£62.00 - £100.00   Open: mar - oct
Map ref no. 08

see p.120

Jill & Ken Hookham-Bassett
Stourcastle Lodge Gough's Close
Sturminster Newton DT10 1BU Dorset
Tel: (01258) 472320   Fax 01258 473381

Near Rd: B.3092
Stourcastle Lodge was rebuilt in the 18th century. Jill & Ken run the lodge in a friendly & relaxed manner, but offer a professional service with a high standard of cuisine & excellent accommodation. All of the tastefully furnished bedrooms are en-suite & overlook the pretty south-facing garden. Guests may unwind in the secluded garden during the warmer months or toast their toes in front of the log fire on wintery evenings. Stourcastle Lodge is an ideal base for exploring Dorset & its many attractions. A warm welcome awaits you.

enquiries@stourcastle-lodge.co.uk
www.stourcastle-lodge.co.uk   £88.00 - £96.00
Open: all year   Map ref no. 09

Anthea & Michael Hipwell
Gold Court House St. John's Hill   Wareham BH20 4LZ
Dorset
Tel: (01929) 553320   Fax 01929 553320

Near Rd: A.351
Gold Court House is a charming Georgian house with walled garden on a small square on the south-side of Wareham. It offers 3 light & airy double or twin rooms with private bathrooms & all facilities at hand, at your request. Wareham is ideally situated for exploring the magnificent coastline of South Dorset & the Isle of Purbeck. Anthea & Michael are always pleased to help & advise on the numerous places of interest, sporting activities & where to dine. (Evening meals are available Nov - Feb.) Children over 10 years welcome.

info@goldcourthouse.co.uk www.goldcourthouse.co.uk
£65.00 - £70.00 Open: all year (excl.xmas & new year)
Map ref no. 11

Sarah Hood
The Old Bank Burton Street Marnhull
Sturminster Newton DT10 1PH Dorset
Tel: (01258) 821019

Near Rd: B.3092
The Old Bank is a comfortable, friendly 18th Century house in the centre of an attractive Dorset village in the heart of Thomas Hardy country. Sarah & Robin welcome you to their home, which is set on a hill overlooking the beautiful Blackmore Vale. Bedrooms are light & airy with Victorian fireplaces & are decorated with cottage furnishings. Enjoy breakfast in the farmhouse kitchen. Relax in the 'secret' cottage garden or on chilly evenings rest in front of the wood burning stove in the sitting room. Shaftesbury, Sherborne, Bath & Salisbury are all within easy reach.

enquiry@theoldbank-marnhull.co.uk
www.theoldbank-marnhull.co.uk   £50.00 - £50.00
Open: all year   Map ref no. 10

Major Christopher Barne
Culeaze   Wareham BH20 7NR   Dorset
Tel: (01929) 471344   Fax 01929 472221

Near Rd: A.35
Culeaze is a lovingly restored Victorian mansion furnished with fine antiques & paintings, set in 3 acres of landscaped gardens in the centre of its small peaceful estate. Situated only 7 miles from the coast in an Area of Outstanding Natural Beauty. The accommodation comprises 3 spacious bedrooms, which are en-suite with bath, some with shower as well. All have T.V., radio, tea-making facilities, fridge & electric blankets. Dinner is a culinary delight, all home-cooking using local produce. Children over 13 years welcome.

majorbarne@ukonline.co.uk   www.culeaze.com
£70.00 - £70.00 Open: ALL YEAR
Map ref no. 12

Stourcastle Lodge

Gough's Close Sturminster Newton DT10 1BU

Tel:(01258) 472320 Fax 01258 473381

email:enquiries@stourcastle-lodge.co.uk www.bestbandb.co.uk

Tania Petford
The Seaham   3 Waterloo Place   Weymouth   DT4 7NU
Dorset
Tel: (01305) 782010

Near Rd: A.354
Situated just across the road from Weymouth's golden sandy beach, The Seaham is ideally located to allow you to enjoy all that this historic seaside town & the surrounding area has to offer. The vibrant town centre & the busy picturesque harbour are within easy walking distance, yet far enough away for you to be able to escape from the hustle and bustle. 5 stylish double bedrooms to choose from all with en-suite facilities, TV, beverage refreshment tray, ironing facilities & hair dryer. Breakfast is served in the elegant dining room & of course, includes a traditional full English breakfast. A perfect base for a relaxing holiday.

stay@theseaham.co.uk   www.theseaham.co.uk
£54.00 - £78.00   Open: all year
Map ref no. 13

John & Sara Turnbull
Thornhill   Holt   Wimborne   BH21 7DJ
Dorset
Tel: (01202) 889434

Near Rd: A.31
Visitors are warmly welcomed to this large, thatched family house located in rural surroundings 3 1/2 miles from Wimborne. A large, pretty garden. Hard tennis court is available for guests use. The accommdoation includes double, twin & single rooms. 1 private bathroom, & another which may be shared. There is also a comfortable sitting room in which to relax with colour T.V. & coffee/tea-making & laundry facilities. There are plenty of good local pubs. Thornhill is very well situated for exploring the coast, New Forest & Salisbury area. A delightful home.

scturnbull@lineone.net   www.bestbandb.co.uk
£50.00 - £54.00   Open: ALL YEAR
Map ref no. 14

Gloucestershire

Gloucestershire

The landscape is so varied the people speak not of one Gloucestershire but of three Cotswold, Vale & Forest. The rounded hills of the Cotswolds sweep & fold in graceful compositions to form a soft & beautiful landscape in which nestle many pretty villages. To the east there are wonderful views of the Vale of Berkeley & Severn, & across to the dark wooded slopes of the Forest of Dean on the Welsh borders.

Hill Forts, ancient trackways & long barrows of neolithic peoples can be explored, & remains of many villas from late Roman times can be seen. A local saying "Scratch Gloucester & find Rome" reveals the lasting influence of the Roman presence. Three major roads mark the path of invasion & settlement. Akeman street leads to London, Ermine street & the Fosse Way to the north east. A stretch of Roman road with its original surface can be seen at Blackpool Bridge in the Forest of Dean, & Cirencester's museum reflects its status as the second most important Roman city in the country.

Offa's Dyke, 80 miles of bank & ditch on the Welsh border was the work of the Anglo-Saxons of Mercia who invaded in the wake of the Romans. Cotswold means "hills of the sheepcotes" in the Anglo-Saxon tongue, & much of the heritage of the area has its roots in the wealth created by the wool industry here.

Fine Norman churches such as those at Tewkesbury & Bishops Cleeve were overshadowed by the development of the perpendicular style of building made possible by the growing prosperity. Handsome 15th century church towers crown many wool towns & villages as at Northleach, Chipping Camden & Cirencester, & Gloucester has a splendid 14th century cathedral.

Wool & cloth weaving dominated life here in the 14th & 15th centuries with most families dependent on the industry. The cottage craft of weaving was gradually overtaken by larger looms & water power. A water mill can be seen in the beautiful village of Lower Slaughter & the cottages of Arlington Row in Bibury were a weaving factory. At Witney you can still buy the locally made blankets.

Arlington Row, Bibury

Gloucestershire

Gloucestershire Gazeteer

Areas of outstanding natural beauty.
The Cotswolds, Malvern Hills & the Wye Valley.

Houses & Castles

Ashleworth Court - Ashleworth
15th century limestone Manor house.

Badminton House - Badminton
Built in the reign of Charles II. Stone
newel staircase.

Berkeley Castle - Berkeley
12th century castle - still occupied by the
Berkeley family. Magnificent collections of
furniture, paintings, tapestries & carved timber
work. Lovely terraced gardens & deer park.

Chavenage - Tetbury
Elizabethan Cotswold Manor house,
Cromwellian associations.

Clearwell Castle - Nr. Coleford
A Georgian neo-Gothic house said to be oldest
in Britain, recently restored.

Court House - Painswick
Cotswold Manor house - has original court room
& bedchamber of Charles I. Splendid panelling
& antique furniture.

Dodington House - Chipping Sodbury
Perfect 18th century house with superb
staircase. Landscape by Capability Brown.

Horton Court - Horton
Cotswold manor house altered & restored in
19th century.

Kelmscott Manor - Nr. Lechlade
16th century country house - 17th century
additions. Examples of work of William Morris,
Rosetti & Burne-Jones.

Owlpen Manor - Nr. Dursley
Historic group of traditional Cotswold stone
buildings. Tudor Manor house with church,
barn, court house & a grist mill. Holds a rare set
of 17th century painted cloth wall hangings.

Snowshill Manor - Broadway
Tudor house with 17th century facade. Unique
collection of musical instruments & clocks, toys.

Sudeley Castle - Winchcombe

12th century - home of Katherine Parr, is rich in
historical associations, contains art treasures &
relics of bygone days.

Cathedrals & Churches

Bishops Cleeve (St. Michael & All Saints)
12th century with 17th century gallery.
Magnificent Norman west front & south porch.
Decorated chancel. Fine window.

Bledington (St.Leonards)
15th century glass in this perpendicular
church, Norman bellcote. Early English
east window.

Buckland (St. Michael)
13th century nave arcades. 17th century oak
panelling, 15th century glass.

Cirencester (St. John the Baptist)
A magnificent church - remarkable exterior, 3
storey porch, 2 storey oriel windows, traceries &
pinnacles. Wine-glass pulpit c.1450. 15th
century glass in east window, monuments in
Lady chapel.

Gloucester Cathedral
Birthplace of Perpendicular style in 14th century.
Fan vaulting, east windows commemorate
Battle of Crecy - Norman Chapter House.

Hailes Abbey - Winchcombe
14th century wall paintings, 15th century tiles,
glass & screen, 17th century pulpit.
Elizabethan benches.

Iron Acton (St. James the Less)
Perpendicular - 15th century memorial cross.
19th century mosaic floors, Laudian alter rails,
Jacobean pulpit, effigies.

Newland (All Saints)
13th century, restored 18th century. Pinnacled
west tower, effigies.

Prinknash Abbey - Gloucester
14th & 16th century - Benedictine Abbey.

Tewkesbury Abbey - Tewkesbury
Dates to Norman times, contains Romanesque
& Gothic styles.14th C. monuments.

Yate (St. Mary)
Splendid perpendicular tower.

Gloucestershire

Museums & Galleries

Bishop Hooper's Lodgings - Gloucester
3 Tudor timber frame buildings - museum of
domestic life & agriculture in Gloucester since 1500.

Bourton Motor Museum - Bourton-on-the-Water
Collection of cars & motor cycles.

Cheltenham Art Gallery - Cheltenham.
Gallery of Dutch paintings, collection of oils,
watercolours, pottery, porcelain, English &
Chinese furniture.

City Wall & Bastion - Gloucester
Roman & medieval city defences in an
underground exhibition room.

Stroud Museum - Cirencester
Depicts earlier settlements in the area & has a
very fine collection of Roman antiquities.

Historic Monuments

Chedworth Roman Villa - Yanworth
Remains of Romano-British villa.

Belas Knap Long Barrow - Charlton Abbots
Neolithic burial ground - three burial chambers
with external entrances.

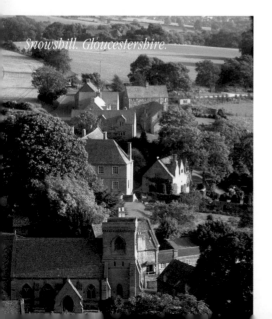

Snowshill. Gloucestershire.

Hailes Abbey - Stanway
Ruins of beautiful medieval abbey built by son
of King John, 1246.

Witcombe Roman Villa - Nr. Birdlip
Large Roman villa - Hypocaust & mosaic
pavements preserved.

Ashleworth Tithe Barn - Ashleworth
15th century tithe barn - 120 feet long - stone
built, interesting roof timbering.

Odda's Chapel - Deerhurst
Rare Saxon chapel dating back to 1056.

Hetty Pegler's Tump - Uley Long Barrow
Fairly complete, chamber is 120 feet long.

Other things to see & do

**Cheltenham International Festival of Music &
Literature - Annual event.**

Cotswolds Farm Park
Dozens of rare breeds of farm animals.

**Gloucestershire Warwickshire Railway -
Toddington**
The Friendly Line in the Cotswolds operates
steam and diesel services over a 20 mile
round trip between Toddington and
Cheltenham Racecourse.

The World of Mechanical Music - Northleach
A living museum of the various kinds of self-
playing musical instruments and automata.
Horology sculpture.

Painswick Rococo Garden - Painswick
The Rococo Garden is situated in a hidden 6
acre Cotswold valley. The Garden is famous
for its display of snowdrops and newly
planted maze.

Dean Heritage Centre - Cinderford
Objects from the museum collection are displayed
in five new museum galleries to tell the history of
the Forest of Dean and its people.

Bird Park & Gardens - Burton on the Water
Seven acres of woodland, river and gardens
inhabited by over 500 birds; flamingos, pelicans
and penguins to parrots, hornbills, & toucans.

Three Choirs Vineyard - Newent
Visit the 75 acres of peaceful vineyard. Wine tasting.

GLOUCESTERSHIRE

Map reference

00 Stagg	12 Paton
01 Bolton	13 Metcalfe
01 Wright	14 Annis
02 Thornely	15 Hodges
03 Moodie	16 Rodger
04 Gamez	17 Whitton
05 Gisby	18 Hayward
06 Wilson	19 Dean
07 Yardley	20 McGrigor
08 Keyser	21 Mason
09 Parsons	22 Atkinson
10 Baxter	23 Adams
11 Rackley	24 Solomon

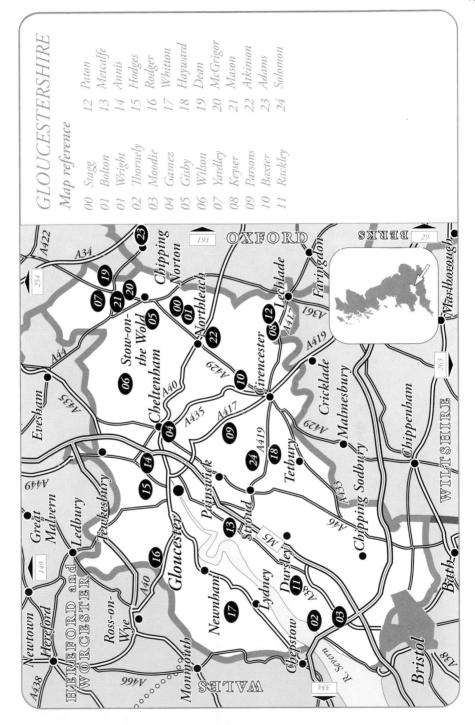

Clapton Manor

Clapton-on-the-Hill Bourton-on-the-Water GL54 2LG

Tel:(01451) 810202 Mobile 07967 144416 email:bandb@claptonmanor.co.uk www.claptonmanor.co.uk

Richard & Pat Stagg
Coombe House Rissington Road
Bourton-on-the-Water GL54 2DT Gloucestershire
Tel: (01451) 821966   Fax 01451 810477

Near Rd: A.429
Coombe House is a charming, peaceful house in lovely gardens with 1st floor sun terrace. Only a 5 mins' easy riverside walk from the centre of the village & restaurants. Offering 6 pretty en-suite bedrooms, thoughtfully equipped with plenty of welcoming extras. Guests' sitting room & attractive dining room where traditional/continental breakfast is served. Parking available. Perfect base for exploring the Cotswolds, Hidcote Gardens, Sudeley Castle, Oxford, Blenheim, Stratford-upon-Avon & Warwick Castle. Children over 12 years welcome.

info@coombehouse.net   www.coombehouse.net
£65.00 - £80.00 Open: feb - dec (excl. xmas)
Map ref no. 00

Julia Wright
Farncombe Clapton-on-the-Hill Bourton-on-the-Water
GL54 2LG   Gloucestershire Tel: (01451) 820120
Mobile 07714 703142 Fax 01451 820120

Near Rd: A.429, A.40
Come & share the peace, tranquillity & superb views of Farncombe, & eat, drink & sleep - smoke-free - 700ft above sea level & only 2 miles from delightful Bourton-on-the-Water. There are 2 attractive doubles with showers, & 1 twin-bedded room en-suite. A spacious dining room, with tea/coffee-making facilities, & a comfortable T.V. lounge. Tourist information, maps & books, & current menus for your choice when eating out. Children over 12. Numerous walks & drives, with easy access to all the attractions & places of interest.

julia@farncombecotswolds.com
www.farncombecotswolds.com £48.00 - £48.00
Open: mid jan - mid dec   Map ref no. 01

see p.126

James & Karin Bolton
Clapton Manor   Clapton-on-the-Hill
Bourton-on-the-Water GL54 2LG   Gloucestershire
Tel: (01451) 810202   Mobile 07967 144416

Near Rd: A.40, A.429
Clapton Manor dates from 1550 & sits at the top of a very quiet village with stunning views. It is an informal yet elegant family home with children & dogs. Guests have their own sitting room with log fire, lots of books & the latest magazines. There are 2 bedrooms (1 can be a twin or a double). Each bedroom is beautifully furnished throughout & has en-suite facilities. Lovely gardens where chickens waddle preparing to lay eggs for your breakfast. Fantastic walking (or even running!) straight from the house.

bandb@claptonmanor.co.uk   www.claptonmanor.co.uk
£80.00 - £95.00 Open: all year (excl.xmas & new year)
Map ref no. 01

Mrs Ann Thornely
Eastcote Cottage Crossways Lane Thornbury Bristol
BS35 3UE   Gloucestershire
Tel: (01454) 413106   Fax 01454 281812

Near Rd: A.38
Eastcote is a charming 200-year-old stone house located in a lovely rural setting, with splendid views across open countryside. The accommodation includes 2 comfortable bedrooms with all modern amenities to ensure a restful stay. A colour-T.V. lounge is available for guests' use. Eastcote is conveniently situated for the M.4/M.5 interchange for the Cotswolds, with historic Bristol, Bath, Cheltenham & the Wye Valley easily accessible. Private parking is available.

ann@nickthornely.co.uk   www.bestbandb.co.uk
£56.00 - £60.00 Open: all year (excl. xmas)
Map ref no. 02

Rectory Farmhouse

Lower Swell Stow-on-the-Wold Nr. Cheltenham GL54 1LH

Tel:(01451) 832351

email:rectory.farmhouse@cw-warwick.co.uk www.bestbandb.co.uk

see p.128

David & Suzanne Moodie
The Elms   Olveston   Bristol   BS35 4DR
Gloucestershire
Tel: (01454) 614559   Fax 01454 618607

Near Rd: A.38
An elegant Grade II listed village house set in attractive 2-acre gardens with comfortable suite (having its own access) & a self-contained cottage. Convenient for Bristol, M.4/M.5 interchange. Great emphasis is placed on immaculate, luxurious standards & green issues. Breakfasts are organic when possible. Allergy sufferers are welcome & the environment is kept as pollutant free as possible. Guests are respectfully requested not to use scented products. The owners are great animal & garden lovers and keep cats, dogs, hens, ornamental ducks, geese & doves. Hard tennis court available.

b&b@theelmsmoodie.co.uk   www.theelmsmoodie.co.uk
£70.00 - £80.00   Open: all year
Map ref no. 03

Sybil Gisby
Rectory Farmhouse   Lower Swell Nr. Stow-on-the-Wold
Cheltenham   GL54 1LH   Gloucestershire
Tel: (01451) 832351

Near Rd: A.429
Rectory Farmhouse is an historic 17th-century traditional Cotswold farmhouse located in the quiet hamlet of Lower Swell, which lies about 1 mile to the west of the well-known market town of Stow-on-the-Wold. This outstanding home is elegantly furnished throughout & boasts superb double bedrooms, enjoying stunning views over open countryside. All bedrooms are centrally heated & have luxurious en-suite bathrooms. Chipping Campden & Bourton-on-the-Water are just a short drive away. Cheltenham, Oxford & Stratford-upon-Avon are all easily accessible. Children over 16 years welcome.

rectory.farmhouse@cw-warwick.co.uk
www.bestbandb.co.uk   £85.00 - £90.00
Open: all year   Map ref no. 05

see p.130

Penny & Alex Gamez
Georgian House   77 Montpellier Terrace   Cheltenham
GL50 1XA   Gloucestershire
Tel: (01242) 515577   Fax 01242 545929

Near Rd: A.40
Take 3 beautiful bedrooms in an elegant Georgian home, set them among the charming terraces of Montpellier, only 5 mins' from the Promenade, add a warm welcome from your hosts, Penny & Alex, & there you have Georgian House. Each of the beautiful en-suite rooms has colour T.V. with satellite, telephone with modem socket, ironing facilities, trouser press & fridge. The delicious English breakfasts include fresh fruit - the perfect combination! Parking available.

penny@georgianhouse.net   www.georgianhouse.net
£80.00 - £95.00   Open: all year (excl. xmas & new year)
Map ref no. 04

Susie & Jim Wilson
Westward   Sudeley Road   Winchcombe   Cheltenham
GL54 5JB   Gloucestershire
Tel: (01242) 604372   Fax 01242 609198

Near Rd: A.40
The Wilson families share this beautiful Grade II listed Georgian house on the scarp of the Cotswolds above Sudeley Castle, sitting within its own 600-acre estate with spectacular views to the Malverns. The heart of the Cotswolds is very close, with Broadway, Oxford & Stratford within easy reach. The Wilsons combine good food - Susie trained at Prue Leith's - with elegance & comfort in their delightful English family home. 3 elegant en-suite rooms available. Children over 12.

jimw@baldon.co.uk   www.westward-sudeley.co.uk
£80.00 - £100.00   Open: all year (excl. xmas)
Map ref no. 06

Westward

Sudeley Road Winchcombe Cheltenham GL54 5JB

Tel:(01242) 604372 Fax 01242 609198

email:jimw@haldon.co.uk www.westward-sudeley.co.uk

see p.132

Alison & Michael Yardley
Nineveh Farm Campden Road Mickleton
Chipping Campden GL55 6PS Gloucestershire
Tel: (01386) 438923

Near Rd: A.44
Multi-award-winning Nineveh is an attractive 200 year old farmhouse, which is ideally situated for visiting the glorious Cotswolds, Stratford-upon-Avon with its Shakespeare connections, Warwick Castle & Blenheim Palace. With antique furnishings, log fires in winter, flagstone floors & beams, all rooms enjoy superb views over open countryside. Hearty breakfasts are served. Complementary tea & cakes on arrival & free use of cycles (subject to availability.) Good pubs & restaurants in nearby Mickleton village. Children over 12 years welcome.

stay@ninevehfarm.co.uk   www.ninevehfarm.co.uk
£65.00 - £70.00 Open: all year
Map ref no. 07

Shaun & Susanna Parsons
Winstone Glebe   Winstone   Cirencester GL7 7LN
Gloucestershire
Tel: (01285) 821451

Near Rd: A.417
A small Georgian rectory overlooking a Saxon church in a Domesday-listed village, & enjoying spectacular rural views. Ideally situated for exploring Cotswold market towns, with their medieval churches, antique shops & rich local history. 3 bedrooms, each with private/en-suite bathroom. Being an Area of Outstanding Natural Beauty, there are signposted walks. The more energetic can borrow a bicycle & explore, or just enjoy warm hospitality & good food cooked by Susanna. Single supplement. Evening meals & animals by arrangement.

sparsons@winstoneglebe.com   www.winstoneglebe.com
£74.00 - £84.00 Open: all year (excl. xmas)
Map ref no. 09

Mrs James Keyser
Lady Lamb Farm Meysey Hampton   Cirencester
GL7 5LH   Gloucestershire
Tel: (01285) 712206   Fax 01285 712206

Near Rd: A.417
Lady Lamb Farm is a Cotswold-stone farmhouse, surrounded by countryside & situated less than a mile from the small market town of Fairford. 2 attractively furnished guest rooms, each with T.V. & tea/coffee-making facilities. (1 is en-suite.) A swimming pool & tennis court are available. Set on the edge of the Cotswolds, Bath, Oxford & many Cotswold towns, & wonderful gardens are within easy reach. Cotswold Water Park offers a wide range of watersports. Golf, riding & fishing are available nearby. Single supplement. Animals by arrangement.

jekeyser1@aol.com   www.bestbandb.co.uk
£65.00 - £65.00 Open: all year
Map ref no. 08

Mrs Bridget Baxter
The Old House Calmsden   Nr. Cirencester GL7 5ET
Gloucestershire
Tel: (01285) 831240

Near Rd: A.429
The 17th-century Old House is situated in a peaceful rural hamlet, with lovely views & a pretty garden. The 3 bedrooms are light, sunny & restful with all amenities to ensure you have a comfortable stay. Food is delicious, organic & free range where possible & is served in the panelled dining room. Bread is baked daily. Fresh flowers abound. There is an excellent pub 1 1/2 miles away & plenty more to choose from within 15 minutes drive. Animals by arrangement. An ideal home for a relaxing short break holiday.

baxter@calmsden.freeserve.co.uk
www.theoldhouse-calmsden.co.uk £65.00 - £80.00
Open: mar - nov   Map ref no. 10

Winstone Glebe

Winstone Cirencester GL7 7LN

Tel:(01285) 821451 email:sparsons@winstoneglebe.com www.winstoneglebe.com

Peter Rackley
Burrows Court Nibley Green North Nibley Dursley
GL11 6AZ Gloucestershire
Tel: (01453) 546230 Fax 01453 546230

Near Rd: A.38
Burrows Court is an historic Grade II listed country house, which is surrounded by open countryside with beautiful views of the Cotswold Edge. Offering accommodation in a fascinating three-storey building consisting of an 18th Century weaving mill & the adjoining Georgian fronted mill-owners house believed to date back to the 13th century. The property is furnished & decorated to a high standard yet it retains much of its original charm & character. 6 en-suite bedrooms with T.V., tea/coffee etc. plus 2 lounges in which to relax. Berkeley Castle, Slimbridge Wildfowl Trust, Bath, Bristol, Cheltenham & Gloucester within easy reach.

burrowscourt@tesco.net www.burrowscourt.co.uk
£55.00 - £68.00 Open: all year
Map ref no. 11

Veronica Metcalfe
The True Heart The Street Frampton-on-Severn
GL2 7ED Gloucestershire
Tel: (01452) 740504

Near Rd: A.38
The True Heart, dating from late Georgian times, was a village pub until the 1960s but has now been transformed into a comfortable homely family run bed & breakfast. It is conveniently & quietly situated in the delightful Severn Vale village of Frampton on Severn, just 5 mins off the M5 motorway between Gloucester & Bristol. It has stunning views from the back of the Gloucester to Sharpness canal, the River Severn & across to the Forest of Dean. Slimbridge, Cheltenham, Bath & the Cotswolds etc. are within easy reach. Great cycling country (cycles available to borrow.) All rooms with T.V., hairdryer, tea/coffee facilities.

veronica@thetrueheart.co.uk www.thetrueheart.co.uk
£70.00 - £75.00 Open: all year
Map ref no. 13

Suzie Paton
Milton Farm Fairford GL7 4HZ
Gloucestershire
Tel: (01285) 712205 Fax 01285 711349

Near Rd: A.417
Milton Farm is a working farm set in spectacular Cotswold countryside, on the edge of this most attractive market town. The impressive Georgian farmhouse has luxuriously spacious & distinctive en-suite bedrooms. Warm hospitality & delicious real farmhouse Aga-cooked breakfasts, from locally sourced quality produce. Superb fine restaurants & traditional pubs locally. Exceptionally welcoming for business guests, walkers, cyclists, fishermen & visitors to the Cotswold Water Park. All bedrooms have wireless Internet access.

stay@milton-farm.co.uk www.milton-farm.co.uk
£50.00 - £70.00 Open: all year (excl.xmas & new year)
Map ref no. 12

Keith & Joyce Annis
Evington Hill Farm Tewkesbury Road The Leigh
Gloucester GL19 4AQ Gloucestershire
Tel: (01242) 680255

Near Rd: A.38
Evington Hill Farm is a delightful 16th-century house, set in 4 acres of grounds & within easy reach of Cheltenham, Gloucester & the Cotswolds. Take refreshment with tea & home-made cake in the sunny conservatory. stay in the charming antique pine furnished bedrooms with their beautiful spacious bathrooms. 1 has a 4-poster bed, all have T.V. & hostess tray. After exploring this wonderful county relax in the beamed sitting room with Tudor fireplace & log burning stove. Games room & hard tennis court for your enjoyment. Parking. 2 holiday cottages available.

evingtonfarm@gmail.com www.evingtonhillfarm.co.uk
£72.00 - £90.00 Open: all year
Map ref no. 14

The Old Farm

Barrel Lane Longhope GL17 0LR

Tel:(01452) 830252 Mobile 0790 5683029

email:BBB@the-old-farm.co.uk www.the-old-farm.co.uk

Mrs Shirley Hodges
The Old Vicarage   Norton   Gloucester GL2 9LR
Gloucestershire
Tel: (01452) 739295/731214   Fax 01452 739091

Near Rd: A.38
A Victorian vicarage in 1 3/4 acres of gardens with views towards the Cotswold escarpment & Malvern Hills, & a footpath from a garden gate leading to a riverside pub & the Severn Way. The accommodation includes 3 delightful guest rooms (2 with en-suite facilities) each with T.V., hairdryer, hospitality tray & fridge. A delicious English country house breakfast is served with a log fire burning in the hearth when chilly. The Old Vicarage is a secluded retreat with a relaxed ambience & only a short drive from Cheltenham, Gloucester & Tewkesbury.

bandb.nov@btconnect.com   www.bestbandb.co.uk
£56.00 - £60.00   Open: all year
Map ref no. 15

Pat & Brian Whitton
Edale House   Folly Road   Parkend   Nr. Lydney
GL15 4JF   Gloucestershire
Tel: (01594) 562835   Fax 01594 564488

Near Rd: A.48
Edale House is a fine Georgian residence facing the cricket green in the village of Parkend at the heart of the Royal Forest of Dean. Once the home of local G.P. Bill Tandy, author of 'A Doctor in the Forest', the house has been tastefully restored to provide comfortable en-suite accommodation with every facility for guests. Enjoy delicious & imaginative cuisine prepared by your hosts. (Evening meals are available Thurs-Mon.) Fully licensed. Children over 12 years welocme. Animals by arrangement. Edale House is the perfect location for a short break holiday.

enquiry@edalehouse.co.uk   www.edalehouse.co.uk
£51.00 - £62.00   Open: all year
Map ref no. 17

see p.134

Lucy Rodger
The Old Farm   Barrel Lane   Longhope GL17 0LR
Gloucestershire
Tel: (01452) 830252   Mobile 0790 5683029

Near Rd: A.40
Nestling in an idyllic valley, this charming 16th-century farmhouse offers tranquillity surrounded by old oak beams, fireplaces & character yet it is within easy reach of the Royal Forest of Dean, Wye Valley, Cheltenham & Cotswolds. Relax with afternoon tea, including home-made cakes, in front of the fire or in the sunny garden. Pretty en-suite bedrooms, including 4-poster. Start your day with a special breakfast made from local produce, free-range eggs from your host's hens & home-made preserves. Good local pub/restaurant. Dogs by arrangement. Children over 12.

BBB@the-old-farm.co.uk   www.the-old-farm.co.uk
£54.00 - £65.00   Open: all year (excl.xmas & new year)
Map ref no. 16

Mrs E Hayward
Hyde Wood House   Cirencester Road   Minchinhampton
GL6 8PE   Gloucestershire
Tel: (01453) 885504   Fax 01453 885504

Near Rd: A.419
A high quality & welcoming family run B & B originally built as a working farmhouse in a rural setting. Although no longer a working farm, it still has stables which retain its character. The house is tastefully furnished with comfortable en-suite bedrooms equipped with T.V., radio & filled with a range of homely extras. A lounge with open fire in winter & in good weather relax in the sun room or garden. Home made cake & biscuits served on arrival. Full English breakfast freshly cooked on the Aga. Close to Minchinhampton centre. Gliding, golf & riding nearby.

info@hydewoodhouse.co.uk   www.hydewoodhouse.co.uk
£55.00 - £60.00   Open: all year (excl.xmas & new year)
Map ref no. 18

Mrs E. M. Dean
Treetops Guest House   London Road   Moreton-in-Marsh
GL56 0HE   Gloucestershire
Tel: (01608) 651036   Fax 01608 651036

Near Rd: A.44
A beautiful family home offering traditional bed & breakfast.
The accommodation includes 6 attractive & tastefully
furnished bedrooms, all with en-suite facilities & 2 of which
are on the ground floor and thus suitable for disabled
persons or wheelchair users. All bedrooms have colour
T.V., radio and tea/coffee-making facilities. Cots and high
chairs are available. Delicious breakfasts served. Delightful
secluded gardens to relax in. Ideally situated for exploring
the Cotswolds. Treetops is an ideal base for a relaxing break
in this lovely county. A warm and homely atmosphere
awaits you here.

treetops1@talk21.com www.treetopscotswolds.co.uk
£55.00 - £60.00   Open: all year (excl. xmas)
Map ref no. 19

Nicholas & Zelie Mason
Lower Farm House   Adlestrop Moreton-in-Marsh
GL56 0YR   Gloucestershire
Tel: (01608) 658756   Fax 01608 659458

Near Rd: A.436
3 miles from Stow-on-the-Wold, this listed Grade II Georgian
farmhouse, in the peaceful village of Adlestrop, is ideally
situated for discovering the Cotswolds. Stratford, Oxford
& Broadway & the wonderful gardens of Hidcote & Kiftsgate
are within easy reach as well as signed walks to explore.
Lower Farm House has 2 acres of landscaped gardens &
guests can enjoy a log fire in winter or sit on the terrace on
those hot balmy days of summer. 2 delightful bedrooms
with en-suite/private bathrooms & glorious views.You will
receive a warm welcome & good food in this elegant family
home. Children & dogs by prior arrangement.

zelie.mason@talk21.com   www.bestbandb.co.uk
£90.00 - £96.00 Open: all year (excl. xmas)
Map ref no. 21

Kiloran McGrigor
Wren House   Donnington   Moreton-in-Marsh
GL56 0XZ   Gloucestershire
Tel: (01451) 831787   Mobile 07802 676673

Near Rd: A.429, A.44
Wren House is an attractive, peacefully situated Cotswold
stone house on the edge of Donnington, a small village 2
miles north of Stow-on-the-Wold. Dating from the 15th-
century, it has been recently renovated & combines original
charm with modern comfort. The bedrooms are simply
yet elegantly decorated & can be either double or twin.
The bathrooms are new & all rooms have a sunny, southern
aspect overlooking an imaginatively planted garden. In
winter a roaring log fire greets you in the drawing room.
Children over 7. Dinner by arrangement.

enquiries@wrenhouse.net   www.wrenhouse.net
£90.00 - £100.00   Open: easter - nov
Map ref no. 20

Margaret & David Atkinson
Cotteswold House Market Place   Northleach GL54 3EG
Gloucestershire
Tel: (01451) 860493   Fax 01451 860493

Near Rd: A.40, A.429
Conveniently situated in Northleach Market Place. This
Grade II listed building (over 400 years old), has bags of
character including beamed ceilings, original wood
panelling, a Tudor archway & a carved fireplace. Once a
wealthy wool merchants home, it is reputed that Queen
Elizabeth I dined here. Stay in the old Hayloft double,
Mullions twin-bedded room or the Tudor suite with 4-poster
bed, canopied corner bath & shower & private lounge. Take
a stroll around the unspoilt town, visit local pubs &
restaurants. Holiday cottage available. Children over 12.

cotteswoldhouse@aol.com www.cotteswoldhouse.com
£65.00 - £80.00 Open: all year
Map ref no. 22

Mrs FJ Adams
Aston House Broadwell Moreton-in-Marsh
Stow-on-the-Wold GL56 0TJ Gloucestershire
Tel: (01451) 830475

Near Rd: A.429

Aston House is set in the quiet village of Broadwell, approx.
1.5 miles from Stow-on-the-Wold & 4 miles from Moreton-
in-Marsh. Centrally situated for visiting all the Cotswold
Villages, while Stratford-upon-Avon, Warwick Castle,
Blenheim Palace, Oxford, Cheltenham, Cirencester &
Gloucester are all within 20–30 miles. There is a 1st floor
twin-bedded room & a double/twin room. Each room is
en-suite (with shower.) A ground floor double room with
private bathroom. All rooms have tea/coffee facilities &
bedtime drinks & biscuits, TV, armchairs, hairdryer & electric
blankets for those colder nights plus fans for summer days.

fja@netcomuk.co.uk www.astonhouse.net
£56.00 - £58.00 Open: mar - oct
Map ref no. 23

Mrs Glynis Solomon
Pretoria Villa Wells Road Eastcombe Stroud GL6 7EE
Gloucestershire Tel: (01452) 770435
Fax 01452 770435 Mobile 07816 323615

Near Rd: A.419

Enjoy luxurious bed & breakfast in a relaxed family country
house set in peaceful secluded gardens. Spacious
tastefully furnished bedrooms, with en-suite/private
facilities. Hospitality trays, hairdryers & bathrobes in all
rooms. Guests have their own comfortable lounge in which
to relax & delicious breakfasts are served in the dining
room. There are many good eating places nearby. Pretoria
Villa is an excellent base from which to explore the
Cotswolds. Personal service & your comfort are
guaranteed in this excellent home.

glynis@gsolomon.freeserve.co.uk
www.bedandbreakfast-cotswold.co.uk £56.00 - £56.00
Open: all year (excl. xmas) Map ref no. 24

Hampshire & The Isle of Wight

Hampshire

Hampshire is located in the centre of the south coast of England & is blessed with much beautiful & unspoilt countryside. Wide open vistas of rich downland contrast with deep woodlands. Rivers & sparkling streams run through tranquil valleys passing nestling villages. There is a splendid coastline with seaside resorts & harbours, the cathedral city of Winchester & the "jewel" of Hampshire, the Isle of Wight.

The north of the county is known as the Hampshire Borders. Part of this countryside was immortalised by Richard Adams & the rabbits of 'Watership Down'. Beacon Hill is a notable hill-top landmark. From its slopes some of the earliest aeroplane flights were made by De

Winchester Cathedral. Winchester. Anthony Gormley's "Sound 11" statue.

Haviland in 1909. Pleasure trips & tow-path walks can be taken along the restored Basingstoke Canal.

The New Forest is probably the area most frequented by visitors. It is a landscape of great character with thatched cottages, glades & streams & a romantic beauty. There are herds of deer & the New Forest ponies wander at will. To the N.W. of Beaulieu are some of the most idyllic parts of the old forest, with fewer villages & many little streams that flow into the Avon. Lyndhurst, the "capital" of the New Forest has a contentious 19th century church constructed in scarlet brickwork banded with yellow, unusual ornamental decoration, & stained glass windows by William Morris.

The Roman city of Winchester became the capital city of Saxon Wessex & is today the capital of Hampshire. It is famous for its beautiful mediaeval cathedral, built during the reign of William the Conquerer & his notorious son Rufus. It contains the great Winchester Bible. William completed the famous Doomsday Book in the city.

The Isle of Wight lies across the sheltered waters of the Solent, & is easily reached by car or passenger ferry. The chalk stacks of the Needles & the multi-coloured sand at Alum Bay are among the best known of the island's natural attractions & there are many excellent beaches & other bays to enjoy. Cowes is a famous international sailing centre with a large number of yachting events throughout the summer.

Hampshire & The Isle of Wight

Hampshire Gazeteer

Areas of outstanding natural beauty.
East & South Hampshire, North Wessex Downs
& Chichester Harbour.

Houses & Castles

Avington Park - Winchester
16th century red brick house, enlarged in 17th
century by the addition of two wings & a
classical portico. Stateroom, ballroom with
wonderful ceiling. Red drawing room, library.

Beaulieu Abbey & Palace House - Beaulieu
12th century Cistercian abbey - the original
gatehouse of abbey converted to palace house
1538. Houses historic car museum.

Breamore House - Breamore
16th century Elizabethan Manor House,
tapestries, furniture, paintings. Also museum.

Jane Austen's Home - Chawston
Personal effects of the famous writer. Here Jane
revised her earlier manuscript novels Sense and
Sensibility, Pride and Prejudice, and wrote
Mansfield Park, Emma and Persuasion.

Broadlands - Romsey
16th century - park & garden created by
Capability Brown. Home of the Earl
Mountbatten of Burma.

Mottisfont Abbey - Nr. Romsey
12th century Augustinian Priory until Dissolution.
Painting by Rex Whistler trompe l'oeil in the
Gothic manner.

Stratfield Saye House - Reading
17th century house presented to the Duke of
Wellington 1817. Now contains his possessions
- also wild fowl sanctuary.

Sandham Memorial Chapel - Sandham, Nr. Newbury
Paintings by Stanley Spencer cover the walls.

The Vyne - Sherbourne St. John
16th century red brick chapel with Renaissance
glass & rare linenfold panelling. Alterations
made in 1654 - classical portico. Palladian
staircase dates form 1760.

West Green House - Hartley Wintney
18th century red brick house set in a walled garden.

Appuldurcombe House - Wroxall - Isle of Wight
The only house in the 'Grand Manner' on the
island. Beautiful English baroque east facade.
House now an empty shell standing in fine park.

Osbourne House - East Cowes - Isle of Wight
Queen Victoria's seaside residence.

Carisbrooke Castle - Isle of Wight
Oldest parts 12th century, but there was a
wooden castle on the mound before that.
Museum in castle.

Cathedrals & Churches

Winchester Cathedral
Largest Gothic church in Europe. Norman &
perpendicular styles, three sets of medieval
paintings, marble font c.1180. Stalls c.1320 with
60 misericords. Extensive medieval tiled floor.

Breamore (St. Mary) - Breamore
10th century Saxon. Double splayed windows,
stone rood.

East Meon (All Saints)
15th century rebuilding of Norman fabric.
Tournai marble front.

Idsworth (St. Hubert)
16th century chapel - 18th century bell turret.
14th century paintings in chancel.

Pamber (dedication unknown)
Early English - Norman central tower, 15th
central pews, wooden effigy of knight c.1270.

Romsey (St. Mary & St. Ethelfleda)
Norman - 13th century effigy of a lady - Saxon
rood & carving of crucifixion, 16th century
painted reredos.

Silchester (St. Mary)
Norman, perpendicular, 14th century effigy of a
lady, 15th century screen, Early English chancel
with painted patterns on south window splays,
Jacobean pulpit with domed canopy.

Winchester (St. Cross)
12th century. Original chapel to Hospital. Style
changing from Norman at east to decorated at
west. Tiles, glass & wall painting.

140

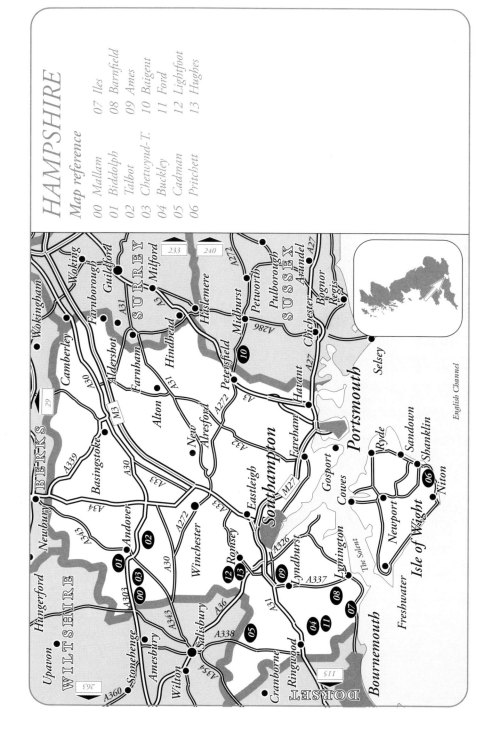

HAMPSHIRE

Map reference

00 Mallam
01 Biddolph
02 Talbot
03 Chetwynd-T.
04 Buckley
05 Cadman
06 Pritchett
07 Iles
08 Barnfield
09 Ames
10 Baigent
11 Ford
12 Lightfoot
13 Hughes

Mrs Carolyn Mallam
Broadwater Amport Nr. Andover SP11 8AY
Hampshire
Tel: (01264) 772240   Fax 01264 772240

Near Rd: A.303
Broadwater is a 17th-century, listed, thatched cottage situated in a peaceful unspoilt village just off the A.303. It is an ideal base for sightseeing in Hampshire, with easy access to the West Country & London. The cottage offers 2 delightful, double/twin-bedded rooms, both with en-suite facilities. Guests have a private & very comfortable sitting/dining room with a traditional open log fire & a very pretty garden to enjoy. Home-made bread. Colour T.V.. Children over 8. years welcome The option of self-catering in a thatched barn is available, on request.

broadwater@dmac.co.uk www.broadwaterbandb.co.uk
£60.00 - £70.00   Open: all year (excl.xmas & new year)
Map ref no. 00

James & Jean Talbot
Church Farm House   Barton Stacey
Andover SO21 3RR   Hampshire
Tel: (01962) 760268   Fax 01962 761825

Near Rd: A.303, A.30
Church Farm is a 15th-century tithe barn with Georgian & modern additions. It features an adjacent coach house & converted groom's cottage, where guests may be totally self-contained, or be welcomed to the log-fired family drawing room & dine on locally produced fresh food. Accommodation is in 4 beautiful bedrooms for guests, all with a private bathroom. T.V. & tea/coffee-making facilities. A swimming pool & croquet lawn are available to guests. Tennis court adjacent. Church Farm is a charming home from which to explore Hampshire.

www.bestbandb.co.uk
£100.00 - £100.00   Open: all year
Map ref no. 02

see p.142

Tom & Fiona Biddolph
May Cottage Thruxton   Nr. Andover SP11 8LZ
Hampshire   Tel: (01264) 771241
Fax 01264 771770 Mobile 07768 242166.

Near Rd: A.303
May Cottage dates back to 1740 & is situated in the heart of this picturesque tranquil village with Post Office & traditional old inn. A most comfortable & tastefully furnished home with 2 doubles & 1 twin room with en-suite/private bathrooms. All with colour T.V. & tea/coffee-making facilities. Guests' have their own sitting/dining room with T.V. An ideal base for visiting ancient cities, stately homes & gardens, yet within easy reach of ports & airports. There are 2 very good local inns which offer food. Parking.

info@maycottage-thruxton.co.uk
www.maycottage-thruxton.co.uk £70.00 - £80.00
Open: all year   Map ref no. 01

Mrs Sarah Chetwynd-Talbot
Gunville House Grateley Andover SP11 8JQ
Hampshire
Tel: (01264) 889206   Fax 01264 889060

Near Rd: A.303
Gunville House is a charming thatched, beamed family house, dating from the 18th century in a secluded, rural situation, 5 mins' from the A.303. The house offers 1 twin bedroom & 1 single, both with en-suite bath & shower, colour T.V. & tea trays. Ideally situated for Salisbury, Winchester, Stonehenge, Marlborough & many famous Hampshire/Wiltshire attractions. Fly fishing, golf. clay pigeon shooting can be arranged locally. Good pub within walking distance. Singlesfrom £35. Children over 5.

pct@onetel.net.uk www.gunvillehouse.co.uk
£70.00 - £70.00   Open: all year
Map ref no. 03

May Cottage

Thruxton Nr. Andover SP11 8LZ

Tel:(01264) 771241 Fax 01264 771770

email:info@maycottage-thruxton.co.uk www.maycottage-thruxton.co.uk

Mrs Wendy Buckley
Tothill House Black Lane Thorney Hill Bransgore
Nr. Christchurch BH23 8DZ Hampshire
Tel: (01425) 674414 Fax 01425 672235

Near Rd: A.35

Tothill House is an Edwardian country house set in 12 acres of woodland. An Area of Outstanding Natural Beauty noted for its flora & fauna. Only 5 mins' from Burley village, a popular New Forest tourist attraction. Offering good food & 3 attractive rooms, 2 with en-suite facilities & 1 with a private bathroom. Each individually decorated, with T.V. & tea-making facilities. Very secluded, and offering peace & tranquillity. There are local sporting & recreational activities, & a variety of places to visit. The perfect spot for a relaxing break. Children over 16.

www.newforest.demon.co.uk/tothillhouse.htm
£70.00 - £70.00 Open: feb - nov
Map ref no. 04

James Pritchett
Under Rock Shore Road Bonchurch Ventnor
Isle of Wight PO38 1RF Hampshire
Tel: (01983) 855274

Near Rd: A.3055

Historical Georgian house set in large secluded gardens near Horseshoe Bay & southern coastal paths, with isolated coves, narrow ravines or chines, soaring cliffs, high chalk downland, & country walks. The accommdoation includes 3 rooms - single/double, double & twin. T.V., tea/coffee making facilities. All have their own bath/shower & W.C.. Guest lounge & terrace, a peaceful, relaxed setting. Picturesque Bonchurch village has literary associations including Thackeray, Dickens & Swinburne. Between Shanklin & Ventnor. Aga cooking.

bestbandb@atlas.co.uk www.under-rock.co.uk
£57.00 - £64.00
Open: ALL YEAR (Excl. Xmas & New Year) Map ref no. 06

Mrs G. Cadman
Cottage Crest Castle Hill Woodgreen
Nr. Fordingbridge SP6 2AX Hampshire
Tel: (01725) 512009

Near Rd: A.338

Cottage Crest was originally a Victorian drovers cottage, the house is situated high in its own 5 acres of grounds with magnificent views across the New Forest & the River Avon valley. It is tastefully furnished with antiques & offers a high standard of comfort. 3 bedrooms, 2 in the main house & 1 in the Garden Suite. All rooms are spacious & have en-suite facilities, TV, tea/coffee etc. For couples who prefer complete privacy 'Sunset Place' (adjacent to the main house) is available on a self-catering basis. Ideal for exploring the New Forest. Children over 8.

lupita_cadman@yahoo.co.uk www.cottage-crest.co.uk
£60.00 - £60.00 Open: all year
Map ref no. 05

Florence Iles
Captiva Lydgate West Road Milford-on-Sea
Lymington SO41 0NU Hampshire
Tel: (01590) 644355 Fax 01590 644185

Near Rd: A.337

Walk through the garden on to Hordle Cliff & the beach in this picturesque village of Milford-on-Sea, south of the New Forest. The spacious en-suite bedroom is tastefully furnished & luxuriously appointed, perfect for a good night's sleep after hiking in the forest, touring Dorset, Wiltshire (Stonehenge & Salisbury) or just walking along the beach. Using fresh & local produce, breakfasts are a gourmet experience with an extensive range of traditional & healthy options. Children over 8 years welcome. An ideal location for a short break holiday.

florence.iles@lineone.net www.captiva.co.uk
£70.00 - £90.00 Open: all year
Map ref no. 07

Ormonde House Hotel

Southampton Road Lyndhurst SO43 7BT

Tel:(02380) 282806 Fax02380 282004

email:enquiries@ormondehouse.co.uk www.ormondehouse.co.uk

Mr R. A. Barnfield
The Nurse's Cottage   Station Road   Sway
Lymington SO41 6BA   Hampshire
Tel: (01590) 683402

Near Rd: B.3055
One of the New Forest's premier accommodations, the former home of Sway's District Nurses has won many awards for hospitality, service, good food & wine, & consideration for disabled guests. Recipient of several Best Breakfast awards, the overnight rates also include Afternoon Tea on arrival, 3-Course Dinner featuring a seasonally-changing menu complemented by the 68-bin wine list. Situated on the ground floor, the 4 cosy bedrooms offer every possible comfort. Less than 2 hours from London, this is an excellent touring centre, with reduced rates for stays of 2 or more nights. Children over 10.

nurses.cottage@lineone.net   www.nursescottage.co.uk
£150.00 - £170.00   Open: all year
Map ref no. 08

Mrs J. E. Baigent
Trotton Farm   Trotton Petersfield GU31 5EN
Hampshire
Tel: (01730) 813618   Fax 01730 816093

Near Rd: A.272
This charming home, set in 200 acres of farmland, offers comfortable & tastefully furnished accommodation in 2 twin-bedded rooms & 1 double-bedded room, each with en-suite shower & modern amenities, including tea/coffee-making facilities. A residents' lounge is available throughout the day. Also a games room & pretty garden for guests' relaxation. Trotton Farm is ideally situated for visiting a variety of local, historical & sporting attractions. It is also very conveniently placed only 1 hour from Gatwick & Heathrow Airports. Single supplement.

baigentfarms@farmersweekly.net
www.bestbandb.co.uk   £50.00 - £60.00
Open: all year   Map ref no. 10

see p.144

Mr. Paul Ames
Ormonde House Hotel   Southampton Road
Lyndhurst SO43 7BT   Hampshire
Tel: (02380) 282806   Fax 02380 282004

Near Rd: A.35
Ormonde House is set back from the main road opposite the open forest; ideal for an early morning walk. Lyndhurst village is just 5 mins' walk & Exbury Gardens, the National Motor Museum & Beaulieu 20 mins' drive. The popular licensed restaurant offers freshly prepared dishes. There are 19 pretty en-suite bedrooms & 4 luxury self-contained suites, all with T.V., 'phone & tea-making facilities, suites have full kitchens. Superior Plus rooms & suites with zip & link king-size beds & whirlpool baths. Dogs very welcome.

enquiries@ormondehouse.co.uk
www.ormondehouse.co.uk   £70.00 - £120.00
Open: all year (excl. xmas)   Map ref no. 09

Robin & Mary Ford
Holmans   Bisterne Close Burley
Ringwood BH24 4AZ Hampshire
Tel: (01425) 402307Fax 01425 402307

Near Rd: A.35, A.31
Holmans is a charming country house in the heart of the New Forest, set in 4 acres with stabling available for guests' own horses. Superb walking, horse riding & carriage driving, with a golf course nearby & pub within walking distance. A warm, friendly welcome is assured at this elegant home, which is ideal for a relaxing break. All bedrooms are tastefully furnished & en-suite with tea/coffee-making facilities, radio, T.V. & hairdryers. Guests' lounge with adjoining orangery & log fires in winter.

www.bestbandb.co.uk
£70.00 - £72.00 Open: all year (excl. xmas)
Map ref no. 11

Mrs Pauline Lightfoot
Crofton Country B & B   Kent's Oak   Awbridge
Romsey SO51 0HH   Hampshire
Tel: (01794) 340333   Fax 01794 340333

Near Rd: A.27
Nestling in 2 acres of garden, Crofton offers quality accommodation within the tranquil setting of a small hamlet in the beautiful Test Valley. A large family room, a twin room & a single room, all tastefully decorated & each with tea/coffee, T.V. & DVD, hairdryer & toiletries. Delicious breakfasts are served in the conservatory. There is a guest lounge as well as a guest kitchen with fridge & microwave. Located just 4 miles north of Romsey, making Salisbury, Winchester, New Forest & south coast resorts easily accessible. Children over 12.

pauline@croftonbandb.com   www.croftonbandb.com
£55.00 - £60.00   Open: all year
Map ref no. 12

Anthea Hughes
Ranvilles Farm House   Romsey SO51 6AA
Hampshire
Tel: (02380) 814481   Fax 02380 814481

Near Rd: A.3090
Ranvilles Farm House dates from the 13th century when Richard De Ranville came from Normandy & settled with his family. Now this Grade II listed house provides a peaceful setting surrounded by 5 acres of gardens & paddock. All rooms, with extra large beds, are attractively decorated & furnished with antiques, & each room has its own en-suite bathroom/shower room & T.V.. 3 miles from the New Forest & just over a mile from Romsey, a small town equidistant from the 2 cathedral cities of Winchester & Salisbury. Single supplement.

info@ranvilles.com   www.ranvilles.com
£50.00 - £65.00   Open: all year
Map ref no. 13

Herefordshire & Worcestershire

Hereford & Worcester

Hereford is a beautiful ancient city standing on the banks of the River Wye, almost a crossing point between England & Wales. It is a market centre for the Marches, the border area which has a very particular history of its own.

Hereford Cathedral has a massive sandstone tower & is a fitting venue for the Three Choirs festival which dates from 1727, taking place yearly in one or the other of the three great cathedrals of Hereford, Worcester & Gloucester.

The county is fortunate in having many well preserved historic buildings. Charming "black & white" villages abound here, romantically set in a soft green landscape.

The Royal Forest of Dean spreads its oak & beech trees over 22,000 acres. There are rich deposits of coal & iron mined for centuries by the foresters, & the trees have always been felled for charcoal. Ancient courts still exist where forest dwellers can & do claim their rights to use the forest's resources.

The landscape alters dramatically as the land rises to merge with the great Black Mountain range at heights of over 2,600 feet. Gospel Pass, takes traffic from Hay-on-Wye to Llanthony with superb views of the upper Wye Valley.

The Pre-Cambrian Malvern Hills form a natural boundary between Herefordshire & Worcestershire & from the highest view points you can see over 14 counties. At their feet nestle pretty little villages such as Eastnor with its 19th century castle in revived Normal style that looks quite mediaeval amongst the parkland gardens.

There are, in fact, five Malverns. The largest predictably known as Great Malvern was a fashionable 19th century spa & is noted for the purity of the water which is bottled & sold countrywide.

The Priory at Malvern is rich in 15th century stained glass & a fine collection of mediaeval tiles made locally. William Langland, the 14th century author of "Piers Ploughman", was educated at the Priory Sir Edward Elgar was born, lived & worked here & his "Dream of Gerontius" had its first performance in Hereford Cathedral in 1902.

Symonds Yat, Herefordshire

Herefordshire & Worcestershire

Hereford & Worcester Gazeteer

Areas of outstanding natural beauty.
The Malvern Hills, The Cotswolds, The Wye Valley.

Historic Houses & Castles

Berrington Hall - Leominster
18th century - painted & plastered ceilings.
Landscape by Capability Brown.

Brilley - Cwmmau Farmhouse - Whitney-on-Wye
17th century timber-framed & stone
tiled farmhouse.

Burton Court - Eardisland
14th century great hall. Exhibition of European
& Oriental costume & curios. Model fairground.

Croft Castle - Nr. Leominster
Castle on the Welsh border - inhabited by Croft
family for 900 years.

Dinmore Manor - Nr. Hereford
14th century chapel & cloister.

Eastnor Castle - Nr. Ledbury
19th century - Castellated, containing pictures &
armour. Arboretum.

Eye Manor - Leominster
17th century Carolean Manor house - excellent
plasterwork, paintings, costumes, books, secret
passage. Collection of dolls.

Hanbury Hall - Nr. Droitwich
18th century red brick house - only two rooms &
painted ceilings on exhibition.

Harvington Hall - Kidderminster
Tudor Manor house with moat, priests
hiding place.

The Greyfriars - Worcester
15th century timber-framed building adjoins
Franciscan Priory.

Hellen's - Much Marcle
13th century manorial house of brick & stone.
Contains the Great hall with stone table -
bedroom of Queen Mary. Much of the original
furnishings remain.

Kentchurch Court - Hereford
14th century fortified border Manor house.
Paintings & Carvings by Grinling Gibbons.

Moccas Court - Moccas
18th century - designed by Adam - Parklands by
Capability Brown - under restoration.

Pembridge Castle - Welsh Newton
17th century moated castle.

Sutton Court - Mordiford
Palladian mansion by Wyatt, watercolours,
embroideries, china.

Cathedrals & Churches

Amestry (St. John the Baptist & St. Alkmund)
16th century rood screen.

Abbey Dore (St. Mary & Holy Trinity)
17th century glass & great oak screen - early
English architecture.

Brinsop (St. George)
14th century, screen & glass, alabaster reredos,
windows in memory of Wordsworth, carved
Norman tympanum.

Bredon (St. Giles)
12th century - central tower & spire. Medieval
heraldic tiles, tombs & early glass.

Brockhampton (St. Eadburgh)
1902. Central tower & thatched roof.

Castle Frome (St. Michael & All Angles)
12th century carved font, 17th century effigies
in alabaster.

Chaddesley Corbett (St. Cassian)
14th century monuments, 12th century font.

Elmley (St. Mary)
12th century & 15th century font, tower,
gargoyles, medieval.

Great Witley (St. Michael)
Baroque - Plasterwork, painted ceiling, painted
glass, very fine example.

Hereford (All Saints)
13th-14th centuries, spire, splendid choir stalls,
chained library.

Hereford Cathedral
Small cathedral. Fine central tower c.1325,
splendid porch, brasses, early English Lady
Chapel with lancet windows. Red sandstone.

Kilpeck (St. Mary & St. David)
Romanesque style - medieval windows.

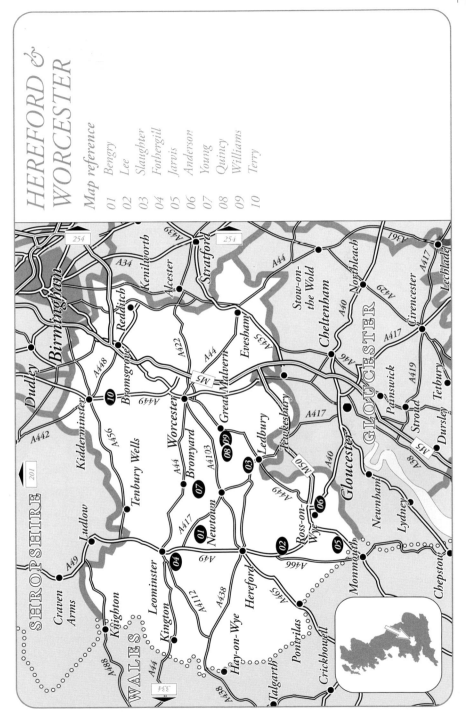

HEREFORD & WORCESTER

Map reference

01 Bengry
02 Lee
03 Slaughter
04 Fothergill
05 Jarvis
06 Anderson
07 Young
08 Quincy
09 Williams
10 Terry

Mr & Mrs J. Bengry
The Vauld Farm The Vauld Marden
Hereford HR1 3HA Herefordshire
Tel: (01568) 797898

Near Rd: A.49
The Vauld Farm is a delightful 16th-century black-&-white former farmhouse, set in a beautiful garden. It retains many period features throughout & affords attractive accommodation. There are 4 charming & elegantly furnished bedrooms, each with an en-suite bathroom, colour T.V. & tea/coffee-making facilities etc. (1 with 4-poster bed.) Hearty breakfasts & delicious evening meals are served in the tastefully decorated dining room. The Vauld is a beautiful home & it is in the perfect location for a relaxing break in Herefordshire.

www.bestbandb.co.uk
£50.00 - £70.00 Open: all year
Map ref no. 01

David & Jennifer Slaughter
Wall Hills House Hereford Road Ledbury HR8 2PR
Herefordshire
Tel: (01531) 632833 Fax 01531 632833

Near Rd: A.438
Walls Hills is a 250 year old Georgian property full of great character & charm and set within the grounds are old Hop Kilns & a listed 15th century Cruck Barn. The large rooms, with their high ceilings, have superb views across the countryside. Bedrooms have en-suite/private facilities; Norfolk lavender toiletries & a tea/coffee tray. David's passion & enthusiasm for cooking & his love of good food, explains why Wall Hills House has received many culinary accolades Ledbury is renowned for its cobbled streets & half-timbered buildings & it is a good place to explore from.

wallbills@tiscali.co.uk www.wallbills.com
£68.00 - £80.00
Open: all year (excl. xmas & new year) Map ref no. 03

Mrs G. Lee
Cwm Craig Farm Bolstone Road Little Dewchurch
Hereford HR2 6PS Herefordshire
Tel: (01432) 840250 Fax 01432 840250

Near Rd: A.49
Spacious Georgian farmhouse, surrounded by superb unspoilt countryside. Situated between the cathedral city of Hereford & Ross-on-Wye, & just a few mins' drive from the Wye Valley. Ideal base for touring the Forest of Dean. All 3 bedrooms have modern amenities, shaver points, tea/coffee-making facilities & an en-suite bathroom. There is a lounge & separated dining room, both with colour T.V.. A delicious full English breakfast is served.

www.bestbandb.co.uk
£50.00 - £54.00 Open: all year
Map ref no. 02

Catherine & Marguerite Fothergill
Highfield Ivington Road Leominster HR6 8QD
Herefordshire
Tel: (01568) 613216

Near Rd: A.44, A.49
Catherine & Marguerite hope you will feel welcome & at home in their elegant Edwardian house & its pleasant rural surroundings. The 3 (1 double & 2 twin) attractive bedrooms are very comfortable & all have a bathroom (1 twin is en-suite.) There is an interesting large garden & a restful T.V. lounge in which you are invited to relax. The homemade food is lovingly prepared & delicious. Reduced rates are available for longer stays.

info@stay-at-bighfield.co.uk
www.stay-at-bighfield.co.uk £54.00 - £58.00
Open: all year Map ref no. 04

Jenny Jarvis
Portland House   Whitchurch   Ross-on-Wye   HR9 6DB
Herefordshire
Tel: (01600) 890757

Near Rd: A.40
Portland House is uniquely placed for you to experience & enjoy an area of outstanding natural beauty, straddling the England & Wales borders. A warm welcome awaits you at this tastefully furnished home (Grade II listed.) Offering spacious en-suite bedrooms all with T.V., service trays & seating areas. Plus larger suites including the Lloyd Suite which overlooks the award-winning garden & is accessibility rated. The Monmouth Suite, which has a gorgeous 4-poster bed & Victorian bathroom & the Ross suite with 2 bedrooms ideal for families. Superb breakfasts from the Aga are served. Dinner by prior arrangement.

j.jarvis@virgin.net   www.portlandguesthouse.co.uk
£55.00 - £80.00   Open: feb - dec
Map ref no. 05

Roger & Judy Young
Dovecote Barn   Stoke Lacy   HR7 4HJ
Herefordshire
Tel: (01432) 820968

Near Rd: A.465
You will be warmly welcomed at this charming Grade II listed 17th-century converted barn set in 2 acres of garden, overlooking peaceful countryside & ideally situated for exploring historic Herefordshire & its many attractions. The accommodation includes 2 well-appointed & tastefully furnished double bedrooms (colour T.V., radio, electric blankets, tea/coffee-making facilities etc.) with private/en-suite bathrooms. Lavish breakfasts, with locally sourced produce are served, & dinners are by arrangement or Roger & Judy will taxi you for free to one of the superb local pubs or restaurants. A delightful home.

dovecotebarn@mail.com   www.dovecotebarn.co.uk
£55.00 - £60.00   Open: all year
Map ref no. 07

Mrs Caroline Anderson
Lea House   Lea   Ross-on-Wye   HR9 7JZ
Herefordshire   Tel: (01989) 750652
Fax 01989 750652 Mobile 07810 200594

Near Rd: A.40
In a small village betwixt the Royal Forest of Dean & the spectacular Wye Valley this 16th-century coaching inn has been prettily refurbished with exposed beams, an inglenook fireplace & imaginative décor - the perfect place to relax. Home-made breads, preserves & freshly squeezed orange juice complement the award-winning breakfasts. The accommodation includes 3 individually styled bedrooms (king-size/twin/family) with en-suite/private bathrooms. Dinner is available on request.

enquiries@leahouse.co.uk   www.leahouse.co.uk
£58.00 - £66.00   Open: all year
Map ref no. 06

Ella Grace Quincy
Old Country House   Old Country Farm   Mathon
Malvern WR13 5PS   Worcestershire
Tel: (01886) 880867

Near Rd: A.4103
A warm welcome awaits you at our 600-year-old family home, in the large and beautiful garden, and 220 acres of traditional farmland close to the Malvern Hills. There are 3 very comfortable double rooms with private or ensuite bathrooms & large reception & sitting rooms. The extensive breakfasts encompass local and organic food wherever possible and we hold a Green Business Award. A haven for cyclists, walkers, nature lovers and seekers of peace. Good eating places. Single rates vary between £35-£55.

ella@oldcountryhouse.co.uk
www.oldcountryhouse.co.uk   £60.00 - £90.00
Open: all year   Map ref no. 08

Jon & Judith Williams
Wyche Keep   22 Wyche Road   Malvern   WR14 4EG
Worcestershire
Tel: (01684) 567018   Fax 01684 892304

Near Rd: B.4218
Wyche Keep is a unique arts-&-crafts castle-style house, perched high on the Malvern Hills, built by the family of Sir Stanley Baldwin, Prime Minister, to enjoy spectacular 60-mile views, with a long history of elegant entertaining. The accommodation includes 3 large, tastefully furnished double suites, 1 with 4-poster. Traditional English cooking is a speciality, & guests can savour memorable 4-course candlelit dinners, selected from fresh local vegetables & game, served in a 'house party' atmosphere. There is ample private parking.

wychekeep@aol.com   www.wychekeep.co.uk
£70.00 - £80.00   Open: all year
Map ref no. 09

Pauline Terry
Garden Cottages Crossway Green   Hartlebury
Worcester DY13 9SL   Worcestershire
Tel: (01299) 250626

Near Rd: A. 449
Garden Cottages is an 'L' shaped oak beamed former farm cottage, which is set in 5 acres of grounds. The cottage has been sensitively converted to include all modern comforts yet much of its original character has been retained. The comfortable bedrooms have en-suite/private facilities, hospitality tray, T.V., hairdryer etc. A delicious Aga cooked full English breakfast is served, using fresh local produce. Dinner by arrangement, although there are good local pubs & restaurants. Parking. Worcester, Birmingham, the M.5 & the Cotswolds are within easy reach.

accommodation@gardencottages.co.uk
www.gardencottages.co.uk   £65.00 - £70.00
Open: all year (excl. xmas & new year) Map ref no. 10

Kent

Kent is best known as "the garden of England". At its heart is a tranquil landscape of apple & cherry orchards, hop-fields & oast-houses, but there are also empty downs, chalk sea-cliffs, rich marshlands, sea ports, castles & the glory of Canterbury Cathedral.

The dramatic chalk ridgeway of the North Downs links the White Cliffs of Dover with the north of the county which extends into the edge of London. It was a trade route in ancient times following the high downs above the Weald, dense forest in those days. It can be followed today & it offers broad views of the now agricultural Weald.

The pilgrims who flocked to Canterbury in the 12th-15th centuries, (colourfully portrayed in Chaucer's Canterbury Tales), probably used the path of the Roman Watling Street rather than the high ridgeway.

Canterbury was the cradle of Christianity in southern England & is by tradition the seat of the Primate of All England. This site, on the River Stour, has been settled since the earliest times & became a Saxon stonghold under King Ethelbert of Kent. He established a church here, but it was in Norman times that the first great building work was carried out, to be continued in stages until the 15th century. The result is a blending of styles with early Norman work, a later Norman choir, a vaulted nave in Gothic style & a great tower of Tudor design. Thomas Becket was murdered on the steps of the Cathedral in 1170. The town retains much of its mediaeval character with half-timbered weavers' cottages, old churches & the twin towers of the west gate.

Two main styles of building give the villages of Kent their special character. The Kentish yeoman's house was the home of the wealthier farmers & is found throughout the county. It is a timber-frame building with white lath & plaster walls & a hipped roof of red tiles. Rather more modest in style is a small weatherboard house, usually painted white or cream. Rolvenden & Groombridge have the typical charm of a Kentish village whilst Tunbridge Wells is an attractive town, with a paved parade known as the Pantiles & excellent antique shops.

Harty Church. Isle of Sheppey. Kent.

Kent

Kent Gazeteer

Areas of outstanding natural beauty.
Kent Downs.

Historic Houses & Castles

Aylesford, The Friars - Nr. Maidstone
13th century Friary & shrine of Our Lady, (much restored), 14th century cloisters - original.

Allington Castle -Nr. Maidstone
13th century. One time home of Tudor poet Thomas Wyatt. Restored early 20th century. Icons & Renaissance paintings.

Black Charles - Nr. Sevenoaks
14th century Hall house - Tudor fireplaces, beautiful panelling.

Boughton Monchelsea Place - Nr. Maidstone
Elizabethan Manor House - grey stone battlements - 18th century landscaped park, wonderful views of Weald of Kent.

Chartwell - Westerham
Home of Sir Winston Churchill.

Chiddingstone Castle - Nr. Edenbridge
18th century Gothic revival building encasing old remains of original Manor House - Royal Stuart & Jacobite collection. Ancient Egyptian collection - Japanese netsuke, etc.

Eyehorne Manor - Hollingbourne
15th century Manor house,17th century additions.

Cobham Hall - Cobham
16th century house - Gothic & Renaissance - Wyatt interior. Now school for girls.

Fairfield - Eastry, Sandwich
13th-14th centuries - moated castle. Was home of Anne Boleyn. Beautiful gardens with unique collection of classical statuary.

Knole - Sevenoaks
15th century - splendid Jacobean interior - 17th & 18th century furniture. One of the largest private houses in England.

Leeds Castle - Nr. Maidstone
Built in middle of the lake, it was the home of the medieval Queens of England.

Lullingstone Castle - Eynsford
14th century mansion house - frequented by Henry VIII & Queen Anne. Still occupied by descendants of the original owners.

Long Barn - Sevenoaks
14th century house - said to be home of William Caxton. Restored by Edwin Lutyens; 16th century barn added to enlarge house. Galleried hall - fine beaming & fireplaces. Lovely gardens created by Sir Harold Nicholson & his wife Vita Sackville-West.

Owletts - Cobham
Carolean house of red brick with plasterwork ceiling & fine staircase.

Owl House - Lamberhurst
16th century cottage, tile hung; said to be home of wool smuggler. Charming gardens.

Penshurst Place - Tonbridge
14th century house with medieval Great Hall perfectly preserved.English Gothic. Birthplace of Elizabethan poet, Sir Philip Sidney Fine staterooms, splendid picture gallery, famous toy museum. Tudor gardens & orchards.

Saltwood Castle - Nr. Hythe
Medieval - very fine castle & is privately occupied. Was lived in by Sir Ralph de Broc, murderer of Thomas a Becket.

Squerreys Court - Westerham
Manor house of William & Mary period, with furniture, paintings & tapestries of time. Connections with General Wolfe.

Stoneacre - Otham
15th century yeoman's half-timbered house.

Cathedrals & Churches

Brook (St. Mary)
11th century paintings in this unaltered early Norman church.

Brookland (St. Augustine)
13th century & some later part. Crown-post roofs, detached wooden belfry with conical cap. 12th century lead font.

Canterbury Cathedral
12th century wall paintings, 12th & 13th century stained glass. Very fine Norman crypt. Early

Kent

perpendicular nave & cloisters which have heraldic bosses. Wonderful central tower.

Charing (St. Peter & St. Paul)
13th & 15th century interior with 15th century tower. 17th century restoration.

Cobham (St. Mary)
16th century carved & painted tombs - unequalled collection of brasses in county.

Elham (St. Mary the Virgin)
Norman wall with 13th century arcades, perpendicular clerestory. Restored by Eden.

Lullingstone (St. Botolph)
14th century mainly - 16th century wood screen. Painted glass monuments.

Newington-on-the-Street (St. Mary the Virgin)
13th & 14th century - fine tower. 13th century tomb. Wall paintings.

Rochester Cathedral
Norman facade & nave, otherwise early English. 12th century west door. 14th century doorway to Chapter room.

Stone (St. Mary)
13th century - decorated - paintings, 15th century brass, 16th century tomb.

Woodchurch (All Saints)
13th century, having late Norman font & priest's brass of 1320.

Museums & Galleries

Royal Museums - Canterbury
Archaeological, geological, mineralogical exhibits, natural history, pottery & porcelain. Engravings, prints & pictures.

Westgate - Canterbury
Museum of armour, etc. in 14th century gatehouse of city.

Dartford District Museum - Dartford
Roman, Saxon & natural history.

Deal Museum - Deal
Prehistoric & historic antiquities.

Dicken's House Museum - Broadstairs
Personalia of Dickens; prints, costume & Victoriana.

Down House - Downe
The home of Charles Darwin for 40 years, now his memorial & museum.

Dover Museum - Dover
Roman pottery, ceramics, coins, zoology, geology, local history, etc.

Faversham Heritage Society - Faversham
1000 years of history & heritage.

Folkestone Museum & Art Gallery - Folkestone
Archeology, local history & sciences.

Herne Bay Museum - Herne Bay
Stone, Bronze & Early Iron Age specimens. Roman material from Reculver excavations. Items of local & Kentish interest.

Museum & Art Gallery - Maidstone
16th century manor house exhibiting natural history & archaeolgical collections. Costume Gallery, bygones, ceramics, 17th century works by Dutch & Italian painters.

Historic Monuments

Eynsford Castle - Eynsford
12th century castle remains.

Rochester Castle - Rochester
Storied keep -1126-39. Roman Fort & Anglo-Saxon Church - Reculver - Excavated remains of 3rd century fort.

Little Kit's Coty House - Aylesford
Ruins of burial chambers from 2 long barrows.

Lullingstone Roman Villa - Lullingstone
Roman farmstead excavations.

Roman Fort & Town - Richborough
Roman 'Rutupiae' & fort.

Dover Castle - Dover
Keep built by Henry II in 1180. Outer curtain built 13th century.

Gardens

Chilham Castle Gardens - Nr. Canterbury
25 acre gardens of Jacobean house, laid out by Tradescant. Lake garden, fine trees & birds of prey. Jousting & medieval banquets.

Great Comp Gardens - Nr. Borough Green
Outstanding 7 acre garden with old brick walls.

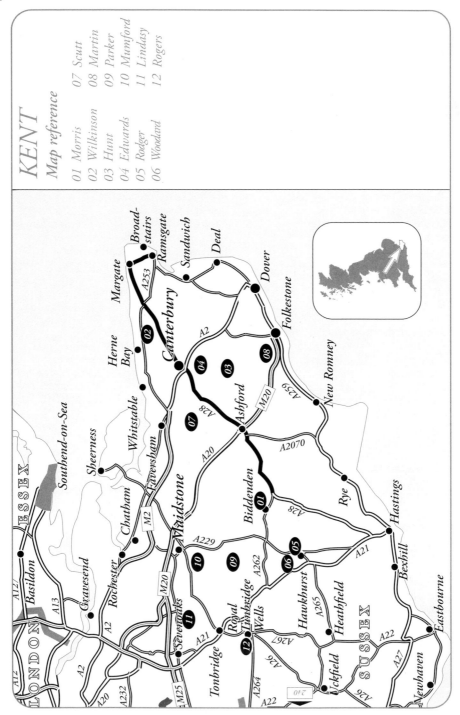

KENT

Map reference

01 Morris
02 Wilkinson
03 Hunt
04 Edwards
05 Rodger
06 Woodard
07 Scutt
08 Martin
09 Parker
10 Mumford
11 Lindsay
12 Rogers

Mrs Susan Morris
Tudor Cottage 25 High Street Biddenden
Ashford TN27 8AL   Kent
Tel: (01580) 291913

Near Rd: A.262
Tudor Cottage is a beautiful 15th century house in the centre of the charming and historic village of Biddenden with 2 excellent restaurants & a traditional English pub nearby. The accommodation includes 3 delightful double bedrooms 2 en-suite, 1 with private facilities, each well-equipped with colour TV and tea/coffee making facilities. Tudor Cottage is an ideal loaction from which to explore the beautiful countryside of Kent and East Sussex. Also, castles, museums, gardens & a host of other attractions. Children over 5 years welcome.

suemorris.biddenden@virgin.net
www.tudorcottagebiddenden.co.uk £50.00 - £60.00
Open: all year   Map ref no. 01

Nick & Anne Hunt
Bower Farm House Bossingham Road Stelling Minnis
Canterbury CT4 6BB Kent
Tel: (01227) 709430

Near Rd: A.2
The house is a 17th Century Kentish Farmhouse with exposed beams and inglenook fireplaces. The two guest rooms are charmingly appointed with tea/coffee, radios & private facilities. The large dinning area adjoins a guest lounge with TV. Home laid eggs, home baked bread are part of a full English Breakfast. The front gate opens onto the largest common in the SE & there are plenty of footpaths and nature reserves in the area. Orchids abound at the right time of year, yet Canterbury with its cathedral is only a 10 minute drive away.

nick@bowerbb.freeserve.co.uk
www.bowerfarmhouse.co.uk   £56.00 - £56.00
Open: all year (excl. xmas) Map ref no. 03

Kathy Wilkinson
Chislet Court Farm   Chislet Canterbury CT3 4DU
Kent
Tel: (01227) 860309   Fax 01227 860444

Near Rd: A.28, A.299
A listed Queen Anne farmhouse, set in mature gardens with views overlooking the surrounding countryside & the ancient village church. The accommodation includes 2 large comfortable bedrooms, which are en-suite & have T.V. etc. & overlook the garden & church. Guests are welcome to wander round the garden or relax in the conservatory - where breakfast is served. Chislet Court Farm is an ideal base for exploring Canterbury & the beautiful Kent countryside.

kathy@chisletcourtfarm.com
www.chisletcourtfarm.com £70.00 - £70.00
Open: all year (excl. xmas) Map ref no. 02

Madeleine Edwards
Elmstone Court Out Elmstead Lane Barham
Canterbury CT4 6PH Kent
Tel: (01227) 830433   Fax 01227 832405

Near Rd: A.2
The dream of losing yourself down a country lane & happening upon an unexpected treasure...fulfil the dream. Grade II listed Elmstone Court is a special place to stay. Your hosts undertake to provide the best accommodation & cuisine, all set in the beautiful Elham Valley, an Area of Outstanding Natural Beauty, yet only 20 mins' from Eurotunnel, Dover ferry port & Ashford International station. Canterbury, Whitstable Harbour & beaches are nearby. Bedrooms offer en-suite shower rooms etc.

info@elmstonecourt.com www.elmstonecourt.com
£90.00 - £110.00 Open: all year
Map ref no. 04

Lynne Rodger
The Wren's Nest   Hastings Road   Hawkhurst
Cranbrook TN18 4RT   Kent
Tel: (01580) 754919   Fax 01580 754919

Near Rd: A.21
Built in traditional Kentish style, with oak beams & vaulted ceilings, The Wren's Nest suites have been designed specifically for the comfort & pleasure of guests. The suites are spacious & beautifully furnished & are well-equipped with T.V., tea/coffee-making facilities, tourist information literature, etc. & excellent en-suite bathrooms. The suites are entered via their own front door allowing absolute privacy. Hearty English breakfasts are served in the main house. An idyllic rural setting, well-placed for touring, walking & birdwatching. Children over 8 years welcome. Also self-catering cottages available.

ian.w.rodger@capgemini.com www.bestbandb.co.uk
£65.00 - £65.00 Open: mar - dec
Map ref no. 05

Mrs Corrine Scutt
Leaveland Court Leaveland   Faversham ME13 0NP
Kent
Tel: (01233) 740596   Fax 01233 740015

Near Rd: A.251
Guests are guaranteed a warm welcome on their arrival at this enchanting 15th-century timbered farmhouse set in delightful gardens. The house is situated in a quiet rural setting, between Leaveland church & woodlands, & surrounded by a 500-acre downland farm. Ideally placed with the M2 & Faversham 5 mins, Canterbury 20 mins & 30 mins to channel ports. The attractive bedrooms have en-suite facilities. A heated outdoor swimming pool is available. Caring hosts, generous breakfasts & a relaxed atmosphere ensure an enjoyable stay. Many guests return to repeat the experience.

email@leavelandcourt.co.uk
www.leavelandcourt.co.uk   £60.00 - £70.00
Open: feb - nov   Map ref no. 07

Susan Woodard
Southgate-Little Fowlers   Rye Road   Hawkhurst
Cranbrook TN18 5DA Kent
Tel: (01580) 752526   Fax 01580 752526

Near Rd: A.268
17th-century historical country house with antique furnishings & a warm, welcoming atmosphere. Beautiful bedrooms, 1 king-size 4-poster, 1 king-size brass bed or a delightful twin, each with an en-suite bathroom. All have wonderful views & many thoughtful extras. Superb breakfast served either in the magnificent Victorian room or original Victorian conservatory housing impressive Muscat vine & collection of plants. Few mins' walk to 15th-century inns for dinner. Near to Bodiam, Scotney, Rye, Sissinghurst, Battle & Dixter. Children over 10.

Susan.Woodard@southgate.uk.net
www.southgate.uk.net   £66.00 - £80.00
Open: all year (excl. xmas)   Map ref no. 06

Mrs Mary Martin
Pigeonwood House   Arpinge   Folkestone CT18 8AQ
Kent
Tel: (01303) 891111   Mobile 07967 925867

Near Rd: A.260
Pigeonwood House is the original, 19th-century farmhouse of the surrounding area, positioned in rural tranquillity in chalk downland. The accommodation includes 2 tastefully furnished guest bedrooms, which have beautiful panoramic views over the surrounding countryside & many guests return for the homely, relaxing atmosphere. Delicious breakfasts are served. Pigeonwood House is ideally situated for touring historic Kent, with its famous gardens & castles as well as having the Channel tunnel & ports close by. Children over 6 are welcome.

mary@pigeonwood.com   www.pigeonwood.com
£35.00 - £75.00 Open: all year
Map ref no. 08

Jordans

Sheet Hill Plaxtol Sevenoaks TN15 0PU

Tel:(01732) 810379

www.bestbandb.co.uk

see p.159

Mrs Annie Parker
*West Winchet   Winchet Hill   Goudhurst TN17 1JX
Kent
Tel: (01580) 212024   Fax 01580 212250*

Near Rd: A.262
West Winchet is an elegant Victorian house surrounded by parkland in a secluded & peaceful setting. The accommodation includes 2 beautifully decorated rooms, 1 double with en-suite bathroom & 1 twin with en-suite shower room. Each with colour T.V., radio & tea/coffee-making facilities. Both rooms are on the ground floor, & the twin-bedded room has French windows opening onto the terrace & into the garden. A magnificent drawing room for guests' use. This is an ideal touring centre for Kent & East Sussex. 2 1/2 miles mainline station (London 55 mins). Children over 5 years.

annie@jpa-ltd.co.uk   www.bestbandb.co.uk
£65.00 - £70.00   Open: all year (excl.xmas & new year)
Map ref no. 09

Mrs Jo Lindsay N.D.D., A.T.D.
*Jordans   Sheet Hill   Plaxtol
Sevenoaks TN15 0PU Kent
Tel: (01732) 810379*

Near Rd: A.227, A.25
Beautiful, picture-postcard, 15th-century Tudor house (awarded a 'Historic Building of Kent' plaque) in the picturesque village of Plaxtol, among orchards & parkland. The house has been featured on T.V. & is beautifully furnished, with leaded windows, inglenook fireplaces, massive oak beams & an enchanting old English garden with rambler roses & espalier trees. Within easy reach are Ightham Mote, Leeds & Hever Castles, Penshurst, Chartwell & Knole. 3 lovely rooms, 2 with en-suite/private facilities. London 35 mins' by train, & easy access to airports. Children over 12 years.

www.bestbandb.co.uk   £72.00 - £76.00
Open: mid jan - mid dec
Map ref no. 11

Pamela & Rodney Mumford
*Merzie Meadows Hunton Road Nr. Marden
Maidstone TN12 9SL Kent
Tel: (01622) 820500   Fax 01622 820500*

Near Rd: A.229
Merzie Meadows is a unique country home, set in 20 acres of conservation areas, small woodland & 3 acres of formal garden. Peaceful yet near places to visit including Sissinghurst, Leeds Castle, Scotney, amongst the many; along with the beautiful gardens that Kent has to offer. The delightful en-suite bedrooms are spacious, comfortable & are contained in separate wings of the house, with fine views over the grounds & countryside beyond. Lovely inns & restaurants nearby for evening meals.

pamela@merziemeadows.co.uk
www.merziemeadows.co.uk £70.00 - £80.00
Open: all year   Map ref no. 10

Richard & Sue Rogers
*Ash Tree Cottage 7 Eden Road
Tunbridge Wells TN1 1TS Kent
Tel: (01892) 541317*

Near Rd: A.21
Ash Tree Cottage is situated in a quiet private road just above the famous Pantiles, & within a few mins' walk of the high street & railway station. Accommodation is in 2 charming & attractively furnished bedrooms with good en-suite bathrooms, radio, colour T.V., tea/coffee-making facilities & plenty of tourist information to help you make the most of your stay. There is an excellent choice of restaurants & country pubs nearby, & many places of interest are within easy reach.

rogersashtree@excite.com   www.smoothhound.co.uk/
hotels/ashtreecottage.html   £65.00 - £75.00
Open: all year (excl.xmas & new year)   Map ref no. 12

Leicestershire, Nottinghamshire & Rutland

Leicestershire

Rural Leicestershire is rich in grazing land, a peaceful, undramatic landscape broken up by the waterways that flow through in the south of the county.

The River Avon passes on its way to Stratford, running by 17th century Stanford Hall & its motorcycle museum. The Leicester section of the Grand Union Canal was once very important for the transportation of goods from the factories of the Midlands to London Docks. It passes through a fascinating series of multiple locks at Foxton. The decorative barges, the 'narrow boats' are pleasure craft these days rather than the life-blood of the closed community of boat people who lived & worked out their lives on the canals.

Rutland

The smallest county in England holds within its boarders Rutland Water, one of Europe's largest reservoirs & an attractive setting for sailing, fishing or enjoying a trip on the pleasure cruiser. There is also the Rutland Theatre at Tolethorpe Hall, where a summer season of Shakespeare's plays is presented in the open air.

This smallest of counties produces two world renowned foods. Melton Mowbray is famous for its pork pies and Rutland is also the centre of Stilton cheese country. The "King of Cheeses" is made mainly in the Vale of Belvoir, with it's famous castle. where Leicestershire meets Nottinghamshire.

Nottinghamshire

Nottinghamshire has a diversity of landscape from forest to farmland, from coal mines to industrial areas.

The north of the county is dominated by the expanse of Sherwood Forest, smaller now than in the time of legendary Robin Hood & his Merry Men, but still a lovely old woodland of Oak & Birch.

The Dukeries are so called because of the numerous ducal houses built in the area & there is beautiful parkland on these great estates that can be visited. Clumber Park, for instance has a huge lake & a double avenue of Limes.

Newstead Abbey was a mediaeval priory converted into the Byron family home in the 16th century.

Newstead Abbey. Nottinghamshire.

Leicestershire, Nottinghamshire & Rutland

Leicestershire Gazeteer
Areas of outstanding natural beauty.
Charnwood Forest, Rutland Water.

Historic Houses & Castles
Belvoir Castle - Nr. Grantham
Overlooking the Vale of Belvoir, castle rebuilt
in 1816, with many special events including
jousting tournaments. Home of the Duke of
Rutland since Henry VIII. Paintings, furniture,
historic armoury, military museums &
magnificent state room.
Belgrave Hall - Leicester
18th century Queen Anne house - furnishing of
18th & 19th centuries.
Langton Hall - Nr. Market Harborough
Privately occupied - perfect English country
house from medieval times - drawing rooms
have 18th century Venetian lace.
Oakham Castle - Oakham
Norman banqueting hall of late 12th century.
Stanford Hall - Nr Lutterworth
17th century William & Mary house - collection
of Stuart relics & pictures, antiques &
costumes of family from Elizabeth I onward.
Motor cycle museum.
Stapleford Park - Nr. Melton Mowbray
Old wing dated 1500, restored 1663. Extended
to mansion in 1670. Collection of pictures,
tapestries, furniture & Balston's Staffordshire
portrait figures of Victorian age.

Cathedrals & Churches
Breedon-on-the-Hill (St. Mary & St. Hardulph)
Norman & 13th century. Jacobean canopied
pew, 18th century carvings.
Empingham (St. Peter)
14th century west tower, front & crocketed spire.
Early English interior double piscina, triple sedilla.
Lyddington (St. Andrew)
Perpendicular in the main - medieval wall
paintings & brasses.
Staunton Harol (Holy Trinity)
17th century - quite unique Cromwellian church.

Museums & Galleries
**Bosworth Battlefield Visitor Centre - Nr
Market Bosworth**
Exhibitions, models, battlefield trails at site of
1485 Battle of Bosworth where Richard III lost
his life & crown to Henry.
**Leicestershire Museum of Technology -
Leicester**
Beam engines, steam shovel, knitting machinery
& other aspects of the county's industrial past.
Leicester Museum & Art Gallery - Leicester
Painting collection.
18th & 19th century, watercolours & drawings,
20th century French paintings, Old Master &
modern prints. English silver & ceramics &
special exhibitions.
Jewry Wall Museum & Site - Leicester
Roman wall & baths site adjoining museum
of archaeology.
Melton Carnegie Museum-Melton Mowbray
Displays of Stilton cheese, pork pies & other
aspects of the past & present life of the area.
Rutland County Museum - Oakham
Domestic & agricultural life of Rutland,England's
smallest county.
**Donnington Racing Car Collection - Castle
Donington**
Large collection of grand prix racing cars &
racing motorcycles, adjoining Donington Park
racing circuit.
**Wygson's House Museum of Costume -
Leicestershire**
Costume, accessories & shop settings in late
medieval buildings.
The Bellfoundry Museum - Loughborough
Moulding, casting, tuning & fitting of bells, with
conducted tours of bellfoundry.

Historic Monuments
The Castle - Ashby-de-la-Zouch
14th century with tower added in 15th century.
Kirby Muxloe Castle - Kirby Muxloe
15th century fortified manor house with
moat ruins.

Leicestershire, Nottinghamshire & Rutland

Other things to see & do

Belton House. Nr Grantham

Twycross Zoo - Nr. Atherstone
Gorillas, orangutans, chimpanzees, gibbons, elephants, giraffes, lions & many other animals.

The Battlefield Line Nr. Market Bosworth
Steam railway & collection of railway relics, adjoining Bosworth Battlefield.

Great Central Railway - Loughborough
Steam railway over 5-mile route in Charnwood Forest area, with steam & diesel museum.

Rutland Railway Museum - Nr. Oakham
Industrial steam & diesel locomotives. wagons from quarries, mines & factories.

Nottinghamshire Gazeteer

Historic Houses & Castles

Holme Pierrepont Hall - Nr. Nottingham
Outstanding red brick Tudor manor, in continuous family ownership, with 19th century courtyard garden.

Newark Castle - Newark
Dramatic castle ruins on riverside site, once one of the most important castles of the north.

Newstead Abbey - Nr. Mansfield
Priory converted to country mansion, home of poet Lord Byron with many of his possessions & manuscripts on display. Beautiful parkland, lakes & gardens.

Nottingham Castle - Nottingham
17th century residence on site of medieval castle. Fine collections of ceramics, silver, Nottingham alabaster carvings, local historical displays.

Wollaton Hall - Nottingham
Elizabethan mansion now housing natural history exhibits. Stands in deer park, with Industrial Museum in former stables, illustrating the city's bicycle, hosiery, lace, pharmaceutical & other industries.

Cathedrals & Churches

Egmanton (St. Mary)
Magnificent interior by Comper. Norman doorway & font. Canopied rood screen, 17th century altar.

Newark (St. Mary Magdalene)
15th century. 2 painted panels of "Dance of Death". Reredos by Comper.

Southwell Cathedral
Norman nave, unvaulted, fine early English choir. Decorated pulpitum, 6 canopied stalls, fine misericords. Octagonal chapter house.

Terseval (St. Catherine)
12th century - interior 17th century unrestored.

Museums & Galleries

Castlegate Museum - Nottingham
Row of Georgian terraced houses showing costume & textile collection. Lace making equipment & lace collection.

Nottinigham Castle Museum - Nottingham
Collections of ceramics, glass & silver. Alabaster carvings.

D.H. Lawrence Birthplace - Eastwood
Home of the novelist & poet as it would have been at the time of his birth, 1885.

Millgate Museum of Social & Folk Life - Newark

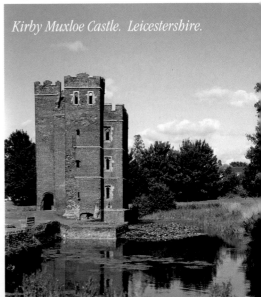

Kirby Muxloe Castle. Leicestershire.

164

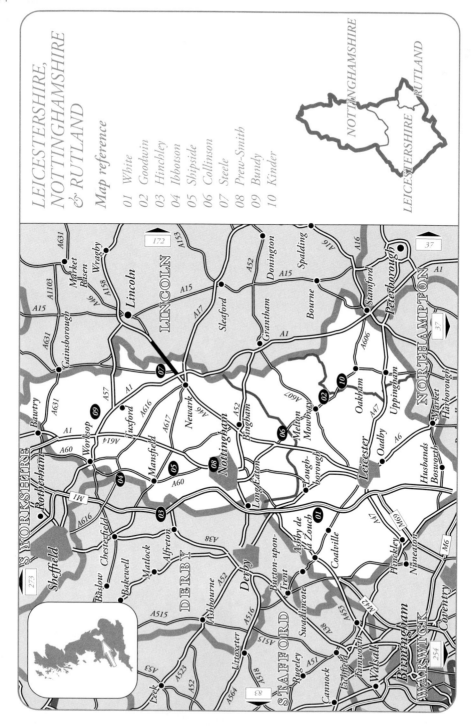

LEICESTERSHIRE, NOTTINGHAMSHIRE & RUTLAND

Map reference

01 White
02 Goodwin
03 Hinchley
04 Ibbotson
05 Shipside
06 Collinson
07 Steele
08 Prew-Smith
09 Bundy
10 Kinder

NOTTINGHAMSHIRE

LEICESTERSHIRE

RUTLAND

172

37

A631

Market Rasen

Wragby

A153

A158

A46

A1103

A15

A631

Gainsborough

Lincoln

LINCOLN

A15

A52

Donington

Spalding

91V

A16

Sleaford

A15

A17

Grantham

Bourne

A1

Stamford

Peterborough

37

A1

NORTHAMPTON

A631

Bawtry

A57

A1

Tuxford

A616

A617

Newark

A46

A52

A52

209V

Bingham

A52

Melton Mowbray

02

A606

10

Oakham

A47

Uppingham

A6

Market Harborough

Worksop

A60

A614

Mansfield

A60

05

08

Nottingham

Long Eaton

Lough-borough

06

Leicester

Oadby

A47

Husbands Bosworth

S YORKSHIRE

273

Sheffield

Rotherham

M1

A1616

Chesterfield

03

Alfreton

Matlock

Bakewell

Baslow

A38

DERBY

Ashbourne

A515

A52

A516

Derby

Burton-upon-Trent

09

04

A38

01

Ashby de la Zouch

Coalville

A42

A453

Hinckley

M69

Nuneaton

M6

Coventry

254

WARWICK

STAFFORD

83

A515

Uttoxeter

A518

Leek

A53

A523

A52

A564

Cannock

Rugeley

Swadlincote

A51

Lichfield

Tamworth

A453

A38

A51

Walsall

Birmingham

M42

A606

A447

A1

Carolyn Voce & Audrey White
Abbots Oak Country House Warren Hills Road
Abbots Oak   Coalville LE67 4UY Leicestershire
Tel: (01530) 832328   Fax 01530 832328

Near Rd: A.50, A.511

A Grade II listed building with a wealth of oak panelling, & including the staircase reputedly from Nell Gwynn's town house. Set in mature gardens & woodland, with natural granite outcrops. The accommodation includes 3 delightful rooms, all with en-suite bathrooms. Open fires create a warm & welcoming atmosphere, & Carolyn's superb dinners are served in the candlelit dining room. Stratford, Belvoir Castle & Rutland Water can all be reached within the hour, making this an excellent touring base. A tennis court & billiard room are available for guests use.. Children over 6 years are welcome.

admin@abbotsoak.com   www.abbotsoak.com
£65.00 - £100.00   Open: all year
Map ref no. 01

Mrs Betty Hinchley
Titchfield House 300/302 Chesterfield Road North
Mansfield NG19 7QU Nottinghamshire
Tel: (01623) 810356/810921   Fax 01623 810356

Near Rd: A.617

Titchfield House is 2 houses converted into 1 family-run guest house, offering 6 comfortably furnished bedrooms, a lounge with colour T.V., a kitchen for guests' use, a bathroom & showers. A delicious full English breakfast is served, with lighter options available. It also has an adjoining garage. The property is situated near to Mansfield, which is a busy market town. Sherwood Forest & the beautiful Peak District are also both easily accessible. Titchfield Guest House is a very handy location for touring this lovely area, & for onward travel. A warm & friendly welcome is assured. Dogs by arrangement.

www.bestbandb.co.uk
£40.00 - £42.00   Open: all year
Map ref no. 03

Mrs Sue Goodwin
Hillside House 27 Melton Road Burton Lazars
Melton Mowbray LE14 2UR Leicestershire
Tel: (01664) 566312   Fax 01664 501819

Near Rd: A.606

Charmingly converted farm buildings with superb views over open countryside, in the small village of Burton Lazars. Comfortable accommodation is offered in 1 double & 2 twin-bedded rooms, each with an en-suite/private bathroom. All of the rooms have tea/coffee-making facilities & colour T.V.. There is a pleasant garden to relax in on sunny days. Close to Melton Mowbray, famous for its pork pies & Stilton cheese, & with Burghley House, Belvoir Castle & Rutland Water within easy reach. Children over 10 years. Single supplement.

billhs27@aol.com www.hillside-house.co.uk
£50.00 - £50.00   Open: all year (excl. xmas & new year)
Map ref no. 02

June M. Ibbotson
Blue Barn Farm Langwith Mansfield NG20 9JD
Nottinghamshire
Tel: (01623) 742248   Fax 01623 742248

Near Rd: A.616

An enjoyable visit is guaranteed at this family-run, 250-acre farm, set in tranquil countryside on the edge of Sherwood Forest (Robin Hood country). 3 guest bedrooms, each with modern amenities including h&c, tea/coffee-making facilities & a guest bathroom with shower. 1 bedroom is en-suite. A colour-T.V. lounge & garden are also available. Guests are very welcome to walk around the farm. Many interesting places, catering for all tastes, only a short journey away. Self-catering cottage available, sleeps 8 plus cot.

bluebarnfarm@supanet.com
www.bluebarnfarm-notts.co.uk £48.00 - £50.00
Open: all year (excl.xmas & new year)   Map ref no. 04

Holly Lodge

Ricket Lane Blidworth Mansfield NG21 0NQ

Tel:(01623) 793853 Fax 01623 490977

email:ann.hollylodge@ukonline.co.uk www.bestbandb.co.uk

see p.166

Ann Shipside
Holly Lodge   Ricket Lane   Blidworth
Mansfield NG21 0NQ Nottinghamshire
Tel: (01623) 793853   Fax 01623 490977

Near Rd: A.60
Holly Lodge is situated just off the A.60, 10 miles north of Nottingham. This attractive former hunting lodge stands in 15 acres of grounds. The 4 comfortable & attractive, en-suite guest rooms are housed within the converted stables & have colour T.V. & tea/coffee-making facilities. There are panoramic countryside views on all sides, with woodland walks, tennis, golf & riding nearby. In the evening, dinner is available at one of the good restaurants, which are closeby. There is ample parking. Holly Lodge is ideally situated for a peaceful, rural holiday base with a relaxed & friendly atmosphere.

ann.hollylodge@ukonline.co.uk
www.hollylodgenotts.co.uk £62.00 - £66.00
Open: all year   Map ref no. 05

Jerry & Jillie Steele
The Old Vicarage Holme Road Langford
Newark NG23 7RT   Nottinghamshire
Tel: (01636) 705031   Fax 01636 708728

Near Rd: A.1133
A mile from Newark showground & 2 miles from the A.1, this fine Victorian vicarage stands in secluded grounds next to one of the oldest churches in Nottinghamshire. It is reputed that Mary Queen of Scots stayed at Langford as a guest of the Earl of Shrewsbury. Southwell's beautiful minster & the cathedral city of Lincoln are nearby, Newark with its pretty shops & wonderful restaurants is 3 miles away. Jerry bakes the bread & vegetables come from the enchanting garden. Rooms are generously proportioned with large Victorian baths. Single supplement. Evening meals & animals by prior arrangement. Children over 12.

jillie.steele@virgin.net   www.bestbandb.co.uk
£70.00 - £80.00 Open: all year
Map ref no. 07

Hilary Collinson
Sulney Fields   Colonel's Lane   Upper Broughton
Melton Mowbray LE14 3BX Nottinghamshire
Tel: (01664) 822204   Fax 01664 823976

Near Rd: A.606
Sulney Fields is situated in a quiet position on the edge of a small village & offers spacious accommodation with spectacular views over the Vale of Belvoir. Each of the 3 attractive bedrooms has private facilities & a T.V. & tea/coffee-making facilities. (2 of the rooms have access via a stair lift.) A delicious full English breakfast is served from 07.30 until 09.30 each day. An ideal base, within easy reach of Nottingham, Loughborough, Leicester & Melton Mowbray. A choice of pubs within 1 mile.

hillyc@hotmail.com www.bestbandb.co.uk
£50.00 - £60.00 Open: all year (excl. xmas)
Map ref no. 06

Mrs Suzanne Prew-Smith
The Yellow House 7 Littlegreen Road   Woodthorpe
Nottingham NG5 4LE   Nottinghamshire
Tel: (0115) 9262280

Near Rd: A.60
The Yellow House is a 1930's semi-detached house, which is set in a very quiet road. The house is very comfortable & the bedroom is elegantly decorated in cream & green, has T.V. & tea/coffee-making facilities & its own en-suite shower room. Breakfast may be taken on the terrace in fine weather. The city centre is 2 miles away & Sherwood Forest is 20 mins' to the north. Suzanne, an ex-model & much travelled, is happy to collect you from the station & extends a friendly welcome on arrival. Single supplement.

suzanne.prewsmith1@btinternet.com
www.bestbandb.co.uk   £35.00 - £55.00
Open: all year   Map ref no. 08

Nigel & Sue Bundy
The Barns Country Guest House   Mansfield Road
Morton Retford DN22 8HA Nottinghamshire
Tel: (01777) 706336

Near Rd: A.1

The Barns Country Guest House is an ideal location for couples. This beautifully converted 18th-century barn boasts oak beams & pretty bedrooms, all en-suite with full facilities, with a 4-poster room for special occasions. Enjoy a delicious Aga-cooked breakfast including those suitable for vegetarians, served in a spacious yet comfortable dining room. This is an interesting base for touring, located at Babworth, home of the Pilgrim Fathers, Robin Hood country & Clumber Park. Children over 8 years are welcome. A warm & friendly atmosphere awaits you.

enquiries@thebarns.co.uk   www.thebarns.co.uk
£60.00 - £82.00 Open: all year (excl.xmas & new year)
Map ref no. 09

Mrs Georgiana Kinder
Torr Lodge Main Street Barrow
Nr.Oakham LE15 7PE Rutland
Tel: (01572) 813396

Near Rd: A.1

A warm welcome awaits you at Torr Lodge, Barrow, in the heart of scenic Rutland, England's smallest county. Belvoir Castle, Burghley House & Geoff Hamilton's famous gardens are all within easy reach, as is Rutland Water. Georgiana has been in the hospitality business for many years & offers tastefully furnished en-suite accommodation with colour T.V., tea/coffee-making facilities etc. Enjoy delicious home-cooking from the Aga & hearty breakfasts, which set you up for the day. Dinner is available by arrangement. Children over 12 years.

reservations@torrlodge.co.uk www.torrlodge.co.uk
£56.00 - £56.00 Open: all year
Map ref no. 10

Lincolnshire

Lincolnshire

Lincolnshire is an intriguing mixture of coast & country, of flat fens & gently rising wolds.

The Lincolnshire Coast is host to two very different experiences: The "seaside" Coast and the Rural Coast. There are the popular resorts of Skegness & Mablethorpe as well as the unbroken tranquillity of the Rural Coast. Gibraltar Point, Saltfleetby, Crook Bank, Moggs Eye reward those seeking the natural coastline. A haven for nature lovers, birdwatchers,& conservationists. These wild stretches of sand are some of Lincolnshire's greatest natural assets.

Fresh vegetables for much of Britain are produced in the rich soil of the Lincolnshire fens, & windmills punctuate the skyline. There is a unique 8-sailed windmill at Heckington. In spring the fields are ablaze with the red & yellow of tulips. The bulb industry flourishes around Spalding & Holbeach, & in early May tulip flowers in abundance decorate the huge floats of the Spalding Flower Parade.

The city of Lincoln has cobbled streets & ancient buildings & a very beautiful triple-towered Cathedral which shares its hill-top site with the Castle, both dating from the 11th century. There is a 17th century library by Wren in the Cathedral, which has amongst its treasures one of the four original copies of Magna Carta.

Boston has a huge parish church with a distinctive octagonal tower which can be seen for miles across the surrounding fenland, known locally as "The Boston Stump". The Guildhall Museum displays many aspects of the town's history, including the cells where the early Pilgrim Fathers were imprisoned after their attempt to flee to the Netherlands to find religious freedom. They eventually made the journey & hence to America.

One of England's most outstanding towns is Stamford. It has lovely churches, ancient inns & other fine buildings in a mellow stone.

Sir Isaac Newton was born at Woolsthorpe Manor & educated at nearby Grantham where there is a museum which illustrates his life & work.

The poet Tennyson was born in the village of Somersby, where his father was Rector.

Burghley House. Stamford.

Lincolnshire

Lincolnshire Gazeteer

Areas of outstanding natural beauty.
Lincolnshire Wolds.

Historic Houses & Castles

Auborn House - Nr. Lincoln
16th century house with imposing carved
staircase & panelled rooms.

Belton House - Grantham
House built 1684-88 - said to be by Christopher
Wren - work by Grinling Gibbons & Wyatt also.
Paintings, furniture, porcelain, tapestries, Duke
of Windsor mementoes. A great English house
with formal gardens, extensive grounds, orangery.

Doddington Hall - Doddington, Nr. Lincoln
16th century Elizabethan mansion with elegant
Georgian rooms & gabled Tudor gatehouse.
Fine furniture, paintings, porcelain, etc. Formal
walled knot gardens, roses & wild gardens.

Burghley House - Stamford
Elizabethan - England's largest & grandest
house of the era. Famous for its beautiful
painted ceilings, silver fireplaces & art treasures.

Gumby Hall - Burgh-le-Marsh
17th century manor house. Ancient gardens.

Harrington Hall - Spilsby
Mentioned in the Domesday Book - has
medieval stone base - Carolinean manor house
in red brick. Some alterations in 1678 to
mullioned windows. Panelling, furnishings of
17th & 18th century.

Marston Hall - Grantham
16th century manor house. Ancient gardens.

The Old Hall - Gainsborough
Fine medieval manor house built in 1480's with
original kitchen, rebuilt after original hall
destroyed during Wars of the Roses. Tower &
wings, Great Hall. First meeting place of the
"Dissenters", later known as the Pilgrim Fathers.

Woolsthorpe Manor - Grantham
Small 17th century Manor house. Birthplace of
Sir Isaac Newton.

Fydell House - Boston
18th century house, now Pilgrim College.

Lincoln Castle - Lincoln
William the Conqueror castle, with complete
curtain wall & Norman shell keep. Towers & wall
walk. Unique prisoners' chapel.

Tattershall Castle - Tattershall
100 foot high brick keep of 15th century moated
castle, with fine views over surrounding country.

Cathedrals & Churches

Addlethorpe (St. Nicholas)
15th century - medieval stained glass -
original woodwork.

Boston (St. Botolph)
14th century decorated - very large parish
church. Beautiful south porch, carved stalls.

Brant Broughton (St. Helens)
13th century arcades - decorated tower & spire -
perpendicular clerestory. Exterior decoration.

Ewerby (St. Andrew)
Decorated - splendid example of period - very
fine spire. 14th century effigy.

Fleet (St. Mary Magdalene)
14th century - early English arcades -
perpendicular windows - detached tower
& spire.

Folkingham (St. Andrew)
14th century arcades - 15th century windows -
perpendicular tower - early English chancel.

Gedney (St. Mary Magdalene)
Perpendicular spire (unfinished). Early English
tower. 13th-14th century monuments, 14th-15th
century stained glass.

Grantham (St. Wulfram)
14th century tower & spire - Norman pillars -
perpendicular chantry 14th C. vaulted crypt.

Lincoln Cathedral - Lincoln
Magnificent triple-towered Gothic building on
fine hill-top site. Norman west front, 13th century
- some 14th century additions. Norman work
from 1072. Angel choir - carved & decorated
pulpitum - 13th century chapter house - 17th
century library by Wren (containing one of the
four original copies of Magna Carta).

St. Botolph's Church - Boston

Lincolnshire

Parish church, one of the largest in the country, 272 foot octagonal tower dominating the fens.

Long Sutton (St. Mary)
15th century south porch, medieval brass lectern, very fine early English spire.

Louth (St. James)
Early 16th century - medieval Gothic - wonderful spire.

Scotter (St. Peter)
Saxon to perpendicular - early English nave - 15th century rood screen.

Stow (St. Mary)
Norman - very fine example, particularly west door. Wall painting.

Silk Willoughby (St. Denis)
14th century - tower with spire & flying buttresses. 15th-17th century pulpit.

Stainfield (St. Andrew)
Small, Queen Anne style - medieval armour & early needlework.

Theddlethorpe (All Saints)
14th century - 15th century & reredos of 15th century, 16th century parcloses, 15th century brasses - some medieval glass.

Wrangle (St. Mary the Virgin & St. Nicholas)
Early English - decorated - perpendicular - Elizabethan pulpit. 14th C. east window & glass.

Museums & Galleries

Alford Manor House - Alford
Tudor manor house - thatched - folk museum. Nearby windmill.

Boston Guildhall Museum - Boston
15th century building with mayor's parlour, court room & cells where Pilgrim Fathers were imprisoned in 1607. Local exhibits.

Lincoln Cathedral Library - Lincoln
Built by Wren housing early printed books & medieval manuscripts.

Lincoln Cathedral Treasury - Lincoln
Diocesan gold & silver plate.

Lincoln City & Country Museum - Lincoln
Prehistoric, Roman & medieval antiquities.

Museum of Lincolnshire Life - Lincoln

Domestic, agricultural, industrial & social history of the county. Edwardian room & shop settings.

Usher Gallery - Lincoln
Paintings, watches, miniatures, porcelain, silver, coins & medals. Temporary exhibitions. Tennyson collection. Works of English watercolourist Peter de Wint.

Grantham Museum - Grantham
Archeology, prehistoric, Saxon & Roman. Local history with special display about Sir Isaac Newton, born nearby & educated in Grantham.

Church Farm Museum - Skegness
Farmhouse & buildings with local agricultural collections & temporary exhibitions & special events.

Stamford Museum - Stamford
Local history museum, with temporary special exhibitions.

Battle of Britain Memorial Flight - Coningsby
Lancaster bomber, five Spitfires, two Hurricanes two Chipmunks & a Dakota with other Battle of Britain memorabilia.

National Cycle Museum - Lincoln
Development of the cycle.

Stamford Steam Brewery Museum - Stamford
Complete Victorian steam brewery with 19th century equipment.

Other things to see & do

Springfield - Spalding
Show gardens of the British bulb industry, & home of the Spalding Flower Parade each May. Summer bedding plants & roses.

Butlins Funcoast World - Skegness
Funsplash Water World with amusements & family entertainment.

Castle Leisure Park - Tattershall
Windsurfing, water-skiing, sailing, fishing & other sports & leisure facilities.

Long Sutton Butterfly Park - Long Sutton
Walk-through tropical butterfly house with outdoor wildflower meadows & pets corner.

Skegness Natureland Marine Zoo - Skegness
Seal sanctuary with aquaria & pets corner.

LINCOLNSHIRE

Map reference

01 Brotherton
02 Armstrong
03 Sharman
04 Clarke

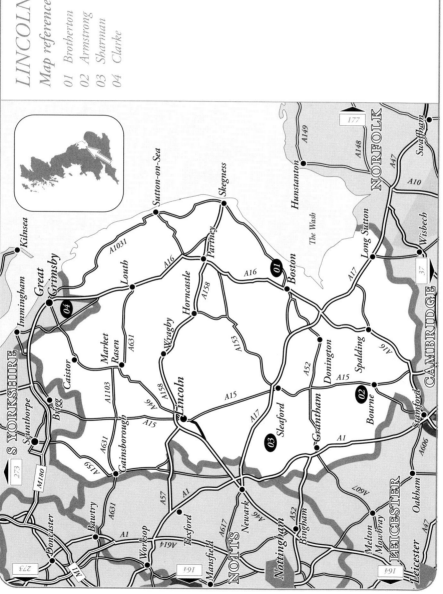

Mr & Mrs Michael Brotherton
The Old Vicarage Wrangle Boston PE22 9EP
Lincolnshire
Tel: (01205) 870688   Fax 01205 871857

Near Rd: A.52
The Old Vicarage is a beautiful Queen Anne house in tranquil Wrangle. 9 miles north of historic Boston. Boston Church - the Stump - is the largest parish church in England & is well known the world over. Boston has historic links with the Pilgrim Fathers. Wrangle lies at the edge of the Fens, on the corner of the Wash. The Brothertons love entertaining & offer great comfort & top-class home-cooking, based on local & home-grown produce. Animals by arrangement. The Old Vicarage is an elegant home from which to explore Lincolnshire.

jb141@aol.com www.bestbandb.co.uk
£45.00 - £55.00 Open: all year (excl. xmas)
Map ref no. 01

Mrs J. Sharman
Gelston Grange Farm Nr. Marston
Grantham NG32 2AQ Lincolnshire
Tel: (01400) 250281

Near Rd: A.1, A.17
A warm welcome awaits you at Gelston Grange, a period farmhouse dated 1840, with many original features. Set in a large garden, it overlooks open countryside & has ample parking. All bedrooms are en-suite, designed with comfort in mind & are pleasing to the eye, with many thoughtful extras. Delicious full English breakfasts are served in the dining room, with a log fire on chilly mornings. Approx. 3 miles from A.1 or A.17. Central for Lincoln, Grantham, Stamford & Newark. A home from home. Children over 10 years. Single supplement.

janet@gelstongrange.com www.gelstongrange.com
£60.00 - £60.00 Open: mid jan - mid dec
Map ref no. 03

Mrs Chantal Armstrong
Cawthorpe Hall Cawthorpe Bourne PE10 0AB
Lincolnshire
Tel: (01778) 423830   Fax 01778 426620

Near Rd: A.15
Ozric & Chantal will give you a friendly welcome in this fine, old listed house, surrounded by wonderful trees, large mixed borders & acres of fragrant roses for the distillation of unique English rose oil & rose water, distilled at Cawthorpe. The rooms are bright, spacious & comfortably furnished with bathrooms en-suite. English breakfast with local produce is served in the studio filled with paintings & interesting objects gathered from different parts of the world. Good pubs nearby for evening meals.

chantal@rosewater.co.uk www.cawthorpebandb.co.uk
£70.00 - £80.00 Open: all year (excl. xmas & new year)
Map ref no. 02

Nicola Clarke
The Old Farmhouse Low Road Hatcliffe
Nr.Grimsby DN37 0SH Lincolnshire
Tel: (01472) 824455   Mobile 07818 272523

Near Rd: A.18
Situated in the Wolds, The Old Farmhouse is an 18th-century treasure recently renovated to a very high standard. Stunning inside & out, & set in a truly peaceful location overlooking a gentle valley. A large comfortable lounge with inglenook fireplace & old beams is provided for you to relax in. 2 beautifully furnished bedrooms with all amenities. An excellent choice of local pubs. Well-placed for golf, country walks, the coast & horse racing. Covered parking & horse livery available. Children over 7 years.

clarky.hatcliffe@btinternet.com www.bestbandb.co.uk
£60.00 - £60.00 Open: all year (excl. xmas & new year)
Map ref no. 04

Norfolk

Norfolk

One of the largest of the old counties, Norfolk is divided by rivers from neighbouring counties & pushes out into the sea on the north & east sides. This is old East Anglia.

Inland there is great concentration on agriculture where fields are hedged with hawthorn which blossoms like snow in summer. A great deal of land drainage is required & the area is crisscrossed by dykes & ditches - some of them dating back to Roman times.

The Norfolk Broads were formed by the flooding of mediaeval peat diggings to form miles & miles of inland waterways, navigable & safe. On a bright summer's day, on a peaceful backwater bounded by reed & sedge, the Broads seem like paradise. Here are hidden treasures like the Bittern, that shyest of birds, the Swallowtail butterfly & the rare Marsh orchid.

Contrasting with the still inland waters is a lively coastline which takes in a host of towns & villages as it arcs around The Wash. Here are the joys of the seaside at its best, miles of safe & sandy golden beaches to delight children, dunes & salt marshes where bird-life flourishes, & busy ports & fishing villages with pink-washed cottages.

Cromer is a little seaside town with a pier & a prom, cream teas & candy floss, where red, white & blue fishing boats are drawn up on the beach.

Hunstanton is more decorous, with a broad green sweeping down to the cliffs. Great Yarmouth is a boisterous resort. It has a beach that runs for miles, with pony rides & every amusement imaginable.

It is possible to take a boat into the heart of Norwich, past warehouses, factories & new penthouses, & under stone & iron bridges. Walking along the riverbank you reach Pulls Ferry where a perfectly proportioned grey flint gateway arcs over what was once a canal dug to transport stone to the cathedral site. Norwich Cathedral is magnificent, with a soaring spire, beautiful cloisters & fine 15th century carving preserved in the choir stalls. Cathedral close is perfectly preserved as is the cobbled street of Elm Hill.

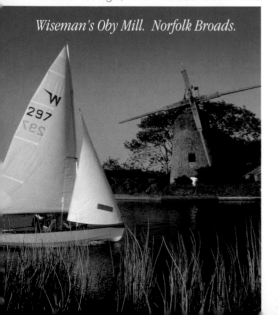

Wiseman's Oby Mill. Norfolk Broads.

Norfolk

Norfolk Gazeteer
Areas of outstanding beauty.
Norfolk coast (part).

Historic Houses & Castles
Anna Sewell House - Great Yarmouth
17th century Tudor frontage. Birthplace of
writer Anna Sewell.
Blicking Hall - Aylsham
Great Jacobean house. Fine Russian tapestry,
long gallery with exceptional ceiling.
Formal garden.
Felbrigg Hall - Nr. Cromer
17th century, good Georgian interior. Set in
wooded parklands.
Holkham Hall - Wells
Fine Palladian mansion of 1734. Paintings,
statuary, tapestries, furnishings & formal garden
by Berry.
Houghton Hall - Wells
18th century mansion. Pictures, china &
staterooms. Herd of white deer & peacocks.
Oxburgh Hall - Oxborough
Late 15th century moated house. Fine
gatehouse tower. Needlework by Mary Queen
of Scots.
Wolterton Hall - Nr. Norwich
Built 1741 with tapestries, porcelain, furniture.
Trinity Hospital - Castle Rising
17th century, nine brick & tile almshouses, court
chapel & treasury.

Cathedrals & Churches
Attleborough (St. Mary)
Norman with late 14th century. Fine rood
screen & frescoes.
Barton Turf (St. Michael & All Angles)
Magnificent screen with painting of the Nine
Orders of Angles.
Beeston-next-Mileham (St. Mary)
14th century. Perpendicular clerestory tower &
spire. Hammer Beam roof, parclose screens,
benches, front cover. Tracery in nave &
chancel windows.

Cawston (St. Agnes)
Tower faced with freestone. Painted screens,
wall paintings, tower, screen & gallery. 15th
century angel roof.
East Harding (St. Peter & St. Paul)
14th century, some 15th century alterations.
Monuments of 15th-17th century. Splendid
medieval glass.
Erpingham (St. Mary)
14th century military brass of John de
Erpingham, 16th C. Rhenish glass. Fine tower.
Gunton (St. Andrew)
18th century. Robert Adam - classical interior in
dark wood - gilded.
King's Lynn (St. Margaret)
Norman foundation. Two fine 14th century
Flemish brasses, 14th century screens, reredos
by Bodley, interesting Georgian pulpit with
sounding board.
Norwich Cathedral
Romanesque & late Gothic with 15th century
spire. Perpendicular lierne vaults in nave,
transepts and presbytery.
Ranworth (St. Helens)
15th century screen, very fine example. Sarum
Antiphoner, 14th century illuminated manuscript
- East Anglian work.
Salle (St. Peter & St. Paul)
15th century. Highly decorated west tower &
porches. Medieval glass, pulpit with 15th
century panels & Jacobean tester. Stalls,
misericords, brasses & monuments,
sacrament font.
Terrington (St. Clement)
Detached perpendicular tower. Western front
has fire-light window & canopied niches.
Georgian panelling west of nave.17th C. painted
font cover. Jacobean commandment boards.
Trunch (St. Botolph)
15th C. screen with painted panels, medieval
glass, famous font canopy with fine carving &
painting,ringer's gallery, Elizabethan monument.
Wiggenhall (St. Germans)
17th century pulpit, table, clerk's desk & chair,

Norfolk

bench ends 15th century.

Wymondham (St. Mary & St. Thomas of Canterbury)
Norman origins including arcades & triforium windows, 13th century font fragments, complete 15th century font. 15th century clerestory & roof. Comper reredos, famous Corporas Case, rare example of 13th century Opus Anglicanum.

Museums & Galleries

Norwich Castle Museum
Art collection, local & natural history.

Strangers Hall - Norwich
Medieval mansion furnished as museum of urban domestic life in 16th-19th centuries.

St. Peter Hungate Church Museum - Norwich
15th century church for the exhibition of ecclesiastical art & East Anglican antiquities.

Sainsbury Centre for Visual Arts - University, Norwich
Collection of modern art, ancient, classical & medieval art, Art Nouveau, 20th century constructivist art.

Bridewell Museum of Local Industries - Norwich
Crafts, industries & aspects of city life.

Museum of Social History - King's Lynn
Exhibition of domestic life & dress, etc., noted glass collection.

Bishop Bonner's Cottages
Restored cottages with coloured East Anglia pargetting, c. 1502, museum of archaeological discoveries, exhibition of rural crafts.

The Guildhall - Thetford
Duleep Singh Collection of Norfolk & Suffolk portraits.

Shirehall Museum - Walsingham
18th century court room having original fittings, illustrating Walsingham life.

Historic Monuments

Binham Priory & Cross - Binham
12th century ruins of Benedictine foundation.

Caister Castle - Great Yarmouth
15th century moated castle - ruins. Now motor museum.

The Castle - Burgh Castle
3rd century Saxon fort - walls - ruin.

Mannington Hall - Saxthorpe
Saxon church ruin in gardens of 15th century moated house.

Castle Rising - Castle Rising
Splendid Norman keep & earthworks.

Castle Acre Priory & Castle Gate - Swaffham

Other things to see & do

African Violet Centre - Terrington St. Clements.
60 varieties of African Violets. Talks & Tours.

Norfolk Lavender Centre - Heacham
Open to the public in July & August. Demonstrations of harvesting & distilling the oil.

Thetford Forest
Forest walks, rides & picnic places amongst conifers, oak, beech & birch.

Sheringham Park - Sheringham
Designed in 1812 by Humphry Repton, the great landscape designer. Viewing towers with spectacular views of the coast and countryside.

Butterfly and Wildlife Park
The Butterfly and Wildlife Park offers a unique day out, with hundreds of exotic butterflies flying around you in a tropical setting.

Church Farm - Stow Bardolph - Rare Breeds Centre
Church farm was a new attraction in 2004 with an extensive variety of rare breeds in the grounds of the Stow Bardolph estate.

Fritton Lake Countryworld - Great Yarmouth
Acres of unspoilt countryside beside one of the most beautiful lakes in East Anglia.

Snettisham Park - Nr Kings Lynn
The complete countryside experience, with deer safari, discovery trail, farm animals, tractor rides, riding stables,

Dinosaur Adventure Park - Lenwade
For a monster day out full of fun & discovery.

NORFOLK
Map reference

01 James
02 Morrish
03 Birkbeck
04 Ellis
05 Pugh
06 Douglas
07 Meynell
08 Allingham

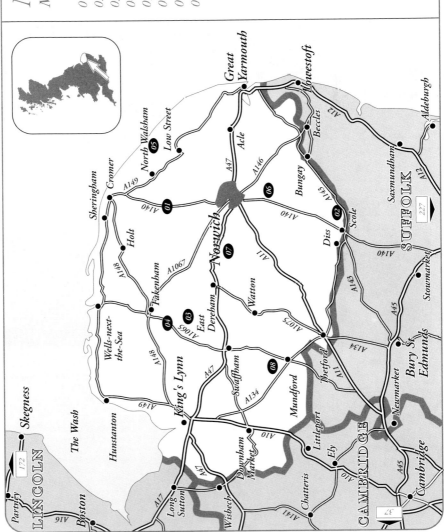

Marc James & Charles Kirkman
The Old Pump House   2 Holman Road
Aylsham NR11 6BY   Norfolk
Tel: (01263) 733789   Fax 01263 734513

Near Rd: A.140
This comfortable 1750's house owned by Marc James & Charles Kirkman, faces the old thatched pump & is a minute from Aylsham's church & historic market place. It offers 5 bedrooms (including one 4-poster) in a relaxed & elegant setting, with T.V., tea/coffee facilities & hairdryers in all rooms. English breakfast with free-range eggs & local produce (or vegetarian breakfast) is served in the pine-shuttered sitting room overlooking the garden. Aylsham is central for Norwich, the coast, the Broads, National Trust houses, steam railways & unspoilt countryside. Dinner by prior arrangement from Oct to May. Parking.

theoldpumphouse@btconnect.com
www.theoldpumphouse.com £55.00 - £85.00
Open: all year (excl.xmas & new year) Map ref no. 01

John & Hermione Birkbeck
Litcham Hall   Lexham Road   Litcham
Kings Lynn PE32 2QQ   Norfolk
Tel: (01328) 701389   Fax 01328 701164

Near Rd: A.1065
This Grade II listed house was built in 1781 & has been owned by only 3 families during its history. The house is beautifully furnished with a sitting room available to guests. The attractive bedrooms, all 16ft sq., with large windows overlooking the garden, have private bathrooms, 2 of the rooms are en-suite. John & Hermione came to Litcham in 1967 & have much enjoyed restoring the house & garden. Now our guests can take advantage of our efforts. Single occupancy supplement. Use of pool, by arrangement. Evening meals are available, min. 4 persons. A delightful home for a relaxing break in Norfolk.

b.birkbeck67@amserve.com   www.bestbandb.co.uk
£60.00 - £70.00 Open: all year
Map ref no. 03

Angela & John Morrish
Grove Thorpe   Grove Road   Brockdish
Diss IP21 4JR   Norfolk
Tel: (01379) 668305

Near Rd: A.143
Award-winning Grove Thorpe set in the Waveney Valley, a paradise for lovers of rural life. Grade II listed country house nestling in 10 acres of secluded grounds with private fishing lake. Inglenook fireplaces & a wealth of beams create a warm ambience, afternoon tea around a log fire in winter or watch the birds & ducks from the gardens in summer. Bedrooms are en-suite with every luxury catered for, antique furniture, 4 with super King-size beds. also a separate ground-floor suite (Garden Cottage). Dinner is available from Nov to Mar by arrangement. Children over 12.

b-b@grovethorpe.co.uk www.grovethorpe.co.uk
£66.00 - £78.00 Open: all year (excl.xmas & new year)
Map ref no. 02

Elisabeth Ellis
Manor House Farm   Wellingham   Nr. Fakenham
Kings Lynn PE32 2TH   Norfolk
Tel: (01328) 838227Fax 01328 838348

Near Rd: A.1065
Tucked away in the heart of rural Norfolk surrounded by lovely gardens next to the tiny 13th-century church. Conservation - award-winning farm. Beautifully converted old stables. 2 en-suite double/twin bedrooms with extra large beds. A sitting room with woodburner & small kitchen. The emphasis here is on charm & comfort. Stripped pine, lovely rugs, artefacts, complete the restful ambience. A delicious breakfast, using home produced fruit, eggs & bacon etc. 20 mins' North Norfolk Coast & close to Sandringham. Wheelchair friendly. Children over 10.

www.bestbandb.co.uk
£70.00 - £80.00 Open: all year
Map ref no. 04

Mrs Wendy Pugh
Mill Common House   Mill Common Road Ridlington
North Walsham NR28 9TY Norfolk
Tel: (01692) 650792   Fax 01692 651480

Near Rd: A.149

Mill Common House is an elegant Georgian farmhouse set in a quiet rural location, close to the market town of North Walsham & only 1 mile from sandy beaches. Standing in its own mature grounds, beside the original brick & flint buildings dating back more than 200 years. The 2 attractive bedrooms, with all amenities, a large conservatory & open log fires on cooler days all add to the relaxed atmosphere & surroundings, typical of comfortable stylish living. An ideal place to stay for a short break & perfect for exploring Norfolk. Children over 12 years. Evening meals by arrangement.

johnpugh@millcommon.freeserve.co.uk
www.millcommonhouse.co.uk   £56.00 - £78.00
Open: all year (excl. xmas)   Map ref no. 05

Mrs Deborah Meynell
The Buttery   Berry Hall   Honingham
Norwich NR9 5AX   Norfolk
Tel: (01603) 880541

Near Rd: A.47

Originally the dairy for Berry Hall, the Buttery is a unique thatched building, which has been beautifully converted into a self-contained tranquil place to stay. The accommodation consists of an attractive mezzanine bedroom (up a steep wooden staircase), a lovely sitting room with a large comfortable sofabed (as an alternative), a bathroom with Jacuzzi & a small country kitchen filled with all the ingredients for you to make a delicious full English breakfast. Walk in the beautiful woods and meadows, or use The Buttery as a convenient base to explore the delights of Norfolk.

thebuttery@paston.co.uk   www.bestbandb.co.uk
£80.00 - £90.00 Open: all year
Map ref no. 07

Joanna Douglas
Greenacres Farmhouse   Woodgreen Long Stratton
Norwich NR15 2RR   Norfolk
Tel: (01508) 530261   Fax 01508 530261

Near Rd: A.140

A period 17th-century farmhouse on a 30-acre common with ponds & wildlife, only 10 miles from Norwich. All of the en-suite/private bedrooms (2 double/1 twin) are tastefully furnished to complement the oak beams & period furniture, with tea/coffee-making facilities & T.V.. The beamed sitting room with inglenook fireplace invites you to relax. A sunny dining room encourages you to enjoy a leisurely breakfast. Snooker table & tennis court. Therapeutic massage, aromatherapy & reflexology service available. Enjoy the peace & tranquillity of this home.

greenacresfarm@tinyworld.co.uk
www.abreakwithtradition.co.uk   £50.00 - £65.00
Open: all year   Map ref no. 06

Wendy Allingham
Colveston Manor Mundford   Thetford IP26 5HU
Norfolk
Tel: (01842) 878218

Near Rd: A.1065

Colveston Manor is a peaceful, 18th-century award winning farmhouse in a delightful setting in the heart of Breckland. Offering 4 attractive bedrooms, some en-suite, including 1 ground floor single room. An attractive guest lounge with log fire in winter. The Allinghams specialise in delicious cooking from the Aga, using all local produce whenever possible. National Trust Properties, Cathedrals, gardens & the coast are all within easy reach & Sandringham is just a few miles away. A wonderful base for birdwatching. Also superb walks and facilities in the Thetford Forest.

mail@colveston-manor.co.uk
www.colveston-manor.co.uk   £55.00 - £65.00
Open: all year   Map ref no. 08

Northumbria

Northumbria

Mountains & moors, hills & fells, coast & country are all to be found in this Northern region which embraces four counties - Northumberland, Durham, Cleveland & Tyne & Wear.

Saxons, Celts, Vikings, Romans & Scots all fought to control what was then a great wasteland between the Humber & Scotland.

Northumberland

Northumberland is England's Border country, a land of history, heritage & breathtaking countryside. Hadrian's Wall, stretching across the county from the mouth of the Tyne in the west to the Solway Firth, was built as the Northern frontier of the Roman Empire in 122 AD. Excavations

along the Wall have brought many archaeological treasures to light. To walk along the wall is to discover the genius of Roman building & engineering skill. They left a network of roads, used to transport men & equipment in their attempts to maintain discipline among the wild tribes.

Through the following centuries the Border wars with the Scots led to famous battles such as Otterburn in 1388 & Flodden in 1513, & the construction of great castles including Bamburgh & Lindisfarne. Berwick-on-Tweed, the most northerly town, changed hands between England & Scotland 13 times.

Northumberland's superb countryside includes the Cheviot Hills in the Northumberland National Park, the unforgettable heather moorlands of the Northern Pennines to the west, Kielder Water (Western Europe's largest man-made lake), & 40 miles of glorious coastline.

The Farne Islands lie two to three miles off the Northumberland coast. Holy Island, or Lindisfarne, is reached by a narrow causeway that is covered at every incoming tide. Here St. Aidan of Iona founded a monastery in the 7th century, & with St. Cuthbert set out to Christianise the pagan tribes. The site was destroyed by the Danes, but Lindisfarne Priory was built by the monks of Durham in the 11th century to house a Benedictine community. The ruins are hauntingly beautiful.

Bamburgh Castle. Northumberland.

Northumbria

Durham

County Durham is the land of the Prince Bishops, who with their armies, nobility, courts & coinage controlled the area for centuries. They ruled as a virtually independent State, holding the first line of defence against the Scots.

In Durham City, the impressive Norman Castle standing proudly over the narrow mediaeval streets was the home of the Prince Bishops for 800 years.

Durham Cathedral, on a wooded peninsula high above the River Wear, was built in the early 12th century & is undoubtably one of the world's finest buildings, long a place of Christian pilgrimage.

The region's turbulent history led to the building of forts & castles. Some like Bowes & Barnard Castle are picturesque ruins whilst others, including Raby, Durham & Lumley still stand complete.

The Durham Dales of Weardale, Teesdale & the Derwent Valley cover about one third of the county & are endowed with some of the highest & wildest scenery. Here are High Force, England's highest waterfall, & the Upper Teesdale National Nature Reserve.

The Bowes Museum at Barnard Castle is a magnificent French-style chateau & houses an important art collection. In contrast is the award-winning museum at Beamish which imaginatively recreates Northern life at the turn of the century.

Cleveland

Cleveland, the smallest 'shire' in England, has long been famous for its steel, chemical & shipbuilding industries but it is also an area of great beauty. The North Yorkshire National Park lies in the south, & includes the cone-shaped summit of Roseberry Topping, "Cleveland's Matterhorn".

Cleveland means 'land of cliffs', & in places along the magnificent coastline, cliffs tower more than 600 feet above the sea, providing important habitat for wild plants & sea-birds.

Tyne & Wear

Tyne & Wear takes its name from the two rivers running through the area, & includes the large & lively city of Newcastle-on-Tyne & Weardale.

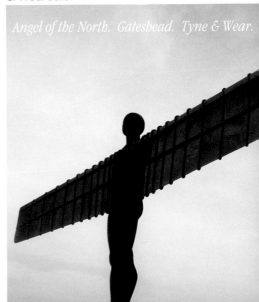

Angel of the North. Gateshead. Tyne & Wear.

Northumbria

Northumbria Gazeeter

Areas of Outstanding Natural Beauty
The Heritage Coast, the Cheviot Hills, the North
Pennine chain.

Historic Houses & Castles

Alnwick Castle - Alnwick
A superb medieval castle of the 12th century.
Bamburgh Castle-Bamburgh
A restored 12th century castle with
Norman keep.
Callaly Castle - Whittingham
A 13th century Pele tower with 17th century
mansion. Georgian additions.
Durham Castle - Durham
Part of the University of Durham. A Norman
castle - began in 1072 restoration continues.
Lindisfarne Castle - Holy Island
An interesting 14th century castle.
Ormesby Hall - Nr. Middlesbrough
A mid 18th century house.
Raby Castle - Staindrop, Darlington
14th century with some later alteration . Fine art
& furniture. Large gardens.
Wallington Hall - Combo
A 17th C. house with much alteration & addition.
Washington Old Hall - Washington
Jacobean manor house, parts of which date
back to 12th century.

Cathedrals & Churches

Brancepeth (St. Brandon)
12th century with superb 17th century
woodwork. Part of 2 medieval screens. Flemish
carved chest.
Durham Cathedral
A superb Norman cathedral. A unique Galilee
chapel & early 12th century vaults.
Escombe
An interesting Saxon Church with sundial.
Hartlepool (St. Hilda)
Early English with fine tower & buttresses.
Hexham (St. Andrews)
Remains of a 17th century church with Roman

dressing. A unique night staircase.
Jarrow (St. Pauls)
Bede worshipped here. Strange in that it was
originally 2 churches until 11th century.
Medieval chair.
Newcastle (St. Nicholas)
14th century with an interesting lantern tower.
Heraldic font. Roundel of 14th century glass.
Morpeth (St. Mary the Virgin)
Fine medieval glass in east window - 14th
century.
Pittington (St. Lawrence)
Late Norman nave with wall paintings. Carved
tombstone - 13th century.
Skelton (St. Giles)
Early 13th century with notable font, gable
crosses, bell-cote & buttresses.
Staindrop (St. Mary)
A fine Saxon window.
Priests dwelling
Neville tombs & effigies.

Museums & Galleries

Aribea Roman Fort Museum - South Shields
Interesting objects found on site.
Berwick-on-Tweed Museum - Berwick
Special exhibition of interesting local finds.
Bowes Museum - Bernard Castle
European art from medieval to 19th century.
**Captain Cook Birthplace Museum -
Middlesbrough**
Cook's life & natural history discoveries relating
to his travels.
Clayton Collection - Chollerford
A collection of Roman sculpture, weapons &
tools from forts.
Corbridge Roman Station - Corbridge
Roman pottery & sculpture.
Dormitory Musuem - Durham Cathedral
Relics of St. Cuthbert.
Medieval seats & manuscripts.
Gray Art Gallery - Hartlepool
19th-20th century art & oriental antiquities.
Gulbenkian Museum of Oriental Art - Durham

Northumbria

Chinese pottery & porcelain, Chinese jade & stone carvings, Chinese ivories, Chinese Japenese & Tibetan art. Egyptian & Mesopotamian antiquities.

Jarrow Hall - Jarrow
Excavation finds of Saxon & medieval monastery.Fascinating information room dealing with early Christian sites in England.

Keep Museum - Newcastle-upon-Tyne
Medieval collection.

Laing Art Gallery - Newcastle-upon-Tyne
17th-19th C. British arts, porcelain, glass & silver.

National Music Hall Museum - Sunderland
19th-20th century costume & artefacts associated with the halls.

Preston Hall Museum - Stockton-on-Tees
Armour & arms, toys, ivory period room.

The Hatton Gallery
Housing a fine collection of Italian paintings.

Museum of Antiquities
Prehistoric, Roman & Saxon collection with an interesting reconstruction of a temple.

Beamish North of England Open Air Museum
European Museum of the Year

Chantry Bagpipe Museum - Morpeth

Darlington Museum & Railway Centre

Historic Monuments

Ariiea Roman Fort - South Shields
Remains which include the gateways & headquarters.

Barnard Castle - Barnard Castle
17th century ruin with interesting keep.

Bowes Castle - Bowes
Roman Fort with Norman keep.

The Castle & Town Walls - Berwick-on-Tweed
12th century remains, reconstructed later.

Dunstanburgh Castle - Alnwick
14th century remains.

Egglestone Abbey - Barnard Castle
Remains of a Poor House.

Finchdale Priory - Durham
13th century church with much remaining.

Hadrian's Wall - Housesteads

Several miles of the wall including castles & site museum.

Mithramic Temple - Carrawbrough
Mithraic temple dating back to the 3rd century.

Norham Castle - Norham
The partial remains of a 12th century castle.

Prudhoe Castle - Prudhoe
Dating from the 12th century with additions. Bailey & gatehouse well preserved.

The Roman Fort - Chesters
Extensive remains of a Roman bath house.

Tynemouth Priory & Castle - Tynemouth
11th century priory - ruin - with 16th century towers & keep.

Vindolanda - Barton Mill
Roman fort dating from 3rd century.

Warkworth Castle - Warkworth
Dating from the 11th century with additions. A great keep & gatehouse.

Warkworth Hermitage - Warkworth
An interesting 14th century Hermitage.

Lindisfarne Priory - Holy Island (Lindisfarne)
11th century monastery. Island accessible only at low tide.

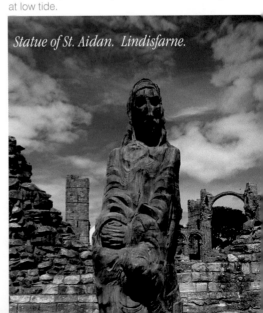

Statue of St. Aidan. Lindisfarne.

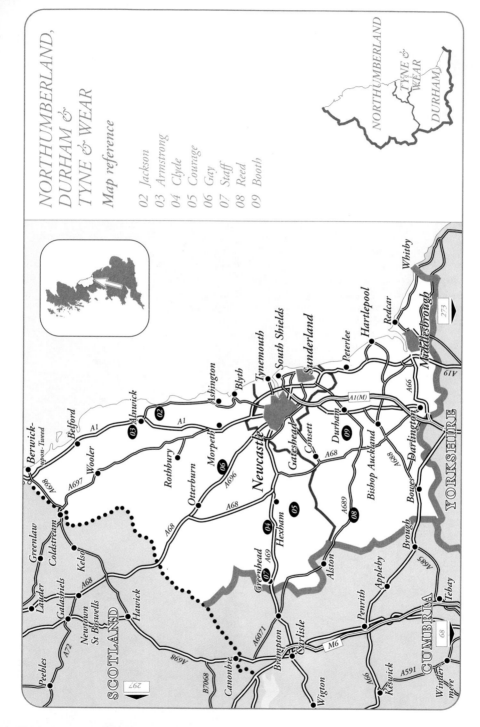

NORTHUMBERLAND, DURHAM & TYNE & WEAR

Map reference

02 Jackson
03 Armstrong
04 Clyde
05 Courage
06 Gay
07 Staff
08 Reed
09 Booth

NORTHUMBERLAND
TYNE & WEAR
DURHAM

see p.186

Dorothy Jackson
Bilton Barns Farmhouse Alnmouth Alnwick NE66 2TB
Northumberland
Tel: (01665) 830427 Fax 01665 833909

Near Rd: A.1
Dating back to 1715, Bilton Barns has fantastic views over Alnmouth & Warkworth Bay, only 1 1/2 miles away. The spacious & beautifully furnished rooms are all en-suite, centrally heated & with colour T.V. & tea/coffee-making facilities; or stay in one of the attractive suites, 1 of which has a 4-poster bed, all have comfortable beamed lounges in which to relax & unwind. Choose delicious Craster kippers from the extensive breakfast menu. Alnwick Gardens & Castle are easily accessible being only 5 miles away. Bilton Barns is an excellent base from which to explore Northumbria & its many attractions.

dorothy@biltonbarns.com www.biltonbarns.com
£60.00 - £70.00 Open: all year (excl. xmas)
Map ref no. 02

Ian & Angela Clyde
Allerwash Farmhouse Newbrough Hexham NE47 5AB
Northumberland
Tel: (01434) 674574 Fax 01434 674574

Near Rd: A.69
Allerwash is an elegant Regency farm house which is full of character & has secluded gardens surrounded by rolling countryside. Bedrooms are stylishly decorated & include private facilities. Open fires in the 2 drawing rooms add to the warmth of the house, & elegant furnishings plus antiques & paintings make this a real house of distinction. You will be well looked after in the licensed dining room, as Angela has many cookery awards to her credit. The Roman Wall, the Lake District, the Northumberland coast & many castles, country houses & gardens are within easy reach. Children over 8. Animals by arrangement.

www.bestbandb.co.uk
£95.00 - £95.00 Open: all year
Map ref no. 04

Mr & Mrs Charles Armstrong
North Charlton Farm North Charlton
Alnwick NE67 5HP Northumberland
Tel: (01665) 579443 Fax 01665 579407

Near Rd: A.1
Afternoon tea with home-baking is served on arrival in the visitors lounge at North Charlton Farm. The house has just been completely restored & is beautifully furnished with antiques, yet offers every modern comfort in elegant surroundings. Enjoy breakfast in the dining room with views out to the sea (Full English, Craster kippers, home-made preserves & more). The Armstrongs also have a Household & Farming Museum at North Charlton, which is a real 'treasure trove'. Children over 10 years welcome.

stay@northcharltonfarm.co.uk
www.northcharltonfarm.co.uk £60.00 - £70.00
Open: apr - oct Map ref no. 03

Elizabeth Courage
Rye Hill Farm Slaley Nr. Hexham NE47 0AH
Northumberland
Tel: (01434) 673259

Near Rd: A.68, A.69
Rye Hill Farm dates back some 300 years & is a traditional livestock unit in beautiful countryside just 5 miles south of Hexham. Recently, some of the stone barns adjoining the farmhouse have been converted into superb modern guest accommodation. There are 3 attractive bedrooms, all with private facilities, & all have radio, colour T.V. & tea/coffee-making facilities. Delicious home-cooked meals are served. Perfect for a get-away-from-it-all holiday. Single occupancy from £30 per night.

info@ryehillfarm.co.uk www.ryehillfarm.co.uk
£50.00 - £75.00 Open: all year
Map ref no. 05

Bilton Barns Farmhouse

Alnmouth Alnwick NE66 2TB

Tel: (01665) 830427 Fax 01665 833909

email:dorothy@biltonbarns.com www.biltonbarns.com

Celia & Stephen Gay
Shieldhall   Wallington by Kirkharle
Morpeth   NE61 4AQ   Northumberland
Tel: (01830) 540387   Fax 01830 540490

Near Rd: A.696, B.6342
Standing alone in an Area of Outstanding Natural Beauty, overlooking the National Trust estate of Wallington, this charmingly restored 17th century house, cottages & later farm buildings were once home to the family of Capability Brown. The recently converted en-suite bedrooms open into a pretty courtyard with an ancient well & attractive raised patios. Each room takes its name from the wood used for their furniture & fittings. Stephen, with his sons, make bespoke & restore antique furniture. Celia & daughter Sarah are excellent cooks, creating delicious breakfast & dinners for guests. Children 12 + & dogs by arrangement.

stay@shieldhallguesthouse.co.uk
www.shieldhallguesthouse.co.uk £64.00 - £76.00
Open: all year (excl.xmas & new year)   Map ref no. 06

Mrs Barbara Reed
Lands Farm   Westgate-in-Weardale
Bishop Auckland DL13 1SN   Durham
Tel: (01388) 517210   Fax 01388 517210

Near Rd: A.689
You will be warmly welcomed to Lands Farm, an old stone-built farmhouse within walking distance of Westgate village. A pretty walled garden with stream meandering by. The accommodation is in centrally heated, tastefully furnished double & family rooms with luxury en-suite facilities, colour T.V., tea/coffee-making facilities. A full English breakfast or Continental alternative is served in the attractive dining room. Lands Farm is an ideal base for touring being within easy reach of Durham, Hadrian's Wall, the Beamish Museum, etc. & for walking. A delightful home, which is perfect for a short break holiday.

barbara@landsfarm.fsnet.co.uk   www.bestbandb.co.uk
£50.00 - £54.00   Open: all year
Map ref no. 08

Brian & Pauline Staff
Holmhead   Hadrian's Wall   Greenhead via Bampton
CA8 7HY   Northumberland
Tel: 016977 47402   Fax 016977 47402

Near Rd: A.69
Holmhead was once a farm but is now a comfortable guest house and cottage . It stands on the line of the Hadrian's Wall World Heritage Site & is built with stones taken from it circa. 1800. 4 cosy bedrooms each with shower/toilet , 2 with king- size beds . The guests lounge has lovely views of the village and distant moors or the ruined castle & the river . Evening Meals are available using fresh local organic produce wherever possible . Award winning organic wines are also available . Your host, Pauline, is expert on Hadrian's Wall and is happy to help you plan your visit.

holmhead@hadrianswall.freeserve.co.uk
www.holmhead.com   £60.00 - £66.00
Open: all year (excl.xmas & new year)   Map ref no. 07

Roger & Pauline Booth
Ivesley   Waterhouses   Durham   DH7 9HB
Durham
Tel: (0191) 3734324   Fax 0191 3734757

Near Rd: A.68
Ivesley is an elegantly furnished country house set in the middle of 220 acres approached by England's oldest beech avenue which is over 650 years old. All rooms are decorated to a high standard. 3 bedrooms are en-suite & 2 sharing a bathroom. An ideal centre for walking, sightseeing & mountain biking. Durham 7 miles. Wine cellar. Excellent cuisine. Adjacent equestrian centre with comprehensive facilities. Children over 8, dogs & horses welcome. Prices include Continental breakfast. Ivesley is handy for Durham University & the Beamish Museum.

ivesley@msn.com   www.ridingholidays.co.uk
£63.00 - £63.00   Open: all year (excl.xmas & new year)
Map ref no. 09

Oxfordshire

Oxfordshire

Oxfordshire is a county rich in history & delightful countryside. It has prehistoric sites, early Norman churches, 15th century coaching inns, Regency residences, distinctive cottages of black & white chalk flints & lovely Oxford, the city of dreaming spires.

The countryside ranges from lush meadows with willow-edged river banks scattered with small villages of thatched cottages, to the hills of the Oxfordshire Cotswolds in the west, the wooded Chilterns in the east & the distinctive ridge of the Berkshire Downs in the south. "Old Father Thames" meanders gently across the county to Henley, home of the famous regatta.

The ancient track known as the Great

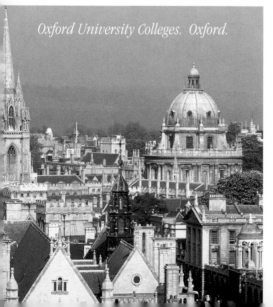

Oxford University Colleges. Oxford.

Ridgeway runs across the shire, & a walk along its length reveals barrows, hill forts & stone circles. The 2,000 year old Uffington Horse cut into the chalk of the hillside below an ancient hill fort site, is some 360 feet in length & 160 feet high.

The Romans built villas in the county & the remains of one, including a magnificent mosaic can be seen at North Leigh. In later centuries lovely houses were built. Minster Lovell stands beside the Windrush; Rousham house with its William Kent gardens is situated near Steeple Aston & beside the Thames lies Elizabethan Mapledurham House with its working watermill.

At Woodstock is Blenheim Palace, the largest private house in Britain & birthplace of Sir Winston Churchill. The statue of King Alfred stands in the market town of Wantage, commemorating his birth there, & Banbury has its cross, made famous in the old nursery rhyme.

Oxford is a town of immense atmosphere with fine college buildings around quiet cloisters, & narrow cobbled lanes. It was during the 12th century that Oxford became a meeting place for scholars & grew into the first established centre of learning, outside the monasteries, in England. The earliest colleges to be founded were University College, Balliol & Merton. Further colleges were added during the reign of the Tudors, as Oxford became a power in the kingdom.

Oxfordshire

Oxfordshire Gazeteer
Areas of Oustanding Natural Beauty.
The North Wessex Downs. The Chiltern Hills.
The Cotswolds.

Historic Houses & Castles
Ashdown House - Nr. Lambourn
17th century, built for Elizabeth of Bohemia, now
contains portraits associated with her. Mansard
roof has cupola with golden ball.
Blenheim Palace - Woodstock
Sir John Vanbrugh's classical masterpiece.
Garden designed by Vanbrugh & Henry Wise.
Further work done by Capability Brown who
created the lake. Collection of pictures
& tapestries.
Broughton Castle- Banbury.
14th century mansion with moat -interesting
plaster work fine panelling & fire places.
Chasleton House - Moreton-in-Marsh
17th century, fine examples of plaster work &
panelling. Still has original furniture & tapestries.
Topiary garden from1700.
Grey Court - Henley-on-Thames
16th century house containing 18th century
plasterwork & furniture. Medieval ruins. Tudor
donkey-wheel for raising water from well.
Mapledurham House - Mapledurham
16th century Elizabethan house. Oak staircase,
private chapel, paintings, original moulded
ceilings. Watermill nearby.
Milton Manor House - Nr. Abingdon
17th century house designed by Inigo Jones -
Georgian wings, Gothic library, walled garden &
pleasant grounds, two lakes & woodland walks.
Rousham House - Steeple Ashton
17th century - contains portraits & miniatures.
University of Oxford Colleges
University college 1249
Balliol 1263
Merton 1264
St. Edmund Hall 1270
Hertford 1284
Exeter 1314
The Queen's 1340
Oriel 1326
Lincoln 1427
New 1438
All Souls 1438
Magdalen 1458
Brasenose 1509
Corpus Christi 1516
Christ Church 1546
Trinity 1554
St. John's 1555
Jesus 1571
Wadham 1610
Pembroke 1624
Worcester 1714
Keble 1868
Nuffield 1937

Cathedrals & Churches
Abingdon (St. Helen)
14th-16th century perpendicular. Painted roof.
Georgian stained & enamelled glass.
Burford (St. John the Baptist)
15th century. Sculptured table tombs in
churchyard.
Chislehampton (St. Katherine)
18th century. Unspoilt interior of Georgian
period. Bellcote.
Dorchester (St. Peter & St. Paul)
13th century knight in stone effigy. Jesse
window.
East Hagbourne (St. Andrew)
14th -15th century. Early glass, wooden roofs,
18th century tombs.
North Moreton (All Saints)
13th century with splendid 14th century chantry
chapel - tracery.
Oxford Cathedral
Smallest of our English cathedrals. Stone spire
form 1230. Norman arcade has double arches,
choir vault.
Ryecote (St. Michael & All Angels)
14th C.benches & screen base.17th C.altar-
piece & communion rails, good ceiling.

Oxfordshire

Stanton Harcourt (St. Michael)
Early English - old stone & marble floor. Early screen with painting, monuments of 17th -19th century.

Yarnton (St. Bartholomew)
13th century - late perpendicular additions. Jacobean screen. 15th century alabaster reredos.

Museums & Galleries

The Ashmolean Museum of Art & Archaeology - Oxford
British, European, Mediterranean, Egyptian & Near Eastern archaeology. Oil paintings of Italian, Dutch, Flemish, French & English schools. Old Master watercolours, prints, drawings, ceramics, silver, bronzes & sculptures. Chinese & Japanese porcelain, lacquer & painting, Tibetan, Islamic & Indian art.

Christ Church Picture Gallery - Oxford
Old Master drawings & paintings.

Museum of Modern Art - Oxford
Exhibitiors of contemporary art.

Museum of Oxford - Oxford
Many exhibits depicting the history of Oxford & its University.

The Rotunda - Oxford
Privately owned collection of dolls' houses 1700-1900, with contents such as furniture, china, silver, dolls, etc.

Oxford University Museum - Oxford
Entomological, zoological, geological & mineralogical collections.

Pendon Museum of Miniature Landscape & Transport - Abingdon.
Showing in miniature the countryside & its means of transport in the thirties, with trains & thatched village. Railway relics.

Town Museum - Abingdon
17th C. building exhibiting fossil, archaeological items & collection of charters & documents.

Tolsey Museum - Burford
Seals, maces, charters & bygones - replica of Regency room, period furnishings & clothing.

Historic Monuments

Uffington Castle & White Horse - Uffington
White horse cut into the chalk - iron age hill fort.

Rollright Stones - Nr. Chipping Norton
77 stones placed in circle - an isolated King's stone & nearby an ancient burial chamber.

Minster Lovell House - Minster Lovell
15th century medieval house - ruins.

Deddington Castle - Deddington

Other things to see & do

Didcot railway centre - Didcot
A large collection of locomotives etc., from Brunel's Great Western Railway.

Filkins - Nr. Burford
A working wool mill where rugs & garments are woven in the traditional way.

University of Oxford Botanic Garden - Oxford
Founded by the Earl of Danby, Henry Danvers as a physic garden in 1621, this is the oldest botanic garden in Britain. It houses a good collection of trees and plants. It has tropical greenhouses, Bog Garden and Rock Garden.

Museum of the History of Science - Oxford
Changing exhibitions featuring famous scientists or discoveries throughout history.

The Bodleian Library - Oxford
This is the main research library of the University of Oxford. It is also a copyright deposit library and its collections are used by scholars from around the world. Other buildings within the site include Duke Humfrey's Library above the Divinity School, the Old Schools Quadrangle with its Great Gate and Tower, the Radcliffe Camera & Britain's first circular library. The Library and the Radcliffe Camera are open Mondays – Fridays in term time.

Sheldonian Theatre - Oxford
Built in 1668 from a design created by Christopher Wren. It was named after Gilbert Sheldon, who was Chancellor of the University at the time the construction was funded. It is now used for music recitals and various University ceremonies.

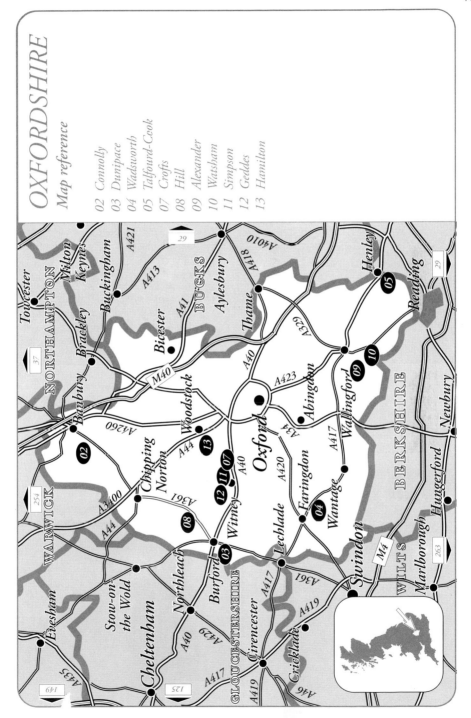

OXFORDSHIRE
Map reference

02 Connolly
03 Dunipace
04 Wadsworth
05 Talfourd-Cook
07 Crofts
08 Hill
09 Alexander
10 Watsham
11 Simpson
12 Geddes
13 Hamilton

The Craven
Fernham Road Uffington Faringdon SN7 7RD
Tel:(01367) 820449 Fax 01367 820351
email:carol@thecraven.co.uk www.thecraven.co.uk

see p.192

Andy Marshall & Sharon Connolly
The Mill House North Newington Road
North Newington Banbury OX15 6AA Oxfordshire
Tel: (01295) 730212 Fax 01295 730363

Near Rd: A.361, B.4035
Referred to in Shakespeare's Henry VI, this peaceful, rurally situated 17th century former mill house, is where husband & wife, Andrew & Sharon, offer a warm welcome to their guests. 3 comfortable en-suite rooms & 4 superbly renovated courtyard cottages are available on a B & B or self-catering basis. Well located for the Cotswolds, Stratford-upon-Avon, Oxford & Blenheim Palace. Good local pubs & restaurants offering evening meals. Attractive lounge & beautiful gardens for guests use. Licensed honesty bar. Ample off road parking.

lamadonett@aol.com www.themillhousebanbury.co.uk
£79.00 - £112.00 Open: all year (excl. xmas)
Map ref no. 02

Mrs Carol Wadsworth
The Craven Fernham Road Uffington
Faringdon SN7 7RD Oxfordshire
Tel: (01367) 820449 Fax 01367 820351

Near Rd: A.420
Roses & clematis cover this pretty 17th-century thatched cottage where breakfast is served around the huge pine table in the farmhouse kitchen. The beautiful beamed bedrooms have lovely views. One of the bedrooms has a 17th-century 4-poster bed with cabbage rose chintz drapes &, as with all bedrooms, hand-embroidered sheets & pillow slips. Daughter, Katie, produces excellent meals using as much local produce as possible. There are glorious walks from the doorstep & a shaggy Old English sheepdog. The Craven is a delightful home.

carol@thecraven.co.uk www.thecraven.co.uk
£70.00 - £95.00 Open: all year
Map ref no. 04

see p.194

Robin & Clare Dunipace
The Glebe House Westwell Burford OX18 4JT
Oxfordshire
Tel: (01993) 822171 Fax 01993 824125

Near Rd: A.40
The Glebe House is a pretty 18th-century Cotswold farmhouse on the edge of the beautiful quiet village of Westwell, 2 miles from historic Burford, with views over open countryside. Offering 2 double rooms, each with private bathroom. Also, an elegantly furnished sitting room & a terrace in the secluded garden. Ideally located for Oxford, Blenheim Palace, Bath, Cirencester, Cheltenham & Stratford. Enjoy a warm welcome, relaxed comfort & delicious food. French spoken. Self-catering option.

clare.dunipace@amserve.net
www.oxford-cotswold-holidays.com £70.00 - £80.00
Open: all year Map ref no. 03

Mr & Mrs Brian Talfourd-Cook
Holmwood Shiplake Row Binfield Heath
Henley RG9 4DP Oxfordshire
Tel: (0118) 9478747 Fax 0118 9478637

Near Rd: A.4155
Holmwood is a large elegant Georgian country house, Grade II listed, furnished with antique, period furniture. There is a galleried hall, carved mahogany doors & marble fireplaces (wood fires in winter). All bedrooms are spacious & have en-suite facilities. The beautiful gardens extend to 3 1/2 acres & have extensive views over the Thames Valley. A good base for London & the South East. Heathrow Airport 30 mins', Reading 4 miles, Henley 2 1/2 miles. Children over 12 years.

wendy.cook@freenet.co.uk www.holmwoodbandb.co.uk
£70.00 - £70.00 Open: all year (excl. xmas)
Map ref no. 05

Holmwood

Shiplake Row Binfield Heath Henley RG9 4DP

Tel:(0118) 9478747 Fax 0118 9478637

email:wendy.cook@freenet.co.uk www.holmwoodbandb.co.uk

Jean A. Crofts
Crofters Guest House   29 Oxford Hill   Witney
Oxford OX28 3JU Oxfordshire
Tel: (01993) 778165   Fax 01993 778165

Near Rd: A.40
Crofters Guest House is situated in a lively market town, 10 miles from the historic city of Oxford, on the edge of the glorious Cotswolds, Blenheim Palace & Burford, & within easy reach of Stratford-upon-Avon. Guests are accommodated in tastefully decorated, comfortable family, double & twin bedrooms, all well-equipped with excellent facilities. En-suite & luxury ground-floor garden rooms are available. A delicious breakfast is served. Your hosts Jean & Peter will make your stay a memorable experience. Arrive as a guest, leave as a friend.

crofters.ghouse@virgin.net
£50.00 - £60.00 Open: all year
Map ref no. 07

Mrs Joanna Alexander
The Well Cottage Caps Lane Cholsey Wallingford
OX10 9HQ Oxfordshire Tel: (01491) 651959
Mobile 07887 958920 Fax 01491 651675

Near Rd: A.329
The Well Cottage is situated in a pretty garden, close to the River Thames, the historic town of Wallingford, the Berkshire Downs & the Ridgway. The cottage has been extended & now offers a secluded garden flat with 2 twin-bedded rooms, each with a private bathroom, T.V. & tea/coffee-making facilities. Each room is beautifully furnished & also has the added bonus of its own private entrance. This is a most charming home for a relaxing break. The Well Cottage is also within easy reach of Oxford & Henley-on-Thames. Single occupancy supplement.

joanna@thewellcottage.com   www.thewellcottage.com
£40.00 - £70.00 Open: all year
Map ref no. 09

see p.196

Veronica Hill
Shipton Grange House   Shipton-under-Wychwood
OX7 6DG   Oxfordshire
Tel: (01993) 831298 Fax 01993 832082

Near Rd: A.361
A unique conversion of a Georgian coach house & stabling situated in the former grounds of Shipton Court. Secluded in its own walled garden, & approached by a gated archway. There are 3 elegantly furnished guest rooms, each with an en-suite/private bathroom, colour T.V. & beverage facilities. Delicious breakfasts served in the attractive dining room. The friendly hosts are animal lovers & have a number of pet dogs. Shipton Grange is a delightful house, & ideal for visiting Oxford, Blenheim, etc. Children over 12 years welcome.

veronica@shiptongrangehouse.com
www.shiptongrangehouse.com   £70.00 - £80.00
Open: all year (excl. xmas) Map ref no. 08

Mrs Maria Watsham
White House Moulsford Wallingford OX10 9JD
Oxfordshire
Tel: (01491) 651397   Fax 01491 652560

Near Rd: A.329
White House is an attractive, detached family home in the picturesque Thameside village of Moulsford on the edge of the Berkshire Downs, close to the Ridgeway & Thames Paths. The accommodation is at ground-floor level with its own separate front door, making access easy for disabled guests. A suite consisting of 1 to 3 bedrooms plus bathroom is available. Offering exclusive occupancy for a couple, group of friends or a family. (Single occupancy from £40.) There is a large garden with croquet lawn, which guests are welcome to enjoy. A delightful home.

mwatsham@tiscali.co.uk www.stayatwhitehouse.co.uk
£60.00 - £60.00 Open: all year (excl. xmas & new year)
Map ref no. 10

Shipton Grange House

Shipton-under-Wychwood OX7 6DG

Tel:(01993) 831298 Fax 01993 832082

email:veronica@shiptongrangehouse.com www.shiptongrangehouse.com

Liz & John Simpson
Field View   Wood Green   Witney OX28 1DE
Oxfordshire
Tel: (01993) 705485   Mobile 07768 614347

Near Rd: A.40
An attractive Cotswold stone house set in 2 acres, situated
on picturesque Wood Green, mid-way between Oxford
University & the Cotswolds. It is an ideal base for touring
& yet is only 8 minutes' walk from the centre of the lively
market town of Witney. A peaceful setting & a warm, friendly
atmosphere await you. The accommodation offered is in
3 comfortable en-suite rooms with all modern amenities,
including tea/coffee-making facilities, colour T.V., radio &
hairdryer.   Capture the quiet of the countryside within
walking distance of the town centre.

bandb@fieldview-witney.co.uk
www.fieldview-witney.co.uk £56.00 - £62.00
Open: all year (excl.xmas & new year)   Map ref no. 11

Mr & Mrs N. Hamilton
Gorselands Hall   Boddington Lane   North Leigh
Witney OX29 6PU Oxfordshire
Tel: (01993) 882292   Fax 01993 883629

Near Rd: A.4095
Gorselands Hall is a lovely old Cotswold stone country
house with oak beams & flagstone floors in a delightful
rural setting, convenient for Oxford (8 miles), Blenheim
Palace (4 miles), the Roman Villa at East End & many of
the lovely Cotswold villages. The accommodation includes
6 attractively furnished en-suite bedrooms, a comfortable
guest sitting room & a large secluded garden with a grass
tennis court. This is very good walking country & there is a
wide choice of excellent eating places within easy reach.
Dogs by arrangement.

hamilton@gorselandshall.com
www.gorselandshall.com £50.00 - £60.00
Open: all year   Map ref no. 13

Bridget Geddes
The Garden House of The Old Vicarage   Minster Lovell
Witney OX29 0RR Oxfordshire
Tel: (01993) 775630   Fax 01993 772534

Near Rd: A.40
Built in the 19th century, the River Windrush trickles through
the garden & the church & ruins of Minster Lovell Hall stand
close by. The Garden House is ideal for a self-catering
arrangement, it is a self-contained cottage on one level
with French windows looking on to the orchard, the use of
which goes with the cottage. Breakfast fixings are provided
for you to take at your leisure. The village pub is within
walking distance. An easy drive from Stratford, Buford,
Cirencester & historic Oxford. A wonderful location for
exploring the Cotswolds .

bridgetgeddes@tiscali.co.uk   www.bestbandb.co.uk
£75.00 - £75.00 Open: all year
Map ref no. 12

Shropshire

Shropshire

Shropshire is a borderland with a very turbulent history. Physically it straddles highlands & lowlands with border mountains to the west, glacial plains, upland, moorlands & fertile valleys & the River Severn cutting through. It has been quarrelled & fought over by rulers & kings from earliest times. The English, the Romans & the Welsh all wanted to hold Shropshire because of its unique situation. The ruined castles & fortifications dotted across the county are all reminders of its troubled life. The most impressive of these defences is Offa's Dyke, an enormous undertaking intended to be a permanent frontier between England & Wales.

Shropshire has great natural beauty, countryside where little has changed with the years. Wenlock Edge & Clun Forest, Carding Mill Valley, the Long Mynd, Caer Caradoc, Stiperstones & the trail along Offa's Dyke itself, are lovely walking areas with magnificent scenery.

Shrewsbury was & is a virtual island, almost completely encircled by the Severn River. The castle was built at the only gap, sealing off the town. In this way all comings & goings were strictly controlled. In the 18th century two bridges, the English bridge & the Welsh bridge, were built to carry the increasing traffic to the town but Shrewsbury still remains England's finest Tudor city.

Massive Ludlow Castle was a Royal residence, home of Kings & Queens through the ages, whilst the town is also noted for its Georgian houses.

As order came out of chaos, the county settled to improving itself & became the cradle of the Industrial Revolution. Here Abraham Darby discovered how to use coke (from the locally mined coal) to smelt iron. There was more iron produced here in the 18th century than in any other county. A variety of great industries sprang up as the county's wealth & ingenuity increased. In 1781 the world's first iron bridge opened to traffic.

There are many fine gardens in the county. At Hodnet Hall near Market Drayton, the grounds cover 60 acres & the landscaping includes lakes & pools, trees, shrubs & flowers in profusion.

Stokesay Castle. Craven Arms.

Shropshire

Shropshire Gazeteer
Areas of Outstanding Natural Beauty.
The Shropshire Hills.

Historic Houses & Castles
Stokesay Castle - Craven Arms
13th century fortified manor house. Still occupied - wonderful setting - extremely well preserved. Fine timbered gatehouse.
Weston Park - Nr. Shifnal
17th century - fine example of Restoration period - landscaping by Capability Brown. Superb collection of pictures.
Shrewsbury Castle - Shrewsbury
Built in Norman era - interior decorations - painted boudoir.
Benthall Hall - Much Wenlock
16th century. Stone House - mullioned windows. Fine wooden staircase - splendid plaster ceilings.
Shipton Hall - Much Wenlock
Elizabethan Manor House - walled garden - medieval dovecote.
Upton Cressett Hall - Bridgnorth
Elizabethan. Manor House & Gatehouse. Excellent plaster work. 14th century great hall.

Cathedrals & Churches
Ludlow (St. Lawrence)
14th century nave & transepts. 15th century pinnacled tower. Restored extensively in 19th century. Carved choir stalls, perpendicular chancel - original glass. Monuments.
Shrewsbury (St. Mary)
14th, 15th, 16th century glass. Norman origins.
Stottesdon (St. Mary)
12th century carvings.Norman font. Fine decorations with columns & tracery.
Lydbury North (St. Michael)
14th C. transept, 15th century nave roof, 17th C. box pews and altar rails. Norman font.
Longor (St. Mary the Virgin)
13th C. with an outer staircase to West gallery.
Cheswardine (St. Swithun)

13th century chapel - largely early English. 19th century glass and old brasses. Fine sculpture.
Tong (St. Mary the Virgin with St. Bartholomew)
15th century. Golden chapel of 1515, stencilled walls, remains of paintings on screens, gilt fan vaulted ceiling. Effigies, fine monuments.

Museums & Galleries
Clive House - Shrewsbury
Fine Georgian House - collection of Shropshire ceramics. Regimental museum of 1st Queen's Dragoon Guards.
Rowley's House Museum - Shrewsbury
Roman material from Viroconium and prehistoric collection.
Coleham Pumping Station - Old Coleham
Preserved beam engines.
Acton Scott Working Farm Museum - Nr. Church Stretton
Site showing agricultural practice before the advent of mechanization.
Ironbridge Gorge Museum - Telford
Series of industrial sites in the Severn Gorge.
Coal Brookdale Museum & Furnace Site
Showing Abraham Darby's blast furnace history. Ironbridge information centre is next to the world's first iron bridge.
Mortimer Forest Museum - Nr. Ludlow
Forest industries of today and yesterday. Ecology of the forest.
Whitehouse Museum of Buildings & Country life - Aston Munslow
4 houses together in one, drawing from every century 13th to 18th, together with utensils and implements of the time.
The Buttercross Museum - Ludlow
Geology, natural & local history of area.
Reader's House - Ludlow
Splendid example of a 16th century town house. 3 storied porch.
Much Wenlock Museum - Much Wenlock
Geology, natural & local history.
Clun Town Museum - Clun

Shropshire

Pre-history earthworks, rights of way.

Historic Monuments

Acton Burnell Castle - Shrewsbury
13th century fortified manor house - ruins only.

Boscobel House - Shifnal
17th century house.

Bear Steps - Shrewsbury
Half timbered buildings. Medieval.

Abbot's House - Shrewsbury
15th century half-timbered.

Buildwas Abbey - Nr. Telford
12th C.- Savignac Abbey - ruins. The church is nearly complete with 14 Norman arches.

Haughmond Abbey - Shrewsbury
12th C.- remains of house of Augustinian canons.

Wenlock Priory - Much Wenlock
13th century abbey - ruins.

Roman Town - Wroxeter
2nd century - remains of town of Viroconium including public baths and colonnade.

Moreton Corbet Castle - Moreton Corbet
13th century keep, Elizabethan features - gatehouse altered 1519.

Lilleshall Abbey
12th century - completed 13th century, West front has notable doorway.

Bridgnorth Castle - Bridgnorth
Ruins of Norman castle whose angle of incline is greater than Pisa.

Whiteladies Priory - Boscobel
12th century cruciform church - ruins.

Old Oswestry - Oswestry
Iron age hill fort covering 68 acres; five ramparts and having an elaborate western portal.

Other things to see & do

Ludlow Festival of Art and Drama - Ludlow
Annual event.

Shrewsbury Flower Show
Every August.

Severn Valley Railway
The longest full guage steam railway in the country.

Hawkstone Park & Follies - Weston-under-Redcastle
England's "most romantic parkland". Cross the Swiss bridge over the Chasm to the thatched Gingerbread Hall. See a dozen counties from the top of the Monument.

Mitchells Fold Stone Circle - Nr. Chirbury
It sits high in the Shropshire hills, on the long ridge of Stapeley Hill, 1000 feet above sea level and close to the Welsh border. Its exposed position gives fine views of the Stiperstones to the east and the Welsh hills to the west.

Mythstories Museum of Myth & Fable - Wem
Brings Shropshire's many legends to life. You can trace the threads of legends across the centuries and you'll thrill to the power of the spoken word at poetry and storytelling events.

Nesscliffe Hill & Humphrey Kynaston's Cave - Nesscliffe
Humphrey Kynaston - Shropshire's answer to Robin Hood. He hid in a cave on Nesscliffe Hill having been outlawed in 1491. In the pine and rhododendron covered hillside you will come to the red sandstone cliff in which Kynaston's cave is cut into the cliff face.

Offa's Dyke - Nr. Oswestry
Offa's Dyke was constructed in the late eighth century on the orders of King Offa. The Dyke is the longest archaeological monument in Britain. The Dyke was originally constructed to mark the boundary between the Kingdom of Mercia and the Welsh Kingdoms to the west; probably intended to serve as a means of regulating access to and from Wales and today lengths of the Dyke form part of the National boundary between England and Wales.

Old Oswestry Hillfort - Oswestry
The Old Oswestry, the most spectacular of Shropshire's hill forts, known as Caer Ogyrfan after King Arthur's father in law, is said to be the birthplace of Queen Guinevere. It is also believed to have been the site for the final battle of the Powys King Cynddylan, the last descendant of King Arthur to rule in Shropshire.

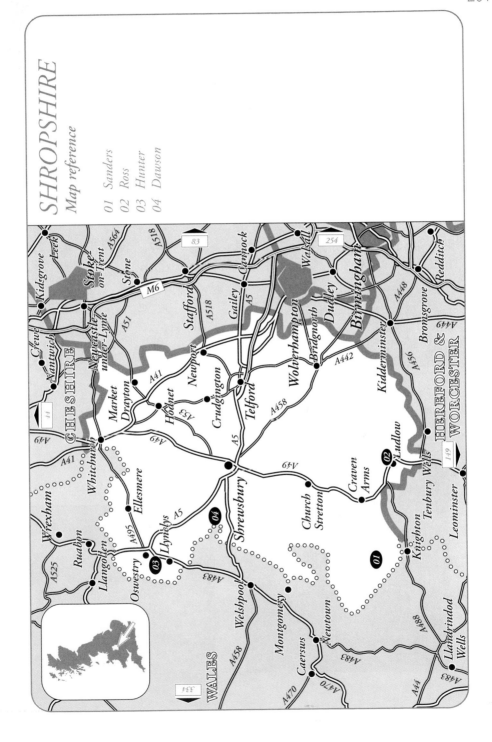

SHROPSHIRE

Map reference

01 Sanders
02 Ross
03 Hunter
04 Dawson

Bromley Court B & B

73/74 Lower Broad Street Ludlow SY8 1PH

Tel:(01584) 876996 Reservations 0845 0656192

email:patricia@ludlowhotels.com www.ludlowhotels.com

see p.204

Mrs Maureen Sanders
Cottage Farm   Clunton   Nr. Craven Arms SY7 0HZ
Shropshire
Tel: (01588) 660555

Near Rd: A.49
Clunton is a small village on the B.4368 between Ludlow & Clun in the beautiful Clun Valley, with superb landscapes & numerous public footpaths. Cottage Farm, which dates back 400 years, has many exposed timbers & stonewalls, which, along with roaring log fires in winter, help to create a wonderful ambience. Maureen Sanders, who enjoys cooking, will provide a 3-course evening meal by arrangement. There are 3 bedrooms (each with tea/coffee facilities) decorated in true country style - 2 doubles (1 en-suite). Plus, a single @ £26.50. Within easy reach of Ludlow & Clun & Stokesay Castles. Children over 12.

bestbandb@hotmail.com   www.bestbandb.co.uk
£51.00 - £55.00   Open: all year (excl. xmas)
Map ref no. 01

Miles Hunter
Pen-Y-Dyffryn Hotel   Rhydycroesau
Oswestry SY10 7JD   Shropshire
Tel: (01691) 653700Fax 01978 211004

Near Rd: A.5
Set almost a thousand feet up in the peaceful Shropshire/ Wales border hills, this silver-stone Georgian rectory has a real 'away from it all' atmosphere. But the historic medieval towns of Chester & Shrewsbury are only a short drive, so civilisation is close by. High-quality local food is served in the restaurant, which is complete with its own log fire. Each of the attractive & tastefully furnished bedrooms is en-suite, with colour T.V., telephone, tea/coffee-making facilities etc. & some even have their own private patios & spa baths. Fully licensed. The hotel is set in excellent walking country. Children over 3 years are welcome.

stay@peny.co.uk   www.peny.co.uk
£106.00 - £152.00   Open: all year (excl. jan 1-24)
Map ref no. 03

see p.202

Patricia & Philip Ross
Bromley Court B & B   73/74 Lower Broad Street
Ludlow SY8 1PH Shropshire
Tel: (01584) 876996   Reservations 0845 0656192

Near Rd: A.49, B.4361
A warm welcome awaits in any of the 3 immaculately furnished & maintained Tudor suites, which open onto a secluded courtyard garden. Take the included Continental breakfast in suite or garden, or enjoy a full English in the breakfast room. This award-winning property is renowned for close attention to detail & provision of many thoughtful extras. Patricia & Philip were seasoned travellers; until they found lovely gourmet Ludlow & Bromley Court. Whitcliffe Common, looking out over town, castle, church, Wenlock Edge & Corvedale is but a step away from your front door.

patricia@ludlowhotels.com   www.ludlowhotels.com
£105.00 - £115.00   Open: all year
Map ref no. 02

Mrs Elizabeth Dawson
Brimford House   Criggion   Shrewsbury SY5 9AU
Shropshire
Tel: (01938) 570235

Near Rd: A.458
Relax & unwind in this elegant Grade II listed Georgian farmhouse, set in tranquil, scenic countryside with breathtaking views of the Shropshire/Welsh border. Take a romantic break with wonderful walks & wildlife; log fires & stylish spacious bedrooms (all en-suite). Farmhouse breakfast served with free range eggs & home-made preserves. Country pub 3 mins' walk or try some of the excellent pubs & restaurants in the area. Private fishing. Shrewsbury & Welshpool only 15 mins' drive. Animals by arrangement.

info@brimford.co.uk www.brimford.co.uk
£55.00 - £65.00   Open: all year
Map ref no. 04

Pen-Y-Dyffryn Hotel

Rhydycroesau Oswestry SY10 7JD

Tel:(01691) 653700 Fax 01978 211004

email:stay@peny.co.uk www.peny.co.uk

Somerset

Somerset

Fabulous legends, ancient customs, charming villages, beautiful churches, breathtaking scenery & a glorious cathedral, Somerset has them all, along with a distinctively rich local dialect. The essence of Somerset lies in its history & myth & particularly in the unfolding of the Arthurian tale.

Legend grows from the bringing of the Holy Grail to Glastonbury by Joseph of Arimathea, to King Arthur's castle at Camelot, held by many to be sited at Cadbury, to the image of the dead King's barge moving silently through the mists over the lake to the Isle of Avalon. Archaeological fact lends support to the conjecture that Glastonbury, with its famous Tor, was an island in an ancient lake. Another island story surrounds King Alfred, reputedly sheltering from the Danes on the Isle of Athelney & there burning his cakes.

Historically, Somerset saw the last battle fought on English soil, at Sedgemoor in 1685. The defeat of the Monmouth rebellion resulted in the wrath of James II falling on the West Country in the form of Judge Jeffreys & his "Bloody Assize".

To the west of the county lies part of the Exmoor National Park, with high moorland where deer roam & buzzards soar & a wonderful stretch of cliffs from Minehead to Devon. Dunster is a popular village with its octagonal Yarn market, & its old world cottages, dominated at one end by the castle & at the other by the tower on Conygar Hill.

To the east the woods & moors of the Quantocks are protected as an area of outstanding natural beauty. The Vale of Taunton is famous for its apple orchards & for the golden cider produced from them.

The south of the county is a land of rolling countryside & charming little towns, Chard, Crewkerne, Ilchester & Ilminster amongst others.

To the north the limestone hills of Mendip are honeycombed with spectacular caves & gorges, some with neolithic remains, as at Wookey Hole & Cheddar Gorge.

Wells is nearby, so named because of the

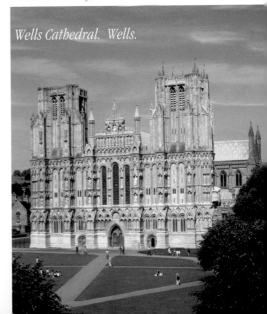

Wells Cathedral. Wells.

Somerset

multitude of natural springs. Hardly a city, Wells boasts a magnificent cathedral set amongst spacious lawns & trees. The west front is one of the glories of English architecture with its sculptured figures & soaring arches. A spectacular feature is the astronomical clock, the work of 14th century monk Peter Lightfoot. The intricate face tells the hours, minutes, days & phases of the moon. On the hour, four mounted knights charge forth & knock one another from their horses.

Bath is one of the most loved historic cities in England. It owes its existence to the hot springs which bubble up five hundred thousand gallons of water a day at a temperature of some 120' F. According to legend, King Bladud appreciated the healing qualities of the waters & established his capital here, calling it Aquae Sulis. He built an elaborate healing & entertainment centre around the springs including reservoirs, baths & hypercaust rooms.

The Roman Baths, not uncovered until modern times, are on the lowest of three levels. Above them came the mediaeval city & on the top layer at modern street level is the elegant Georgian Pump Room.

Edward was crowned the first King of all England in 973, in the Saxon Abbey which stood on the site of the present fifteenth century abbey. This building, in the graceful perpendicular style with elegant fan vaulting, is sometimes called the "lantern of the West", on account of its vast clerestories & large areas of glass.

During the Middle Ages the town prospered through Royal patronage & the development of the wool industry. Bath became a city of weavers, the leading industrial town in the West of England.

The 18th century gave us the superb Georgian architecture which is the city's glory. John Wood, an ambitious young architect laid out Queen Anne's Square in the grand Palladian style, & went on to produce his masterpiece, the Royal Crescent. His scheme for the city was continued by his son & a number of other fine architects, using the beautiful Bath stone. Bath was a centre of fashion, with Beau Nash the leader of a glittering society.

In 1497 John & Sebastian Cabot sailed from the Bristol quayside to the land they called Ameryke, in honour of the King's agent in Bristol, Richard Ameryke. Bristol's involvement in the colonisation of the New World & the trade in sugar, tobacco & slaves that followed, made her the second city in the kingdom in the 18th century. John Cabot is commemorated by the Cabot Tower on grassy Brandon Hill - a fine vantage point for viewing the city.

On the old docks below are the Bristol Industrial Museum & the SS Great Britain, Brunel's famous iron ship. Another achievement of this master engineer, the Clifton Suspension Bridge, spans Bristol's renowned beauty spot, the Clifton Gorge.

Somerset

Somerset Gazeteer

Areas of Outstanding Natural Beauty.
Mendip Hills. Quantock Hills. National Park -
Exmoor. The Cotswolds.

Historic Houses & Castles

Abbot's Fish House - Meare
14th century house.

Barrington Court - Illminster
16th century house & gardens.

Blaise Castle House - Henbury Nr. Bristol
18th century house - now folk museum,
extensive woodlands.

Brympton D'Evercy - Nr. Yeovil
Mansion with 17th century front & Tudor west
front. Adjacent is 13th century priest's house &
church. Formal gardens & vineyard.

Claverton Manor - Nr. Bath
Greek revival house - furnished with 17th, 18th,
19th century American originals.

Clevedon Court - Clevedon
14th century manor house, 13th century hall,
12th century tower. Lovely garden with rare
trees & shrubs. This is where Thackerey wrote
much of 'Vanity Fair'.

Dyrham Park - Between Bristol & Bath
17th century house - fine panelled rooms,
Dutch paintings, furniture.

Dunster Castle - Dunster
13th century castle with fine 17th century
staircase & ceilings.

East Lambrook Manor - South Petherton
15th century house with good panelling.

Gaulden Manor - Tolland
12th century manor. Great Hall having unique
plaster ceiling & oak screen. Antique furniture.

Halsway Manor - Crowcombe
14th century house with fine panelling.

Hatch Court - Hatch Beauchamp
Georgian house in the Palladian style with
China room.

King John's Hunting Lodge - Axbridge
Early Tudor merchant's house.

Lytes Carry - Somerton

14th & 15th century manor house with a chapel
& formal garden.

Montacute House - Yeovil
Elizabethan house with fine examples of
Heraldic Glass, tapestries, panelling & furniture.
Portrait gallery of Elizabethan & Jacobean paintings.

Tintinhull House - Yeovil
17th century house with beautiful gardens.

Priory Park College Bath
18th century Georgian mansion, now Roman
Catholic school.

No. 1 Royal Crescent - Bath
An unaltered Georgian house built 1767.

Red Lodge - Bristol
16th C. house - period furniture & panelling.

St. Vincent's Priory - Bristol
Gothic revival house, built over caves which
were sanctuary for Christians.

St Catherine's Court - Nr. Bath
Small Tudor house - associations with Henry VIII
& Elizabeth I.

Cathedrals & Churches

Axbridge (St. John)

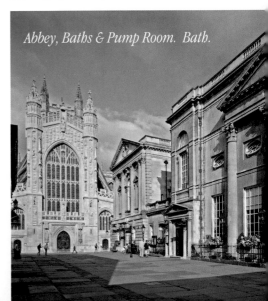

Abbey, Baths & Pump Room. Bath.

Somerset

1636 plaster ceiling & panelled roofs.

Backwell (St. Andrew)
12th to 17th C., 15th C. tower, repaired 17th C..
15th C. tomb & chancel, 16th C. screen, 18th C.
brass chandelier.

Bath Abbey
Perpendicular - monastic church, 15th century
foundation. Nave finished 17th century,
restorations in 1674.

Bishop's Lydeard (St. Mary)
15th C. Notable tower, rood screen & glass.

Bristol Cathedral
Medieval. Eastern halfnave Victorian.
Chapterhouse richly ornamented. Iron screen,
3 fonts.

Bristol (St. Mary Redcliffe)
"fairest parish church in all England".Elizabeth I.

Bristol (St. Stephens')
Perpendicular - monuments, magnificent tower.

Bruton (St. Mary)
Fine 2 towered 15th century church. Georgian
chancel, tie beam roof, Georgian reredos.
Jacobean screen. 15th century embroidery.

Chewton Mendip (St. Mary Magdalene)
12th century with later additions. 12th century
doorway, 15th century bench ends, magnificent
16th century tower & 17th century lecturn.

Crewkerne (St. Bartholomew)
Magnificent west front & roofs, 15th & 16th
century. South doorway dating from 13th
century, wonderful 15th century painted glass &
18th century chandeliers.

East Brent (St. Mary)
Mainly 15th century. Plaster ceiling, painted
glass & carved bench ends.

Glastonbury (St. John)
One of the finest examples of perpendicular
towers. Tie beam roof, late medieval painted
glass, medieval vestment & early 16th century
altar tomb.

High Ham (St. Andrew)
Sumptuous roofs & vaulted rood screen.
Carved bench ends. Jacobean lecturn,
medieval painted glass. Norman font.

Kingsbury Episcopi (St. Martin)
14th-15th century. Good tower with fan vaulting.
Late medieval painted glass.

Long Sutton (Holy Trinity)
15th century with noble tower & magnificent tie
beam roof. 15th century pulpit & rood screen,
tower vaulting.

Martock (All Saints)
13th C. chancel. Nave with tie beam roof,
outstanding of its kind.17th C. paintings of Apostles

North Cadbury (St. Michael)
Painted glass.

Pilton (St. John)
12th century with arcades. 15th century roofs.

Taunton (St. Mary Magdalene)
Highest towers in the county. Five nave roof,
fragments of medieval painted glass.

Trull (All Saints)
15th century with many medieval art treasures.

Wells Cathedral - Wells
Magnificent west front with carved figures.
Splendid tower. Early English arcade of nave &
transepts. 60 fine misericords c.1330. Lady
chapel with glass & star vault. Chapter House &
Bishop's Palace.

Weston Zoyland (St. Mary)
15th century bench ends. 16th century heraldic
glass. Jacobean pulpit.

Wrington (All Souls)
15th century aisles & nave; font, stone pulpit,
notable screens.

Museums & Galleries

Admiral Blake Museum - Bridgewater
Exhibits relating to Battle of Sedgemoor,
archaeology.

American Museum in Britain - Claverton
American decorative arts 17th-19th C.displayed
in series of furnished rooms & galleries of
special exhibits. Paintings, furniture, glass wood
& metal work, textiles, folk sculpture, etc.

Borough Museum - Hendford Manor Hall
Archaeology, firearms collections & Bailward
Costume Collection.

Somerset

Bristol Industrial Museum - Bristol
Collections of transport items of land, sea & air. Many unique items.

Burdon Manor - Washford
14th century manor house with Saxon fireplace & cockpit.

City of Bristol Art Gallery - Bristol
Permanent & loan collections of paintings, English & Oriental ceramics.

Glastonbury Lake Village Museum - Glastonbury
Late prehistoric antiquities.

Gough's Cave Museum - Cheddar
Upper Paleolithic remains, skeleton, flints, amber & engraved stones.

Holburne of Menstrie Museum - Bath
Old Master paintings, silver, glass, porcelain, furniture & miniatures in 18th century building. Work of 20th century craftworkers.

Hinton Priory - Hinton Charterhouse
13th century - ruins of Carthusian priory.

Kings Weston Roman Villa - Lawrence Weston
3rd & 4th C. - mosaics of villa - some walls.

Museum of Costume - Bath
Collection of fashion from17th C. to present day.

Roman Baths - Bath
Roman Museum - Bath
Material from remains of extensive Roman baths & other Roman sites.

Stoney Littleton Barrow - Nr. Bath
Neolithic burial chamber - restoration work 1858.

St. Nicholas Church & City Museum - Bristol
Medieval antiquities relating to local history, Church plate & vestments. Altar-piece by Hogarth.

Temple Church - Bristol
14th & 15th century ruins.

Victoria Art Gallery - Bath
Paintings, prints, drawings, glass, ceramics, watches, coins, etc. Bygones - permanent & temporary exhibitions. Geology collections.

Wookey Hole Cave Museum - Wookey Hole
Remains from Pliocene period. Relics of Celtic & Roman civilization. Exhibition of handmade paper-making.

Historic Monuments

Cleeve Abbey - Cleeve
Ruined 13th century house, with timber roof & wall paintings.

Farleigh Castle - Farleigh Hungerford
14th century remains - museums in chapel.

Glastonbury Abbey - Glastonbury
12th & 13th century ruins of St. Joseph's chapel & Abbot's kitchen.

Muchelney Abbey - Muchelney
15th century ruins of Benedictine abbey.

Other things to see & do

Black Rock Nature Reserve - Cheddar
Circular walk through plantation woodland, downland grazing.

Cheddar Caves
Show caves at the foot of beautiful Cheddar Gorge.

Clifton Zoological Gardens - Bristol
Flourishing zoo with many interesting exhibits and beautiful gardens.

Royal Crescent. Bath.

SOMERSET, BATH & BRISTOL

Map reference

01 John	07 Hill
01 Williams	08 Deacon
01 Greenwood	09 Nurcombe
01 Besley	10 Bale
01 Potter	11 Mott
01 Close	13 Redmond
01 Beckett	14 Knight
01 Huxley	15 Copeland
01 Lanz	16 Orr
02 Tiley	17 Mitchem
04 Priddle	18 Green
04 Rhys-Roberts	19 Frost
05 Jones	20 Nowell
06 Riley	21 Read

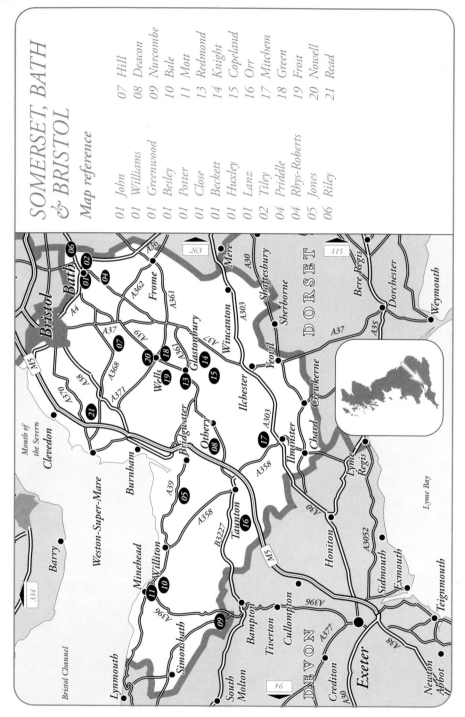

Judy John
Tolley Cottage 23 Sydney Buildings Bath BA2 6BZ
Somerset
Tel: (01225) 463365

Near Rd: A.4
Tolley Cottage, Bath is an elegant Victorian house in a unique & idyllic setting on the Kennet & Avon Canal, yet only a 10 min walk from Bath city centre. The double & twin bedded rooms, both with en suite bathrooms, provide luxurious & stylish accommodation. The furnishings are sophisticated, the art fascinating & the attention to detail ensures guests have a memorable stay. In summer, breakfast is served in the garden overlooking the canal. The breakfast menu includes local organic food when possible. Free parking. Historic sites, museums, shops, galleries & wonderful restaurants are an easy walk away.

jj@judyj.plus.com www.tolleycottage.com
£65.00 - £95.00 Open: all year (excl.xmas & new year)
Map ref no. 01

David & Caroline Greenwood
Number 30 Crescent Gardens Bath BA1 2NB
Somerset
Tel: (01225) 337393 Fax 01225 337393

Near Rd: A.4
Number Thirty is a wonderful Victorian house situated within 5 mins' level walk of the city centre & Roman Baths, the Pump Room, Circus & Royal Crescent. Number Thirty has been completely refurbished & all rooms are light & airy. The bedrooms all have excellent en-suite bathrooms & are tastefully decorated mainly in blue & white. Each one is named after a famous person who has influenced the building or character of this wonderful city. Number Thirty is a charming home from which to explore this historic Bath. Private parking. Children over 12 years welcome.

david.greenwood12@btinternet.com
www.numberthirty.com £79.00 - £109.00
Open: all year Map ref no. 01

Louise Williams
Brocks 32 Brock Street Bath BA1 2LN
Somerset
Tel: (01225) 338374 Fax (01225) 334245

Near Rd: A.4
Brocks is a beautiful Georgian town house built in 1765 by John Wood, situated between the Circus and Royal Crescent. Very close to the Roman Baths, Assembly Rooms, etc. This really is a wonderful part of Bath. This historic house has all modern conveniences, & all of the comfortable & tastefully furnished bedrooms have en-suite facilities. The aim here is to offer guests the highest standards, and personal attention. Brocks is a delightful base from which to explore beautiful Bath.

brocks@brocksguesthouse.co.uk
www.brocksguesthouse.co.uk £72.00 - £90.00
Open: all year (excl.xmas & new year) Map ref no. 01

Chrissie Besley
The Old Red House 37 Newbridge Road
Bath BA1 3HE Somerset
Tel: (01225) 330464 Fax 01225 331661

Near Rd: A.4
This charming Victorian Gingerbread House is colourful, comfortable & warm; full of unexpected touches & intriguing little curiosities. Its leaded & stained glass windows are now double-glazed to ensure a peaceful stay. The extensive breakfast menu, a delight in itself, is served around a large family dining table. Parking is available. Special rates for 3 or more nights. Dinner available at a local riverside pub. A non-smoking home. Children over 5 years welcome.

orh@amserve.com www.oldredhouse.co.uk
£55.00 - £75.00 Open: feb - dec
Map ref no. 01

Cranleigh

159 Newbridge Hill Bath BA1 3PX

Tel:(01225) 310197 Fax 01225 423143

email:cranleigh@btinternet.com www.cranleighguesthouse.com

see p.212

Denise & Colin Potter
Cranleigh   159 Newbridge Hill   Bath BA1 3PX
Somerset
Tel: (01225) 310197   Fax 01225 423143

Near Rd: A.431
Cranleigh has 9 delightfully appointed rooms, all decorated & furnished in their own individual style with every comfort imaginable to ensure the enjoyment of your stay. The regal decor of the 4-poster room offers the perfect choice for a special occasion. Many of the rooms have views over the garden & Avon Valley & all have en-suite/private facilities, colour T.V., phone, radio/alarm, hairdryer & tea/coffee-making facilities. After a hard day visiting the historic sights in the city why not come & relax in the secluded garden with hot tub. Private parking. Licensed. Children over 4 years are welcome.

cranleigh@btinternet.com
www.cranleighguesthouse.com £60.00 - £95.00
Open: all year (excl. xmas)   Map ref no. 01

Derek & Maria Beckett
Cedar Lodge 13 Lambridge   London Road
Bath BA1 6BJ Somerset
Tel: (01225) 423468

Near Rd: A.4, A.46
Within easy level walk to the historic city centre, this beautiful, detached Georgian house offers period elegance with modern amenities. The accommodation includes 3 lovely bedrooms (1 with 4-poster, 1 half-tester, 1 twin), all with en-suite/private bathrooms. Delightful gardens & a comfortable drawing room, with fire, to relax in. A delicious breakfast is served. Cedar Lodge is ideally situated for excursions to Avebury, Stonehenge, Salisbury, Longleat, Wells, Cotswolds, Wales & many other attractions. Secure private parking. Children over 10 years. A very warm welcome awaits you from your most charming hosts.

www.bestbandb.co.uk
£65.00 - £80.00 Open: all year
Map ref no. 01

William & Fiona Close
Weston Lawn   Lucklands Road   Weston
Bath BA1 4AY Somerset
Tel: (01225) 421362

Near Rd: A.4
Welcome to this Georgian family house set in its own grounds complete with fossils & Roman remains. Approx. 1 mile from the centre of Bath & only yards from the Cotswold Way, this is a premium base for city visits, leaving your car on the drive & exploring the surrounding country. The 3 bedrooms carefully furnished for your relaxing stay & with colour T.V, & beverages, are en-suite or with private bathroom. Your breakfast choice is between an extravagant Continental or an Aga cooked English. Evening meals are available at the local pub.

reservations@westonlawn.co.uk
www.westonlawn.co.uk £40.00 - £80.00
Open: all year Map ref no. 01

George & Jane Riley
Dolphin House 8 Northend   Batheaston
Bath BA1 7EN Somerset Tel: (01225) 858915
Fax 01225 858915 Mobile 07801 444521

Near Rd: A.4
Dolphin House is a detached Georgian Grade II listed house with a mature terraced walled garden. Centrally heated & with period furnishings. There is a private suite consisting of a twin-bedded room, lounge & large bathroom. Also, a large double bedroom with private bathroom. T.V. & tea/coffee-making facilities in each room. All meals are served in the privacy of your own room or on the terrace. The historic city of Bath is only 2 1/2 miles away. Children over 12 years welcome.

georgeandjane@hotmail.com
www.dolphinhouse-bath.com £55.00 - £75.00
Open: all year Map ref no. 06

Lavender House

17 Bloomfield Park Bath BA2 2BY

Tel:(01225) 314500 Fax 01225 448564

email:lavenderhouse@btinternet.com www.lavenderhouse-bath.com

see p.214

Carol & Bill Huxley
Lavender House 17 Bloomfield Park Bath BA2 2BY
Somerset
Tel: (01225) 314500 Fax 01225 448564

Near Rd: A.367
Set in a quiet conservation area, within easy reach of Bath city centre. Lavender House is an Edwardian house which offers 5 lovely guest rooms. Each bedroom is individually designed & has a large, luxurious bathroom, colour T.V. & tea/coffee-making facilities. In addition to serving a delicious traditional English breakfast, using free-range & fresh local produce, there are special vegetarian Cordon Vert options. Lavender House is a special place to unwind, relax & be spoiled. Parking. Children over 8 years welcome at this elegant home.

lavenderhouse@btinternet.com
www.lavenderhouse-bath.com £80.00 - £98.00
Open: all year Map ref no. 01

Ian & Carolyn Tiley
Lindisfarne Guest House 41a Warminster Road
Bath BA2 6XJ Somerset
Tel: (01225) 466342

Near Rd: A.36
Your welcoming & knowledgeable hosts, Ian & Carolyn, invite you to enjoy their spacious & comfortable en suite rooms, some overlooking the pretty garden. There are 1 twin, 2 doubles & 1 triple room, all with colour T.V./DVD, refreshment trays & complimentary toiletries. Lindisfarne is easily accessible to Bath but away from the hustle & bustle of the city centre in the semi-rural environment of Bathampton. Good local eating places, & pleasant walks along the Kennet & Avon canal, within easy reach. Children over 8 years welcome.

lindisfarne-bath@talk21.com
www.bath.org/hotel/lindisfarne.htm £55.00 - £65.00
Open: all year (excl. xmas) Map ref no. 02

David & Annie Lanz
Paradise House Hotel 88 Holloway Bath BA2 4PX
Somerset
Tel: (01225) 317723 Fax 01225 482005

Near Rd: A.367
Paradise House was built in the 1720s, on the ancient Roman Fosse Way. The Fosse Way, now a cul-de-sac, is one of the quietest streets in Bath & provides easy access to the city centre. (The Roman Baths are only 7 mins' walk away.) There are 11 attractively furnished & well-appointed bedrooms, each with an en-suite bathroom & delightful 4-poster garden rooms with en-suite jacuzzi. Paradise House enjoys fine views over the Georgian city & has over 1/2 an acre of splendid walled gardens which compete with the golden splendour of the city below. A delightful home.

info@paradise-house.co.uk www.paradise-house.co.uk
£65.00 - £160.00 Open: all year (excl. xmas)
Map ref no. 01

see p.216

Sarah Priddle & John Webster
The Plaine Norton St. Philip Bath BA2 7LT
Somerset
Tel: (01373) 834723 Fax 01373 834101

Near Rd: A.366
The Plaine is a delightful listed building, dating from the 16th century & situated in the heart of an historic conservation village. The accommodation includes 3 beautiful & tastefully furnished en-suite rooms, all with 4-poster beds. Opposite is the famous George Inn - one of the oldest hostelries in England. Delicious breakfasts are prepared with local produce and free-range eggs. The Plaine is in a convenient location for Bath, Wells, Longleat and many beautiful Cotswold villages. Parking. Children over 3 years.

theplaine@easynet.co.uk www.theplaine.co.uk
£65.00 - £80.00 Open: all year (excl.xmas & new year)
Map ref no. 04

The Plaine

Norton St. Philip Bath BA2 7LT

Tel:(01373) 834723 Fax 01373 834101

email:theplaine@easynet.co.uk www.theplaine.co.uk

Mrs Angharad Rhys-Roberts
Honeybatch Cottage   Railway Lane   Wellow
Bath BA2 8QG Somerset
Tel: (01225) 833107

Near Rd: A.36
Honeybatch is a Grade II listed cottage in a beautiful village yet it is also close to Bath. The cottage retains many original features including flagstone floors, a bread oven & winding stairs. The large & attractive double bedroom has en-suite facilities & far-reaching views of the countryside. Peace & comfort abound & Angharad is an aromatherapist (treatments available by arrangement.) Breakfast is taken in the large farmhouse kitchen with Aga & terracotta tiles & is served at the cherrywood refectory table. Children, evening meals & animals by arrangement.

www.bestbandb.co.uk
£55.00 - £70.00   Open: all year
Map ref no. 04

Linda Hill
Harptree Court East Harptree   Nr. Bristol BS40 6AA
Somerset
Tel: (01761) 221729

Near Rd: A.368
A delightful, Grade II listed Georgian country house set in its own extensive parkland extending over 17 acres. Ideally situated for exploring Bath, Wells and Bristol and the Mendip Hills. Our elegant bedrooms are furnished with antiques and all have wonderful views of the gardens. All rooms have a TV with either a video or dvd player. There is large guest sitting room, but our complimentary cream tea can be taken either in front of a roaring fire in winter or outside in the sunshine. Linda's delicious meals are served in the candlelit dining room. Children over 12.

location.harptree@tiscali.co.uk
www.harptreecourt.co.uk   £80.00 - £80.00
Open: all year (excl. xmas)   Map ref no. 07

Mr Stacey & Ms Jones
Stowey Brooke House   18 Castle Street Nether Stowey
Bridgwater TA5 1LN Somerset
Tel: (01278) 733356

Near Rd: A.39
Stowey Brooke House is a Grade II listed property set in a picturesque village in west Somerset. Offering high standards with 2 double bedrooms with brass bedsteads & crisp white cotton bedlinen, plus a pretty twin-bedded room with Dolls House & replica tea shop. All rooms are en-suite with T.V. & tea trays, together with little extras such as mints, chocolates & fresh flowers. The breakfast menu includes full English using local produce, scrambled eggs with smoked salmon, freshly baked croissants & home-made bread. Children by arrangement.

marka@stacey77.fsnet.co.uk
www.stoweybrookehouse.co.uk £60.00 - £65.00
Open: all year   Map ref no. 05

Crispin & Elizabeth Deacon
Saltmoor House Burrowbridge TA7 0RL
Somerset
Tel: (01823) 698092

Near Rd: A.361
Saltmoor House, a Grade II listed building, is an elegant country home overlooking the River Parrett. The property has a delightful walled garden set in 15 acres of pasture. Flagstone floors, log fires & classical wall paintings characterize the stylish interior. The accommodation includes 2 double bedrooms with private bathrooms, 1 double/twin with en-suite facilities. A wide choice is offered for breakfast with home-produced eggs & a superb dinner is always available. The area is wonderfully placed for walking & touring.

saltmoorhouse@aol.com   www.saltmoorhouse.co.uk
£50.00 - £50.00   Open: all year
Map ref no. 08

John & Carole Nurcombe
Marsh Bridge Cottage　Dulverton　TA22 9QG
Somerset
Tel: (01398) 323197

Near Rd: A.396
Marsh Bridge Cottage is peacefully & idyllically situated alongside the sparkling River Barle on the edge of a woodland walkway to Tarr Steps (one of Exmoor's most popular walks & beauty spots. Built in the 1860s as a gamekeeper's cottage it has gradually been attractively extended by Carole & John Nurcombe. All bedrooms are fresh & prettily decorated with luxury bathrooms & lovely river views. Enjoy delicious traditional home-cooking using fresh vegetables from the garden, when in season, & other locally sourced produce. Marsh Bridge Cottage is a lovely base from which to explore Somerset.

carolenurcombe@yahoo.co.uk www.bestbandb.co.uk
£50.00 - £60.00 Open: all year
Map ref no. 09

Mrs Janet Mott
Dollons House　10-12 Church Street　Dunster　TA24 6SH
Somerset
Tel: (01643) 821880

Near Rd: A.358, A.39
17th-century Grade II listed Dollons House nestles beneath the castle in this delightful medieval village in the Exmoor National Park. The accommdoation includes 3 attractive, tastefully furnished & very comfortable en-suite rooms, all well-equipped & each with its own character & special decor. 100 years ago, the local pharmacist had his shop in Dollons, & in the back he made marmalade for the Houses of Parliament. This is a delightful home. Dunster is ideal for exploring Somerset & its many attractions. Pull up outside the front door to unload & your hosts will provide instructions for parking.

jmott@onetel.com www.SmoothHound.co.uk/hotels/
dollons.html　£55.00 - £55.00
Open: all year (excl. xmas)　Map ref no. 11

see p.219

Mrs B. Bale
Conygar House　2A The Ball　Dunster　TA24 6SD
Somerset
Tel: (01643) 821872　Fax 01643 821872

Near Rd: A.39
Conygar House is situated in a quiet road just off the main street of medieval Dunster village. Excelelnt restaurants, bars & shops are all within 1 mins' walking distance. There are wonderful views of castle & moors. Delightful sunny garden & patio for guests' use. Ideal for exploring Exmoor & coast. All rooms decorated & furnished to a high standard throughout. Personal service & your comfort is guaranteed. Dunster Beach is 1 1/2 miles away, Minehead 2 1/2 miles & Porlock 8 miles.

bale.dunster@virgin.net www.conygarhouse.co.uk
£54.00 - £60.00 Open: feb - nov
Map ref no. 10

Mrs Pat Redmond
Number Three Hotel　3 Magdalene Street　Glastonbury
BA6 9EW　Somerset
Tel: (01458) 832129　Fax 01458 834227

Near Rd: M.5 Ex. 23, A.39
Number Three is a beautiful Georgian town house; once the home of Winston Churchill's mother & also Frederick Bligh Bond. 5 individually designed & refurbished rooms, all with en-suite bathrooms, T.V., telephone & tea/coffee-making facilities. 2 rooms are in the main house & 3 are in the Garden House, set within the large walled garden; with wonderful mature trees, floodlit at night. Cars are parked here behind security gates. Number Three stands beside Glastonbury Abbey & is a place of peace & tranquillity.

info@numberthree.co.uk www.numberthree.co.uk
£110.00 - £120.00 Open: all year (excl. xmas)
Map ref no. 13

Number Three Hotel

3 Magdalene Street Glasonbury BA6 9EW

Tel:(01458) 832129 Fax 01458 834227

email:info@numberthree.co.uk www.numberthree.co.uk

Rita & Michael Knight
Mill House   Mill Road   Barton St. David
Somerton TA11 6DF   Somerset
Tel: (01458) 851215   Mobile 07780 961912

Near Rd: A.37, A.303
Ideally situated & beautifully restored, listed Georgian mill house set in a peaceful garden with mill stream. Close to historic Glastonbury & Wells with many National Trust properties & classical gardens also nearby. Fish without leaving the garden, walk or cycle for miles & enjoy birdwatching on the panoramic Somerset Levels. The Mill House offers beautifully decorated, luxury en-suite bedrooms with wonderful views, an elegant Georgian dining room & delicious Aga breakfasts await you. Children over 10 years welcome.

BandB@millhousebarton.co.uk
www.millhousebarton.co.uk   £60.00 - £72.00
Open: feb - dec   Map ref no. 14

Lesley Orr
Causeway Cottage   West Buckland   Taunton TA21 9JZ
Somerset
Tel: (01823) 663458   Fax 01823 663458

Near Rd: A.38, M.5 J.26
Privately tucked away within easy reach of J.26 M.5. A 200-year-old stone cottage standing in a lovely garden with apple orchard & views up to the church. The interior is simple with antique pine & beams. All 3 bedrooms have en-suite facilities & there is a spacious restful sitting room for guests. Lesley is renowned for her cooking. Home-baked bread, free range eggs & farm sausages for breakfast. Causeway Cottage is an informal, relaxed & comfortable family home. Children over 10 yaers. Evening meals by arrangement.

orrs@westbuckland.freeserve.co.uk
www.causewaycottage.co.uk   £60.00 - £65.00
Open: all year   Map ref no. 16

see p.221

Roy Copeland
The Lynch Country House 4 Behind Berry
Somerton TA11 7PD   Somerset
Tel: (01458) 272316   Fax 01458 272590

Near Rd: A.303
The Lynch is a charming small hotel, standing in acres of carefully tended, wonderfully mature grounds. Beautifully refurbished & decorated to retain all its Georgian style & elegance, it now offers 9 attractively presented rooms, some with 4-posters, others with Victorian bedsteads, all with thoughtful extras including bathrobes & magazines. Each room has en-suite/private facilities, 'phone, T.V. & tea/coffee etc. The dining room overlooks the lawns & lake. Single supplement. Children & dogs by arrangement.

the_lynch@talk21.com
www.thelynchcountryhouse.co.uk £60.00 - £95.00
Open: all year (excl.xmas & new year) Map ref no. 15

Mrs Claire Mitchem
Whittles Farm   Beercrocombe   Taunton TA3 6AH
Somerset
Tel: (01823) 480301   Fax 01823 480301

Near Rd: A.358
Guests at Whittles Farm can be sure of a high standard of accommodation & service. A superior 16th-century farmhouse set in 200 acres of pastureland, it is luxuriously carpeted & tastefully furnished in traditional style. Inglenook fireplaces & log-burners add character. There are 2 en-suite bedrooms, individually furnished, with colour T.V. & tea/coffee-making facilities. Super farmhouse food, using own meat, eggs & vegetables, & local Cheddar cheese & butter. Table licence.

dj.CM.MITCHEM@themail.co.uk
www.whittlesfarm.co.uk   £60.00 - £62.00
Open: feb - nov   Map ref no. 17

The Lynch Country House
4 Behind Berry Somerton TA11 7PD
Tel:(01458) 272316 Fax 01458 272590 email:the_lynch@talk21.com www.thelynchcountryhouse.co.uk

see p.223

Tish Hopkins & Mike Green
Tynings House Harters Hill Lane Coxley
Wells BA5 1RF Somerset
Tel: (01749) 675368   Fax 01749 674217

Near Rd: A.39
A former farmhouse, parts of which date back to the 1680s, Tynings is set in its own grounds of some 4 acres & offers relaxed, peaceful & comfortable surroundings. Tynings offers 2 double rooms, which look out over the large garden & 1 twin-bedded room, which looks out over the Mendip hills, all en-suite. Ideally located for many places of interest including the historic & picturesque city of Wells 2 miles away, the mystical Isle of Avalon & Glastonbury 3 miles, as well as the Mendips & the Somerset Levels with its multitude of wildlife. Children over 12 years are welcome. Evening meals by arrangement.

info@tynings.co.uk   www.tynings.co.uk
£52.00 - £70.00   Open: all year (excl. xmas)
Map ref no. 18

Holly & Mary-Ellen Nowell
Beryl   Off Hawkers Lane   Wells BA5 3JP
Somerset
Tel: (01749) 678738   Fax 01749 670508

Near Rd: A.39
Beryl is a precious gem in a perfect setting, situated 1 mile from the cathedral city of Wells. This striking 19th-century Gothic mansion has beautifully furnished, stylishly decorated en-suite bedrooms (which are non-smoking), interesting views & all the accoutrements of luxury living (including a chair lift from ground to first floor). An honesty bar is available for drinks in the exquisite drawing room or on the terrace in summer; a wonderful spot to relax after spending the day exploring Somerset. Holly & Mary-Ellen are charming hosts, & your stay at their delightful home is sure to be memorable.

stay@beryl-wells.co.uk   www.beryl-wells.co.uk
£70.00 - £115.00   Open: all year (excl. xmas)
Map ref no. 20

Mrs Naomi Frost
Southway Farm   Polsham   Wells BA5 1RW
Somerset
Tel: (01749) 673396   Fax 01749 670373

Near Rd: A.39
A friendly welcome is assured at Southway Farm, a Grade II listed Georgian farmhouse, situated half-way between Glastonbury & Wells. Accommodation is in 3 comfortable & spacious, well-equipped en-suite bedrooms. Delicious quality breakfasts are served using local produce & our free-range eggs, home-made bread & preserves, in the elegant dining room at separate tables. Guests can relax in the cosy lounge with T.V., books, magazines & games or in the pretty gardens. Southway Farm is an ideal spot for a relaxing short break.

southwayfarm@ukonline.co.uk
www.southwayfarm.co.uk   £50.00 - £55.00
Open: all year   Map ref no. 19

Mrs Kathlyn Read
Rolstone Court Barn   Hewish Weston-Super-Mare
BS24 6UP   Somerset
Tel: (01934) 820129

Near Rd: A.370, M.5
Enjoy stylish bed & breakfast at this converted barn in a peaceful location on the edge of the Mendips & Somerset Levels, yet handy for Junction 21 of the M.5, convenient for Bristol International Airport & train services from Weston-Super-Mare to London or all points west. It is also ideally situated for visiting the many local beauty spots & as a stopover on the way to Devon & Cornwall. The barn was originally built in the 1880s as a cattle barn & grain store. It was converted in 1988 to provide spacious family accommodation & now offers 3 attractive guest rooms.

read@rolstone-court.co.uk   www.rolstone-court.co.uk
£60.00 - £60.00   Open: ALL YEAR (Excl. Xmas)
Map ref no. 21

Beryl

(off) Hawkers Lane Wells BA5 3JP

Tel:(01749) 678738 Fax 01749 670508

email:stay@beryl-wells.co.uk www.beryl-wells.co.uk

Suffolk

Suffolk

In July, the lower reaches of the River Orwell hold the essence of Suffolk. Broad fields of green and gold with wooded horizons sweep down to the quiet water. Orwell Bridge spans the wide river where yachts and tan-sailed barges share the water with ocean-going container ships out of Ipswich. Downstream the saltmarshes echo to the cry of the Curlew. The small towns and villages of Suffolk are typical of an area with long seafaring traditions. This is the county of men of vision; like Constable and Gainsborough, Admiral Lord Nelson and Benjamin Britten.

The land is green and fertile and highly productive. The hedgerows shelter some of our prettiest wild flowers, & the narrow country lanes are a pure delight. Most

Kentwell Hall, Long Melford.

memorable is the ever-changing sky, appearing higher and wider here than elsewhere in England. There is a great deal of heathland, probably the best known being Newmarket where horses have been trained and raced for some hundreds of years. Gorse-covered heath meets sandy cliffs on Suffolk's coast.

West Suffolk was famous for its wool trade in the Middle Ages, & the merchants gave thanks for their good fortune by building magnificent "Wool Churches". Much-photographed Lavenham has the most perfect black & white timbered houses in Britain, built by the merchants of Tudor times. Ipswich was granted the first charter by King John in 1200, but had long been a trading community of seafarers. Its history can be read from the names of the streets - Buttermarket, Friars Street, Cornhill, Dial Lane & Tavern Street. The latter holds the Great White Horse Hotel mentioned by Charles Dickens in Pickwick Papers. Sadly not many ancient buildings remain, but the mediaeval street pattern and the churches make an interesting trail to follow. The Market town of Bury St. Edmunds is charming, with much of its architectural heritage still surviving, from the Norman Cornhill to a fine Queen Anne House. The great Abbey, now in ruins, was the meeting place of the Barons of England for the creation of the Magna Carta, enshrining the principals of individual freedom, parliamentary democracy and the supremacy of the law.

Suffolk

Suffolk Gazeteer
Areas of Outstanding Natural Beauty.
Suffolk Coast. Heathlands. Dedham Vale.

Historic Houses & Castles
Euston Hall - Thetford
18th C. house with fine collection of pictures.
Gardens & 17th C. Parish Church nearby.
Christchurch Mansion - Ipswich
16th century mansion built on site of 12th
century Augustinian Priory. Gables & dormers
added in 17th century & other alteration &
additions made in 17th & 18th centuries.
Gainsborough's House - Sudbury
Birthplace of Gainsborough, well furnished,
collection of paintings.
The Guildhall - Hadleigh
15th century.
Glemham Hall - Nr Woodbridge
Elizabethan house of red brick - 18th century
alterations. Fine stair, panelled rooms with
Queen Anne furniture.
Haughley Park - Nr. Stowmarket
Jacobean manor house.
Heveningham Hall - Nr. Halesworth
Georgian mansion, English Palladian. Interior in
Neo-Classical style.Garden by Capability Brown.
Ickworth - Nr. Bury St. Edmunds
Mixed architectural styles - late Regency & 18th
century. French furniture, pictures & superb
silver. Gardens with orangery.
Kentwell Hall - Long Melford
Elizabethan mansion in red brick, built in E plan,
surrounded by moat.
Little Hall - Lavenham
15th century hall house, collection of furniture,
pictures, china, etc.
Melford Hall - Nr. Sudbury
16th century - fine pictures, Chinese porcelain,
furniture. Garden with gazebo.
Somerleyton Hall - Nr. Lowestoft
Dating from16th century. Additional work in 19th
century. Carving by Grinling Gibbons.
Tapestries, library, pictures.

Cathedrals & Churches
Bury St. Edmunds (St. Mary)
15th century. Hammer Beam roof in nave,
wagon roof in chancel. Boret monument 1467.
Bramfield (St. Andrew)
Early circular tower. Fine screen & vaulting.
Renaissance effigy.
Bacton (St. Mary)
15th century timbered roof. East Anglian stone
& flintwork.
Dennington (St. Mary)
15th C. alabaster monuments & bench ends.
Aisle & Parclose screens with lofts & parapets.
Earl Stonhay (St. Mary)
14th century - rebuilt with fine hammer roof &
17th century pulpit with four hour-glasses.
Euston (St. Genevieve)
17th century. Fine panelling, reredos may be
Grinling Gibbons.
Framlingham (St. Michael)
15th C. nave & west tower, hammer beam roof
in false vaulting. Chancel was rebuilt in 16th C.
for the tombs of the Howard family, monumental
art treasures. Thamar organ. 1674.
Fressingfield (St. Peter & St. Paul)
15th century woodwork - very fine.
Lavenham (St. Peter & St. Paul)
15th century. Perpendicular. Fine towers. 14th
century chancel screen. 17th century
monument in alabaster.
Long Melford (Holy Trinity)
15th century Lady Chapel, splendid brasses.
15th century glass of note. Chantry chapel with
fine roof. Like cathedral in proportions.
Stoke-by-Nayland (St. Mary)
16th-17th century library, great tower. Fine nave
& arcades. Good brasses & monuments.
Ufford (St. Mary)
Medieval font cover - glorious.

Museums & Galleries
Christchurch Mansion - Ipswich
Country house, collection of furniture, pictures,
bygones, ceramics of 18th C. Paintings by

Suffolk

Gainsborough, Constable & modern artists.

Ipswich Museum - Ipswich
Natural History; prehistory, geology & archaeology to medieval period.

Moyse's Hall Musuem - Bury St. Edmunds
12th century dwelling house with local antiquities & natural history.

Abbot's Hall Museum of Rural Life - Stowmarket
Collections describing agriculture, crafts & domestic utensils.

Gershom-Parkington Collection - Bury St. Edmunds
Queen Anne House containing collection of watches & clocks.

Dunwich Musuem - Dunwich
Flora & fauna; local history.

Historic Monuments

The Abbey - Bury St. Edmunds
Only west end now standing.

Framlingham Castle
12th & 13th centuries - Tudor almshouses.

Bungay Castle - Bungay
12th century. Restored 13th century drawbridge & gatehouse.

Burgh Castle Roman Fort - Burgh
Coastal defences - 3rd century.

Herringfleet Priory - Herringfleet
13th century - remains of small Augustinian priory.

Leiston Abbey - Leiston
14th century - remains of cloisters, choir & trancepts.

Orford Castle - Orford
12th century - 18-sided keep - three towers.

Other things to do

Clare Castle Country Park - Clare
Ancient and modern combine here in a most unusual way. The Castle itself is Norman, but curiously, there is a Victorian railway station inside the castle and the visitor centre is today housed in the old goods shed.

The remains of the old castle moat are now a series of ponds. There is also a charming nature trail along the old railway line.

Dunwich Dingle Marshes Nature Reserve
Coastal grazing marsh, vegetated shingle, saline lagoons and reedbed. Breeding Bitterns and waders including Avocet.

Framlingham Mere Nature Reserve - Framlingham
Circular walk around the Mere and fenland with fine views of Framlingham Castle.

Hadleigh Railway Walk
Two and a half mile walk. Now a local nature reserve open to horseriders and cyclists as well as pedestrians.

Orford Ness National Nature Reserve
8km route over grazing marshes, shingle and areas of historic interest. From 1913 to the mid 1980's this was the base for military research into aerial surveillance and the development of the use of radar.

Snape Maltings - Snape
Snape Maltings is a unique collection of 19th Century maltings set beside the River Alde. There are eight shops, two galleries, a tea shop, restaurant and pub. Attend a concert in the world famous concert hall, enjoy a river trip or just browse through the shops and galleries.

Sutton Hoo Maze Adventure Park - Sutton Hoo
Explore one of the largest maize maze's in the country with great childrens activities. Safari along the banks of the River Deben. Picnic site.

Wyken Hall Vineyard & Gardens
The Elizabethan manor house is surrounded by a romantic, plant- lover's garden including herb garden, knot garden, rose garden (featuring old roses), kitchen garden, wildflower meadows, nuttery, copper beech maze and Millennium Giant Stride. A walk through ancient woodlands leads to Wyken Vineyards, producer of award-winning wines.

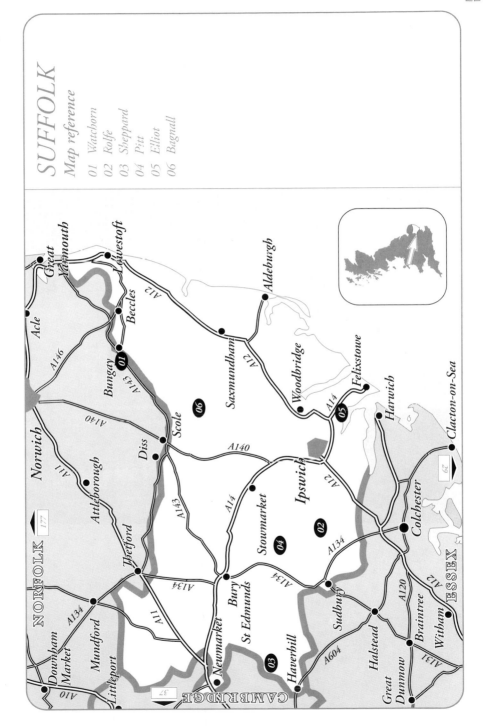

SUFFOLK
Map reference

01 Watchorn
02 Rolfe
03 Sheppard
04 Pitt
05 Elliot
06 Bagnall

NORFOLK 177

CAMBRIDGE 37

ESSEX

Great Yarmouth
Lowestoft
Acle
Beccles
Aldeburgh
A12
A146
Bungay
01
Saxmundham
Woodbridge
Felixstowe
06
Scole
Norwich
A140
Diss
A11
Attleborough
A143
A140
06
A12
A14
Harwich
Clacton-on-Sea
05
29
A14
Ipswich
A12
Stowmarket
04
02
Thetford
Colchester
A134
A1134
Bury St Edmunds
A134
Sudbury
A120
Braintree
Mundford
Downham Market
Littleport
A10
Newmarket
A11
03
Haverhill
A604
Halstead
Great Dunmow
Witham
A131
A12

Mrs Bobbie Watchorn
Earsham Park Farm   Old Railway Road   Earsham
Bungay NR35 2AQ   Suffolk
Tel: (01986) 892180

Near Rd: A.143
Set on a hill with stunning views over the garden, lake & countryside, the farmhouse is a haven of peace & quietness. Wake up to birdsong & delicious award-winning breakfasts featuring home-made bread & preserves, the farms own outdoor reared bacon & sausages & local free-range eggs. Your comfort is considered a priority in the beautifully furnished en-suite rooms, which are spacious & light with extensive facilities, colour T.V.s, tea/coffee-making facilities & many extras including embroidered linen & thick fluffy towels.   Dogs & horses by arrangement.

bestb@earsham-parkfarm.co.uk
www.earsham-parkfarm.co.uk   £64.00 - £84.00
Open: all year   Map ref no. 01

Mrs Jane Sheppard
The Old Vicarage Great Thurlow   Haverhill CB9 7LE
Suffolk Tel: (01440) 783209
Fax 01638 667270   Mobile 07887 717429

Near Rd: A.1307, A.143
Set in mature grounds & woodlands, this delightful Old Vicarage has a friendly family atmosphere. Complete peace & comfort are assured with wonderful views of the Suffolk countryside. Guests are welcome to use the large garden. Open log fires welcome you in winter. The attractively furnished bedrooms have en-suite or private facilities & tea/coffee trays. Evening meals are available with prior notice & there are excellent pubs nearby. Perfectly situated for Newmarket, Cambridge, Long Melford, Lavenham & Constable country. Children over 7. Parking.

info@ebfhorseracing.com www.bestbandb.co.uk
£70.00 - £70.00 Open: all year
Map ref no. 03

Angela Rolfe
Edge Hall 2 High Street   Hadleigh IP7 5AP
Suffolk
Tel: (01473) 822458   Fax 01473 827751

Near Rd: A.1071, A.12, A.14
Edge Hall is a family-run Georgian house in central Hadleigh. Beautifully restored & tastefully modernised, it offers the ultimate luxury en-suite bedrooms, ranging from an antique 4-poster to pretty attic family rooms. Situated in the most picturesque part of Suffolk, it is an ideal base from which to explore the surrounding towns & unspoilt villages. Your hosts pride themselves on making your stay at Edge Hall a truly memorable experience.

r.rolfe@edgehall-hotel.co.uk www.egdehall-hotel.co.uk
£75.00 - £95.00 Open: ALL YEAR
Map ref no. 02

Tim & Gilli Pitt
Lavenham Priory Water Street
Lavenham CO10 9RW   Suffolk
Tel: (01787) 247404   Fax 01787 248472

Near Rd: A.134
A Grade I listed half-timbered 13th-century merchant's house set in the heart of Lavenham. Bedrooms feature Lit Bateau, Polonaise & 4-poster beds with medieval wall paintings, oak floors & massive exposed timbering. True luxury at an affordable price. Lavenham is regarded as one of the finest medieval villages in England with its historic buildings & streets. Leave your car for a while & enjoy England as it used to be. Children over 10.

mail@lavenhampriory.co.uk
www.lavenhampriory.co.uk   £42.50 - £72.50
Open: all year (excl. xmas & new year)   Map ref no. 04

Buttermans

Broke Hall Park Nacton IP10 0ET

Tel:(0173) 655133 email:elliot@buttermans.com www.buttermans.com

see p.229

Tim & Janet Elliot
Buttermans   Broke Hall Park
Nacton IP10 0ET Suffolk
Tel: (01473) 655133

Near Rd: A. 12, A.14
Buttermans is set in the grounds of Broke Hall (the 18th-century home of Admiral Broke). Originally the blacksmiths' forge, this delightful home is just 150 metres from the River Orwell & offers spectacular views across unspoilt countryside, which is designated as an Area of Outstanding Natural Beauty. Each of the bedrooms is beautifully appointed with en-suite bath/shower room, colour T.V. & tea/coffee-making facilities. Home-made bread & local produce are served with a full English breakfast. Evening meals can be arranged.

elliot@buttermans.com   www.buttermans.com
£70.00 - £90.00   Open: mar - oct
Map ref no. 05

Sue Bagnall
Abbey House Monk Soham
Woodbridge IP13 7EN   Suffolk
Tel: (01728) 685225

Near Rd: A.1120
Abbey House is a delightful listed Victorian rectory set in 10 acres of quiet Suffolk countryside. The house is surrounded by secluded gardens with mature trees & several large ponds. Attractively furnished bedrooms, 2 doubles & 1 twin with en-suite or private bathrooms & tea-making facilities. Exclusive use of the dining room & drawing room with colour T.V. & log fire. Outdoor heated swimming pool. Centrally placed for touring East Anglia, within easy reach of Lavenham, Constable country & the coast. Children over 10.

sue@abbey-house.net   www.abbey-house.net
£60.00 - £70.00
Open: ALL YEAR (Excl. Xmas & New Year) Map ref no. 06

Surrey

Surrey

One of the Home Counties, Surrey includes a large area of London, south of the Thames. Communications are good in all directions so it is easy to stay in Surrey & travel either into central London or out to enjoy the lovely countryside which, despite urban development, survives thanks to the 'Green Belt' policy. The county is also very accessible from Gatwick Airport.

The land geographically, is chalk sandwiched in clay, & probably the lack of handy building material was responsible for the area remaining largely uninhabited for centuries. The North Downs were a considerable barrier to cross, but gradually settlements grew along the rivers which were the main routes through. The Romans used the gap created by the River Mole to build Stane Street between London & Chichester, this encouraged the development of small towns. The gap cut by the passage of the River Wey allows the Pilgrims Way to cross the foot of the Downs. Dorking, Reigate & Farnham are small towns along this route, all with attractive main streets & interesting shops & buildings.

Surrey has very little mention in the Domesday Book, &, although the patronage of the church & of wealthy families established manors which developed over the years, little happened to disturb the rural tranquillity of the region. As a county it made little history but rather reflected passing times, although the Magna Carta was signed at Egham in 1215.

The heathlands of Surrey were a Royal playground for centuries. The Norman Kings hunted here & horses became part of the landscape & life of the people, as they are today on Epsom Downs.

Nearness to London & Royal patronage began to influence the area, & the buildings of the Tudor period reflect this. Royal palaces were built at Hampton Court & Richmond, & great houses such as Loseley near Guildford often using stone from the monasteries emptied during the Reformation. Huge deer parks were enclosed & stocked, Richmond, has a wonderful park with deer, lakes & woodland that was enclosed by Charles I.

The Royal Chapel, Hampton Court. Richmond upon Thames.

Surrey

Surrey Gazeteer

Historic Houses & Castles

Albury Park - Albury, Nr. Guildford
A delightful country mansion designed by Pugin.

Clandon Park - Guildford
A fine house in the Palladian style by Leoni. A good collection of furniture & pictures. The house boasts some fine plasterwork.

Claremont - Esher
Superb Palladian house with interesting interior.

Detillens - Limpsfield
A fine 15th century house with inglenook fireplaces & medieval furniture. A large, pleasant garden.

Greathed Manor - Lingfield
An imposing Victorian manor house.

Hatchlands - East Clandon
A National Trust property of the 18th century with a fine Adam interior.

Loseley House - Guildford
A very fine Elizabethan mansion with superb panelling, furniture & paintings.

Polesden Lacy - Dorking
A Regency villa housing the Grevill collection of tapestries, pictures & furnishings. Extensive gardens.

Cathedrals & Churches

Compton (St. Nicholas)
The only surviving 2-storey sanctuary in the country. A fine 17th century pulpit.

Esher (St. George)
A fine altar-piece & marble monument.

Hascombe (St. Peter)
A rich interior with much gilding & painted reredos & roofs.

Lingfield (St. Peter & St. Paul)
15th century. Holding a chained bible.

Ockham (St. Mary & All Saints)
Early church with 13th century east window.

Stoke D'Abernon (St. Mary)
Dating back to Pre-conquest time with additions from the 12th-15th centuries. A fine 13th century painting. Early brasses.

Museums & Galleries

Charterhouse School Museum - Godalming
Peruvian pottery, Greek pottery, archaeology & natural history.

Chertsey Museum - Chertsey
18th-19th century costume & furnishing displayed & local history.

Guildford House - Guildford
The house is 17th century & of architectural interest housing monthly exhibitions.

Guildford Museum - Guildford
A fine needlework collection & plenty of information about local history.

Old Kiln Agricultural - Tilford
A very interesting collection of old farm implements.

Watermill Museum - Haxted
A restored 17th century mill with working water wheels & machinery.

Weybridge Museum - Weybridge
Good archaeological exhibition plus costume & local history.

Other things to do

Hampton Court Palace - East Molesey
Visit the famous hedge maze, Tudor knot garden and the state apartments at this splendid red-brick Tudor Palace, which is set in formal gardens and open parkland along the Thames River.

Royal Botanic Gardens Kew - Richmond
This delightful 300-acre botanical park, once owned by the Royals, features the glass Palm House and other Victorian greenhouses that house a vast variety of exotic plants from around the world.

Kew Palace and Queen Charlotte's Cottage - Richmond
The former home of King George III.

Richmond Park - Richmond
Beautiful parkland with 100s of acres of woodland and lakes. Off-road cycle tracks.

Thorpe Park - Surrey
Amusement theme park; fun for all the family.

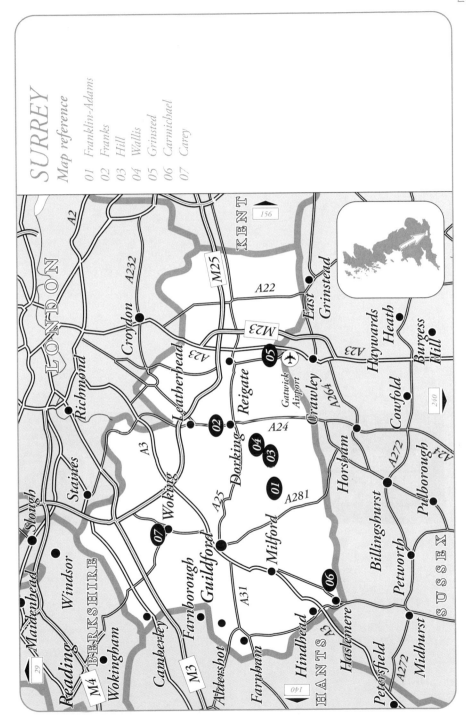

SURREY

Map reference

01 Franklin-Adams
02 Franks
03 Hill
04 Wallis
05 Grinsted
06 Carmichael
07 Carey

Carol Franklin-Adams
High Edser Shere Road   Ewhurst   Cranleigh GU6 7PQ
Surrey
Tel: (01483) 278214   Fax 01483 278200

Near Rd: A.25
High Edser is a large, handsome Grade II listed home, the earliest part built in the 16th century, which is situated in an Area of Outstanding Natural Beauty. There are three attractive & tastefully furnished bedrooms available: two doubles and one twin. A residents' lounge with colour T.V., in which to relax in the evening. Tennis court in grounds, and golf nearby. 35 minutes to Gatwick and London Airports. It is also conveniently situated approximately an hour's drive from London. A delightful home, ideal for a relaxing short break holiday.

carol@highedser.co.uk   www.highedser.co.uk
£50.00 - £65.00   Open: all year
Map ref no. 01

Gill Hill
Bulmer Farm   Pasturewood Road
Holmbury St. Mary   Dorking RH5 6LG   Surrey
Tel: (01306) 730210

Near Rd: A.25
Enjoy a warm welcome at this delightful 17th-century farmhouse, full of character & complete with many beams & an inglenook fireplace. Adjoining the house around a courtyard are 5 very attractive barn-conversion en-suite bedrooms for non-smokers. Farm produce & home-made preserves are provided, whenever possible. Situated in a picturesque village, Bulmer Farm is convenient for London airports. Children over 12 years welcome. A self-catering is also available. A brochure is available on request. Dogs by arrangement.

bestbandb@atlas.co.uk   www.bestbandb.co.uk
£60.00 - £62.00   Open: all year
Map ref no. 03

Mike & Lynda Franks
Denbies Wine Estate   London Road   Dorking RH5 6AA
Surrey
Tel: (01306) 876777   Fax 01306 888930

Near Rd: A.24
Denbies Farmhouse is a tastefully refurbished 7 room guesthouse situated on England's largest vineyard, within easy reach of Heathrow & Gatwick Airports. Bedrooms are large, comfortable & ensuite with T.V., hospitality tray. etc. The conservatory breakfast room gives guests the opportunity to enjoy a full English or Continental breakfast overlooking the spectacular far-reaching views of the vineyard. Denbies visitor centre is nearby, offering lunches, wine tours & tastings, art gallery & gift shop. The town centre & train stations are closeby. Children over 6.

BandB@denbiesvineyard.co.uk
www.denbiesvineyard.co.uk £65.00 - £100.00
Open: all year Map ref no. 02

Ann & Peter Wallis
Park House Farm Hollow Lane Abinger Common
Dorking RH5 6LW Surrey
Tel: (01306) 730101   Fax 01306 730643

Near Rd: A.25
A delightful large family home, tastefully furnished with many antiques.   The guest accommodation is very comfortable with en-suite/private facilities, satellite T.V., tea/coffee-making facilities etc. A delicious breakfast is served. It is set in 25 acres in an Area of Outstanding Natural Beauty within easy reach of Heathrow & Gatwick Airports, many beautiful gardens & National Trust properties. There is a good train service to London. This is ideal walking country, with many good village pubs serving food. Children over 12 years are welcome.

Peterwallis@msn.com
www.smoothhound.co.uk/hotels/parkhous
£60.00 - £70.00   Open: all year   Map ref no. 04

Carole & Adrian Grinsted
The Lawn Guest House 30 Massetts Road Horley
Gatwick RH6 7DF   Surrey
Tel: (01293) 775751   Fax 01293 821803

Near Rd: A.23
A well-appointed Victorian house only 5 mins' from Gatwick Airport & 25 miles to London or Brighton. Very useful as a base for travelling, it is close to the rail station & town centre. There are 12 bedrooms, all with en-suite facilities & all very comfortable & well decorated, with colour T.V., hairdryer, 'phone & tea/coffee-making facilities, etc. A full English breakfast, or a healthy alternative including fruit, yoghurt & muesli, is served in the pleasant dining room. Also, a garden for guests' use. There is a supplement payable for single use of rooms. Parking.

info@lawnguesthouse.co.uk www.lawnguesthouse.co.uk
£58.00 - £63.00 Open: all year
Map ref no. 05

Joan & David Carey
Swallow Barn Milford Green   Chobham
Woking GU24 8AU   Surrey
Tel: (01276) 856030   Fax 01276 856030

Near Rd: A.3046
Situated in quiet, secluded surroundings on the edge of Chobham, attractively converted outbuildings & stables with outdoor swimming pool. 3 bedrooms with en-suite/ private bathrooms, T.V. & tea/coffee-making facilities. An excellent breakfast is served. Ideal for famous golf courses: Sunningdale, Wentworth & Foxhills. For garden lovers, Wisley & Savill Gardens are within easy reach. Convenient for M.3, M.25, Heathrow Airport, Windsor, Ascot & Hampton Court. Woking station 2 miles - London 25 mins' by train. Single supplement charge. Children over 8.

swallowbarn@web-hq.com   www.swallow-barn.co.uk
£45.00 - £90.00 Open: all year
Map ref no. 07

see p.236

Elizabeth Carmichael
Deerfell Blackdown Park Fernden Lane   Haslemere
GU27 3BU Surrey
Tel: (01428) 653409 Fax 01428 656106

Near Rd: A.286, A.283
A warm welcome at a spacious & comfortable stone-built home set in downland countryside, with breathtaking views to the hills & valleys of Surrey/Sussex. 3 pretty rooms with en-suite/private bathrooms, which are comfortable & have tea/coffee facilities & T.V.. Wonderful walks right on doorstep. Light suppers available on request. Close by - village of Lurgashall, Haslemere (4 miles), London (45 mins' by train), Guildford/Chichester (20 miles), Heathrow/ Gatwick Airports 1 hr. Children 6+. Dogs by arrangement.

deerfell@tesco.net   www.deerfell.co.uk
£50.00 - £55.00 Open: mid jan- mid dec
Map ref no. 06

Deerfell

Blackdown Park Fernden Lane Haselmere GU27 3BU

Tel:(01428)653409 Fax:01428656106

email:deerfell@tesco.net www.deerfell.co.uk

Sussex

Sussex

The South Downs of Sussex stretch along the coast, reflecting the expanse of the North Downs of Kent, over the vast stretches of the Weald.

The South Downs extend from dramatic Beachy Head along the coast to Chichester & like the North Downs, they are crossed by an ancient trackway. There is much evidence of pre-historic settlement on the Downs. Mount Caburn, near Lewes, is crowned by an iron age fort, & Cissbury Ring is one of the most important archaeological sites in England. The Long Man of Wilmington stands 226 feet high & is believed to be Nordic, possibly representing Woden, the God of War.

The landscape of the inland Weald ranges from bracken-covered heathlands where deer roam, to the deep woodland stretches of the Ashdown Forest, eventually giving way to soft undulating hills & valleys, patterned with hop-fields, meadows, oast houses, windmills & fruit orchards. Villages like Midhurst & Wadhurst hold the Saxon suffix "hurst" which means wood & we find Bosham & Stedham whose suffix "ham" means homestead or farm.

Battle, above Hastings, is the site of the famous Norman victory & 16th century Bodiam Castle, built as defence against the French in later times, has a beautiful setting encircled by a lily-covered moat.

Sussex has an extensive coastline, with cliffs near Eastbourne at Beachy Head, & at Hastings. Further east, the great flat Romney Marshes stretch out to sea, & there is considerable variety in the coastal towns.

Chichester has a magnificent cathedral & a harbour reaching deep into the coastal plain that is rich in archaeological remains. The creeks & mudflats make it an excellent place for bird watching.

Brighton is the most famous of the Sussex resorts with its Pier, the Promenade above the beaches, the oriental folly of George IV's Royal Pavilion & its Regency architecture. "The Lanes" are a maze of alleys & small squares full of fascinating shops, a thriving antique trade, & many good pubs & eating places. Hastings to the east preserves its "Old Town" where timbered houses nestle beneath the cliffs.

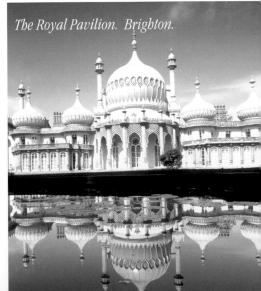

The Royal Pavilion. Brighton.

Sussex

Sussex Gazeteer

Areas of Outstanding Natural Beauty.
The Sussex Downs. Chichester Harbour.

Historic Houses & Castles

Arundel Castle - Arundel
18th century rebuilding of ancient castle, fine
portraits, 15th century furniture.

Cuckfield Park - Cuckfield
Elizabethan manor house, gatehouse. Very fine
panelling & ceilings.

Danny - Hurstpierpoint
16th century - Elizabethan.

Goodwood House - Chichester
18th century - Jacobean house - Fine Sussex
flintwork, paintings by Van Dyck, Canaletto &
Stubbs, English & French furniture, tapestries
& porcelain.

Newtimber Place - Newtimber
Moated house - Etruscan style wall paintings.

Purham - Pulborough
Elizabethan house containing important
collection of Elizabethan, Jacobean & Georgian
portraits, also fine furniture.

Petworth House - Petworth
17th century - landscaped by Capability Brown -
important paintings - 14th century chapel.

St. Mary's - Bramber
15th C. timber framed house - rare panelling.

Tanyard - Sharpthorne
Medieval tannery - 16th & 17th C. additions.

The Thatched Cottage - Lindfield
Close-studded weald house - reputedly Henry
VII hunting lodge.

Uppark - Petersfield
17th century - 18th century interior decorations
remain unaltered.

Alfriston Clergy House - Nr. Seaford
14th century parish priest's house -
pre-reformation.

Battle Abbey - Battle
Founded by William the Conqueror.

Charleston Manor - Westdean
Norman, Tudor & Georgian architectural styles.

Bull House - Lewes
15th century half-timbered house - was home of
Tom Paine.

Bateman's - Burwash
17th C. - watermill - home of Rudyard Kipling.

Bodiam Castle - Nr. Hawkshurst
14th century - noted example of medieval
moated military architecture.

Great Dixter - Northiam
15th century half-timbered manor house - great
hall - Lutyens gardens.

Glynde Place - Nr. Lewes
16th century flint & brick - built around
courtyard-collection of paintings by Rubens,
Hoppner, Kneller, Lely, Zoffany.

**Michelham Priory - Upper Dicker,
Nr. Hailsham**
13th century Augustinian Priory - became Tudor
farmhouse - working watermill, ancient stained
glass, etc., enclosed by moat.

Royal Pavilion - Brighton
Built for Prince Regent by Nash upon classical
villa by Holland. Exotic Building - has superb
original works of art lent by H.M. The Queen.
Collections of Regency furniture also Art
Nouveau & Art Deco in the Art Gallery
& Museum.

Sheffield Park - Nr. Uckfield
Beautiful Tudor House - 18th century alterations
- splendid staircase.

Cathedrals & Churches

Alfriston (St. Andrew)
14th century - transition from decorated style to
perpendicular, Easter sepulchre.

Boxgrove (St. Mary & St. Blaise)
13th C. choir,16th C. painted decoration on
vaulting. Relic of Benedictine priory.16th C.
chantry. Much decoration.

Chichester Cathedral
Norman & earliest Gothic. Large Romanesque
relief sculptures in south choir aisle.

Etchingham (St. Mary & St. Nicholas)
14th C. Old glass, brasses, screen, carved stalls.

Sussex

Hardham (St. Botolph)
11th century - 12th century wall paintings.
Rotherfield (St. Denys)
16th century font cover, 17th century canopied pulpit, glass by Burne-Jones, wall paintings, Georgian Royal Arms.
Sompting (St. Mary)
11th century Saxon tower - Rhenish Helm Spire - quite unique.
Worth (St. Nicholas)
10th century - chancel arch is the largest Saxon arch in England. German carved pulpit c.1500 together with altar rails.
Winchelsea (St. Thomas the Apostle)
14th century - choir & aisles only. Canopied sedilia & piscina.

Museums & Galleries
Barbican House Museum - Lewes
Collection relating to pre-historic, Romano-British & , medieval antiquities of the area. Prints & water colours of the area.
Battle Museum - Battle
Remains from archeological sites in area. Diorama of Battle of Hastings.
Bignor Roman Villa Collection - Bignor
4th century mosaics, Samian pottery, hypocaust, etc.
Brighton Museum & Art Gallery - Brighton
Old Master Paintings, watercolours, ceramics, furniture. Surrealist paintings, Art Nouveau & Art Deco applied art, musical instruments & many other exhibits.
Marlipins Museum - Shoreham
12th century building housing collections of ship models, photographs, old maps, geological specimens, etc.
Royal National Lifeboat Institution Museum - Eastbourne
Lifeboats of all types used from earliest times to present.
Tower 73 - Eastbourne
Martello tower restored to display the history of these forts. Exhibition of equipment, uniforms &

weapons of the times.
The Toy Museum - Rottingdean, Brighton
Toys & playthings from many countries - children's delight.

Other things to see & do
Bewl Water - Nr. Wadhurst
Boat trips, walks, adventure playground.
The Bear Museum - Petersfield
World's First Teddy Bear Museum, Museum shop and Steiff Club Store along with a showcase display of some of the earliest and most interesting bears that will be of interest to collectors.
Chichester Festival Theatre - Chichester
Summer season of plays from May to September.
Goodwood Racecourse - Goodwood
The Cass Sculpture Foundation - Goodwood
Where else in the world can you see a changing display of 70 specially commissioned, monumental sculptures sited in an idyllic landscape and all for sale.
Hollycombe Steam Engine Collection - Liphook
A unique collection of working steam powered attractions providing fun and entertainment for the whole family. The centre-piece is a complete Edwardian Fairground where you can experience all the fun of the fair from the 1870's; from the gentle "Golden Gallopers" to the first "White Knuckle" rides.
Pulborough Brooks - Pulborough
Set in the sheltered Arun valley, in the heart of West Sussex, Pulborough Brooks is a fantastic place for a day out for people of all ages. There is a superb nature reserve and trail with birdwatching hides and viewpoints, a visitor area with gift shop and a tearoom with terrace.
The Wildfowl & Wetlands Trust - Arundel
The new visitor centre at Arundel is surrounded by ancient woodland and overlooked by the town's historic castle. The wetlands at Arundel are home to many rare species of wetland wildlife.

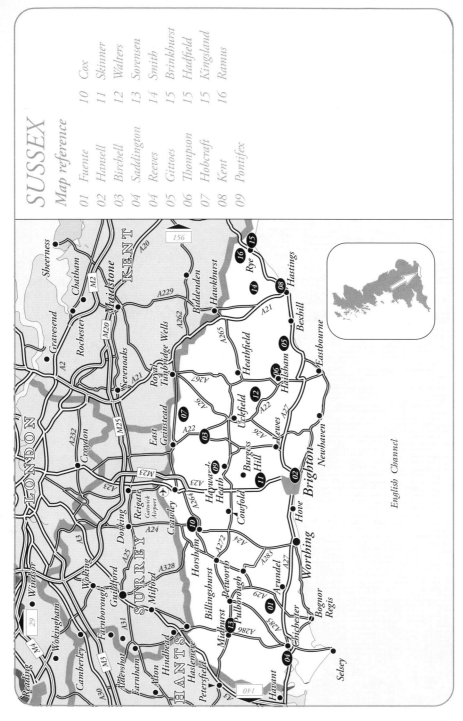

SUSSEX

Map reference

01 Fuente	10 Cox
02 Hansell	11 Skinner
03 Birchell	12 Walters
04 Saddington	13 Sorensen
04 Reeves	14 Smith
05 Gittoes	15 Brinkhurst
06 Thompson	15 Hadfield
07 Hobcraft	15 Kingsland
08 Kent	16 Ramus
09 Pontifex	

English Channel

Charters

Bosham Lane Bosham Chichester PO18 8HG

Tel:01243 572644

email:louise@chartersbandb.co.uk www.chartersbandb.co.uk

Jan Fuente
Mill Lane House   Slindon   Arundel BN18 0RP
Sussex
Tel: (01243) 814440   Mobile 07909 923206

Near Rd: A.29
Partly 17th-century house in beautiful National Trust village of Slindon,backing onto South Downs, with large gardens & views from the 1st floor down to the coast (approx. 5 miles away.)   All bedrooms are en-suite, with tea/coffee-making facilities, hairdryer, colour T.V./video. A delicious full English breakfast is served all year round. Mill Lane House has excellent walking on the doorstep, with pubs & restaurants within short driving distance & many tourist attractions in the surrounding areas of Chichester, Goodwood, Bignor & Arundel.

Jan.Fuente@btopenworld.com
www.Mill-Lane-House.co.uk £65.00 - £85.00
Open: all year   Map ref no. 01

John & Daphne Hansell
Trouville Hotel   11 New Steine   Brighton BN2 1PB
Sussex
Tel: (01273) 697384

Near Rd: A.259
The Trouville is a Regency, Grade II listed townhouse, tastefully restored & furnished.   Accommodation is in 8 attractive & tastefully furnished bedrooms, 6 rooms have en-suite facilities & each room has a colour T.V. & tea/coffee-making facilities. For a romantic or special weekend break, 4-poster rooms are available. Situated in a charming sea-front square, the Trouville is convenient for shopping, the Pavilion, the Lanes, Marina & Conference Centre & the many excellent restaurants which are all within walking distance. A wonderful base for exploring Brighton.

www.bestbandb.co.uk
£65.00 - £85.00   Open: feb - dec
Map ref no. 02

Mrs D. Birchell
Holly House   Beaconsfield Road   Chelwood Gate
Ashdown Forest RH17 7LF Sussex
Tel: (01825) 740484   Fax 01825 740172

Near Rd: A.275
On the edge of the Ashdown Forest, in a rural setting, stands Holly House a 130 year old forest farmhouse. Now converted to form a comfortable family home, which has seen Chelwood Gate change from a hamlet to a pleasant village with 2 churches, 2 good pubs and a well-stocked parish shop. Find a warm welcome with an inviting lounge, very comfortable beds & memorable breakfasts, served in the conservatory overlooking the interesting garden. Children & dogs are welcome by prior arrangement. Holly House is the perfect spot for a relaxing break.

db@hollyhousebnb.co.uk   www.hollyhousebnb.co.uk
£60.00 - £65.00   Open: all year
Map ref no. 03

see p.241

Louise Saddington
Charters   Bosham Lane   Bosham
Chichester PO18 8HG   Sussex
Tel: 01243 572644

Near Rd: A.259
Charters is an attractive home in the heart of the picturesque sailing village of Old Bosham, situated 3 miles west of the Cathedral City of Chichester. Each bedroom (3 double/1 twin, ensuite or private facilities) offers a unique & luxurious style in this comfortable & welcoming house. Just a short walk from the beautiful waterfront with its attractive Saxon Church, waterfront pub & coffee shops. An ideal base for visiting the Theatre, racing at Goodwood, and local beaches & marinas. Nearby is Arundel Castle & Portsmouth, with its naval history.   Children 5+

louise@chartersbandb.co.uk
www.chartersbandb.co.uk £50.00 - £100.00
Open: all year (excl.xmas & new year)   Map ref no. 04

Wartling Place

Wartling Herstmonceux Eastbourne BN27 1RY

Tel:(01323) 832590 Fax 01323 831558

email:accom@wartlingplace.prestel.co.uk www.countryhouseaccommodation.co.uk

Christine Reeves
White Barn Crede Lane Bosham
Chichester PO18 8NX Sussex
Tel: (01243) 573113   Fax 01243 573113

Near Rd: A.259

White Barn is a unique open-plan, single-storey house on different levels in a quiet corner of the beautiful Saxon harbour village of Bosham. The guest accommodation includes 3 privately located en-suite bedrooms, each room is comfortably furnished & has colour T.V. & tea/coffee-making facilities. Delicious breakfasts are served in the the glass walled dining room overlooking the garden. White Barn is ideal for visiting Chichester (3 miles), Goodwood (4 miles), Portsmouth, the South Downs & beaches. Children over 12 years welcome. A charming home for a short break holiday.

chrissie@whitebarn.biz   www.whitebarn.biz
£60.00 - £90.00   Open: all year
Map ref no. 04

Noel Thompson
Hailsham Grange Vicarage Road Hailsham
BN27 1BL   Sussex
Tel: (01323) 844248

Near Rd: A.22, A.295

Hailsham Grange is a former 18th century vicarage built in the Mary-Anne architectural style c.1700, and is situated in the market town of Hailsham within close proximity of the South Downs, Eastbourne, Bexhill-on-Sea, Hastings & Brighton. Royal Tunbridge Wells, Rye, Bodium & Scotney Castles & Romney Marshes are also within driving distance. There are good theatres in Eastbourne & Brighton and Glyndebourne opera is only 15 minutes drive. Hailsham Grange provides accommodation in the classic English style throughout the year. If you really wish to pamper yourself Hailsham Grange is the place for you.

noel-hgrange@amserve.com
www.hailshamgrange.co.uk £75.00 - £110.00
Open: all year   Map ref no. 06

see p.243

Barry & Rowena Gittoes
Wartling Place Wartling Herstmonceux
Eastbourne BN27 1RY Sussex
Tel: (01323) 832590   Fax 01323 831558

Near Rd: A.27, A.271

Award-winning Georgian country house - Wartling exudes classic elegance with antique furntiure & rich fabrics. Each bedroom proudly displays an identity all of its own, some on a grand scale, with magnificent 4-posters, others with a more intimate atmosphere. All are exceptionally comfortable with large en-suite bathrooms. Close to National Trust castles & gardens of Sussex & Kent. Private parking. Self-catering lodge cottage available. Easy access to Glynebourne, Lewes & Brighton.

accom@wartlingplace.prestel.co.uk
www.countryhouseaccommodation.co.uk
£100.00 - £145.00 Open: all year Map ref no. 05

see p.245

Peter Hobcraft
Bolebroke Watermill (Bolebroke Castle)
Edenbridge Road Hartfield TN7 4JJ Sussex
Tel: (01892) 770061   Fax 01892 771041

Near Rd: A.264

A magical watermill, first recorded in 1086 A.D., & an Elizabethan miller's barn offer 5 en-suite rooms of genuine, unspoilt rustic charm, set amid woodland, water & pasture, & used as the idyllic setting for the film 'Carrington'. The mill is complete with machinery, trap doors & very steep stairs. The barn has low doors & beamed ceilings, & includes the enchanting honeymooners' hayloft with a 4-poster bed. (Please note breakfast is taken in the Castle.) Children over 8 years.

bolebrokemill@btinternet.com
www.bolebrokemillhotel.co.uk £79.00 - £99.00
Open: all year   Map ref no. 07

Bolebroke Watermill (Bolebroke Castle)
Edenbridge RoadHartfield TN7 4JJ
Tel:(01892) 770061 Fax 01892 771041 email:bolebrokemill@btinternet.com www.bolebrokemillhotel.co.uk

Brian W. Kent
Parkside House   59 Lower Park Road
Hastings TN34 2LD   Sussex
Tel: (01424) 433096   Fax 01424 421431

Near Rd: A.21

Parkside House is located in a quiet residential conservation area, & it is set in an elevated position opposite a beautiful park. This elegant Victorian house retains all of its original features, but with every modern facility. High standards of hospitality, comfort & good home-cooking are provided, creating an informal, very friendly & welcoming atmosphere. Bedrooms are tastefully furnished & en-suite & offer every luxury. The 'Apricot' room has a beautiful antique French bed. Parkside House is in a quiet location, yet it is only 15 mins' walk from the town centre & sea front.

bkent.parksidehouse@talk21.com
www.bestbandb.co.uk   £55.00 - £65.00
Open: all year   Map ref no. 08

Liz & Chris Cox
Glebe End   Church Street Warnham
Nr. Horsham RH12 3QW   Sussex
Tel: (01403) 261711   Fax 01403 257572

Near Rd: A.24

Glebe End is a fascinating medieval house, with a secluded, sunny, walled garden, set in the heart of Warnham. It retains many original features, including heavy flagstones, curving ships' timbers & an inglenook fireplace. En-suite single, twin & double rooms are charmingly furnished with antiques, paintings & books. 1, with its own staircase, has an adjoining bedroom making it an ideal family suite. All rooms have their own T.V. & hot drinks trays. Breakfasts are delicious. 2 Inns within 5 mins' walk provide lunches & evening meals. 5 National Trust houses & famous gardens - 30 mins' drive. 20 mins' Gatwick.

coxeswarnham@aol.com www.bestbandb.co.uk
£54.00 - £54.00 Open: all year
Map ref no. 10

Roy & Carol Pontifex
The Pilstyes 106 & 108 High Street Lindfield
Haywards Heath RH16 2HS   Sussex
Tel: (01444) 484101

Near Rd: B.2028

The Pilstyes is a Grade II listed village house believed to have been built around 1575. It is arranged as a main house with an attached cottage. (The cottage is let as a holiday home and/or bed and breakfast.) Also, 1 double en-suite room in the main house, which is available for B & B. The cottage has 2 rooms. A 4 poster bedroom & a twin bedded room with bathroom. It is let to one party at a time, so it is totally private. Breakfast is served in the sunny kitchen. Within easy reach of Brighton, Glyndebourne, Ashdown Forest, the Bluebell Railway & Gatwick Airport by car.

carol@pontifexes.co.uk
www.sussex-bedandbreakfast.co.uk   £65.00 - £95.00
Open: all year   Map ref no. 09

Mike & Susie Skinner
Clayton Wickham Farmhouse Belmont Lane
Hurstpierpoint BN6 9EP   Sussex
Tel: (01273) 845698   Fax 01273 841970

Near Rd: A.23

A delightful, secluded 14th-century farmhouse with lovely views, set amidst the beautiful Sussex countryside. The friendly hosts have refurbished their home to a high standard, yet have retained many original features, hence there are a wealth of beams & a huge inglenook fireplace in the drawing room. There are also a variety of tastefully furnished & well-appointed bedrooms, including a super 4-poster en-suite. Excellent 4-course candlelit dinner by arrangement, & lovely 3-acre grounds with tennis court. Ample parking. Animals by arrangement.

susie@cwfbandb.co.uk www.cwfbandb.co.uk
£80.00 - £95.00 Open: all year
Map ref no. 11

Shortgate Manor Farm

Halland Lewes BN8 6PJ

Tel: (01825) 840320 Fax 01825 840320

email:david@shortgate.co.uk www.shortgate.co.uk

see p.247

David & Ethel Walters
Shortgate Manor Farm   Halland   Lewes BN8 6PJ
Sussex
Tel: (01825) 840320   Fax 01825 840320

Near Rd: A.22
It's roses all the way up the poplar-lined drive to wonderful Shortgate Manor Farm set in 8 acres with a 2 acre romantic plantsmans garden with yet more fragrant roses. The elegant en-suite guests bedrooms overlook the beautiful gardens & offer a high degree of comfort with attention to detail & many thoughtful extras. Delicious breakfasts are served in the bright & attractive dining hall. A gently restful & very comfortable home from which to enjoy the many wonderful gardens of Sussex & of course, opera at Glyndebourne. Children over 10 years are welcome. A delightful home .

david@shortgate.co.uk   www.shortgate.co.uk
£65.00 - £80.00   Open: all year
Map ref no. 12

John Smith & Shelagh Franklin
Fairacres   Udimore Road   Broad Oak
Rye TN31 6DG Sussex
Tel: (01424) 883236   Fax 01424 883236

Near Rd: B.2089
Fairacres is a beautifully restored, listed building located in the picturesque village of Broad Oak, on the north side of the Sussex Weald. The village is an ideal location for visiting Tenderden, Battle, Hastings and Rye. John & Shelagh welcome you to their picturesque home, which is full of great charm & character with original beams & inglenook fireplaces. The elegant en-suite bedrooms offer every comfort with hospitality tray, complimentary sherry & port & many thoughtful extras. Comprehensive breakfast menu. Enjoy the restful lounge & the charming garden on warm evenings. Children over 5. Dogs by arrangement.

john-shelagh@fairacres.fsworld.co.uk
www.smoothhound.co.uk/hotels/fairacres.html
£80.00 - £90.00   Open: all year   Map ref no. 14

Erling Sorensen
Amberfold   Heyshott   Midhurst GU29 0DA
Sussex
Tel: (01730) 812385   Fax 01730 813559

Near Rd: A.286
Amberfold is a charming 17th-century listed cottage, situated in quiet, idyllic countryside yet only 5 mins' drive from Midhurst. The accommodation at Amberfold comprises The Lodge, which sports a 4-poster bed & a wet room en-suite, The Cottage with a double bed & en-suite shower plus a 1st floor double bedroom with en-suite bath & shower. All rooms are equipped with T.V., hospitality tray, fridge & hairdryer. An ideal base for exploring Goodwood, Singleton, Chichester & the coast.

erlingamberfold@aol.com   www.amberfold.com
£65.00 - £85.00   Open: mar - oct
Map ref no. 13

Sara Brinkhurst
Little Orchard House   3 West Street   Rye TN31 7ES
Sussex Tel: (01797) 223831
Fax 01797 223831 Mobile 07790 363950

Near Rd: A.259, A.268
This charming Georgian townhouse, with traditional walled garden & Smuggler's Watchtower, is at the heart of ancient Rye. Little Orchard House is a perfect touring base, & it retains many original features. Open fires, antique furnishings & books ensure a peaceful, relaxed atmosphere. Generous country breakfasts feature organic & free-range local products. The 2 lovely en-suite bedrooms have 4-poster beds & include colour T.V., VCR, fridge & hot-drinks tray.

info@littleorchardhouse.com
www.littleorchardhouse.com   £80.00 - £110.00
Open: all year Map ref no. 15

Jeake's House Hotel
Mermaid Street Rye TN31 7ET
Tel:(01797) 222828 Fax 01797 222623 email:stay@jeakeshouse.com www.jeakeshouse.com

see p.249

Jenny Hadfield
Jeake's House Hotel   Mermaid Street   Rye TN31 7ET
Sussex
Tel: (01797) 222828   Fax 01797 222623

Near Rd: A.259
Jeakes House is an outstanding 17th-century Grade II listed building. Retaining original features, including oak beams & wood panelling, & decorated throughout with antiques. 11 comfortable rooms overlook the peaceful gardens, with either en-suite or private facilities, colour T.V. & tea/coffee-making facilities. A 4-poster room is available. Dine in the galleried former Baptist chapel, where a choice of full English, wholefood vegetarian or Continental breakfast is served. Jeake's House is located in one of Britain's most picturesque medieval streets. Private parking. Children over 8 years are welcome.

stay@jeakeshouse.com www.jeakeshouse.com
£90.00 - £122.00   Open: all year
Map ref no. 15

James & Joy Ramus
Barons Grange   Iden   Rye TN31 7UU
Sussex
Tel: (01797) 280478   Fax 01797 280186

Near Rd: A.268
Barons Grange is a charming Georgian farmhouse, combining elegance with home comforts. It is only 2 1/2 miles from the beautiful medieval town of Rye. Set in an acre of lovely gardens with hard tennis court & swimming pool. The bedrooms are all en-suite with colour T.V. & tea/coffee-making facilities. Full English breakfast with home-made preserves is served in the attractive dining room or sun lounge. Light suppers available, on request. The farm is about 700 acres with sheep, orchards & corn. It is an ideal base for visiting the many castles, gardens & other places of interest in the area. Children over 12.

www.bestbandb.co.uk
£50.00 - £65.00   Open: all year (excl. xmas day)
Map ref no. 16

see p.251

Ron & Jo Kingsland
Durrant House 2, Market Street   Rye TN31 7LA
Sussex
Tel: (01797) 223182   Fax 01797 226940

Near Rd: A.259
Durrant House Hotel is a charming listed building located in the centre of ancient Rye. It has 6 comfortable & individually decorated bedrooms, including four-poster & triple rooms, all equipped to a high standard. There are far-reaching views across the marshes from the rear garden, where breakfast may be taken during the summer. The hotel offers an informal & friendly atmosphere, wholesome food & is the perfect location for a relaxing break. Evening meals by arrangement.

info@durranthouse.com www.durranthouse.com
£75.00 - £98.00   Open: feb -dec
Map ref no. 15

Durrant House

2 Market Street Rye TN31 7LA

Tel:(01797) 223182 Fax 01797 226940

email:info@durranthouse.com *www.durranthouse.com*

Warwickshire

Warwickshire

Warwickshire contains much that is thought of as traditional rural England, but it is a county of contradictions. Rural tranquillity surrounds industrial towns, working canals run along with meandering rivers, the mediaeval splendour of Warwick Castle vies with the handsome Regency grace of Leamington Spa.

Of course, Warwickshire is Shakespeare's county, with his birthplace, Stratford-upon-Avon standing at the northern edge of the Cotswolds. You can visit any of half a dozen houses with Shakespearian associations, see his tomb in the lovely Parish church or enjoy a performance by the world famous Royal Shakespeare Company in their theatre on the banks of the River Avon.

Angel framed by a crown of thorns. Coventry Cathedral.

Warwickshire was created as the Kingdom of Mercia after the departure of the Romans. King Offa of Mercia left us his own particular mark - a coin which bore the imprint of his likeness known as his "pen" & this became our penny. Lady Godiva was the wife of an Earl of Mercia who pleaded with her husband to lessen the taxation burden on his people. He challenged her to ride naked through the streets of Coventry as the price of her request. She did this knowing that her long hair would cover her nakedness, & the people, who loved her, stayed indoors out of respect. Only Peeping Tom found the temptation irresistible.

The 15th, 16th, & 17th centuries were the heyday of fine building in the county, when many gracious homes were built. Exceptional Compton Wynyates has rosy pink bricks, twisted chimney stacks, battlements & moats & presents an unforgettably romantic picture of a perfect Tudor House.

Coventry has long enjoyed the reputation of a thriving city, noted for its weaving of silks and ribbons, learned from the refugee Huguenots. When progress brought industry, watches, bicycles & cars became the mainstay of the city. Coventry suffered grievously from aerial bombardment in the war & innumerable ancient & treasured buildings were lost. A magnificent new Cathedral stands besides the shell of the old. Mystery plays enacting the life of Christ are performed in the haunting ruin.

Warwickshire

Warwickshire Gazeteer
Areas of Outstanding Natural Beauty.
The Edge Hills.

Historic Houses & Castles

Arbury Hall - Nuneaton
18th century Gothic mansion - made famous by George Elliot as Cheverel Manor - paintings, period furnishings, etc.

Compton Wynyates
15th century - famous Tudor house - pink brick, twisted chimneys, battlemented walls. Interior almost untouched - period furnishing.

Coughton Court - Alcester
15th century - Elizabethan half-timbered wings. Holds Jacobite relics.

Harvard House - Stratford-upon-Avon
16th century - home of mother of John Harvard, University founder.

Homington Hall - Shipston-on-Stour
17th century with fine 18th century plasterwork.

Packwood House - Hockley Heath
Tudor timber framed house - with 17th century additions. Famous yew garden.

Ragley Hall - Alcester
17th century Palladian - magnificent house with fine collection of porcelain, paintings, furniture, etc. & a valuable library.

Shakespeare's Birthplace Trust Properties - Stratford-upon-Avon

Anne Hathaway's Cottage - Shottery
The thatched cottage home of Anne Hathaway.

Hall's Croft - Old Town
Tudor house where Shakespeare's daughter Susanna lived.

Mary Arden's House - Wilmcote
Tudor farmhouse with dovecote. Home of Shakespeare's mother.

New Place - Chapel Street
Shakespeare's last home - the foundations of his house are preserved in Elizabethan garden.

Birthplace of Shakespeare - Henley Street
Many rare Shakespeare relics exhibited in this half-timbered house.

Lord Leycester Hospital - Warwick
16th century timber framed group around courtyard - hospital for poor persons in the medieval guilds.

Upton House - Edge Hill
Dating from James II reign - contains Brussels tapestries, Sevres porcelain, Chelsea figurines, 18th century furniture & other works of art, including Old Masters.

Warwick Castle - Warwick
Splendid medieval castle - site was originally fortified more than a thousand years ago. Present castle 14th century. Armoury.

Cathedrals & Churches

Astley (St. Mary the Virgin)
17th century - has remains of 14th century collegiate church. 15th century painted stalls.

Beaudesert (St. Nicholas)
Norman with fine arches in chancel.

Brailes (St. George)
15th century - decorated nave & aisles - 14th century carved oak chest

Coventry Cathedral - Coventry
Coventry Cathedral combines majestic medieval ruins with awe-inspiring modern buildings and artworks, as a symbol of resurrection and reconciliation.

Crompton Wynyates
A church of the Restoration period having a painted ceiling.

Lapworth (St. Mary)
13th & 14th century - steeple & north aisle connected by passage.

Preston-on-Stour (The Blessed Virgin Mary)
18th century. Gilded ceiling, 17th century glass.

Tredington (St. Gregory)
Saxon walls in nave - largely14th century, 17th century pulpit. Fine spire.

Warwick (St. Mary)
15th century Beauchamp Chapel, vaulted choir, some 17th century Gothic.

Wooten Wawen (St. Peter)
Saxon. Small 17th century chained library.

254

WARWICKSHIRE
Map reference

02 Lilly	06 Short
03 Lawson	06 Andrews
04 Walliker	06 P. Evans
05 Bowen	06 Tozer
06 Pettitt	07 Spencer
06 Castelli	08 Winter
06 Hughes	

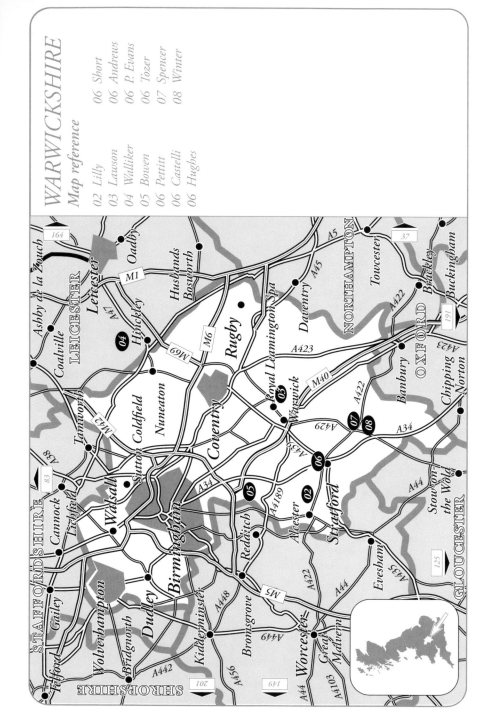

Wendy Lilly
Tudor Rose Cottage   29 Chapel Lane   Aston Cantlow
B95 6HU   Warwickshire
Tel: (01789) 488315

Near Rd: A. 422, A. 3400
A beautiful 15th century cottage in the tranquil, picturesque village of Aston Cantlow ideally situated for visiting the Cotswolds. Stratford-upon-Avon & Warwick are nearby offering a wide range of cultural. & historical attractions. An ideal base for short breaks or longer stays. Country walks are on the doorstep & bicycles are available for use on request. Bedrooms are comfortably furnished with T.V., hairdryer & tea/coffee & have private facilities. Traditional cooked breakfasts & lighter options are available, with vegetarian or special dietary needs accommodated. An idyllic tranquil setting for your visit to Shakespeare country.

enquiries@Tudor-Rose-Cottage.co.uk
www.tudor-rose-cottage.co.uk   £40.00 - £60.00
Open: all year   Map ref no. 02

John & Wendy Walliker
Ambion Court Hotel   The Green   Dadlington
Nuneaton CV13 5JB   Warwickshire
Tel: (01455) 212292   Fax 01455 213141

Near Rd: A.5
Charming, modernised Victorian farmhouse overlooking Dadlington's village green in rolling countryside near Ashby Canal. Rustic character, warm hospitality & exceptional tranquillity abound.   The accommodation includes 7 bedrooms with bathroom, T.V., phone etc; the king-sized Pine Room is particularly imposing.   Relax in the comfortable lounge & cocktail bar, savour the excellent cuisine, or amble to good pubs nearby, feeding the ducks en-route. Well-placed for Coventry, Warwick, Stratford, motorways & airports. Smoking is not permitted in lounge, restaurant & bedrooms.

stay@ambionhotel.co.uk
www.ambionhotel.co.uk   £65.00 - £75.00
Open: all year Map ref no. 04

see p.256

Christine Lawson
8 Clarendon Crescent   Leamington Spa CV32 5NR
Warwickshire
Tel: (01926) 429840   Fax 01926 424641

Near Rd: A.452
Number 8 Clarendon Crescent is a Grade II listed Regency house overlooking a private dell. Situated in a quiet backwater of Leamington. Elegantly furnished with antiques, & offering accommodation in 5 tastefully furnished bedrooms, 4 with en-suite facilities. A delicious full English breakfast is served. Only 5 mins' walk from the town centre. Very convenient for Warwick, Stratford, Stoneleigh Agricultural Centre, Warwick University & the N.E.C.. Children over 4 yrs.

lawson@lawson71.fsnet.co.uk
www.8clarendoncrescent.co.uk £70.00 - £75.00
Open: all year   Map ref no. 03

Christine Bowen
Grange Farm B & B   Forde Hall Lane
Tanworth-in-Arden   Solihull B94 5AX   Warwickshire
Tel: (01564) 742911

Near Rd: A.435
A warm welcome awaits you at this peaceful 17th-century farmhouse, set in 200 acres of beautiful countryside with footpaths & wildlife pools. Grange Farm has sloping floors, oak beams & log fires. There are 3 very attractive en-suite bedrooms with colour T.V., tea/coffee-making facilities, clock/radio alarms & hairdryers. The house is centrally located for easy access to the NEC, NAC, Stratford-upon-Avon, the Cotswolds, Warwick & Worcester. Children over 4 years. Evening meals by arrangement.

enquiries@grange-farm.com www.grange-farm.com
£65.00 - £80.00 Open: all year
Map ref no. 05

8 Clarendon Crescent

Leamington Spa CV32 5NR

Tel:(01926) 429840 Fax 01926424641

email:lawson@lawson71.fsnet.co.uk www.8clarendoncrescent.co.uk

Roger & Joanna Pettitt
Parkfield 3 Broad Walk Stratford-upon-Avon
CV37 6HS Warwickshire
Tel: (01789) 293313

Near Rd: A.3400
Visitors return to Parkfield over & over again. It must be the car park & its central location, but Parkfield also has a special atmosphere - the old Victorian house, the welcoming owners, the en-suite rooms with radio alarms, T.V. & tea/coffee-making facilities & the particular theatre interest. Breakfast is regarded as an individual choice. Parkfield pancakes are famous, but there are other vegetarian choices besides the traditional English breakfast. Children over 5 years welcome. Parkfield, the perfect base for exploring Shakespeare country.

Parkfield@btinternet.com www.ParkfieldBandB.co.uk
£55.00 - £56.00 Open: all year
Map ref no. 06

Paul & Beverley Short
Stretton House 38 Grove Road Stratford-upon-Avon
CV37 6PB Warwickshire
Tel: (01789) 268647 Fax 01789 268647

Near Rd: A.4390
Stretton House is a 'home from home' where a warm & friendly welcome awaits you. Stay in very comfortable accommodation at reasonable prices. Attractive, full en-suite bedrooms & standard rooms, all having colour T.V. & tea/coffee-making facilities. An excellent full English breakfast is served, although naturally vegetarians are catered for. There is limited car parking. Situated opposite lovely Fir Park, within easy reach of the country, yet only 3 mins' walk from the town centre & the main attractions. Children over 5 years welcome.

shortpbshort@aol.com   www.strettonhouse.co.uk
£60.00 - £60.00 Open: all year
Map ref no. 06

Danielle Castelli
Minola House 25 Evesham Place Stratford-upon-Avon
CV37 6HT Warwickshire
Tel: (01789) 293573 Fax 01789 551525

Near Rd: A.439
A comfortable house with a relaxed atmosphere, offering good accommodation in 5 rooms, 1 with private shower, 3 en-suite; all have T.V. & tea/coffee makers. Stratford offers a myriad of delights for the visitor, including the Royal Shakespeare Theatre. Set by the River Avon, this makes a lovely place for a picnic lunch or early evening meal before the performance. Children over 10 welcome. Italian & French spoken. Single occupancy from £45 per night.

www.bestbandb.co.uk
£60.00 - £60.00 Open: all year (excl. xmas)
Map ref no. 06

Patricia Andrews
Melita Private Hotel 37 Shipston Road
Stratford-upon-Avon CV37 7LN Warwickshire
Tel: (01789) 292432 Fax 01789 204867

Near Rd: A.3400
An extremely friendly family-run hotel. Offering pleasant service, good food & accommodation in 12 excellent bedrooms, with en-suite/private facilities, T.V., tea/coffee & 'phones. A comfortable lounge/bar & a beautiful garden for guests to relax in. A pleasant 5-min. walk to Shakespearian properties/theatres, shopping centre & riverside gardens. Superbly situated for Warwick Castle, Coventry & the Cotswolds. On-site private car park.

info@melitahotel.co.uk www.melitahotel.co.uk
£60.00 - £89.00 Open: all year (excl.xmas & new year)
Map ref no. 06

Fulready Manor

Ettington Stratford-upon-Avon CV37 7PE

Tel:(01789) 740152 Fax 01789 740247

email:stay@fulreadymanor.co.uk www.fulreadymanor.co.uk

Philip & Jean Evans
Sequoia House 51 Shipston Road Stratford-upon-Avon
CV37 7LN   Warwickshire
Tel: (01789) 268852 Fax 01789 414559

Near Rd: A.3400
Sequoia House is closed for refurbishment during 2007.
The property will be re-opening in 2008, offering luxury bed
& breakfast accommodation with 5 superior guest rooms.
Please see our website for on-going details of our
refurbishment programme. When we re-open why not visit
us & enjoy our wonderful location, situated across the
River Avon from the Royal Shakespeare Theatre, combined
with warm hospitality & superior accommodation. We very
much look forward to welcoming guests, both old & new,
to Sequoia House in 2008.

info@sequoiahotel.co.uk   www.sequoiahotel.co.uk
Open: from 2008
Map ref no. 06

Paul & Dreen Tozer
Victoria Spa Lodge Bishopton Lane Bishopton
Stratford-upon-Avon CV37 9QY Warwickshire
Tel: (01789) 267985 Fax 01789 204728

Near Rd: A.3400, A 46
Large 19th-century house overlooking Stratford canal, with
ample parking. A royal coat of arms was built into the
gables (with the permission of Queen Victoria) of this
Grade II listed building. The accommodation includes 7
very attractive & comfortable en-suite bedrooms, each
having a hostess tray, colour T.V., radio/alarm & hairdryer.
1 mile from the centre of town. Victoria Spa Lodge is an
excellent base for the Cotswolds & Shakespearian
properties. Pleasant walks along the tow path to Stratford
& Wilmcote. Single supplement.

ptozer@victoriaspalodge.demon.co.uk
www.stratford-upon-avon.co.uk/victoriaspa.htm
£65.00 - £65.00 Open: all year Map ref no. 06

see p.258

Michael & Mauveen Spencer
Fulready Manor Ettington   Stratford-upon-Avon
CV37 7PE   Warwickshire
Tel: (01789) 740152 Fax 01789 740247

Near Rd: A.422
Michael & Mauveen Spencer invite you to experience their
unique home, Fulready Manor. This stunning manor house
is set in 120 acres overlooking its own lake, in the beautiful
south Warwickshire countryside. It is on the doorstep of
the Cotswolds & is only 7 miles from historic Stratford-upon-
Avon. Fulready Manor boasts sumptuously furnished,
individually designed 4-poster bedrooms, all with dramatic
views & en-suite bathrooms. All of the rooms have been
skilfully created by an interior designer. Evening meals
are available by arrangement.

stay@fulreadymanor.co.uk www.fulreadymanor.co.uk
£95.00 - £140.00   Open: all year
Map ref no. 07

Angela Winter
Drybank Farm Fosseway Ettington
Stratford-upon-Avon CV37 7PD Warwickshire
Tel: (01789) 740476

Near Rd: B.4455
Drybank Farm has 15 acres of attractive farmland where
guests can enjoy walking or simply sitting & enjoying the
views of the countryside. Parts of the Farmhouse date
back 500 years & the rooms overlook the garden &
surrounding paddocks. The attractive & recently
refurbished bedrooms are ensuite & have many extras
including a hospitality tray & bath robes to name a couple.
Breakfast is cooked from local farm produce and is served
in the beamed dinning room. Situated within easy reach
of Stratford Upon Avon, Warwick & the Cotswolds.

drybank@btinternet.com www.drybank.co.uk
£70.00 - £76.00 Open: all year (excl. xmas)
Map ref no. 08

Wiltshire

Wiltshire

Wiltshire is a county of rolling chalk downs, small towns, delightful villages, fine churches & great country houses. The expanse of Salisbury Plain is divided by the beautiful valleys of Nadder, Wylye, Ebble & Avon. In a county of open landscapes, Savernake Forest, with its stately avenues of trees strikes a note of contrast. In the north west the Cotswolds spill over into Wiltshire from neighbouring Gloucestershire.

No other county is so rich in archaeological sites. Long barrows and ancient hill forts stand on the skylines as evidence of the early habitation of the chalk uplands. Many of these prehistoric sites are at once magnificent and mysterious. The massive stone arches and monoliths of

Ancient Stone Circle. Stonehenge.

Stonehenge were built over a period of 500 years with stones transported over great distances. At Avebury the small village is completely encircled by standing stones and a massive bank and ditch earthwork. Silbury Hill is a huge, enigmatic man-made mound. England's largest chambered tomb is West Kennet Long Barrow and at Bush Barrow, finds have included fine bronze and gold daggers and a stone sceptre-head similar to one found at Mycenae in Greece.

Some of England's greatest historic houses are in Wiltshire. Longleat is an Elizabethan mansion with priceless collections of paintings, books & furniture. The surrounding park was landscaped by Capability Brown and its great fame in recent years has been its Safari Park, particularly the lions which roam freely around the visiting cars.

Two delightful villages are Castle Combe, nestling in a Cotswold valley, & Lacock where the twisting streets hold examples of buildings ranging from mediaeval half-timbered, to Tudor & Georgian. 13th century Lacock Abbey, converted to a house in the 16th century, was the home of Fox Talbot, pioneer of photography.

There are many notable churches in Wiltshire. In Bradford-on-Avon, a fascinating old town, is the church of St. Lawrence, a rare example of an almost perfect Saxon church. Farley has an unusual brick church thought to have been designed by Sir Christopher Wren.

Wiltshire

Wiltshire Gazeteer

Area of Outstanding Natural Beauty.
The Costwolds & the North Wessex Downs.

Historic Houses & Castles

Corsham Court - Chippenham
16th & 17th centuries from Elizabethan &
Georgian periods. 18th century furniture, British,
Flemish & Italian Old Masters. Gardens by
Capability Brown.

Great Chalfield Manor - Melksham
15th century manor house - moated.

Church House - Salisbury
15th century house.

Chalcot House - Westbury
17th century small house in Palladian manner.

Lacock Abbey - Nr. Chippenham
13th century abbey. In 1540 converted into
house - 18th century alterations. Medieval
cloisters & brewery.

Longleat House - Warminster
16th century - early Renaissance, alterations in
early 1800's. Italian Renaissance decorations.
Splendid state rooms, pictures, books, furniture.
Victorian kitchens. Game reserve.

Littlecote - Nr. Hungerford
15th century Tudor manor. Panelled rooms,
moulded plaster ceilings.

Luckington Court - Luckington
Queen Anne for the most part - fine
ancient buildings.

Malmesbury House - Salisbury
Queen Anne house - part 14th century.
Rococo plasterwork.

Newhouse - Redlynch
17th century brick Jacobean trinity house - two
Georgian wings.

Philips House - Dinton
1816 Classical house.

Sheldon Manor - Chippenham
13th century porch & 15th century chapel in this
Plantagenet manor.

Stourhead - Stourton
18th C. Palladian house, framed landscape gardens.

Westwood Manor - Bradford-on-Avon
15th century manor house - alterations in 16th &
17th centuries.

Wardour Castle - Tisbury
18th century house in Palladian manner.

Wilton House - Salisbury
17th century - work of Inigo Jones & later of
James Wyatt in 1810. Paintings, Kent &
Chippendale furniture.

Avebury Manor - Nr Malborough
Elizabethan manor house - beautiful
plasterwork, panelling & furniture. Gardens
with topiary.

Bowood - Calne
18th century - work of several famous
architects. Gardens by Capability Brown -
famous beechwoods.

Mompesson House - Salisbury
Queen Anne town house -
Georgian plasterwork.

Cathedrals & Churches

Salisbury Cathedral
13th century - decorated tower with stone spire.
Part of original stone pulpitum is preserved.
Beautiful large decorated cloister. Exterior
mostly early English.

Salisbury (St. Thomas of Canterbury)
15th century rebuilding - 12th century font, 14th
& 15th C. glass, 17th C. monuments. 'Doom'
painting over chancel & murals in south chapel.

Amesbury (St. Mary & St. Melor)
13th century - refashioned 15th & restored in
19th century. Splendid timber roofs, stone
vaulting over chapel of north transept,
medieval painted glass, 15th century screen,
Norman font.

Bishops Cannings (St. Mary the Virgin)
13th-15th C. Fine arcading in transept - fine porch
doorway. 17th C. almsbox, Jacobean Holy table.

Bradford-on-Avon (St. Lawrence)
Best known of all Saxon churches in England.

Cricklade (St. Sampson)
12th -16th C. Tudor central tower vault,15th C chapel.

Wiltshire

Inglesham (St. John the Baptist)
Medieval wall paintings, high pews, clear glass, remains of painted screens.

Malmesbury (St. Mary)
Norman - 12th century arcades, refashioning in 14th century with clerestory, 15th century stone pulpitum added. Fine sculpture.

Tisbury (St. John the Baptist)
14th-15th C. 15th-17th C. roofing to nave & aisles. Two storeyed porch & chancel.

Potterne (St. Mary)
13th,14th,15th centuries. Inscribed Norman tub font. Wooden pulpit.

Museums & Galleries

Salisbury & South Wiltshire Museum - Salisbury
Collections showing history of the area in all periods. Models of Stonehenge & Old Sarum - archaeologically important collection.

Devizes Museum - Devizes
Unique archaeological & geological collections, including Sir Richard Colt-Hoare's Stourhead collection of prehistoric material.

Alexander Keiller Museum - Avebury
Collection of items from the Neolithic & Bronze ages & from excavations in district.

Athelstan Museum - Malmesbury
Collection of articles referring to the town - household, coin, etc.

Bedwyn Stone Museum - Great Bedwyn
Open-air museum showing where Stonehenge was carved.

Lydiard Park - Lydiard Tregoze
Parish church of St. Mary & a splendid Georgian mansion standing in park & also permanent & travelling exhibitions.

Borough of Thamesdown Museum & Art Gallery - Swindon
Natural History & Geology of Wiltshire, Bygones, coins, etc. 20th century British art & ceramic collection.

Great Western Railway Museum - Swindon
Historic locomotives. Visit this local steam railway & ride upon a fully functioning locomotive.

Other things to do

Studley Grange Garden & Leisure Park - Wroughton
Butterfly World - Rain or shine, summer or winter you can walk amongst some of the most beautiful butterflies in the world. Flying freely against a backdrop of tropical plants and flowers, listen to water falling into fish filled pools or just sit, relax and unwind for a while. A mini beasts display.

Corsham Heritage Centre - Corsham
In the home of William Arnold, 17th Century clothier, discover the stories of the two great industries of the woollen trade and quarrying of golden Bath stone used to create Corsham's architectural heritage and historical buildings throughout the world. Interactive and hands on displays in the exhibition rooms. Temporary exhibitions throughout the year.

Keynes Country Park - Nr Cricklade
Blue Flag beach, lakeside walks, adventure playgrounds, BBQ & picnic sites, nature reserves, lakeside cafe, high ropes course, bike hire, boat hire and outdoor pursuits centre.

Calne Heritage Centre - Calne
Calne Heritage Centre explains the town's rich history, from Anglo-Saxon to present time. Set in the former town library, exhibitions include details of how the town, its businesses and residents have changed over time.

Westonbirt Arboretum - Nr. Tetbury
Explore one of the largest and oldest man-made tree collections in the world. Over 18,000 rare and beautiful trees and shrubs, laid out over 600 glorious acres. Bluebells, magnolias, and rhodedendrons, 100 champion trees and the Japanese maples in Autumn. Spectacular Illuminated Trail, the unique Festival of the Wood and the Firework Concert in July. Free weekend guided walks with friendly, expert volunteers.

WILTSHIRE

Map reference

01 Roberts
02 Denning
03 Sexton
05 Stafford
06 Daniel
07 Read
08 Eavis
10 Green

10 Barker
11 Lawrence
12 Robathan
13 Sykes
14 Mertens
15 Fergie-Woods
16 Hocken

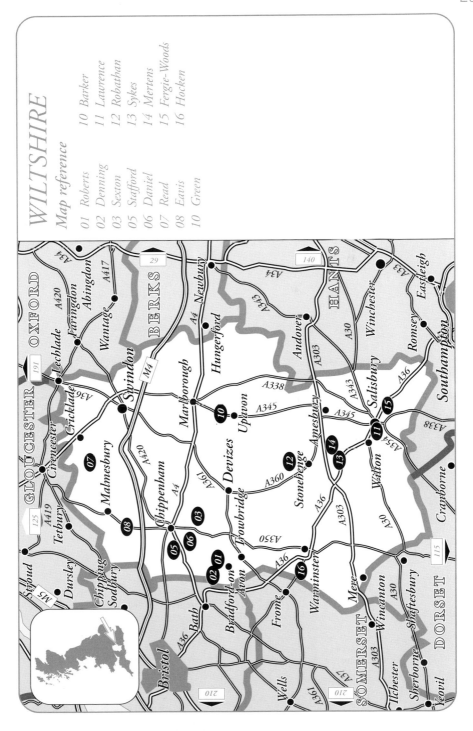

see p.265

Peter & Priscilla Roberts
Bradford Old Windmill   4 Masons Lane
Bradford-on-Avon   Bath   BA15 1QN   Wiltshire
Tel: (01225) 866842   Fax 01225 866648

Near Rd: A.363
A cosy, relaxed atmosphere greets you at this converted windmill high on the hill above the town. The old stone tower overflows with character, & with the many finds picked up by Peter & Priscilla on their backpacking trips around the world. All of the unusually shaped bedrooms have en-suite bathrooms & are tastefully furnished with your comfort in mind. Imaginative healthy & unhealthy breakfasts are served beneath the massive grain weighing scales. Delicious evening meals by arrangement. Bradford Old Windmill is only 5 mins' walk from the town centre. Children over 6 years welcome.

bbbw@bradfordoldwindmill.co.uk
www.bradfordoldwindmill.co.uk   £59.00 - £109.00
Open: mar - oct   Map ref no. 01

Elaine Sexton
The Old Rectory   Cantax Hill   Lacock
Chippenham   SN15 2JZ   Wiltshire
Tel: (01249) 730335   Fax 01249 730166

Near Rd: A.350
Situated in the medieval village of Lacock, The Old Rectory, built in 1866, is a fine example of Victorian Gothic architecture, with creeper-clad walls & mullioned windows. It stands in 12 acres of its own carefully tended grounds, which include a tennis court & croquet lawn for guests use. The Old Rectory offers 6 very attractive, tastefully furnished bedrooms (1room is on the ground floor), all with en-suite/private facilities etc. A good breakfast menu is available. The house is an excellent choice for a relaxing short break holiday & for those who wish to explore the delights of the glorious West Country.

sexton@oldrectorylacock.co.uk
www.oldrectorylacock.co.uk   £60.00 - £75.00
Open: all year (excl. xmas)   Map ref no. 03

Elizabeth & John Denning
Burghope Manor   Winsley   Bradford-on-Avon
BA15 2LA   Wiltshire
Tel: (01225) 723557   Fax 01225 723113

Near Rd: A.36
This lovely old home has stood here for 7 centuries overlooking the wonderful valley below - 5 miles from Bath & 1 1/2 miles from Bradford-on-Avon. Although steeped in history, Burghope Manor is first & foremost a living family home, which has been carefully modernised so that the wealth of historical features may complement the present-day comforts. A village pub & restaurant are nearby. Evening meals for groups only. Children over 10 years. Single occupancy supplement.

info@burghope.co.uk
www.burghope.co.uk   £95.00 - £100.00
Open: all year (excl.xmas & new year) Map ref no. 02

Gill Stafford
Pickwick Lodge Farm   Guyers Lane   Corsham   SN13 0PS
Wiltshire
Tel: (01249) 712207   Fax 01249 701904

Near Rd: A.4
A delightful 17th-century Cotswold stone farmhouse, set in peaceful surroundings. 3 well-appointed & tastefully furnished bedrooms, each with an en-suite/private bathroom, radio, T.V. & tea/coffee-making facilities. Hearty & delicious breakfasts are served. Ideally situated for visiting many sites of historical interest, such as the Wiltshire White Horses, Avebury & Stonehenge; many stately homes & National Trust properties within easy reach. Ample car parking. Children over 12 years.

b&b@pickwickfarm.co.uk   www.pickwickfarm.co.uk
£60.00 - £65.00   Open: all year (excl.xmas & new year)
Map ref no. 05

The Old Rectory

Cantax Hill Lacock SN15 2JZ

Tel: (01249)730335 Fax: 01249 730166

email:sexton@oldrectorylacock.co.uk www.oldrectorylacock.co.uk

Jenny & Peter Daniel
Heatherly Cottage Ladbrook Lane Gastard   Corsham
SN13 9PE   Wiltshire
Tel: (01249) 701402   Fax 01249 701412

Near Rd: A.4
17th-century Heatherly Cottage is situated in a quiet lane approx. 9 miles from Bath. Close to the National Trust village of Lacock where several films have been made. The guests' accommodation is in a separate wing of the house with its own entrance. There is one ground-floor twin & 2 first-floor double rooms (1 with queen-size bed), all en-suite & with T.V. etc. Each room is tastefully furnished throughout. A full English breakfast is served with free-range eggs from the Daniels' own hens, or Continental with croissants. Children over 9 years.

pandj@heatherly.plus.com
www.SmoothHound.co.uk/hotels/heather3.html
£62.00 - £65.00 Open: all year Map ref no. 06

Mrs Ross Eavis
Manor Farm Corston   Malmesbury SN16 0HF
Wiltshire
Tel: (01666) 822148   Fax 01666 826565

Near Rd: A.429
Relax & unwind in this charming award-winning 17th-century farmhouse, situated on a mixed working farm. The accommodation includes 4 bedrooms, all with colour T.V. & hospitality trays. Eat your hearty breakfast in a dining room with a large inglenook fireplace. Ideal base for 1 night or longer stays for exploring the Cotswolds, Bath, Stonehenge, Lacock & many stately homes. Or just while away the time relaxing in the pretty walled garden. Meals are available at the local pub, which is within walking distance. Children over 12.

ross@johneavis.wanadoo.co.uk
www.manorfarmbandb.co.uk £50.00 - £60.00
Open: all year (excl.xmas & new year) Map ref no. 08

Mrs Claire Read
Leighfield Lodge Farm   Malmesbury RoadLeigh
Cricklade SN6 6RH   Wiltshire
Tel: (01666) 860241   Fax 01666 860241

Near Rd: A.419
Leighfield Lodge is a lovely old farmhouse in a secluded & rural setting. It is built on the site of a former Royal hunting lodge. Discover en-suite rooms with comfortable beds, crisp cotton bedlinen, power showers, colour T.V. & tea/coffee-making facilities. Experience good traditional cooking using locally sourced food where possible. Evening meals are available by prior arrangement. Guests' sitting room available. Well situated for Oxford, Bath, Stonehenge, Avebury, Thames Path & the Cotswolds. Brochure available.

claireread@leighfieldlodge.fsnet.co.uk
www.leighfieldlodge.com £60.00 - £70.00
Open: all year Map ref no. 07

Peter & Cherry Barker
The Old Dairy House Sharcott Pewsey SN9 5PA
Wiltshire
Tel: (01672) 562287

Near Rd: A.345
Situated in the quiet hamlet of Sharcott just outside Pewsey, this 300 year old thatched red-brick house is a blissful place to stay. It stands in 5 acres of park-like grounds, overlooking the headwaters of the River Avon, & taking in a water meadow, a wooded area & a lake. 2 spacious en-suite bedrooms, both attractively decorated. Also a sitting room on the first floor (with TV). Breakfast is served in the modern conservatory, which overlooks the garden. Good local eateries for evening meals. A good base for visits to Bath, Salisbury, Marlborough and Winchester.

sharcott.pewsey@virgin.net
business.virgin.net/sharcott.pewsey £70.00 - £70.00
Open: all year (excl. xmas) Map ref no. 10

Isabel Green
The Manor Upavon Pewsey SN9 6EB
Wiltshire
Tel: (01980) 635115

Near Rd: A.342
The Manor is a charming, spacious 17th-century thatched house, nestling in a quiet location in the village yet within walking distance of 2 pubs. It is surrounded by 8 acres leading to the River Avon. The interior has been recently renovated to a high standard & rooms are tastefully furnished throughout. The en-suite bedrooms & beds are extremely comfortable & many guests have commented on the wonderfully relaxed atmosphere. Upavon is very well situated for all the historical interest of Wiltshire, including Salisbury, Stonehenge, Avebury & Marlborough etc. Evening meals & animals by arrangement.

isabelbgreen@botmail.com
www.themanorupavon.co.uk £70.00 - £80.00
Open: all year Map ref no. 10

Dick & Joan Robathan
Maddington House Maddington Street Shrewton
Salisbury SP3 4JD Wiltshire
Tel: (01980) 620406

Near Rd: A.360
Maddington House is the family home of Dick & Joan Robathan. It is an elegant 17th-century Grade II listed house in the centre of the pretty village of Shrewton - about 2 1/2 miles from Stonehenge & 11 miles from Salisbury. The accommdoation includes 3 attractive & comfortabley furnished guest rooms, all with en-suite facilities. The village has 3 pubs, all within easy walking distance. Maddington House is a delightful home, & the perfect base for a relaxing short break holiday. Children over 12 years. Also self-catering cottages are available.

rsrobathan@freenet.co.uk
www.maddingtonhouse.co.uk £60.00 - £70.00
Open: all year Map ref no. 12

Mrs J Lawrence
Stratford Lodge 4 Park Lane Salisbury SP1 3NP
Wiltshire
Tel: (01722) 325177 Fax 01722 325177

Near Rd: A.345
Stratford Lodge is tucked away in a quiet lane overlooking Victoria Park & it has all the charm of the Victorian era when the house was built. The comfortable bedrooms are en-suite & decorated in pastel colours with co-ordinating fabrics. All of the food at Stratford Lodge is prepared with great care & includes local produce & fresh herbs, vegetables & fruit. The dinner menu, which changes daily, always offers vegetarian dishes (special diets with notice.) After exploring Salisbury, relax in the sheltered & secluded garden or retire to the sitting room with log fire, in winter.

enquiries@stratfordlodge.co.uk
www.stratfordlodge.co.uk £79.50 - £82.00
Open: all year Map ref no. 11

Mrs Christine Sykes
Elm Tree Cottage Chain Hill Stapleford
Salisbury SP3 4LH Wiltshire
Tel: (01722) 790507 Mobile 07786 880275

Near Rd: A.36, B.3083
Elm Tree Cottage is a 17th-century character cottage with inglenook & beams & a pretty flower garden to relax in. The bedrooms, each with an en-suite/private bathroom, are light & airy, attractively decorated & have colour T.V. & tea/coffee-making facilities. The atmosphere is relaxed & warm, & breakfast is served as required. Situated in a picturesque village, there are views across various valleys, & it is a good centre for Salisbury, Wilton, Longleat, Stonehenge, Avebury, Lacock, Bath, Glastonbury & Wells. Animals by arrangement.

enquiries@elmtreecottage.com
www.elmtreecottage.com £56.00 - £58.00
Open: feb - nov Map ref no. 13

Mill House

Berwick St. James Salisbury SP3 4TS

Tel:(01722) 790331 Fax 01722 790753 email:bestbandb@atlas.co.uk www.millhouse.org.uk

see p.268

Michael Mertens (son) & Diana Gifford Mead
Mill House Berwick St. James Salisbury SP3 4TS
Wiltshire
Tel: (01722) 790331 Fax 01722 790753

Near Rd: A.36, A.303
Stonehenge is only 3 miles away. Diana welcomes you to
The Mill House set in acres of nature reserve abounding in
wild flowers & infinite peace. An island paradise with the
River Till running through the working mill & gardens.
Diana's old fashioned roses long to see you as do the
lovely walks, antiquities & houses. Built by the miller in
1785, the bedrooms all have tea/coffee-making facilities &
colour T.V.. Fishing or swimming in the mill pool & close to
golf course & riding. Attention to healthy & organic food.
Sample superb cuisine at the Boot Inn. Children over 5
years. Restricted smoking.

www.millhouse.org.uk
£70.00 - £70.00 Open: all year
Map ref no. 14

Mrs J. Hocken
Bugley Barton Warminster BA12 8HD
Wiltshire
Tel: (01985) 213389

Near Rd: A.362
Ideally placed for trips to Bath, Salisbury, Longleat,
Stonehenge & Stourhead; Bugley provides the perfect
opportunity to stay in a truly elegant & comfortable Grade
II listed Georgian house. Julie & Brian are easy-going &
friendly. Home-made cake & delicious breakfasts are
served in the huge farmhouse kitchen overlooking the
fountain. The spacious & well-equipped en-suite guest
rooms overlook the beautiful garden & have many
thoughtful added touches. Good local pubs, parking & a
train station within easy reach. Single supplement.
Children over 12 years.

bugleybarton@aol.com www.bestbandb.co.uk
£70.00 - £75.00 Open: all year (excl.xmas & new year)
Map ref no. 16

Ian & Annette Fergie-Woods
Witherington Farm Nr.Downton Salisbury SP5 3QT
Wiltshire
Tel: (01722) 710222

Near Rd: A.36
Ian & Annette offer you award-winning accommodation in
their oak-beamed Grade II listed 17th-century farmhouse.
2 of the attractive bedrooms have stunning views to the
Wiltshire Downs, the 3rd room is in the very oldest part of
the house, overlooking the old farmyard. Each room is
furnished to a high standard & has en-suite/private facilities.
A beautiful 2-acre garden surrounds the house. The farm
extends to 600 acres. If you are looking for peace & quiet
this is the place for you & only 15 mins' drive from Salisbury.
Children over 12.

bandb@witheringtonfarm.co.uk
www.witheringtonfarm.co.uk £60.00 - £80.00
Open: all year (excl. xmas) Map ref no. 15

Yorkshire

Yorkshire

England's largest county is a region of beautiful landscapes, of hills, peaks, fells, dales & forests with many square miles of National Park. It is a vast area taking in big industrial cities, interesting towns & delightful villages. Yorkshire's broad rivers sweep through the countryside & are an angler's paradise. Cascading waterfalls pour down from hillside & moorland.

The North sea coast can be thrilling, with wild seas & cliff-top walks. Staithes & Robin Hoods Bay are fascinating old fishing villages. Whitby is an attractive port with Abbey, the small town tumbles in red-roofed tiers down to the busy harbour from which Captain Cook sailed.

The Yorkshire Dales form one of the finest landscapes in England. From windswept

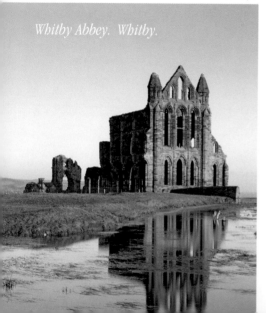

Whitby Abbey. Whitby.

moors to wide green valleys the scenery is incomparable. A network of dry stone walls covers the land; some are as old as the stone-built villages but those which climb the valley sides to the high moors are the product of the 18th century enclosures.

Each of the Dales has a distinctive character; from the remote upper reaches of Swaledale & Wensleydale, where the air sings with the sound of wind, sheep, & curlew, over to Airedale & the spectacular limestone gorges of Malham Cove & Gordale Scar, & down to the soft meadows & woods of Wharfedale where the ruins of Bolton Priory stand beside the river.

The North Yorks National Park, where the moors are ablaze with purple fire of heather in the late summer, is exhilarating country. There is moorland to the east also, on the Pennine chain; famous Ilkley Moor with its stone circle known as the twelve apostles, & the Haworth Moors around the plain Yorkshire village where the Bronte sisters lived. York is the finest mediaeval city in England. It is encircled by its limestone city walls with four Great Gates. Within the walls are the jumbled roof line, dog-leg streets & sudden courtyards of a mediaeval town. Half timbered buildings with over-sailing upper storeys jostle with Georgian brick houses along the network of narrow streets around The Shambles & King Edward Square. York Minster stands in timeless majesty, at the heart of the city.

Yorkshire

Yorkshire Gazeteer
Areas of Outstanding Natural Beauty.
The North Yorkshire Moors. The Yorkshire Dales.

Historic Houses & Castles.

Carlton Towers
17th century, remodelled in later centuries.
Paintings, silver, furniture, pictures. Carved
woodwork, painted decorations, examples of
Victorian craftmanship.

Castle Howard - Nr. York
18th C.- celebrated architect, Sir John Vanbrugh
- paintings, costumes, furniture by Chippendale,
Sheraton, Adam. Not to be missed.

East Riddlesden Hall - Keighley
17th century manor house with fishponds &
historic barns, one of which is regarded as very
fine example of medieval tithe barn.

Newby Hall - Ripon
17th century Wren style extended by Robert
Adam. Gobelins tapestry, Chippendale
furniture, sculpture galleries with Roman
rotunda, statuary. Award- winning gardens.

Nostell Priory - Wakefield
18th century, Georgian mansion, Chippendale
furniture, paintings.

Burton Constable Hall - Hull
16th century, Elizabethan, remodelled in
Georgian period. Stained glass, Hepplewhite
furniture, gardens by Capability Brown.

Ripley Castle - Harrogate
14th century, parts dating during 16th & 18th
centuries. Priest hole, armour & weapons,
beautiful ceilings.

The Treasurer's House - York
17th & 18th centuries, splendid interiors,
furniture, pictures.

Harewood House - Leeds
18th century - Robert Adam design,
Chippendale furniture, Italian & English
paintings. Sevres & Chinese porcelain.

Benningbrough Hall - York
18th century. Highly decorative woodwork, oak
staircase, friezes etc. Splendid hall.

Markenfield Hall - Ripon
14th to 16th century - fine Manor house
surrounded by moat.

Heath Hall - Wakefield
18th century, palladian. Fine woodwork &
plasterwork, rococo ceilings, excellent furniture,
paintings & porcelain.

Bishops House - Sheffield
16th century. Only complete timber framed
yeoman farmhouse surviving. Vernacular
architecture. Superb.

Skipton Castle- Skipton
One of the most complete & well preserved
medieval castles in England.

Cathedral & Churches

York Minster
13th century. Greatest Gothic Cathedral north
of the Alps. Imposing grandeur - superb
Chapter house, contains half of the medieval
stained glass of England. Outstandingly
beautiful.

York (All Saints, North Street)
15th century roofing in parts - 18th century pulpit
wonderful medieval glass.

Ripon Cathedral
12th century - though in some parts Saxon in
origin. Decorated choir stalls - gables
buttresses. Church of 672 preserved in crypt,
Caxton Book, ecclesiastic treasures.

Bolton Percy (All Saints)
15th century. Maintains original glass in east
window. Jacobean font cover. Georgian pulpit.
Interesting monuments.

Rievaulx Abbey
12th century, masterpiece of Early English
architecture. One of three great Cistercian
Abbeys built in Yorkshire. Impressive ruins.

Campsall (St. Mary Magdalene)
Fine Norman tower - 15th century rood screen,
carved & painted stone altar.

Fountains Abbey - Ripon
Ruins of England's greatest medieval abbey -
surrounded by wonderful landscaped gardens.

Yorkshire

Enormous tower, vaulted cellar 300 feet long.

Whitby (St. Mary)
12th century tower & doorway, 18th century
remodelling - box pews much interior woodwork
painted - galleries. High pulpit. Table tombs.

Whitby Abbey - Whitby (St. Hilda)
7th century superb ruin - venue of Synod of 664.
Destroyed by the Vikings, restored 1078.
Magnificent north transept.

Halifax (St. John the Baptist)
12th century origins, showing work from each
succeeding century - heraldic ceilings.
Cromwell glass.

Beverley Minster - Beverley
14th century. Fine Gothic Minster - remarkable
medieval effigies of musicians playing
instruments. Founded as monastery in 700.

Bolton Priory - Nr. Skipton
Nave of Augustinian Priory, now Bolton's Parish
Church, amidst ruins of choir & transepts, in
beautiful riverside setting.

Selby Abbey - Selby
11th century Benedictine abbey of which the
huge church remains. Roof & furnishings
are modern after a fire of 1906, but the
stonework is intact. Reputedly the birth place of
Henry I - 1068.

Museums & Galleries

**Aldborough Roman Museum -
Boroughbridge**
Remnants of Roman period of the town - coins,
glass, pottery, etc.

Great Ayton
Home of Captain Cook, explorer & seaman.
Exhibits of maps, etc.

Art Gallery - City of York
Modern paintings, Old Masters, watercolours,
prints, ceramics.

Lotherton Hall - Nr. Leeds
Museum with furniture, paintings, silver, works of art
from the Leeds collection & oriental art gallery.

National Railway Museum - York
Devoted to railway engineering & its development.

York Castle Museum
The Kirk Collection of bygones including
cobbled streets, shops, costumes, toys,
household & farm equipment - fascinating
collection.

Cannon Hall Art Gallery - Barnsley
18th century house with fine furniture & glass,
etc. Flemish & Dutch paintings. Also houses
museum of the 13/18 Royal Hussars.

Mappin Art Gallery - Sheffield
Works from18th,19th & 20th century.

Graves Art gallery-Sheffield.
British portraiture. European works & examples
of Asian & African art. Loan exhibitions are held.

Royal Pump Room Museum - Harrogate
Original sulphur well used in the Victorian Spa.
Local history costume & pottery.

Bolling Hall - Bradford
A period house with mixture of styles -
collections of 17th century oak furniture,
domestic utensils, toys & bygones.

Georgian Theatre - Richmond
Oldest theatre in the country - interesting
theatrical memorabilia.

Jorvik Viking Centre - York
Recently excavated site in the centre of York
showing hundreds of artifacts dating from the
Viking period. One of the most important
archaeological discoveries last century.

Abbey House Museum - Kirkstall, Leeds
Illustrated past 300 years of Yorkshire life.
Shows 3 full streets from 19th century with
houses, shops & workplaces.

Piece Hall - Halifax
Remarkable building - constructed around huge
quadrangle - now Textile Industrial Museum, Art
Gallery & has craft & antique shops.

**National Museum of Photography, Film &
Television - Bradford**
Displays look at art & science of photography,
film & T.V. Britain's only IMAX arena.

The Colour Museum - Bradford
Explore the world of colour. Discover the story
of dyeing & textile printing.

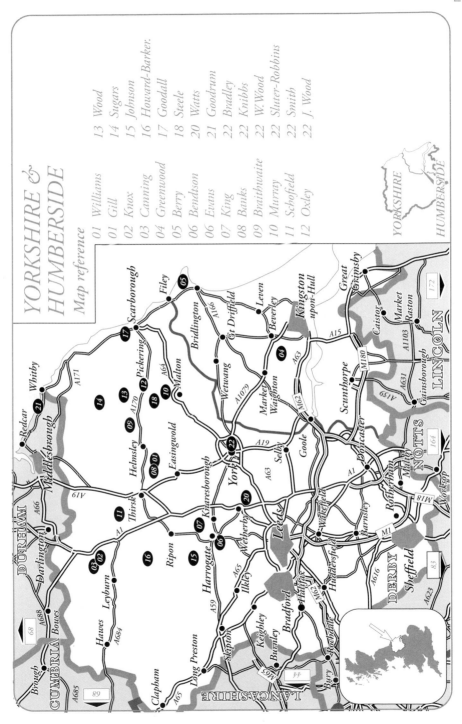

YORKSHIRE & HUMBERSIDE
Map reference

01 Williams
01 Gill
02 Knox
03 Canning
04 Greenwood
05 Berry
06 Bendson
06 Evans
07 King
08 Banks
09 Braithwaite
10 Murray
11 Schofield
12 Oxley

13 Wood
14 Sugars
15 Johnson
16 Howard-Barker
17 Goodall
18 Steele
20 Watts
21 Goodrum
22 Bradley
22 Knibbs
22 W.Wood
22 Sluter-Robbins
22 Smith
22 J.Wood

see p.275

Paul & Pat Williams
Daleside   East End Ampleforth YO62 4DA
Yorkshire
Tel: (01439) 788266

Near Rd: A.170
Daleside is listed the oldest house in this charming stone village, with 400-year-old cruck beams & oak panelling. The house has been sympathetically restored, with the 2 en-suite guests' rooms (1 twin-bedded, 1 double with half-tester bed) overlooking the garden. There are 2 inns in the village & other good restaurants nearby for evening meals. Ampleforth is on the edge of the North York Moors National Park, with excellent walks all around. Children from 10 years are welcome. Daleside is the perfect location for a relaxing break in Yorkshire.

dalesidepaul@hotmail.com www.bestbandb.co.uk
£65.00 - £73.00 Open: all year (excl. xmas & new year)
Map ref no. 01

Mrs Patricia Knox
Mill Close Farm   Patrick Brompton   Bedale DL8 1JY
Yorkshire
Tel: (01677) 450257   Fax 01748 813612

Near Rd: A.684
Award-winning farmhouse surrounded by beautiful rolling countryside at the foothills of the Yorkshire Dales. Offering luxurious en-suite bedrooms, 2 with spa baths, 1 with a 4-poster suite. Bedrooms have super king-size beds, guest fridges with complimentary fruit, handmade chocolates & spring water. Mill Close Farm is set in a very tranquil location with exceptional views, perfect for a short break holiday A lovely walled garden with pond & waterfall. Traditional & speciality breakfasts are prepared with local produce. A colour brochure is available.

pat@millclose.co.uk www.millclose.co.uk
£65.00 - £85.00 Open: all year (excl. xmas & new year)
Map ref no. 02

Phillip Gill & Anton Van Der Horst
Shallowdale House   West End Ampleforth YO62 4DY
Yorkshire
Tel: (01439) 788325   Fax 01439 788885

Near Rd: A.170
This is an outstanding modern country house, with 2 acres of hillside garden, on the southern edge of the North York Moors National Park, 20 miles north of York. Each of the 3 spacious guest rooms, furnished with style & attention to detail, enjoys stunning views of the unspoilt countryside. Imaginative meals are prepared from fresh seasonal ingredients. Drinks licence. Award-winning Shallowdale House is a perfect place to unwind when exploring Herriot country & York. Children over 12.

stay@shallowdalehouse.co.uk
www.shallowdalehouse.co.uk £85.00 - £105.00
Open: all year (excl. xmas & new year) Map ref no. 01

Mrs Canning
Elmfield Country House   Arrathorne Bedale DL8 1NE
Yorkshire
Tel: (01677) 450558   Fax 01677 450557

Near Rd: A.684
Located in its own grounds in the country. Enjoy a relaxed, friendly atmosphere in spacious surroundings, with a high standard of furnishings. 9 en-suite bedrooms comprising twin-bedded, double & family rooms. 2 rooms have been adapted for disabled guests & another has a 4-poster bed. All rooms have satellite colour T.V., 'phone, radio/alarm & tea/coffee makers. A games room & solarium are also available. Excellent farmhouse cooking. Residential licence. A delightful home. Single supplement.

stay@elmfieldhouse.freeserve.co.uk
www.elmfieldhouse.co.uk £60.00 - £80.00
Open: all year   Map ref no. 03

Mill Close Farm

Patrick Brompton Bedale DL8 1JY

Tel:(01677) 450257 Fax 01748 813612

email:pat@millclose.co.uk www.millclose.co.uk

Laura & Charlie Greenwood
Rudstone Walk Country Accommodation   South Cave
Nr. Beverley HU15 2AH   Yorkshire
Tel: (01430) 422230   Fax 01430 424552

Near Rd: A.1034
Rudstone Walk is renowned for its hospitality & good food. Accommodation is in the very tastefully converted farm buildings, adjacent to the main farmhouse where meals are served. Each of the attractive bedrooms has excellent en-suite facilities, colour T.V., telephone, hairdryer & internet access. Rudstone Walk provides a peaceful retreat after a tiring day. It is ideal for a relaxing break, & is within easy reach of historic York & many other attractions. Animals by arrangement. Special offer breaks Nov - May, stay 3 nights for the price of 2.

admin@rudstone-walk.co.uk
www.rudstone-walk.co.uk   £68.00 - £68.00
Open: all year   Map ref no. 04

Gill & Kristian Bendtson
Ashwood House 7 Spring Grove Harrogate HG1 2HS
Yorkshire
Tel: (01423) 560081   Fax 01423 527928

Near Rd: A.61
Ashwood House is a charming 5-bedroomed Edwardian house retaining many of its original features. Situated in a quiet, residential cul-de-sac mins' from the town centre. The attractive en-suite bedrooms are spacious, some with 4-poster beds, all with hospitality tray, colour T.V., hairdryer & complimentary toiletries. A delicious breakfast is served from lovely Royal Copenhagen china in the elegant dining room. A high standard of service & a warm welcome is assured at this charming home. Scandinavian languages spoken. Children over 7 years welcome.

ashwoodhouse@aol.com   www.ashwoodhouse.co.uk
£65.00 - £70.00 Open: all year (excl. xmas & new year)
Map ref no. 06

Lesley Berry & Geoffrey Miller
The Manor House Flamborough Bridlington YO15 1PD
Yorkshire   Tel: (01262) 850943
Fax 01262 850943 Mobile 07718 415234

Near Rd: B.1255
Flamborough Manor, dating from c.1770, offers spacious, comfortable accommodation. Pefectly situated to explore the Flamborough Heritage Coast & the famous gannet colony & puffins (early summer) at Bempton RSPB Sanctuary. Burton Agnes Hall, Sledmere House, Castle Howard, the North York Moors, Robin Hood's Bay, Whitby, York, Beverley & Scarborough are all nearby. The larger en-suite room features an imposing 17th century Portuguese bed; the 2nd has a Victorian brass bed & private bathroom. Children over 8. Dinner by arrangemnt.

gm@flamboroughmanor.co.uk
www.flamboroughmanor.co.uk   £76.00 - £86.00
Open: all year (excl. xmas)   Map ref no. 05

Kath & Bob Evans
Shannon Court 65 Dragon Avenue Harrogate HG1 5DS
Yorkshire
Tel: (01423) 509858   Fax 01423 530606

Near Rd: A.59
Shannon Court is a charming Victorian house hotel, overlooking the 'Stray' in High Harrogate. Enjoy real home cooking in this charming home. Accommodation is in 8 delightful & tastefully furnished bedrooms, all of which are en-suite & have every modern comfort including radio/alarm, colour T.V. & tea/coffee-making facilities. The hotel is licensed for residents & their guests. Close to town centre, railway station & conference centre, with easy parking & direct main routes for moors & dales. Shannon Court Hotel is an excellent touring base.

shannon@courthotel.freeserve.co.uk
www.shannon-court.com   £67.00 - £73.00
Open: all year (excl. new year) Map ref no. 06

Oldstead Grange

Oldstead Coxwold Helmsley YO61 4BJ

Tel:(01347) 868634

email:anne@yorkshireuk.com www.yorkshireuk.com

Clive & Gill King
Fountains House Burton Leonard   Nr. Harrogate
HG3 3RU   Yorkshire
Tel: (01765) 677537

Near Rd: A.61
Fountains House is a charming 18th-century limestone cottage with lovely south-facing garden; situated in the pretty village of Burton Leonard halfway between Harrogate & Ripon, ideally placed for both town & country. The accommodation includes 2 twin/double rooms with en-suite facilities, colour T.V. & hospitality tray, delightfully furnished & decorated to a high standard. Delicious breakfasts are cooked to order & include home-made preserves & freshly baked bread from the Aga. Evening meals available by prior arrangement. Parking. Children over 11 years are welcome.

info@fountainshouse.co.uk www.fountainshouse.co.uk
£58.00 - £68.00 Open: all year
Map ref no. 07

Chris & Sarah Braithwaite
Plumpton Court High Street   Nawton Helmsley
YO62 7TT   Yorkshire
Tel: (01439) 771223

Near Rd: A.170
A family-run 17th-century guest house set in the foothills of the North York Moors. Plumpton Court is ideally situated for exploring historic York & exploring the east coast. There are 9 en-suite, comfortable, tastefully furnished & well-appointed bedrooms including 2 luxury king-size bedrooms, all with clock/radio, tea/coffee-making facilities & colour T.V.. There is a comfortable lounge in which guests may relax, with a cosy real fire & a small bar. Delicious breakfasts are served in the comfortable dining room. Chris's scrambled eggs are a real treat. Children over 12 years. A gated car park & garden.

mail@plumptoncourt.com www.plumptoncourt.com
£52.00 - £55.00 Open: all year (excl. xmas & new year)
Map ref no. 09

see p.277

Mrs Anne Banks
Oldstead Grange Oldstead Coxwold Helmsley
YO61 4BJ   Yorkshire
Tel: (01347) 868634

Near Rd: A.170
A 17th-century historic farmhouse set amidst superb National Park countryside. Stay in a relaxed, uncomplicated friendly atmosphere uniquely combined with exceptionally high quality accommodation. 3 spacious en-suite bedrooms, including a special 4-poster suite, each with really comfortable king-size beds, T.V., robes, fresh flowers & home-made chocolates. Breakfasts feature freshly prepared traditional & speciality dishes & for dinner there are renowned eating places in the local picturesque villages. Children over 10.

anne@yorkshireuk.com   www.yorkshireuk.com
£68.00 - £88.00 Open: all year
Map ref no. 08

Mrs Judith Murray
Manor Farm   Little Barugh Malton YO17 6UY
Yorkshire
Tel: (01653) 668262   Fax 01653 668600

Near Rd: A.169
Manor Farm is a charming Georgian manor house set in spacious grounds with hard tennis court, croquet lawn & views to the Howardian Hills. The accommodation includes 3 very attractive bedrooms, with either an en-suite or a private bathroom. Excellent cooking caters for all tastes. Manor Farm is within easy reach of historic York, Scarborough, the Moors, Castle Howard & Flamingoland. Reduced rates are available for stays of 3 nights or more. Dogs, & children over 5, are most welcome. Minimum 2 nights stay applies.

cphmurray@compuserve.com www.bestbandb.co.uk
£60.00 - £70.00 Open: all year
Map ref no. 10

Rose Cottage Farm B & B

Main Street Cropton Pickering YO18 8IIL

Tel:(01751) 417302

www.bestbandb.co.uk

see p.279

Mike & Pauline Schofield
Elmscott   Hatfield Road   Northallerton   DL7 8QX
Yorkshire
Tel: (01609) 760575

Near Rd: A.684, A.167
Elmscott is a charming property which is set in a delightful landscaped garden. It is situated close to the centre of Northallerton, which is a thriving market town. Your hosts offer 2 attractively furnished bedrooms, each with an en-suite bathroom, tea/coffee-making facilities & colour T.V. A delicious breakfast is served. Elmscott is located mid-way between the North Yorkshire Moors & the beautiful Yorkshire Dales National Parks, with their famous 'Herriott' connections. This really is a lovely home, perfect for a relaxing short break holiday.

elmscott@freenet.co.uk
www.elmscottbedandbreakfast.co.uk   £56.00 - £56.00
Open: all year Map ref no. 11

Mrs Joan Wood
Rose Cottage Farm B & B Main Street   Cropton
Pickering YO18 8HL   Yorkshire
Tel: (01751) 417302

Near Rd: A.170
A warm welcome awaits you at Rose Cottage Farm. Your hosts aim to provide good food using home produce & comfortable accommodation in a cosy informal atmosphere. The 3 spacious & attractively decorated en-suite rooms include colour T.V. & tea/coffee-making facilities. Guests may relax in the cosy lounge, which has cruck beams & many original features. Afternoon tea is served on arrival & evening meals can be taken in the attractive conservatory dining room. Easy access to the beautiful moors, coast & York.

bestbandb@atlas.co.uk
www.smoothhound.co.uk   £52.00 - £60.00
Open: all year Map ref no. 13

see p.281

Mrs Pat Oxley
17 Burgate   Pickering YO18 7AU
Yorkshire
Tel: (01751) 473463

Near Rd: A.170
17 Burgate is a stylishly renovated town house only a few minutes walk from the town centre, the historic castle & North Yorkshire Moors Steam Railway. 17 is a fusion of traditional standards of service with up to date amenities & elegant decor to meet the needs of the modern traveller. There is a comfy restful lounge with well-stocked bar, log burning stove & outside a terrace & patio, ideal for warm summer evenings. 17 is the perfect retreat whatever the occasion. Relax & indulge. Children over 10 welcome.

info@17burgate.co.uk   www.17burgate.co.uk
£75.00 - £99.00 Open: all year (excl. xmas)
Map ref no. 12

Linda Sugars
Sevenford House Rosedale Abbey Pickering YO18 8SE
Yorkshire
Tel: (01751) 417283

Near Rd: A.170
Originally a vicarage, & built from the stones of Rosedale Abbey, Sevenford House stands in 4 acres of lovely gardens in the heart of the beautiful Yorkshire Moors National Park. There are 3 tastefully furnished, en-suite bedrooms, with T.V., radio & tea/coffee-making facilities, offering wonderful views overlooking valley & moorland. A relaxing guests' lounge/library with an open fire. An excellent base for exploring the region. Riding & golf locally. Also, ruined abbeys, Roman roads, steam railways, the beautiful coastline & pretty fishing towns.

sevenford@aol.com   www.sevenford.com
£55.00 - £60.00 Open: all year
Map ref no. 14

Sevenford House

Rosedale Abbey Pickering YO18 8SE

Tel:(01751) 417283

email:sevenford@aol.com www.sevenford.com

see p.283

Mrs Maggie Johnson
Mallard Grange Aldfield   Nr. Fountains Abbey Ripon
HG4 3BE   Yorkshire
Tel: (01765) 620242   Mobile 07720 295918

Near Rd: B.6265, A.1
Mallard Grange is a rambling 16th-century farmhouse nestling in glorious countryside nestling between Yorkshire Dales & Moors. A special place, warm, welcoming, relaxed & informal with lots of character & style. The accommodation includes 4 en-suite bedrooms, which are generously spacious, well-equipped & thoughtfully furnished to ensure an exceptionally comfortable stay. Delicious breakfasts with emphasis on local flavour are served. There are excellent country inns & restaurants nearby for evening meals.

maggie@mallardgrange.co.uk
www.mallardgrange.co.uk £70.00 - £85.00
Open: all year (excl. xmas & new year) Map ref no. 15

Mrs C Goodall
Holly Croft 28 Station Road   Scalby
Scarborough YO13 0QA Yorkshire
Tel: (01723) 375376   Fax 01723 360563

Near Rd: A.171
Holly Croft is a Victorian detached house 3 miles north of Scarborough & 1 mile from the cliffs of the Cleveland Way. It is ideal for touring the North Yorks Moors & walks, coast or countryside. Wholesome breakfasts, cooked on the Aga, are served in the south-facing conservatory or around the polished mahogany dining table depending on the season. Dinner is available by prior arrangement (min. 4 persons). Holly Croft is furnished with comfort in mind. There are 2 delightful bedrooms & an elegant guest lounge with a log fire in winter. Children over 5.

www.holly-croft.co.uk £65.00 - £70.00
Open: all year (excl. xmas & new year)
Map ref no. 17

Graham & Liz Howard-Barker
Bank Villa   Masham Nr. Ripon HG4 4DB
Yorkshire
Tel: (01765) 689605

Near Rd: A.6108
Set in half an acre of terraced garden, this welcoming Grade II listed home has recently been renovated & refurbished to a high standard. It offers guests 2 delightful lounges in which to relax & 6 double bedrooms, each with radio, 4 with en-suite or private facilities, 2 with private shower. Bank Villa is an excellent spot for a relaxing break & it is an ideal base from which to explore the Yorkshire Dales, tour around, walk, horse-ride or fish. Children over 5 years. A warm welcome awaits you.

bankvilla@btopenworld.com   www.bankvilla.com
£50.00 - £85.00   Open: all year
Map ref no. 16

Chris & Malcolm Steele
Wildsmith House Marton Sinnington YO62 6RD
Yorkshire
Tel: (01751) 432702

Near Rd: A.170
A former farmhouse, originating from 1720, Wildsmith House is full of character & charm. Set on the village green, at the edge of the North Yorkshire Moors. The accommodation includes 2 spacious en-suite rooms, decorated & furnished to a high standard, with colour T.V. & tea/coffee-making facilities. Guest sitting room with log fires. Ideally situated for exploring the region with its historic houses, abbeys, unspoilt villages & city of York. Children over 12 years welcome.

wildsmithhouse@talk21.com
www.pb-design.com/swiftlink/bb/1102.htm
£54.00 - £60.00 Open: mar - oct Map ref no. 18

Mallard Grange

Aldfield Fountains Abbey Nr. Ripon HG4 3BE
Tel:(01765) 620242 Mobile 07720 295918
email:maggie@mallardgrange.co.uk www.mallardgrange.co.uk

David & Anne Watts
Four Gables   Oaks Lane   Boston Spa
Wetherby LS23 6DS   Yorkshire
Tel: (01937) 845592

Near Rd: A.659
Visitors will love this special art-and-craft movement house with its wealth of original features, stripped oak & terracotta floors, fireplaces & beautiful ceilings. A feature of the house is its gardens of over 1/2 an acre which contain many interesting plants & a croquet lawn. Enjoy the peaceful setting, down a private lane, yet only 3 mins' walk from the bustling Georgian stone village of Boston Spa with all its facilities, shops, restaurants, pubs & riverside walks. There are 3 attractive en-suite bedrooms, separate guests dining room & living room, log fires in winter. Single supplement. Children over 3 years.

info@fourgables.co.uk   www.fourgables.co.uk
£65.00 - £73.00   Open: all year (excl. xmas & new year)
Map ref no. 20

see p.285

Adrian Bradley
Barbican House   20 Barbican Road   York YO10 5AA
Yorkshire
Tel: (01904) 627617   Fax 01904 647140

Near Rd: A.19
Welcome to Barbican House, a wonderful restored Victorian villa, overlooking the famous medieval city walls & York Minster. 8 delightful rooms, each individually decorated to compliment the charm & character of the period. All rooms are en-suite & have T.V., 4 superior rooms with DVD players & king-size beds - 1 ground floor. 1 twin & 2 doubles with king-size beds & 2 doubles, all with complimentary sherry, tea/coffee & fresh flowers. A full English breakfast is served in the attractive dining room, with a vegetarian alternative & fresh fruit platter always available. Car park. Broadband WiFi internet access available. Children over 8.

info@barbicanhouse.co.uk   www.barbicanhouse.co.uk
£62.00 - £78.00   Open: all year (excl. xmas & new year)
Map ref no. 22

Mrs Ashley Goodrum
Cliffemount Hotel Runswick Bay   Whitby TS13 5HU
Yorkshire
Tel: (01947) 840103   Fax 01947 841025

Near Rd: A.174
As the name implies, this privately run hotel is situated on a clifftop with panoramic views over Runswick Bay. Built in the 1920s with later additions, the hotel is tastefully decorated throughout. There are 20 comfortably furnished bedrooms, all are en-suite, & the majority have spectacular sea views. Cliffemount, with its warm & friendly atmosphere, also enjoys a good reputation for its high standard of food. Fully licensed. Log fires in winter. Animals by arrangement.

cliffemount@runswickbay.fsnet.co.uk
www.cliffemounthotel.co.uk £68.00 - £110.00
Open: all year (excl. xmas)   Map ref no. 21

Ian Knibbs & Joanne Pease
The Dairy Guesthouse 3 Scarcroft Road   York
YO23 1ND   Yorkshire
Tel: (01904) 639367

Near Rd: A.59, A.64   Dating from 1890 & tastefully renovated throughout, The Dairy retains many of its original features. Situated within walking distance of the centre & York Minster, it is just 200 yards from the medieval city walls. Offering 5 bedrooms, all with colour T.V., HiFi & hot drink facilities. A 4-poster room is available & most rooms are en-suite. A private & relaxing flower-filled courtyard is available for guests use. The breakfast menu ranges from traditional English to wholefood, vegetarian & vegan. Families are always welcome.

stay@dairyguesthouse.co.uk
www.dairyguesthouse.co.uk £56.00 - £75.00
Open: all year (excl. xmas & jan)   Map ref no. 22

Barbican House

20 Barbican Road York YO10 5AΛ

Tel:(01904) 627617 Fax 01904 647140

email:info@barbicanhouse.co.uk www.barbicanhouse.co.uk

Wendy Wood
Curzon Lodge & Stable Cottages 23 Tadcaster Road
York YO24 1QG   Yorkshire
Tel: (01904) 703157   Fax 01904 703157

Near Rd: A.1036
Curzon Lodge is a charming 17th-century Grade II listed house & oak-beamed stables within city conservation area overlooking York racecourse. Once a home of the Terry 'chocolate' family, guests are now invited to share the unique atmosphere in 10 delightful & fully-equipped en-suite rooms, some with Four-poster & brass beds. Country antiques, prints, books, fresh flowers & complimentary sherry in the cosy sitting room lend traditional ambience. Delicious English breakfasts. Restaurants are just 1-min walk away. Parking in grounds. Warm & relaxed hospitality.

admin@curzonlodge.com
www.smoothhound.co.uk/hotels/curzon £65.00 - £82.00
Open: all year (excl. xmas)   Map ref no. 22

Allan & Julie Smith
City Guest House 68 Monkgate   York YO31 7PF
Yorkshire
Tel: (01904) 622483

Near Rd: A.1036
A warm & friendly welcome is assured in this family-run Victorian guest house (built in 1840) & only a short distance from the ancient bar walls, Minster & many of York's historical landmarks. The tastefully furnished bedrooms boast a stylish interior & come with a host of thoughtful touches. 6 bedrooms are en-suite & 1 has private facilities. A wide range of breakfasts including vegetarian, full English & Continental, are served in the spacious dining room. Guests are welcome to relax in the cosy lounge. Children over 12 years welcome.

info@cityguesthouse.co.uk www.cityguesthouse.co.uk
£64.00 - £72.00 Open: all year (excl. xmas)
Map ref no. 22

Miss Kim & Mrs Ann Sluter-Robbins
Arnot House 17 Grosvenor Terrace Bootham
York YO30 7AG Yorkshire
Tel: (01904) 641966

Near Rd: A.19
Overlooking Bootham Park, only 5 mins' walk from the York Minster & city centre. Award-winning Arnot House is a Victorian town house built for a wealthy merchant in 1865. The house is beautifully decorated throughout, & there are fine antiques & paintings. Many of its original features have been retained, including marble fireplaces & ornate coving. The accommodation includes 4 attractive bedrooms, which have either Victorian brass or wooden beds & every facility. An excellent location foem which to explore York.

kim.robbins@virgin.net www.arnothouseyork.co.uk
£65.00 - £70.00 Open: feb - dec
Map ref no. 22

see p.287

June & Keith Wood
Ascot House 80 East Parade York YO31 7YH
Yorkshire
Tel: (01904) 426826   Fax 01904 431077

Near Rd: A.1036
Ascot House is a family-run Victorian villa built in 1869. There are 15 en-suite rooms of character, many having four-poster or canopy beds. Each is well-equipped with T.V., tea/coffee facilities, etc. Delicious traditional English or vegetarian breakfasts are served in the attractive dining room. Ascot House is only 15 mins' walk to the historic city centre with its ancient narrow streets, medieval churches, Roman, Viking & National Railway Museums & the York Minster. Licensed. Sauna available. Car park.

admin@ascothouseyork.com www.ascothouseyork.com
£60.00 - £80.00 Open: all year (excl. xmas week)
Map ref no. 22

Ascot House

80 East Parade York YO31 7YH

Tel:(01904) 426826 Fax 01904 431077

email:admin@ascothouseyork.com www.ascothouseyork.com

Eilean Donan Castle
Highland
Scotland

Scotland

Scotland

Scotland's culture & traditions, history & literature, languages & accents, its landscape & architecture, even its wildlife set it apart from the rest of Britain. Much of Scotland's history is concerned with the struggle to retain independence from England.

The Romans never conquered the Scottish tribes, but preferred to keep them at bay with Hadrian's Wall, stretching across the Border country from Tynemouth to the Solway Firth.

Time lends glamour to events, but from the massacre of Glencoe to the Highland Clearances, much of Scotland's fate has been a harsh one. Robert the Bruce did rout the English enemy at Bannockburn after scaling the heights of Edinburgh Castle to take the city, but in later years Mary, Queen of Scots was to spend much of her life imprisoned by her sister Elizabeth I of England. Bonnie Prince Charlie (Charles Edward Stuart) led the Jacobite rebellion which ended in defeat at Culloden.

These events are recorded in the folklore & songs of Scotland. The Border & Highland Gatherings & the Common Ridings are more than a chance to wear the Tartan, they are reminders of national pride.

Highland Games are held throughout the country where local & national champions compete in events like tossing the caber & in piping contests. There are sword dances & Highland flings, the speciality of young men & boys wearing the full dress tartan of their clan.

Scotland's landscape is rich in variety from the lush green lowlands to the handsome splendour of the mountainous Highlands, from the rounded hills of the Borders to the far-flung islands of the Hebrides, Orkney & Shetland where the sea is ever-present. There are glens & beautiful lochs deep in the mountains, a spectacular coastline of high cliffs & white sandy beaches, expanses of purple heather moorland where the sparkling water in the burns runs brown with peat, & huge skies bright with cloud & gorgeous sunsets.

Argyll & The Islands

This area has ocean & sea lochs, forests

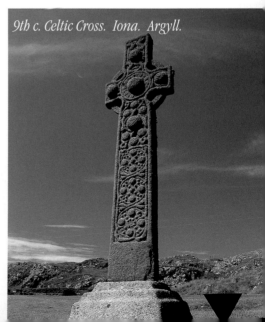

9th c. Celtic Cross. Iona. Argyll.

Scotland

& mountains, 3000 miles of coastline, about 30 inhabited islands, the warming influence of the Gulf Stream & the tallest tree in Britain (in Strone Gardens, near Loch Fyne).

Sites both historic & prehistoric are to be found in plenty. There is a hilltop fort at Dunadd, near Crinan with curious cup-&-ring carvings, & numerous ancient sites surround Kilmartin, from burial cairns to grave slabs.

Kilchurn Castle is a magnificent ruin in contrast to the opulence of Inveraray. Both are associated with the once-powerful Clan Campbell. There are remains of fortresses built by the Lords of the Isles, the proud chieftains who ruled the west after driving out the Norse invaders in the 12th century.

Oban is a small harbour town accessible by road & rail & the point of departure for many of the islands including Mull.

Mull is a peaceful island with rugged seascapes, lovely walks & villages, a miniature railway & the famous Mull Little Theatre. It is a short hop from here to the tiny island of Iona & St. Columba's Abbey, cradle of Christianity in Scotland.

Coll & Tiree have lovely beaches & fields of waving barley. The grain grown here was once supplied to the Lords of the Isles but today most goes to Islay & into the whisky. Tiree has superb windsurfing.

Jura is a wilder island famous for its red deer. The Isles of Colonsay & Oronsay are joined at low water.

Gigha, 'God's Isle', is a fertile area of gardens with rare & semitropical plants. The Island of Staffa has Fingal's Cave.

The Borders, Dumfries &Galloway

The borderland with England is a landscape of subtle colours & contours from the round foothills of the Cheviots, purple with heather, to the dark green valley of the Tweed.

The Lammermuir Hills sweep eastwards to a coastline of small harbours & the spectacular cliffs at St. Abbs Head where colonies of seabirds thrive.

The Border towns, set in fine countryside, have distinctive personalities. Hawick, Galashiels, Selkirk & Melrose all played their parts in the various Border skirmishes of this historically turbulent region & then prospered with a textile industry which survives today. They celebrate their traditions in the Common Riding ceremonies.

The years of destructive border warfare have left towers & castles throughout the country. Roxburgh was once a Royal castle & James II was killed here during a seige. Now there are only the shattered remains of the massive stone walls. Hermitage Castle is set amid wild scenery near Hawick & impressive Floors Castle stands above Kelso.

Scotland

At Jedburgh the Augustine abbey is remarkably complete, & a visitors centre here tells the story of the four great Border Abbeys; Jedburgh itself, Kelso, Dryburgh & Melrose.

The lovely estate of Abbotsford where Sir Walter Scott lived & worked is near Melrose. A prolific poet & novelist, his most famous works are the Waverley novels written around 1800. His house holds many of his possessions, including a collection of armour. Scott's View is one of the best vantage points in the borderlands with a prospect of the silvery Tweed & the three distinctive summits of the Eildon Hills.

There are many gracious stately homes. Manderston is a classical house of great luxury, & Mellerstain is the work of the Adam family. Traquair was originally a Royal hunting lodge. Its main gates were locked in 1745 after a visit from Bonnie Prince Charlie, never to be opened until a Stuart King takes the throne.

Dumfries & Galloway to the south-west is an area of rolling hills with a fine coastline.

Plants flourish in the mild air here & there are palm trees at Ardwell House & the Logan Botanic Garden.

Lowland

The Firth of Clyde & Glasgow in the west, & the Firth of Forth with Edinburgh in the east are both areas of rich history, tradition & culture.

Edinburgh is the capital of Scotland & amongst the most visually exciting cities in the world. The New Town is a treasure trove of inspired neo-classical architecture, & below Edinburgh Castle high on the Rock, is the Old Town, a network of courts, closes, wynds & gaunt tenements around the Royal Mile.

The Palace of Holyrood House, home of Mary, Queen of Scots for several years overlooks Holyrood Park & nearby Arthur's Seat, is a popular landmark.

The City's varied art galleries include The Royal Scottish Academy, The National Gallery, Portrait Gallery, Gallery of Modern Art & many other civic & private collections.

The Royal Museum of Scotland displays superb historical & scientific material. The

Smoking of the salmon at Inverawe. Strathclyde.

Scotland

Royal Botanic Gardens are world famous.

Cultural life in Edinburgh peaks at Festival time in August. The official Festival, the Fringe, the Book Festival, Jazz Festival & Film Festival bring together artistes of international reputation.

The gentle hills around the city offer many opportunities for walking. The Pentland Hills are easily reached, with the Lammermuir Hills a little further south. There are fine beaches at Gullane, Yellowcraigs, North Berwick & at Dunbar.

Tantallon Castle, a 14th century stronghold, stands on the rocky Firth of Forth, & 17th century Hopetoun House, on the outskirts of the city is only one of a number of great houses in the area.

North of Edinburgh across the Firth of Forth lies the ancient Kingdom of Fife. Here is St. Andrews, a pleasant town on the seafront, an old university town & Scotland's ecclesiastical capital, but famous primarily for golf.

Glasgow is the industrial & business capital of Scotland. John Betjeman called it the 'finest Victorian city in Britain' & many buildings are remarkable examples of Victorian splendour, notably the City Chambers.

Many buildings are associated with the architect Charles Rennie MacKintosh; the Glasgow School of Art is one of them. Glasgow Cathedral is a perfect example of pre-Reformation Gothic architecture.

Glasgow is Scotland's largest city with the greatest number of parks & fine Botanic Garden. It is home to both the Scottish Opera & the Scottish Ballet, & has a strong & diverse cultural tradition from theatre to jazz. Its museums include the matchless Burrell Collection, & the Kelvingrove Museum & Art Gallery, which houses one of the best civic collections of paintings in Britain, as well as reflecting the city's engineering & shipbuilding heritage.

The coastal waters of the Clyde are world famous for cruising & sailing, with many harbours & marinas. The long coastline offers many opportunities for sea-angling from Largs to Troon & Prestwick, & right around to Luce Bay on the Solway.

There are many places for birdwatching on the Estuary, whilst the Clyde Valley is famous for its garden centres & nurseries.

Paisley has a mediaeval abbey, an observatory & a museum with a fine display of the famous 'Paisley' pattern shawls.

Further south, Ayr is a large seaside resort with sandy beach, safe bathing & a racecourse. In the Ayrshire valleys there is traditional weaving & lace & bonnet making, & Sorn, in the rolling countryside boasts its 'Best Kept Village' award.

Culzean Castle is one of the finest Adam houses in Scotland & stands in spacious grounds on the Ayrshire cliffs.

Robert Burns is Scotland's best loved

Scotland

poet, & 'Burns night' is widely celebrated. The region of Strathclyde shares with Dumfries & Galloway the title of 'Burns Country' . The son of a peasant farmer, Burns lived in poverty for much of his life. The simple house where he was born is in the village of Alloway. In the town of Ayr is the Auld Kirk where he was baptised & the foot- bridge of 'The Brigs of Ayr' is still in use. The Tam O'Shanter Inn is now a Burns museum & retains its thatched roof & simple fittings. The Burns Trail leads on to Mauchline where Possie Nansie's Inn remains. At Tarbolton the National Trust now care for the old house where Burns founded the 'Batchelors Club' debating society.

Perthshire, Loch Lomond & The Trossachs

By a happy accident of geology, the Highland Boundary fault which separates the Highlands from the Lowlands runs through Loch Lomond, close to the Trossachs & on through Perthshire, giving rise to marvellous scenery.

In former times Highlanders & Lowlanders raided & fought here. Great castles like Stirling, Huntingtower & Doune were built to protect the routes between the two different cultures.

Stirling was once the seat of Scotland's monarchs & the great Royal castle is set high on a basalt rock. The Guildhall & the Kirk of the Holy Rude are also interesting buildings in the town, with Cambuskenneth

Abbey & the Bannockburn Heritage Centre close by.

Perth 'fair city' on the River Tay, has excellent shops & its own repertory theatre. Close by are the Black Watch Museum at Balhousie Castle, & the Branklyn Gardens, which are superb in May & June.

Scone Palace, to the north of Perth was home to the Stone or Scone of Destiny for nearly 500 years until its removal to Westminster. 40 kings of Scotland were crowned here.

Pitlochry sits amid beautiful Highland scenery with forest & hill walks, two nearby distilleries, the famous Festival theatre, Loch Faskally & the Dam Visitor Centre & Fish Ladder.

In the Pass of Killiecrankie, a short drive

The Pass of Glencoe. Highlands.

Scotland

away, a simple stone marks the spot where the Highlanders charged barefoot to overwhelm the redcoat soldiers of General MacKay.

Famous Queen's View overlooks Loch Tummel beyond Pitlochry with the graceful peak of Schiehallion completing a perfect picture.

Other lochs are picturesque too; Loch Earn, Loch Katrine & bonnie Loch Lomond itself, & they can be enjoyed from a boat on the water. Ospreys nest at the Loch of the Lowes near Dunkeld.

Mountain trails lead through Ben Lawers & the 'Arrocher Alps' beyond Loch Lomond. The Ochils & the Campsie Fells have grassy slopes for walking. Near Callander are the Bracklinn Falls, the Callander Crags & the Falls of Leny.

Wooded areas include the Queen Elizabeth Forest Park & the Black Wood of Rannoch which is a fragment of an ancient Caledonian forest. There are some very tall old trees around Killiecrankie, & the world's tallest beech hedge - 26 metres high - grows at Meikleour near Blairgowrie.

Creiff & Blairgowrie have excellent golf courses set in magnificent scenery.

The Grampians, Highlands & Islands

This is spacious countryside with glacier-scarred mountains & deep glens cut through by tumbling rivers. The Grampian Highlands make for fine mountaineering & walking.

There is excellent skiing at Glenshee, & a centre at the Lecht for the less experienced, whilst the broad tops of the giant mountains are ideal for cross-country skiing. The chair-lift at Glenshee is worth a visit at any season.

The Dee, The Spey & The Don flow down to the coastal plain from the heights. Some of the world's finest trout & salmon beats are on these rivers.

Speyside is dotted with famous distilleries from Grantown-on-Spey to Aberdeen, & the unique Malt Whisky Trail can be followed.

Royal Deeside & Donside hold a number of notable castles. Balmoral is the present Royal family's holiday home, & Kildrummy is a romantic ruin in a lovely garden. Fyvie Castle has five dramatic towers & stands in peaceful parkland. Nearby Haddo House, by contrast, is an elegant Georgian home.

There is a 17th century castle at Braemar, but more famous here is the Royal Highland Gathering. There are wonderful walks in the vicinity - Morrone Hill, Glen Quoich & the Linn O'Dee are just a few.

The city of Aberdeen is famed for its sparkling granite buildings, its university, its harbour & fish market. It also has long sandy beaches & lovely year-round flower displays, of roses in particular.

Scotland

Around the coast are fishing towns & villages. Crovie & Pennan sit below impressive cliffs. Buckie is a typical small port along the picturesque coastline of the Moray Firth.

The Auld Kirk at Cullen has fine architectural features & elegant Elgin has beautiful cathedral ruins. Pluscarden Abbey, Spynie Palace & Duffus Castle are all nearby.

Nairn has a long stretch of sandy beach & a golf course with an international reputation. Inland are Cawdor Castle & Culloden Battlefield.

The Northern Highlands are divided from the rest of Scotland by the dramatic valley of the Great Glen. From Fort William to Inverness, sea lochs, canals & the depths of Loch Ness form a chain of waterways linking both coasts.

Here are some of the wildest & most beautiful landscapes in Britain. Far Western Knoydart, the Glens of Cannich & Affric, the mysterious lochs, including Loch Morar, deeper than the North Sea, & the marvellous coastline; all are exceptional.

The glens were once the home of crofting communities, & of the clansmen who supported the Jacobite cause. The wild scenery of Glencoe is a favourite with walkers & climbers, but it has a tragic history. Its name means 'the glen of weeping' & refers to the massacre of the MacDonald clan in 1692.

South of Inverness lie the majestic Cairngorms. The Aviemore centre provides both summer & winter sports facilities here.

To the north of Loch Ness are the remains of the ancient Caledonian forest where red deer & stags are a common sight on the hills. Rarer are sightings of the Peregrine Falcon, the Osprey, & the Golden Eagle.

To the west are The Hebrides - beautiful and haunting islands. Here there is an abundance of habitats, peaceful, unspoilt and natural. The fresh water & sea lochs are unsurpassed in their beauty. Whales, dolphins, seals & puffins can all be seen in the clear waters around the islands. The Hebrides are a place where traditional music and crafts live side by side with a lively and modern culture.

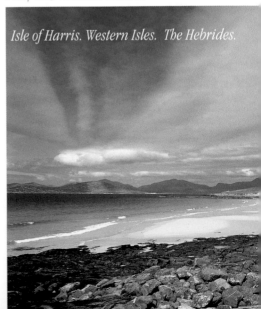

Isle of Harris. Western Isles. The Hebrides.

Scotland

Scotland Gazeteer

Areas of outstanding natural beauty.
It is almost impossible to choose any particular area of Scotland as having a more beautiful aspect than another - the entire country is a joy to the traveller. The rugged Highlands, the great glens, tumbling waters, tranquil lochs - the deep countryside or the wild coastline.

Historic Houses & Castles

Bachelors' Club - Tarbolton
17th century house - thatched - where Burns & friends formed their club - 1780.

Bowhill - Nr. Selkirk
18th-19th century - home of the Duke of Bucceleugh & Queensberry. Has an outstanding collection of pictures by Canaletto, Claude, Gainsborough, Reynolds & Leonardo da Vinci. Superb silver, porcelain & furniture. 16th & 17th century miniatures.

Blair Castle - Blair Atholl
Home of the Duke of Atholl, 13th century Baronial mansion - collection of Jacobite relics, armour, paintings, china & many other items.

Burn's Cottage - Alloway
Birthplace of Robert Burns - 1659 - thatched cottage - museum of Burns' relics.

Cawdor Castle - Nairn
14th century fortress - like castle - has always been the home of the Thanes of Cawdor - background to Shakespeare's Macbeth.

Culzean Castle & Country Park - Maybole
Fine Adam house & spacious gardens perched on Ayrshire cliff.

Drum Castle - Nr. Aberdeen
Dating in part from 13th century, it has a great square tower.

Drumlanrigg Castle - Nr. Thornhill
17th century castle of pale pink stone - romantic & historic - wonderful art treasures including a magnificent Rembrandt & a huge silver chandelier. Beautiful garden setting.

Dunrobin Castle - Golspie
Ancient seat of the Earls & Dukes of Sutherland.

Dunvegan Castle - Isle of Skye
13th century - has always been the home of the Chiefs of McLeod.

Edinburgh Castle
Fortress standing high over the town - famous for military tattoo.

Eilean Donan Castle - Wester Ross
13th century castle, Jacobite relics.

Glamis Castle - Angus
17th century remodelling in Chateau style - home of the Earl of Strathmore & Kinghorne. Very attractive castle - lovely grounds by Capability Brown.

Hopetoun House - South Queensferry
Very fine example of Adam architecture & has a fine collection of pictures & furniture. Splendid landscaped grounds.

Inverary Castle - Argyll
Home of the Dukes of Argyll. 18th century - Headquarters of Clan Campbell.

Linlithgow Palace - Linlithgow
The birthplace of Mary, Queen of Scots.

Manderston - Duns
Great classical house with only silver staircase in the world. Stables, marble dairy, formal gardens.

Scone Palace - Perth
has always been associated with seat of Government of Scotland from earliest times. The Stone of Destiny was removed from the Palace in 1296 & taken to Westminster Abbey. Present palace rebuilt in early 1800's still incorporating parts of the old. Lovely gardens.

Stirling Castle - Stirling
Royal Castle.

Traquair House - Innerleithen
A unique & ancient house being the oldest inhabited home in Scotland. It is rich in associations with every form of political history & after Bonnie Prince Charlie passed through its main gates in 1745 no other visitor has been allowed to use them. There are treasures in the house dating from 12th century, & it has an 18th century library. A priest's room with secret stairs.

Scotland

Cathedrals & Churches

Dunfermline Abbey - Dunfermline
Norman remains of beautiful church. Modern east end & tower.

Edinburgh (Church of the Holy Rood)
15th century - was divided into two in 17th century & re-united 1938. Here Mary, Queen of Scots was crowned.

Glasgow (St. Mungo)
12th-15th century cathedral - 19th century interior. Central tower with spire.

Kirkwall (St. Magnus)
12th century cathedral with very fine nave.

Falkirk Old Parish Church - Falkirk
The spotted appearance (faw) of the church (kirk) gave the town its name. The site of the church has been used since 7th century, with succesive churches built upon it. The present church was much rebuilt in 19th century. Interesting historically.

St Columba's Abbey - Iona

Museums & Galleries

Agnus Folk Museum - Glamis
17th century cottages with stone slab roots, restored by the National Trust for Scotland & houses a fine folk collection.

Mary, Queen of Scots' House - Jedburgh
Life & times of the Queen along with paintings.

Andrew Carnegie Birthplace - Dunfermline
The cottage where he was born is now part of a museum showing his life's work.

Aberdeen Art Gallery & Museum - Aberdeen
Sculpture, paintings, watercolours, prints & drawings. Applied arts. Maritime museum exhibits.

Provost Skene's House - Aberdeen
17th century house now exhibiting local domestic life, etc.

Highland Folk Museum - Kingussie
Examples of craft work & tools - furnished cottage with mill.

West Highland Museum - Fort William
Natural & local hsitory. Relics of Jacobites & exhibition of the '45 Rising.

Clan Macpherson House - Newtonmore
Relics of the Clan.

Glasgow Art Gallery & Museum - Glasgow
Archaeology, technology, local & natural history. Old Masters, tapestries, porcelain, glass & silver, etc. Sculpture.

Scottish National Gallery - Edinburgh
20th century collection - paintings & sculpture - Arp, Leger, Giacometti, Matisse, Picasso. Modern Scottish painting.

National Museum of Antiquities in Scotland - Edinburgh
Collection from Stone Age to modern times - Relics of Celtic Church, Stuart relics, Highland weapons, etc.

Gladstone Court - Biggar
Small indoor street of shops, a bank, schoolroom, library, etc.

Burns' Cottage & Museum - Alloway
Relics of Robert Burns - National Poet.

Inverness Museum & Art Gallery - Inverness
Social history, archaeology & cultural life of the Highlands. Display of the Life of the Clans.

Kirkintilloch - Nr. Glasgow
Auld Kirk Museum. Local history, including archaeological specimens from the Antonine Wall (Roman). Local industries, exhibitions, etc.

Pollock House & Park - Glasgow
18th century house with collection of paintings, etc. The park is the home of the award-winning Burrel Collection.

Historic Monuments

Aberdour Castle - Aberdour
14th century fortification - part still roofed.

Balvenie Castle - Dufton
15th century castle ruins.

Cambuskenneth Abbey - Nr. Stirling
12th century abbey - seat of Bruce's Parliament in 1326. Ruins.

Dryburgh Abbey - Dryburgh
Remains of monastery.

SCOTLAND

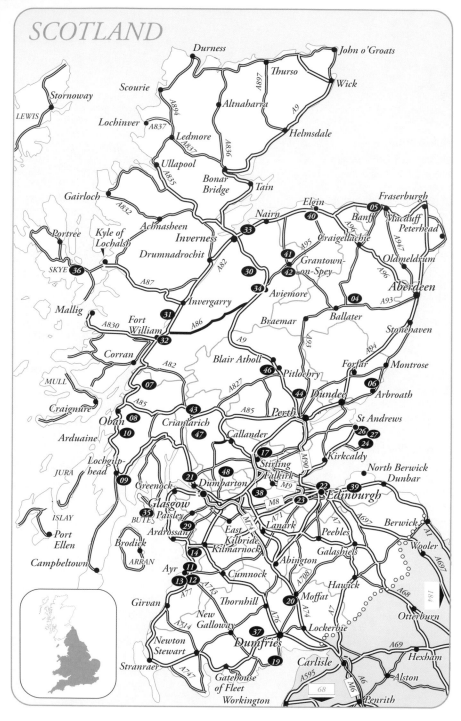

LEWIS
Stornoway
Durness
John o'Groats
Scourie
Thurso
Wick
A897
A894
Altnaharra
A9
Lochinver
A837
Helmsdale
Ledmore
A837
A836
Ullapool
A835
Bonar
Bridge
Tain
Gairloch
A832
Elgin
Fraserburgh
05
Nairn
Banff
Macduff
40
Peterhead
Portree
Achnasheen
Inverness
33
A96
Craigellachie
A947
Kyle of
Lochalsh
Drumnadrochit
41
Grantown-
on-Spey
Oldmeldrum
A96
SKYE
36
A87
A82
30
42
Aberdeen
34
Aviemore
A93
Mallig
31
A86
Braemar
04
Ballater
A830
Fort
William
Invergarry
Stonehaven
32
A9
A82
A93
A94
Corran
A82
Blair Atholl
Forfar
Montrose
46
Pitlochry
06
MULL
07
A827
Dundee
Arbroath
A85
43
44
Craignure
A85
08
Perth
St Andrews
Oban
Crianlarich
26 27
Arduaine
10
47
Callander
24
17
Stirling
Kirkcaldy
Lochgilp-
head
21
48
Falkirk
North Berwick
JURA
09
Greenock
Dumbarton
38
M9
Dunbar
22
39
ISLAY
Glasgow
23
Edinburgh
35
Paisley
M8
BUTES
29
East
Lanark
A69
Port
Ellen
Ardrossan
Kilbride
Peebles
Berwick
Brodick
14
Kilmarnock
Galashiels
Wooler
Campbeltown
ARRAN
Ayr
11
Cumnock
Abington
A708
Hawick
13 12
A713
Thornhill
A74
Otterburn
Girvan
A77
20
Moffat
A7
New
Galloway
A76
Lockerbie
Newton
37
A69
Stewart
Dumfries
Hexham
Stranraer
A747
19
Carlisle
Alston
Gatehouse
of Fleet
A595
M6
68
Workington
Penrith

SCOTLAND
Map references

Julia Chambers
Tigh na Geald   Ballater Road   Aboyne AB34 5HY
Aberdeenshire
Tel: (013398) 86668   Fax 013398 85606

Near Rd: A.93
Tigh na Geald is a beautifully restored Victorian house overlooking the village green in the centre of Aboyne on Royal Deeside. With both Aberdeen City one way & Balmoral Castle the other, both only 30 mins' drive away, it is the perfect base for touring. It is close to the golf course & gliding strip & within easy walking distance of the shops, the tennis courts & the river bank. It offers immediate access to the hills & mountains & is at the start point of the famous whisky trail. Shooting & fishing can be arranged. Offering 1 large double bedroom & 1 large twin-bedded room, both with spacious en-suite bathroom facilities.

chambers@planet-talk.co.uk www.bestbandb.co.uk
£50.00 - £70.00   Open: all year
Map ref no. 04

Kirstin de Morgan
Ethie Castle By Arbroath DD11 5SP
Angus
Tel: (01241) 830434   Fax 01241 830432

Near Rd: A.92
A warm welcome awaits you at the de Morgan family home. An ancient sandstone fortress dating from the 14th century, former home of Cardinal David Beaton Abbot of Arbroath & the Earls of Northesk. Ethie is reputed to be Scotland's second oldest inhabited castle. Immortalised by Sir Walter Scott as "Knockwhinnock" in his novel 'The Antiquary'. Ethie is now a haven of hospitality & peace with 3 elegant & tastefully furnished guest rooms with all amenities. Who can resist the famous Arbroath smokie? Animals by arrangement. A wonderful base from which to explore this region & its many attractions.

kmydemorgan@aol.com www.ethiecastle.com
£85.00 - £95.00   Open: all year
Map ref no. 06

Hazel Watt
Balwarren B & B Ordiquhill Cornhill
Banff AB45 7HR Aberdeenshire
Tel: (01466) 751688   Fax 01466 751688

Near Rd: A.95
Balwarren is a 30-acre croft in the heart of Aberdeenshire. It is teeming with wildlife; ducks, herons & buzzards to name but a few inhabit the wood by the pond, along with badgers, roe deer & night owls. There are 2 lovely & immaculate twin-bedded rooms, each with en-suite facilities. Also, a sunny sitting room with a wood burning stove & a small garden in which to relax. Delicious breakfasts are served & include home-made jams & chutneys. Situated close to 'castle & whisky country',

balwarren@tiscali.co.uk
www.balwarrenbedandbreakfast.com £56.00 - £56.00
Open: MAR - NOV Map ref no. 05

Earle & Stella Broadbent
Lochside Cottage Fasnacloich Appin PA38 4BJ
Argyll
Tel: (01631) 730216   Fax 01631 730216

Near Rd: A.828
Total peace on the shore of Loch Baile Mhic Chailen, in an idyllic glen of outstanding beauty. There are many walks from the cottage garden; or visit Fort William, Glencoe & Oban, from where you can board a steamer to explore the Western Isles. At the end of the day, a warm welcome awaits you: a delicious home-cooked dinner, a log fire & the certainty of a perfect night's sleep in one of 3 tastefully furnished en-suite bedrooms. Children & animals are welcome by prior arrangement.

broadbent@lochsidecottage.fsnet.co.uk
www.lochsidecottage.fsnet.co.uk £60.00 - £70.00
Open: ALL YEAR Map ref no. 07

Patsy & John Cugley
Sithe Mor House Kilcrenan   Loch Awe PA35 1HF
Argyll
Tel: (01866) 833234

Near Rd: B.845
Sithe Mor House is on the shores of Loch Awe and has its own bay, beach, jetty & private fishing rights on the loch. The 2 main en suite bedrooms have beautiful original frieze plasterwork, 20 feet domed ceilings & stunning views over the the loch & luxury en suite bathrooms. With its antlers, portraits & antiques this 1880's house oozes a Scots baronial feel. Fine local produce is a highlight at dinner. Kilts are encouraged & you can even borrow one for dinner. Dine at a long Georgian table in a dining room adorned with Boat Race memorabilia including family oars with Oxbridge College crests dating from 1861.

patsy@sithemor.com www.sithemor.com
£70.00 - £110.00   Open: ALL YEAR
Map ref No. 08

Alasdair & Melissa Oatts
Glenmore Country House B & B Kilmelford By Oban
PA34 4XA   Argyll
Tel: (01852) 200314

Near Rd: A.816
Glenmore dates from the 1850s & retains many original architectural features. This attractive family home is furnished throughout with antiques & interesting pictures. It is superbly situated with spectacular views down Loch Melfort. The accommodation comprises 1 attractive double bedroom & 1 family suite, each with private facilities. Excellent breakfasts are served. There is a lovely drawing room with open fire in which to relax. Glenmore is in an ideal location for exploring Argyll, with fishing, boat trips, horse riding & National Trust for Scotland gardens nearby. Animals by arrangement.

oatts@glenmore22.fsnet.co.uk
www.glenmorecountryhouse.co.uk £60.00 - £90.00
Open: all year (excl. xmas & new year) Map ref no. 10

Hamish & Charlotte Nicol
Allt-na-Craig Tarbert Road Ardrishaig
Lochgilphead PA30 8EP   Argyll
Tel: (01546) 603245

Near Rd: A.83
Hamish & Charlotte warmly welcome all their guests to Allt-na-Craig, a lovely old Victorian mansion set in picturesque grounds overlooking Loch Fyne. Accommodation is in 5 comfortable en-suite bedrooms with tea/coffee makers, hairdryers & T.V. A guests' drawing room with open fire & dining room is also available. This is a perfect base for outdoor activities, like hill-walking, fishing, golf, riding & windsurfing, or for visiting the islands. Delicious evening meals by arrangement.

information@allt-na-craig.co.uk
www.allt-na-craig.co.uk £80.00 - £110.00
Open: all year (excl. xmas) Map ref no. 09

Caroline McDonald
The Crescent 26 Bellevue Crescent Ayr KA7 2DR
Ayrshire
Tel: (01292) 287329   Fax 01292 286779

Near Rd: A.70
Built in 1898 at the height of Victorian splendour, No. 26 The Crescent lies amidst an impressive row of imposing terraced houses. Its location allows guests complete peace & quiet, yet enjoys close proximity & easy access to Ayr's busy shopping centre & seafront. The charming rooms have all been individually styled & decorated & include the Grand 4-poster bedroom, the ground floor Yellow room with French doors opening onto the garden or any of the other equally delightful bedrooms. Children over 8.

carrie@26crescent.freeserve.co.uk
www.26crescent.freeserve.co.uk £60.00 - £70.00
Open: all year (excl. xmas & new year) Map ref no. 11

Helen Martin
Greenan Lodge 39 Dunure Road Ayr KA7 4HR
Ayrshire
Tel: (01292) 443939

Near Rd: A.719
A warm welcome is assured at Greenan Lodge. Located on the coastal route (A.719) 2 miles from Ayr town centre. Handy for Prestwick Airport. Set in the heart of Burns country. A perfect base for Ayr races, Brig o' Doon, Turnberry, Troon & Prestwick golf courses & nearby Culzean Castle. All of the attractive bedrooms are on the ground floor with en-suite facilities. Relax & unwind in the comfort of the lounge & enjoy breakfast in the conservatory style dining room. With ample off-street parking, Greenan Lodge is ideal for a relaxing short break holiday.

helen@greenanlodge.com www.greenanlodge.com
£60.00 - £70.00 Open: all year
Map ref no. 12

Sheila Payne
Glenfoot House   Dundonald KA2 9HG
Ayrshire
Tel: (01563) 850311

Near Rd: A.77
Glenfoot is a former Georgian manse lying amidst beautiful Ayrshire countryside surrounding the 14th-century Dundonald Castle, which was built by Robert Stewart to mark his succession to the throne as Robert II in 1371. It is an ideal base for exploring Glasgow, the Isle of Arran & the Argyle Peninsula. For golfers the championship courses at Troon, Prestwick & Turnberry are within easy reach. The house is warm, comfortable & tastefully furnished & the upstairs drawing room has fine views. You will be warmly welcomed & cosseted at Glenfoot.

alan@onyxnet.co.uk www.aboutscotland.com
£80.00 - £80.00 Open: ALL YEAR
Map ref no. 14

Mrs Agnes Gemmell
Dunduff House   Dunure   Ayr KA7 4LH
Ayrshire
Tel: (01292) 500225   Fax 01292 500222

Near Rd: A.77
A warm friendly welcome awaits you at Dunduff House. Situated just south of Ayr at the coastal village of Dunure, this family-run beef & sheep unit of some 600 acres is only 15 mins' from the shore. Excellent accommodation, yet homely & comfortable. Bedrooms have panoramic coastal views over Arran, the Holy Isle, Mull of Kintyre & Ailsa Craig. Each is well-equipped & has beverage facilities, T.V. & an en-suite or private bathroom. Good location for exploring south-west Scotland & ideal for Culzean Castle, Robert Burns' Cottage & the Heritage Trail.

gemmelldunduff@aol.com www.gemmelldunduff.co.uk
£65.00 - £65.00 Open: feb - nov
Map ref no. 13

Adrian & Jane O'Dell
Westbourne House   10 Dollar Road Tillicoultry
Stirling FK13 6PA   Clackmannanshire
Tel: (01259) 750314   Mobile 0776 6984311

Near Rd: A.91
A fascinating Victorian mill-owner's mansion set within wooded grounds beneath the Ochil Hills. The atmosphere at Westbourne is warm & friendly. All 3 bedrooms are comfortably furnished, 2 en-suite (1 ground floor) & 1 with private bathroom. All have T.V., etc. Enjoy Aga-cooked breakfasts including Jane's famous porridge & smoked salmon with scrambled eggs. Ideally situated for visiting central Scotland, Stirling (15 mins) & Edinburgh, Glasgow, St Andrews & the Trossachs (1hr.) Many golf courses, an equestrian centre & hill-walking in the Ochils. Parking.

info@westbournehouse.co.uk
www.westbournehouse.co.uk   £50.00 - £54.00
Open: all year (excl. xmas & new year) Map ref no. 17

see p.304

Angus Fordyce
Cavens House   Kirkbean By Dumfries DG2 8AA
Dumfriesshire
Tel: (01387) 880234   Fax 01387 880467

Near Rd: A.710
Formerly an old mansion with a strong American historical connection, Cavens, now a charming small country house hotel, offers 6 comfortable en-suite bedrooms. There are 2 lounges with open fires, which add to the ambience of the house. Standing in 11 acres of gardens & woodland, it is ideal for those wishing to explore the joys of the Solway Coast, with its beautiful scenery & beaches. Sailing, walking, golfing, shooting, fishing & riding by arrangement. Award-winning cuisine; 3-course dinner with coffee. Children over 12 years welcome. Dogs by arrangement.

enquiries@cavens.com   www.cavens.com
£110.00 - £160.00 Open: ALL YEAR
Map ref no. 19

Stewart & Gillian Macdonald
Kirkton House   Darleith Road Cardross Dumbarton
G82 5EZ   Dunbartonshire
Tel: (01389) 841951   Fax (01389) 841868

Near Rd: A.814
Experience a blend of "olde worlde" charm, modern amenities & superb views at this converted 18/19th-century farmstead, set in a tranquil countryside location yet handy for Glasgow City (34 mins by train/car), Glasgow Airport (25 mins by car), Loch Lomond, The Trossachs & the main West Highland route. Accommodation is in 6 attractive & well-appointed en-suite bedrooms including 4 family rooms. Private car parking. Real fire on chilly evenings in lounge with 'Freeview' TV. Original stone walls & old "swee" for the cooking pots in the dining room.

bbiw@kirktonhouse.co.uk www.kirktonhouse.co.uk
£50.00 - £60.00 Open: feb - nov
Map ref no. 21

Mr & Mrs Ash-Kuri
Hartfell House   Hartfell Crescent   Moffat DG10 9AL
Dumfriesshire
Tel: (01683) 220153

Near Rd: A.701
Hartfell House is a splendid Victorian manor house located in a rural setting overlooking the hills, yet only a few mins' walk from the town. It is a listed building known locally for its fine interior woodwork. The accommodation includes 7 spacious & tastefully furnished bedrooms, each with en-suite facilities. Breakfasts are delicious. Standing in gardens of lawns & trees, & providing an atmosphere of peaceful relaxation. Perfect for a short break holiday. A warm welcome awaits all guests at Hartfell House. Animals by arrangement.

enquiries@hartfellhouse.co.uk
www.hartfellhouse.co.uk £60.00 - £60.00
Open: all year (excl. jan, feb & xmas) Map ref no. 20

Carole Wilson
Ben Cruachan Guest House   17 McDonald Road
Edinburgh
Tel: (0131) 556 3709

Near Rd: A.1
Guests are assured of a warm welcome & a friendly atmosphere at this attractive house, situated 1 km from Princes Street - one of Britain's best, most pleasant & undoubtedly most picturesque shopping venues. Offering comfortable en-suite bedrooms, well-equipped with every comfort in mind & serving an excellent breakfast. (Family room available.) Centrally situated within easy reach of the castle, Royal Mile, Holyrood Palace, shops, theatres & restaurants. Unrestricted parking & on all main bus routes. A good base from which to explore Edinburgh.

bencruachan@btinternet.com www.bencruachan.com
£60.00 - £100.00 Open: all year
Map ref no. 22

Kirkton House

Darleith Road Cardross Dumbarton G82 5EZ

Tel:(01389) 841951 Fax(01389) 841868 email:bbiw@kirktonhouse.co.uk www.kirktonhouse.co.uk

Joyce Sandeman
Sandeman House   33 Colinton Road
Edinburgh EH10 5DR
Tel: (0131) 4478080

Near Rd: A.702
Built in 1860, Sandeman House is a charming family home which has been sympathetically restored by Neil & Joyce Sandeman. The accommodation includes 3 bedrooms, which are individually furnished & are bright & tastefully decorated to a very high standard. Each has an en-suite/ private bathroom, colour T.V., tea/coffee-making facilities, hairdryer etc. A delicious full traditional Scottish breakfast is served including home-made preserves. Shops, bars & restaurants are close by. Sandeman House is within easy reach of most of the city's attractions, making it an ideal base from which to explore Edinburgh.

joycesandeman@freezone.co.uk
www.sandemanhouse.co.uk £70.00 - £100.00
Open: all year   Map ref no. 22

Edward & Felicity Stanley
Joppa Turrets Guesthouse 1 Lower Joppa   Joppa
Edinburgh EH15 2ER
Tel: (0131) 6695806   Fax 0131 6695806

Near Rd: A.1
This charming guest house is set in a peaceful location on a mile of sandy seaside, which will really add to your unmissable Edinburgh experience.   Joppa has been a popular resort for over 100 years, & whilst the donkey rides are no more, the peace remains. The cosy pretty bedrooms all have sea views & private or shared facilities. Good restaurants are within a few mins' walk. There is an excellent & frequent bus service into the city centre for all that Edinburgh has to offer. A delightful home. Children over 3. (Please note: the guest house is located at the beach end of Morton Street).

stanley@joppaturrets.co.uk   www.joppaturrets.com
£58.00 - £84.00   Open: all year (excl. xmas)
Map ref no. 22

Ian Hamilton
Kew House & Apartments 1 Kew Terrace   Murrayfield
Edinburgh EH12 5JE
Tel: (0131) 3130700   Fax 0131 3130747

Near Rd: A.8
Forming part of a listed Victorian terrace, Kew House and Apartments lies within walking distance of the city centre, & is convenient for Murrayfield rugby stadium & the tourist attractions. Meticulously maintained throughout, it offers attractive bedrooms, all thoughtfully equipped. Licensed lounge offering a supper & snack menu. Free internet access with wi-fi is also available. The 2 adjacent serviced apartments offer two bedrooms, bathroom, kitchen etc. (max. 3 people in each.) 2 night minimum here with Continental breakfast & daily maid service included.

info@kewhouse.comw ww.kewhouse.com
£70.00 - £150.00   Open: all year
Map ref no. 22

Dorothy Vidler
Kenvie Guest House   16 Kilmaurs Road   Edinburgh
EH16 5DA
Tel: (0131) 6681964   Fax 0131 6681926

Near Rd: A.1, A.7, A.68
Kenvie Guest House is charming, comfortable, warm, friendly & inviting. This small Victorian town house is ideally situated in a quiet residential street, 1 small block from the main road, leading to the city centre (an excellent bus service) & the bypass to all routes. Offering, for your comfort, lots of caring touches, including complimentary tea/coffee-making facilities, colour T.V. & no-smoking rooms. Private facilities are also available. Delicious breakfasts are served. You are guaranteed a warm welcome from Richard & Dorothy.

dorothy@kenvie.co.uk www.kenvie.co.uk
£52.00 - £80.00 Open: all year
Map ref no. 22

Kildonan Lodge Hotel

27 Craigmillar Park Edinburgh EH16 5PE

Tel:(0131) 6672793 Fax 0131 6679777

email:info@kildonanlodgehotel.co.uk www.kildonanlodgehotel.co.uk

see p.306

Maggie Urquhart
Kildonan Lodge Hotel   27 Craigmillar Park
Edinburgh EH16 5PE
Tel: (0131) 6672793   Fax 0131 6679777

Near Rd: A.701
Ideally situated close to the city centre, Kildonan Lodge with its own private car park, is an outstanding example of Victorian elegance providing the perfect setting for your visit to Scotland's capital. Relax in the elegant lounge & enjoy a 'dram' from the Honesty Bar.   Each of the individually designed en-suite bedrooms have colour T.V., free broadband wireless internet, hairdryer & complimentary sherry & shortbread. In selected rooms there are beautiful 4-poster beds & spa baths.

info@kildonanlodgehotel.co.uk
www.kildonanlodgehotel.co.uk £69.00 - £150.00
Open: all year (excl. xmas)   Map ref no. 22

Michael Gilbert
Frederick House Hotel 42 Frederick Street
Edinburgh EH2 1EX
Tel: (0131) 2261999   Fax 0131 6247064

Near Rd: A.8
Frederick House Hotel is perfectly situated in the very heart of Edinburgh's city centre, a stones' throw from Princes Street. All of the 45 tastefully decorated bedrooms feature en-suite bathrooms (with bath & shower); Continental breakfast is served in your room. Your hosts' aim is to make your stay as comfortable & relaxing as possible, with all modern conveniences combined together with an 'olde worlde' atmosphere. Frederick House Hotel is very central for exploring Edinburgh's main attractions.

frederickhouse@ednet.co.uk
www.townhousehotels.co.uk £50.00 - £130.00
Open: all year   Map ref no. 22

Mrs Lyn Redmayne
Kingsley Guest House 30 Craigmillar Park
Edinburgh EH16 5PS
Tel: (0131) 6673177   Fax 0131 6678439

Near Rd: A.701
A warm, friendly welcome awaits you at this Victorian terraced villa. The accommdoation includes 5 comfortably furnished bedrooms, each with either en-suite or private facilities, colour T.V. & tea/coffee-making facilities. A delicious full English or Continental breakfast is served. Kingsley Guest House is conveniently situated in the south of the city, with an excellent bus service at the door to & from the city centre which has many tourist attractions. Private parking is available.

lyn.kingsley@virgin.net
www.kingsleyguesthouse.co.uk £46.00 - £82.00
Open: all year   Map ref no. 22

see p.308

Gerald Della-Porta
Gerald's Place 21B Abercromby Place
Edinburgh EH3 6QE
Tel: (0131) 5587017   Mobile 077 6601 6840

Near Rd: A.1
Your host Gerald, welcomes you to his delightful home full of character, colour & comforts. The accommodation includes 2 double bedrooms (each with one king-size bed or 2 3ft beds of supreme comfort & quality) with 2 private bathrooms (each with power shower & bath tub). It is the ideal place for 2 couples travelling together. Breakfast is an organic feast. Abercromby Place is at the very centre of the city, only 6 mins' walk from Waverley station. One of the finest streets in Edinburgh.

gerald@geraldsplace.com
www.geraldsplace.com £59.00 - £119.00
Open: all year   Map ref no. 22

Gerald's Place

21B Abercromby Place Edinburgh EH3 6QE

Tel:(0131) 5587017 Mobile 077 6601 6840

email:gerald@geraldsplace.com www.geraldsplace.com

see p.310

Cecilia & Tommy Leishman
Ellesmere Guest House 11 Glengyle Terrace
Edinburgh EH3 9LN
Tel: (0131) 229 4823

Near Rd: A.702
Guests are made welcome at this very elegant tastefully restored Victorian town house, quietly situated overlooking golf links in the centre of Edinburgh. The attractive bedrooms are all en-suite, decorated to a very high standard & well-equipped with every comfort in mind. Delicious breakfasts are served. Ellesmere is 'A home away from home.'; perfect for a short break holiday in Edinburgh. Convenient for the castle, Princes Street, Royal Mile, International Conference Centre, theatres & many good restaurants. Children over 14 years welcome.

celia@edinburghbandb.co.uk
www.edinburghbandb.co.uk £70.00 - £100.00
Open: ALL YEAR Map ref no. 22

Susan Virtue
The Town House 65 Gilmore Place
Edinburgh EH3 9NU
Tel: (0131) 2291985

Near Rd: A.702
Attractive Victorian town house, located in the city centre. Theatres & restaurants are only minutes walk away. The Town House has been fully restored & tastefully decorated throughout, retaining many original architectural features. The bedrooms are tastefully furnished & individually decorated, all have en-suite bath or shower & w.c., radio/alarm, colour T.V., hairdryer & tea/coffee-making facilities. Parking is situated at the rear of the house. A most comfortable self-catering apartment is also available. Children over 9 years.

susan@thetownhouse.com www.thetownhouse.com
£70.00 - £100.00 Open: all year
Map ref no. 22

Navin Varma
Ailsa Craig Hotel 24 Royal Terrace
Edinburgh EH7 5AB
Tel: (0131) 5566055/5561022 Fax 0131 5566055

Near Rd: A.1
Ailsa Craig Hotel is situated in the heart of Edinburgh near the city centre in one of the most prestigious terraces. This elegant Georgian town house hotel is situated only 10 minutes walk from Princes Street, Waverly Station & many of Edinburgh's major attractions. The accommodation includes 16 tastefully furnished & decorated bedrooms, all with en-suite facilities, telephone, hairdryer, colour T.V. & tea/coffee-making facilities. A delicious breakfast & good evening meals are served in the dining room. A good base for exploring Edinburgh.

ailsacraighotel@ednet.co.uk
www.townhousehotels.co.uk £50.00 - £100.00
Open: ALL YEAR Map ref no. 22

David Jack & Yoke Holm
Ravensdown Guest House 248 Ferry Road
Edinburgh EH5 3AN
Tel: (0131) 5525438

Near Rd: A.1
Ravensdown is a friendly and stylish guest house which provides excellent value high quality bed & breakfast accommodation in central Edinburgh. A spacious Edwardian house built in the early 1900's with spectacular views of the city skyline. 7 en suite rooms, one with private facilities. Free parking, plus lock up parking for bikers. Wireless Internet Access. Full Scottish breakfast. Within walking distance of the Royal Botanic Garden. 10 min bus ride into the city, 5 mins to Leith, 20 mins to airport. Golfing parties & families welcome. Dutch & English spoken

david@ravensdownhouse.com
www.ravensdownhouse.com £60.00 - £100.00
Open: all year Map ref no. 22

Elmview

15 Glengyle Terrace Edinburgh EH3 9LN

Tel:(0131) 228 1973

email:nici@elmview.co.uk www.elmview.co.uk

Ellesmere Guest House

11 Glengyle Terrace Edinburgh EII3 9LN

Tel:(0131) 229 4823

email:celia@edinburghbandb.co.uk   www.edinburghbandb.co.uk

Alan & Angela Vidler
Rowan Guest House   13 Glenorchy Terrace
Edinburgh EH9 2DQ
Tel: (0131) 6672463   Fax 0131 6672463

Near Rd: A.701
Quietly located in a leafy conservation area but only a mile from the Castle & Royal Mile, Rowan Guest House is an excellent base for exploring the city. This warm, welcoming home, built in 1880, retains many original features. The comfortable & tastefully furnished bedrooms have tea/coffee-making facilities, colour T.V., hairdryer & radio/clock alarm. The delicious breakfast includes porridge & freshly baked scones & special diets are catered for with notice. There are many good restaurants nearby & free parking just outside the house.

angela@rowan-house.co.uk   www.rowan-house.co.uk
£54.00 - £82.00   Open: all year
Map ref no. 22

Irene Robins
Sonas Guest House   3 East Mayfield   Newington
Edinburgh EH9 1SD
Tel: (0131) 6672781

Near Rd: A.701, A.7
Sonas Guest House is a delightful Victorian villa, cira 1876, built for the directors of the railways. It is quietly situated 1 mile from the centre of Edinburgh. The well-appointed en-suite bedrooms have a colour T.V., tea/coffee-making facilities & hairdryer. Delicious Scottish breakfasts are served. Irene & Dennis wish to welcome you to an idyllic base for exploring the attractions of historic Edinburgh. Private parking available. Many guests favour them with a return visit. Stay at 'Sonas' Gaelic for bliss & enjoy true Scottish hospitality.

info@sonasguesthouse.com www.sonasguesthouse.com
£50.00 - £90.00   Open: ALL YEAR
Map ref no. 22

see p.311

Robin & Nici Hill
Elmview 15 Glengyle Terrace
Edinburgh EH3 9LN
Tel: (0131) 228 1973

Near Rd: A.702
Robin & Nici Hill's luxurious bed & breakfast is situated in the heart of Edinburgh within easy walking distance of Edinburgh Castle & Princes Street (1 km). Elmview is a wonderful base from which to enjoy your stay in Edinburgh. Each bedroom has been elegantly furnished throughout & all have en-suite facilities. Direct-dial 'phones, fridges & fresh flowers are but a few of the thoughtful extras in each bedroom. A delightful home.

nici@elmview.co.uk www.elmview.co.uk
£80.00 - £110.00   Open: 01 mar - 01 dec
Map ref no. 22

Alan Drummond
Parklands Guest House 20 Mayfield Gardens
Edinburgh EH9 2BZ
Tel: (0131) 6677184   Fax 0131 6672011

Near Rd: A.701
Parklands is an attractive Victorian terraced house conveniently located 1 1/2 miles from Princes Street & all the main tourist attractions. There are 6 bedrooms, each is furnished to a high standard & is fully equipped with en-suite/private facilities, colour T.V. & tea/coffee makers. A full Scottish breakfast is served. Nearby are many excellent restaurants. Parklands is family-run with a friendly atmosphere. You are assured of a warm welcome.

reservations@parklands-guesthouse.co.uk
www.parklands-edinburgh.co.uk   £46.00 - £80.00
Open: ALL YEAR   Map ref no. 22

see p.314

Derek & Elizabeth Scott
Ashcroft Farmhouse   East Calder
Nr. Edinburgh EH53 0ET
Tel: (01506) 881810   Fax 01506 884327

Near Rd: A.71, B.7015
Ashcroft is a new farmhouse set in beautifully landscaped gardens, enjoying lovely views of the surrounding farmland. Situated only 10 miles from Edinburgh, 5 miles from the airport, city bypass, M.8/M.9, Ingliston & Livingston. Bedrooms, including a 4-poster, are attractively furnished in pine with co-ordinating fabrics & are very comfortable. Regular bus/train service nearby to city centre (20 mins). Choice of delicious breakfasts with local produce. Children over 12. Parking. Elizabeth was runner-up in the UK Landlady of the Year awards 2005.

ashcroftinfo@aol.com   www.ashcroftfarmhouse.com
£70.00 - £80.00   Open: all year
Map ref no. 23

Peter & Catherine Erskine
Cambo House   Kingsbarns St. Andrews KY16 8QD
Fife
Tel: (01333) 450313   Fax 01333 450987

Near Rd: A. 917
This impressive Victorian house lies at the heart of the 1200 acre estate, which has been home to Peter's family since 1688 & is set among picturesque fishing villages & near historic St Andrews yet only 1 1/2 hours from Edinburgh & the Highlands. There are 2 comfortable & elegantly furnished bedrooms (1 with 4-poster), each with en-suite/ private facilities. Unwind in the restful atmosphere of the Victorian walled garden, woodland walks to sea or elegant sitting room overlooking the fountain. Evening meals & animals by prior arrangement.

cambo@camboestate.com   www.camboestate.com
£90.00 - £126.00 Open: all year (excl. xmas & new year)
Map ref no. 27

Sandy & Frippy Fyfe
Kinkell House   St. Andrews KY16 8PN
Fife
Tel: (01334) 472003   Fax 01334 475248

Near Rd: A.917
Kinkell is a family home near St. Andrews where Sandy & Frippy Fyfe offer a warm welcome, good food & informal hospitality. The accommodation includes 3 very comfortable & tastefully furnished en-suite guest rooms. Kinkell runs down to the sea & has spectacular views of the coast & St. Andrews as well as access to walks on the coast. Some of the attractions of the area include golf, historic buildings, scenic villages, the sea & wonderful beaches. An elegant home.

info@kinkell.com www.kinkell.com
£80.00 - £80.00   Open: all year
Map ref no. 26

Janet Anderson
East Lochhead Country House Largs Road
Lochwinnoch PA12 4DX   Glasgow
Tel: (01505) 842610   Fax 01505 842610

Near Rd: A.760
A large 100-year-old Scottish farmhouse commanding beautiful views over Barr Loch & the Renfrewshire hills. Offering 3 beautifully furnished bedrooms with panoramic views, and en-suite facilities, T.V. & tea/coffee. Delicious breakfasts. Special diets catered for. Only 15 mins from Glasgow & 25 mins from Prestwick airports. An ideal base for visiting Glasgow, the Clyde coast, islands of Arran & Bute, the Trossachs/Loch Lomond or golfing in Ayrshire. Self-catering holiday cottages also available.

admin@eastlochhead.co.uk   www.eastlochhead.co.uk
£75.00 - £80.00   Open: all year
Map ref no. 29

Ashcroft Farmhouse

East Calder Nr.Edinburgh EH53 0ET

Tel:(01506) 881810 Fax 01506 884327

email:ashcroftinfo@aol.com www.ashcroftfarmhouse.com

see p.316

John Gardner
Feith Mhor Lodge   Station Road   Carrbridge
Nr. Aviemore PH23 3AP   Inverness-shire
Tel: (01479) 841621

Near Rd: A.9
Situated in a peaceful but accessible valley, 25 miles south of Inverness, Feith Mhor Lodge ('Fay Moor') offers bed & breakfast accommodation in an elegant Victorian country home with 6 comfortable &tastefully furnished en-suite bedrooms with all amenities. Your hosts specialise in party bookings for groups enjoying the sporting activities of the area. Shooting, fishing, falconry & golf parties can all be exclusively booked on a full-board basis. Evening meals are available by arrangement. (Restricted smoking areas).

feith.mhor@btinternet.com   www.feithmhor.co.uk
£45.00 - £56.00   Open: all year
Map ref no. 30

Mrs Joan Campbell
The Grange   Grange Road   Fort William PH33 6JF
Inverness-shire
Tel: (01397) 705516

Near Rd: A.82
Tucked away in its own grounds, The Grange sits quietly overlooking Loch Linnhe, yet it is only 10 mins' walk from the town centre & good local restaurants. Log fires, crystal, fresh flowers, antiques, loch views, all add to the charm of this luxury B & B in the breathtaking scenery of the Scottish Highlands. One night is not enough to enjoy The Grange or the area surrounding, whether it be walking in famous Glen Nevis, sailing on Loch Linnhe or visiting the distillery. It really is the perfect location for a relaxing Highland holiday.

info@thegrange-scotland.co.uk
www.thegrange-scotland.co.uk £98.00 - £115.00
Open: mar - nov   Map ref no. 32

Margaret & James Cairns
Invergloy House   Nr. Spean Bridge   Fort William
PH34 4DY   Inverness-shire
Tel: (01397) 712681

Near Rd: A.82
A really interesting Scottish coach house, dating back 120 years, offering 2 charming & comfortable rooms (1 double & 1 twin-bedded room), each with modern facilities including an en-suite bath or shower room. Only 5 miles north of the village of Spean Bridge towards Inverness, it is signposted on the left, along a wooded drive. Guests have use of own comfortable sitting room, overlooking Loch Lochy in 50 acres of superb woodland filled with rhododendron & azaleas. Fishing is available from the private beach. Children over 8 years welcome.

cairns@invergloy-house.co.uk
www.invergloy-house.co.uk £64.00 - £64.00
Open: ALL YEAR (Excl. Xmas & New Year) Map ref no. 31

Mrs Sandra Henderson
The Gantocks   Achintore Road   Fort William PH33 6RL
Inverness-shire
Tel: (01397) 702050

Near Rd: A.82
Imagine being in a boat with no waves, then you are breakfasting at The Gantocks. Unrestricted views over Loch Linnhe to the Argour Hills, a world away from stress. This period house has had a major overhaul with everything expected of a luxury B & B including power showers & king-size beds. Tasty breakfast treats are carefully prepared on the Aga. Quietly located less than 1 mile from the town centre. Parking. Sandra & Allan are happy to book tickets, tours or dinner & provide much information to enhance your enjoyment of the outdoor capital of the UK.

boxfamily@hotmail.co.uk
www.thegantocksfortwilliam.co.uk   £70.00 - £100.00
Open: mar - nov   Map ref no. 32

The Grange

Grange Road Fort William PH33 6JF

Tel (01397) 705516

email:info@thegrange-scotland.co.uk   www.thegrange-scotland.co.uk

see p.318

Christine & William MacDonald
Ashburn House Achintore Road Fort William PH33 6RQ
Inverness-shire
Tel: (01397) 706000   Fax 01397 702024

Near Rd: A.82
Ashburn is a splendid Victorian house personally run by Highland hosts. It is quietly situated by the shores of Loch Linnhe only 600 yards from the town centre & among others the renowned Crannog Seafood Restaurant. This really is an excellent base for touring the Highlands. Sample an imaginative Highland breakfast, served at your own individual table, complemented with freshly baked scones from the Aga. The guest accommodation includes 7 attractive en-suite bedrooms, 4 with super-king-size beds & 3 single rooms. Parking. Weekly rates are available. Single rooms from £40.

christine@no-1.fsworld.co.uk www.highland5star.co.uk
£80.00 - £100.00   Open: ALL YEAR
Map ref no. 32

Mrs Helen Gillies
Balcraggan House   Feshiebridge   Kincraig
Kingussie PH21 1NG Inverness-shire
Tel: (01540) 651488

Near Rd: A.9, B.970
Set in the heart of the Cairngorm National Park, Balgraggan House offers a unique setting for a relaxing holiday. Bedrooms include a large double room & a twin-bedded room with antique Dutch beds. Each room has en-suite facilities, T.V. & welcome tray. There is also a separate shower room on the ground floor. In the evening one can relax in the elegant drawing room with open fire on chilly evenings. The list of activities in the area is endless along with the wildlife (red squirrels are frequent visitors to the bird table in the garden, as are woodpeckers) so come & experience it for yourself at Balcraggan House.

balcraggan@kincraig.com   www.visitkincraig.com
£54.00 - £54.00 Open: all year
Map ref no. 34

Mrs Margaret Pottie
Easter Dalziel Farmhouse   Dalcross   Inverness IV2 7JL
Inverness-shire
Tel: (01667) 462213   Fax 01667 462213

Near Rd: A.96, B.9039 This Scottish farming family offer the visitor a friendly Highland welcome on their 200-acre stock/arable farm. There are 3 charming bedrooms are available in the delightful early-Victorian farmhouse. The lounge has log fire & colour T.V.. Delicious home cooking & baking served, including a choice of breakfasts. Ideal for exploring the scenic Highlands, Whisky trail & sandy beaches. Local attractions are Cawdor Castle, Culloden, Fort George, Loch Ness & nearby Castle Stuart. A delightful home. Animals by arrangement.

BBB@easterdalzielfarm.co.uk
www.easterdalzielfarm.co.uk £42.00 - £50.00
Open: all year (excl. xmas & new year) Map ref no. 33

Tony & Beryl Harrison
Balmory Hall   Ascog PA20 9LL
Isle of Bute
Tel: (01700) 500669   Fax 01700 500669

Near Rd: A.844
Experience the delights of this beautifully restored Victorian mansion house, set within its own extensive natural grounds, located on the east coast of the Isle of Bute. Appointed with all modern comforts in mind & with that touch of elegance, which is synonymous with the Victorian age. Enjoy the peaceful serenity of the bright, exceptionally spacious public rooms & the warmth of the cosy bedrooms & bathrooms. Leave all stresses behind; relax & enjoy. A delightful home. Children over 12 years welcome.

tony@balmoryhall.com   www.balmoryhall.com
£120.00 - £160.00   Open: all year
Map ref no. 35

Ashburn House

Achintore Road Fort William PH33 6RQ

Tel:(01397) 706000 Fax 01397 702024

www.bestbandb.co.uk

Mrs Hilary Prall
Shorefield House Edinbane By Portree IV51 9PW
Isle of Skye
Tel: (01470) 582444   Fax 01470 582414

Near Rd: A.850
Shorefield House nestles peacefully in the village of
Edinbane with undisturbed views of Loch Greshornish &
sunsets over the peninsula. A range of comfortable, high-
quality en-suite accommodation & a warmth of hospitality
adds a special touch to your stay. A la carte breakfasts
make use of local produce & special diets are catered for
where possible. Excellent (category 1) disabled facilities.
A very good children's play area. Close to Dunvegan Castle
& the Talisker Distillery. Shorefield House is an ideal spot
for your stay on Skye.

shorefieldhouse@aol.com   www.shorefield.com
£60.00 - £80.00 Open: Mid MAR - OCT
Map ref no. 36

Elsie Hunter
Easter Glentore Farmhouse Slamannan Road
Greengairs Airdrie ML6 7TJ   Lanarkshire
Tel: (01236) 830243   Fax 01236 830243

Near Rd: A.73, B.803
Easter Glentore dates back to 1705 & provides quality
ground-floor accommodation, with 3 delightful bedrooms
with en-suite or private facilities & a tea/coffee tray. Great
care is taken to ensure guests' comfort. Relax & enjoy a
homely atmosphere, home-made shortbread, scones,
cakes & preserves. A choice of breakfasts. Guests' lounge
with panoramic views. A working sheep farm with private
woodlands, ideally situated for Stirling, Glasgow &
Edinburgh, Falkirk Wheel - 8 miles & with easy access to
M.8. M.74, M.9 & M.80. Children over 5.

info@easterglentorefarm.com
www.easterglentorefarm.com £56.00 - £58.00
Open: all year Map ref no. 38

see p.320

Catriona & Willie Dickson
Chipperkyle Kirkpatrick Durham Castle Douglas
DG7 3EY   Kirkcudbrightshire
Tel: (01556) 650223   Fax 01556 650223

Near Rd: A.75
Chipperkyle is a beautiful 18th-century Georgian house,
without a hint of formality. The Dicksons are both engaging
& sociable & will endeavour to make you feel at ease in
their elegant family home. Bedrooms are light & charming,
decorated with cast iron beds, excellent furniture & masses
of books. Drawing room with open log fire. 200 acres of
grazing land with a dog, cats, donkeys & free-ranging hens.
Threave & Logan gardens, Drumlanrig & Culzean castles
are within an easy drive. Golf courses nearby. The place
& the people are simply among the best.

bestbandb@chipperkyle.co.uk www.chipperkyle.co.uk
£90.00 - £90.00 Open: all year
Map ref no. 37

Michael & Barbara Williams
Eaglescairnie Mains Gifford Haddington EH41 4HN
Lothian
Tel: (01620) 810491   Fax 01620 810491

Near Rd: A. 1, B.6368
Eaglescairnie Mains is a beautifully furnished Georgian
farmhouse in the centre of a 350 acre conservation award-
winning working farm - peace & tranquillity yet only 30 mins
from Edinburgh. All the bedrooms enjoy wonderful views
over the garden towards the Lammermuir Hills & there's a
stunning coral-walled sitting room with deep chintz sofas
& a log fire. Play tennis or walk the farm, explore Edinburgh,
play one of the numerous golf courses, sample the golden
liquid from the only lowland whisky distillery, or visit the
Sea Bird Centre or Concorde at the Museum of Flight.

williams.eagles@btinternet.com
www.eaglescairnie.com   £60.00 - £80.00
Open: all year (excl. xmas) Map ref no. 39

Chipperkyle

Kirkpatrick Durham Castle Douglas DG7 3EY

Tel:(01556) 650223 Fax 01556 650223

email:bestbandb@chipperkyle.co.uk www.chipperkyle.co.uk

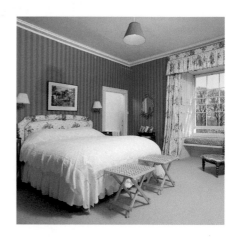

see p.322

Mr & Mrs John Maclean
Westfield House   Nr.Elgin IV30 8XL
Morayshire
Tel: (01343) 547308   Fax 01343 551340

Near Rd: A.96
The Macleans have lived at Westfield House since 1862. The carpet in the hall is clan tartan, the oak stair is hung with portraits, standards & the odd ceremonial sword. The bedrooms are tastefully furnished & are warm & inviting. Guests have their own sitting room & breakfast is served in the large dining room. Dinner is available if ordered in advance. Although, there are lots of good places to eat nearby. The house is situated on the family arable farm. There are walks locally, good beaches nearby & the house is convenient for many golf courses, distilleries & castles.

veronicamaclean@hotmail.com
£80.00 - £80.00 Open: all year (excl. xmas & new year)
Map ref no. 40

Gwen & Michael Stewart
The Pines   Woodside Avenue Grantown-on-Spey
PH26 3JR   Morayshire
Tel: (01479) 872092

Near Rd: A.95
A timeless atmosphere of peaceful tranquillity prevails at this spacious accommodation. Interesting objet d'art, a library, 2 dining rooms serving good country house food increase the sense of heritage in this fine 19th-century Scottish country house. All of the attractive bedrooms have en-suite facilities & their own distinctive style & furnishings. The peaceful, large maturing garden with its small woodland area provides pleasant private walks. Children over 12 years are welcome. Animals by arrangement. A delightful spot in which to relax & unwind.

info@thepinesgrantown.co.uk
www.thepinesgrantown.co.uk   £90.00 - £125.00
Open: mar - oct (& by arrangement)   Map ref no. 42

Val Dickinson
An Cala Guest House   Woodlands Terrace
Grantown on Spey PH26 3JU   Morayshire
Tel: (01479) 873293   Fax 01479 873293

Near Rd: A.95
An Cala is a large comfortable Victorian house retaining many of its original features. Set in 1/2 an acre, there are plenty of on-site parking spaces & gardens to relax in. Overlooked by woods yet within 10 minutes walking distance of the town centre. All rooms have en-suite facilities, doubles are king-size, including a magnificent mahogany 4-poster bed bought from Castle Grant. T.V., tea/coffee, hairdryers etc. in all rooms. Your hosts aim to provide relaxing & comfortable accommodation with lovely gardens to enjoy. Children over 3.

ancala@globalnet.co.uk   www.ancala.info
£56.00 - £62.00 Open: all year (excl. xmas)
Map ref no. 41

Gordon Gaughan
The Lodge House   Crianlarich FK20 8RU
Perthshire
Tel: (01838) 300276   Fax 01838 300276

Near Rd: A.82
Although just by the roadside, The Lodge is secluded & all rooms enjoy an excellent view of the surrounding hills & glens. With only 6 rooms (all of which are comfortable & tastefully furnished), your hosts aim to provide a personal service & compliment this with good Scottish home-cooking. In the small, informal bar, there is an extensive selection of malts for guests to enjoy both before & after dinner. The Lodge House is the perfect location for a relaxing break in this lovely part of Scotland.

stay@lodgehouse.co.uk   www.lodgehouse.co.uk
£55.00 - £55.00 Open: all year
Map ref no. 43

The Pines

Woodside Avenue Grantown-on-Spey PH26 3JR

Tel:(01479) 872092

email:info@thepinesgrantown.co.uk www.thepinesgrantown.co.uk

Mrs Jo Andrew
Letter Farm Loch of Lowes Dunkeld PH8 0HH
Perthshire
Tel: (01350) 724254 Fax 01350 724341

Near Rd: A.923
Situated next to Loch of Lowes Wildlife Reserve, home to nesting osprey, this family-run stock farm is a peaceful haven for guests seeking peace & tranquillity. The accommodation includes 3 attractive & spacious en-suite bedrooms, 1 ground-floor with king-size bed. There is a large guest T.V. lounge, with log fire on cooler evenings. Full breakfast menu with local & homemade produce. Dinner by arrangement. Enjoy afternoon tea on the patio whilst watching the birdlife. Come & treat yourselves to an unforgettable stay. Children over 12.

letterlowe@aol.com www.letterfarm.co.uk
£55.00 - £65.00 Open: MAY - OCT
Map ref no. 44

Elizabeth Sanderson
Tigh Dornie Aldclune Killiecrankie
Pitlochry PH16 5LR Perthshire
Tel: (01796) 473276 Fax 01796 473276

Near Rd: A.9
Tigh Dornie is situated amid beautiful Perthshire scenery, approx 5 miles north of Pitlochry. Offering attractive accommodation in 2 very comfortable & tastefully furnished guest bedrooms, each with an en-suite bathroom, colour T.V. & tea/coffee-making facilities. A good breakfast is served. A warm & friendly welcome is assured from your hosts, who will ensure that your stay is a memorable one. This is an ideal spot for touring Scotland. There is ample car parking. Children over 12 years welcome.

tigh_dornie@btinternet.com
www.btinternet.com/~tigh_dornie/ £50.00 - £54.00
Open: EASTER - OCT Map ref no. 46

see p.324

Gretta & Douglas Maxwell
Craigroyston House 2 Lower Oakfield Pitlochry
PH16 5HQ Perthshire
Tel: (01796) 472053 Fax 01796 472053

Near Rd: A.9
Craigroyston House is quietly situated in its own grounds, this fine Victorian villa has direct access from the grounds to the town centre. The accommodation includes spacious en-suite bedrooms, some with 4-poster beds & original antique pieces, which are beautifully decorated in keeping with the period. So are the comfortable lounge with seasonal log fire & the dining room with views to the south, where guests can enjoy a hearty traditional Scottish breakfast. There is safe off-street parking. A charming home from which to explore this region.

reservations@craigroyston.co.uk
www.craigroyston.co.uk £50.00 - £66.00
Open: all year Map ref no. 46

Sue Mathieson
Easter Dunfallandy House Logierait Road Pitlochry
PH16 5NA Perthshire
Tel: (01796) 474128

Near Rd: A.9, A.924 Perfectly situated in a quiet elevated rural position overlooking the tummel Valley, mountains & Pitlochry. The house is completely non-smoking & all attractive rooms are en-suite with every comfort to make your stay enjoyable. This is the perfect base for touring. Enjoy afternoon tea on arrival, relax in the gardens & prepare yourself for the best breakfast you may ever have eaten in the 19th century dining room, with a range of local produce & Sue's home-made bread & preserves. Come & unwind & enjoy a few days of the Easter Dunfallandy experience. Animals by arrangement.

sue@dunfallandy.co.uk www.dunfallandy.co.uk
£60.00 - £74.00 Open: all year
Map ref no. 46

Easter Dunfallandy House

Logierait Road Pitlochry PH16 5NA

Tel:(01796) 474128

email:sue@dunfallandy.co.uk www.dunfallandy.co.uk

see p.326

see p.327

Mrs Cara Wilson
Creag-Ard House   Lochard Road   Aberfoyle   FK8 3TQ
Stirlingshire
Tel: (01877) 382297   Fax 01877 382297

Near Rd: B.829
Nestling in 3 acres of beautiful gardens, Creag-Ard House, a lovely Victorian home, enjoys some of the most magnificent scenery in Scotland; overlooking Loch Ard with superb views of Ben Lomond in a peaceful setting & yet only 1 mile from Aberfoyle. A warm welcome awaits. A choice of 6 delightful en-suite bedrooms. Enjoy the delicious Scottish breakfast looking out at the views. Private trout fishing & boat hire. Beautiful countryside for walking & cycling. The perfect spot for exploring the Trossachs. Children over 12. Animals by arrangement.

cara@creag-ardhouse.co.uk
www.creag-ardhouse.co.uk   £70.00 - £90.00
Open: mar - oct Map ref no. 47

Laird Andrew Haslam
Culcreuch Castle Hotel & Country Park   Fintry   G63 0LW
Stirlingshire
Tel: (01360) 860555   Fax 01360 860556

Near Rd: A.811, A.81
Retreat to 700 years of history at magical Culcreuch, the ancestral fortalice & clan castle of the Galbraiths, home of the Barons of Culcreuch, & now a country house hotel where the Laird and his family extend an hospitable welcome. Set in 1,600 spectacular acres, yet only 19 miles from central Glasgow & 17 miles from Stirling. 13 well-appointed bedrooms with en-suite or private facilities. 4-poster bedroom supplement. Elegant period-style decor, antiques & log fires. Animals by arrangement.

info@culcreuch.com   www.culcreuch.com
£76.000 - £160.00   Open: ALL YEAR
Map ref no. 48

Creag-Ard House

Lochard Road Aberfoyle FK8 3TQ

Tel:(01877) 382297 Fax 01877 382297

email:cara@creag-ardhouse.co.uk www.creag-ardhouse.co.uk

Culcreuch Castle Hotel & Country Park
Fintry G63 0LW
Tel:(01360) 860555 Fax 01360 860556 email:info@culcreuch.com www.culcreuch.com

Beaumaris Castle
Isle of Anglesey
Wales

Wales

Wales

Wales is a small country with landscapes of intense beauty. In the north are the massive mountains of the Snowdonia National Park, split by chasms & narrow passes, & bounded by quiet vales & moorland. The Lleyn peninsula & the Isle of Anglesey have lovely remote coastlines.

Forests, hills & lakeland form the scenery of Mid Wales, with the great arc of Cardigan Bay in the west.

To the south there is fertile farming land in the Vale of Glamorgan, mountains & high plateaux in the Brecon Beacons, & also the industrial valleys. The coastline forms two peninsulas, around Pembroke & the Gower.

Welsh, the oldest living language of Europe spoken & used, most obviously in the north, & is enjoying a resurgence in the number of its speakers.

From Taliesin, the 6th century Celtic poet, to Dylan Thomas, Wales has inspired poetry & song. Every August, at the Royal National Eisteddfod, thousands gather to compete as singers, musicians & poets, or to listen & learn. In the small town of Llangollen, there is an International Music Eisteddfod for a week every July.

North Wales.

North Wales is chiefly renowned for the 850 miles of the Snowdonia National Park. It is a land of mountains & lakes, rivers & waterfalls & deep glacier valleys. The scenery is justly popular with walkers & pony-trekkers, but the Snowdon Mountain Railway provides easy access to the summit of the highest mountain in the range with views over the "roof of Wales".

Within miles of this wild highland landscape is a coastline of smooth beaches & little fishing villages.

Barmouth has mountain scenery on its doorstep & miles of golden sands & estuary walks. Bangor & Llandudno are popular resort towns.

The Lleyn peninsula reaches west & is an area of great charm. Abersoch is a dinghy & windsurfing centre with safe sandy beaches. In the Middle Ages pilgrims would come to visit Bardsey, the Isle of 20,000 saints, just off Aberdaron, at the tip of the peninsula.

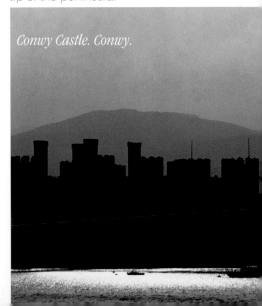

Conwy Castle. Conwy.

Wales

The Isle of Anglesey is linked to the mainland by the handsome Menai Straits Suspension Bridge. Beaumaris has a 13th century castle & many other fine buildings in its historic town centre.

Historically North Wales is a fiercely independent land where powerful local lords resisted first the Romans & later the armies of the English Kings.

The coastline is studded with 13th century castles. Dramatically sited Harlech Castle, famed in fable & song, commands the town, & wide sweep of the coastline.

The great citadel of Edward I at Caernarfon comprises the castle & the encircling town walls. In 1969 it was the scene of the investiture of His Royal Highness Prince Charles as Prince of Wales.

There are elegant stately homes like Plas Newydd in Anglesey & Eriddig House near Wrexham, but it is the variety of domestic architecture that is most charming. The timber-frame buildings of the Border country are seen at their best in historic Ruthin set in the beautiful Vale of Clwyd. Further west, the stone cottages of Snowdonia are built of large stones & roofed with the distinctive blue & green local slate. The low, snow-white cottages of Anglesey & the Lleyn Peninsula are typical of the "Atlantic Coast" architecture that can be found on all the western coasts of Europe. The houses are constructed of huge boulders with tiny windows & doors.

Mid Wales

Mid Wales is farming country where people are outnumbered three to one by sheep. A flock of ewes, a lone shepherd & a Border Collie are a common sight on these green hills. Country towns like Old Radnor, Knighton & Montgomery with its castle ruin, have a timeless quality. The market towns of Rhyader, Lampeter & Dolgellau have their weekly livestock sales & annual agricultural festivals, including the Royal Welsh Show at Builth Wells in July.

This is the background to the craft of weaving practised here for centuries. In the valley of the River Tefi & on an upper tributary of the Wye & the Irfon, there are tiny riverbank mills which produce the colourful Welsh plaid cloth.

Towards the Snowdonia National Park in the North, the land rises to the scale of true mountains. Mighty Cader Idris & the expanses of Plynlimon, once inaccessible to all but the shepherd & the mountaineer, are now popular centres for walking & pony trekking with well signposted trails.

The line of the border with England is followed by a huge earth work of bank & ditch. This is Offa's Dyke, built by the King of Mercia around 750 A.D. to deter the Welsh from their incessant raids into his kingdom. Later the border was guarded by the castles at Hay-on-Wye, Builth Wells, Welshpool, & Chirk which date from mediaeval times.

North from Rhayader, lies the Dovey

Wales

estuary & the historic town of Machynlleth. This is where Owain Glyndwr's parliament is thought to have met in 1404, & there is an exhibition about the Welsh leader in the building, believed to have been Parliament House.

The Cambrian Coast (Cardigan Bay) has sand dunes to the north & cliffs to the south with sandy coves & miles of cliff walks.

Aberystwyth is the main town of the region with two beaches & a yachting harbour, a Camera Obscura on the cliff top & some fine walks in the area.

South Wales

South Wales is a region of scenic variety. The Pembrokeshire coastline has sheer cliffs, little coves & lovely beaches. Most of the area is National Park with an 80 mile foot path running along its length, passing pretty harbour villages like Solva & Broad Haven.

A great circle of Norman Castles stands guard over South Pembrokeshire, Roch, Haverfordwest, Tenby, Carew, Pembroke & Manorbier.

The northern headland of Saint Brides Bay is the most westerly point in the country & at the centre of a tiny village stands the Cathedral of Saint David, the Patron Saint of Wales.

The Preseli Hills hold the vast prehistoric burial chambers of Pentre Ifan, & the same mountains provided the great blue stones used at faraway Stonehenge.

Laugharne is the village where Dylan Thomas lived & worked in what was a boat-house & is now a museum.

In the valleys, towns like Merthyr Tydfil, Ebbw Vale & Treorchy were in the forefront of the boom years of the Industrial Revolution. Now the heavy industries are fast declining & the ravages of the indiscriminate mining & belching smoke of the blast furnaces are disappearing. The famous Male Voice Choirs & the love of rugby football survives.

Cardiff, the capital of Wales, is a pleasant city with acres of parkland, the lovely River Taff, & a great castle, as well as a new civic centre, two theatres & the ultra-modern St. David's Concert Hall. It is the home of the Welsh National Opera. Cardiff - a capital city embracing the 21st century.

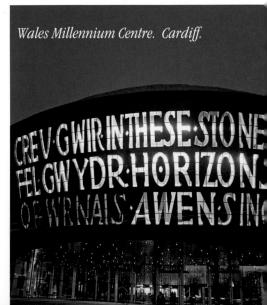

Wales Millennium Centre. Cardiff.

Wales

Wales Gazeteer

Areas of Outstanding Natural Beauty.
The Pembrokeshire Coast. The Brecon
Beacons. Snowdonia. Gower.

Historic Houses & Castles

Cardiff Castle - Cardiff
Built on a Roman site in the 11th century.
Caerphilly Castle - Caerphilly
13th century fortress.
Chirk Castle - Nr. Wrexham
14th century Border Castle. Lovely gardens.
Coity Castle - Coity
Medieval stronghold - three storied round tower.
Gwydir Castle - Nr. Lanrwst
Royal residence in past days - wonderful Tudor
furnishings. Gardens with peacocks.
Penrhyn Castle - Bangor
Neo-Norman architecture 19thC.- large grounds
with museum & exhibitions. Victorian garden.
Picton Castle - Haverfordwest
12th century - lived in by the same family
continuously. Fine gardens.
Caernarfon Castle - Caernarfon
13th century - castle of great importance to
Edward I.
Conway Castle - Conwy
13th C. - one of Edward I's chain of castles.
Powis Castle - Welshpool
14th century. Reconstruction work in 17th
century. Murals, furnishings, tapestries &
paintings, terraced gardens.
Pebroke Castle - Pembroke
12th century Norman castle with huge keep &
immense walls. Birthplace of Henry VII.
Plas Newydd - Isle of Anglesey
18th century Gothic style house.
Home of the Marquis of Anglesey.
Stands on the edge of the Menai Strait looking
across to the Snowdonia Range. Famous for
the Rex Whistler murals.
The Tudor Merchant's House - Tenby
Built in 15th century.
Tretower Court & Castle - Crickhowell

Medieval - finest example in Wales.

Cathedrals & Churches

St. Asaph Cathedral
13th century - 19th century restoration. Smallest
of Cathedrals in England & Wales.
Holywell (St. Winifred)
15th century well chapel & chamber - fine
example.
St. Davids (St. David)
12th century Cathedral - splendid tower - oak
roof to nave.
Gwent (St. Woolos)
Norman Cathedral - Gothic additions - 19th
century restoration.
Abergavenny (St. Mary)
14th century church of 12th century Benedictine
priory.
Llanengan (St. Engan)
Medieval church - very large with original roof &
stalls 16th century tower.
Esyronen
17th century chapel, much original interior
remaining.
Llangdegley (St. Tegla)
18th century Quaker meeting house - thatched
roof - simple structure divided into school room
& meeting room.
Llandaff Cathedral (St. Peter & St. Paul)
Founded in 6th century - present building began
in 12th century. Great damage suffered in
bombing during war, restored with Epstein's
famous figure of Christ.

Museums & Galleries

**National Museum of Wales - Cardiff (also
Turner House)**
Geology, archaeology, zoology, botany,
industry, & art exhibitions.
**Welsh Folk Museum - St. Fagans Castle -
Cardiff**
13th century walls curtaining a 16th century
house. Now a most interesting folk museum.
County Museum - Carmarthen

Wales

Roman jewellery, gold, etc. Romano British & Stone Age relics.

National Library of Wales - Aberystwyth
Records of Wales & Celtic areas. Great historical interest.

University College of Wales Gallery
Aberystwyth Travelling exhibitions of painting & sculpture.

Museum & Art Gallery - Newport
Specialist collection of English watercolours - natural history, Roman remains, etc.

Legionary Museum - Caerleon
Roman relics found on the site of legionary fortress at Risca.

Nelson Museum - Monmouth
Interesting relics of Admiral Lord Nelson & Lady Hamilton.

Bangor Art Gallery - Bangor
Exhibitions of contemporary paintings & sculpture.

Bangor Museum of Welsh Antiquities - Bangor
History of North Wales is shown. Splendid exhibits of furniture, clothing, domestic objects, etc. Also Roman antiquities.

Narrow Gauge Railway Museum - Tywyn
Rolling stock & exhibitions of narrow gauge railways of U.K.

Museum of Childhood - Menai Bridge
Charming museum of dolls & toys & children's things.

Brecknock Museum - Brecon
Natural history, archaeology, agriculture, local history, etc.

Glynn Vivian Art Gallery & Museum - Swansea
Ceramics, old & contemporary, British paintings & drawings, sculpture, loan exhibitions.

Stone Museum - Margam
Carved stones & crosses from pre-historic times.

Plas Mawr - Conwy
A beautiful Elizabethan town mansion house in its original condition. Now holds the Royal Cambrain Academy of Art.

Historic Monuments

Rhuddlan Castle - Rhuddlan
13th century castle - interesting diamond plan.

Valle Crucis Abbey - Llangollen
13th century Cistercian Abbey Church.

Other things to do

Anglesey Angora Workshop - Llangefni - Anglesey
Visit the gentle angora rabbits in all colours and their young. See the clipping of their coat. The yarn from fibre and the exquisitely soft and warm garments made from their coats.

Ewe-Phoria - Corwen - Conwy
Fascinating insight into the work of the shepherd and his sheepdog. Sheepdog demonstrations. Sheep shearing. Meet the lambs and puppies.

Vale of Rheidol Railway - Aberystwyth
One of the Great Little Trains of Wales, was the last steam railway owned by British Rail.

Nash Point. Vale of Glamorgan.

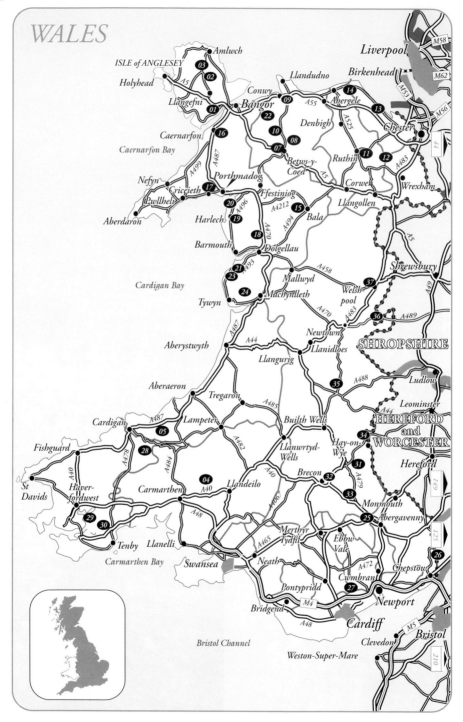

WALES

ISLE of ANGLESEY

Liverpool

Amlwch

Holyhead

Llangefni

Bangor

Caernarfon

Caernarfon Bay

Nefyn

Criccieth

Pwllheli

Aberdaron

Porthmadog

Harlech

Barmouth

Cardigan Bay

Tywyn

Aberystwyth

Aberaeron

Cardigan

Fishguard

St Davids

Haver-
fordwest

Tenby

Llanelli

Carmarthen Bay

Swansea

Bristol Channel

Llandudno

Conwy

Denbigh

Betws-y-
Coed

Ffestiniog

Dolgellau

Mallwyd

Machynlleth

Llangurig

Tregaron

Lampeter

Llandeilo

Carmarthen

Neath

Bridgend

Birkenhead

Abergele

Chester

Ruthin

Corwen

Wrexham

Llangollen

Bala

Welsh-
pool

Shrewsbury

Newtown

Llanidloes

SHROPSHIRE

Ludlow

Leominster

Builth Wells

Llanwrtyd-
Wells

Brecon

Hay-on-
Wye

HEREFORD
and
WORCESTER

Hereford

Merthyr
Tydfil

Ebbw
Vale

Pontypridd

Monmouth

Abergavenny

Cumbran

Chepstow

Newport

Cardiff

Clevedon

Bristol

Weston-Super-Mare

WALES
Map references

01	Roberts	18	Anderson-Kaye	32	P. Jackson
02	Bown	19	Stenberg	33	C. Jackson
03	Hughes	20	Williams	34	Newall
04	Dent	21	Davies	35	Millan
05	Lewis	22	Morgan	36	Bright
07	Betteney	23	Chadwick	37	S. Jones
07	Bidwell	24	Howkins		
07	Howard	25	Harris		
08	Pitman	26	Vrettos		
09	Vaughan	27	Price		
10	Nichols	28	Vickers		
11	J. Spencer	29	Lort-Phillips		
12	Parry	30	Fielder		
13	M. Jones	31	Meredith		
14	Steele-Mortimer				
15	Hind				
16	Bayles				
17	Williamson				

ANGLESEY
FLINTSHIRE
CONWY
DENBIGHSHIRE
WREXHAM
GWYNEDD
CEREDIGION
POWYS
PEMBROKESHIRE
CARMARTHENSHIRE
MONMOUTH-SHIRE
SWANSEA
NEATH & PORT TALBOT
CARDIFF
NEWPORT
VALE OF GLAMORGAN

1 BRIDGEND
2 RHONDA CYNON TAFF
3 MERTHYR TYDFIL
4 CAERPHILLY
5 BLAENAU GWENT
6 TORFAEN

Plas Alltyferin

Pontargothi Nantgaredig Carmarthen SA32 7PF

Tel:(01267) 290662 Fax 01267 290662 email:dent@alltyferin.co.uk www.alltyferin.co.uk

Marian Roberts
Bodlawen   Brynsiencyn   Isle of Anglesey   LL61 6TQ
Anglesey
Tel: (01248) 430379

Near Rd: A.480
A beautiful large house in a glorious location looking onto
Snowdonia & Caernarfon Castle, a short walk to the shore
of the tranquil Menai Strait. Ideally based for touring
Anglesey & the mainland, its sights & beaches. Close to
Plas Newydd (National Trust), the Sea Zoo & the Foel open
farm. All bedrooms have en-suite facilities, colour T.V. &
beverage tray. The lounge & dining room are exquisitly
furnished & there is a grand piano. Your host, Marian, a
well-known soprano soloist, is Welsh speaking & very
welcoming. Children over 7 years.

marion@bodlawen.co.uk   www.bodlawen.co.uk
£55.00 - £60.00   Open: mar - nov
Map ref no. 01

Margaret Hughes
Llwydiarth Fawr Farm   Llanerchymedd   Isle of Anglesey
LL71 8DF   Anglesey
Tel: (01248) 470321/470540

Near Rd: A.55
Secluded Georgian mansion set in 800 acres of woodland
& farmland, with lovely open views. Ideal touring base for
the island's coastline, Snowdonia & North Wales coast.
Offering 3 delightfully furnished bedrooms with en-suite
facilities & T.V.. Full central heating, log fires. Enjoy a 'Taste
of Wales' with delicious country cooking using farm & local
produce. Personal attention & a warm Welsh welcome to
guests, who will enjoy the scenic walks & private fishing
from this award-winning home. Conveniently located for
Holyhead-to-Ireland crossings.

llwydiarth@hotmail.com
www.angleseyfarms.com/llwydia.htm   £70.00 - £80.00
Open: all year   Map ref no. 03

see p.336

Mrs Jane Bown
Drws-Y-Coed   Llannerch-Y-Medd   Isle of Anglesey
LL71 8AD   Anglesey
Tel: (01248) 470473

Near Rd: A.5025, A.55
Enjoy wonderful panoramic views of Snowdonia &
countryside at this beautifully appointed farmhouse on a
large main working farm. It is centrally situated to explore
the island. Comfortable & tastefully decorated/furnished
en-suite bedrooms with all facilities & attention to detail.
An inviting spacious lounge with antiques & log fire. The
excellent breakfasts are served in the cosy dining room.
Grade II listed farm buildings. Pleasant walks. Drws-Y-
Coed is only 25 mins to Holyhead Port.

drwsycoed2@hotmail.com
www.smoothhound.co.uk/hotels/drwsycoed.html
£60.00 - £70.00   Open: all year   Map ref no. 02

Charlotte & Gerard Dent
Plas Alltyferin   Pontargothi   Nantgaredig
Carmarthen SA32 7PF   Carmarthenshire
Tel: (01267) 290662   Fax 01267 290662

Near Rd: A.40
Alltyferin is a classic Georgian country house (Grade II
listed), lying in the hills above the beautiful Towy Valley
overlooking a Norman hill fort & down to the rushing salmon
River Cothi. 2 spacious twin bedrooms, each with en-suite/
private bathroom & stunning views. Guests are welcomed
as friends of the family & encouraged to relax in the drawing
room (log fires in winter) or to wander through 270 acres
of woodland, fields & river valley. Delicious breakfasts
served. Good pubs & restaurants. Castles, beaches, the
National Botanic Garden nearby. Children over 10.

dent@alltyferin.co.uk   www.alltyferin.co.uk
£50.00 - £70.00   Open: all year (excl. xmas)
Map ref no. 04

Wervil Grange Farm
Pentregat Llangranog Llandysul SA44 6HW
TEL:01239 654252

www.bestbandb.co.uk

see p.338

Mrs Ionwen Lewis
Wervil Grange Farm   Pentregat   Llangranog
Llandysul SA44 6HW   Ceredigion
Tel: (01239) 654252

Near Rd: A.487
A warm welcome awaits you at this superb & luxurious
Welsh Georgian farmhouse offering a very high standard
of accommodation. The comfortable farmhouse is
beautifully decorated & furnished, all bedrooms are en-
suite. It is a traditional stock-rearing farm with a flock of
breeding ewes & a herd of Pedigree Welsh Black cattle.
Free fishing on the farm. Only 10 mins' from Llangranog
beach in Cardigan Bay, which is home to the only resident
population of bottle-nosed dolphins in Welsh waters - they
are regular visitors to this part of the coast. Your hosts aim
is to provide you with an unforgettable holiday.

www.bestbandb.co.uk
£60.00 - £60.00   Open: all year
Map ref no. 05

Marion & Bill Betteney
The Acorns Holyhead Road   Betws-y-Coed LL24 0AR
Conwy
Tel: (01690) 710395

Near Rd: A.5
The Acorns offers quality accommodation, & is ideal for a
special break or holiday in this beautiful part of the
Snowdonia National Park. This bed & breakfast suite is of
an open plan design with a king size double bed, lounge
area, dining area, & bathroom. It has been recently
refurbished to a high standard & is tastefully decorated
throughout. A luxury continental style breakfast is provided.
The suite is well equipped with TV, hairdryer etc. A perfect
location for a honeymoon, anniversary, or romantic break.
For stays of 3 nights or more a complimentary bottle of
wine, drinks, & fruit are provided to enhance your stay.

betteneym@aol.com   www.betys-y-coed-breaks.co.uk
£70.00 - £90.00   Open: all year
Map ref no. 07

Mr & Mrs Bidwell
The Courthouse (Henllys) Old Church Road
Betws-y-Coed LL24 0AL Conwy
Tel: (01690) 710534   Fax 01690 710884

Near Rd: A.5
Charming accommodation is provided in this Victorian
property, a former police station & magistrate's court, set
in a peaceful riverside garden within the village. Modern
comforts include colour T.V.s, hospitality trays & en-suite
facilities in every room except the former prison cell, which
has its own private bathroom. Breakfast is served in the
former court room. Bodnant Gardens, Port Meirion,
Snowdon Mountain Railway & the castles of North Wales
are all within easy reach.

gillian.bidwell@btconnect.com
www.guesthouse-snowdonia.co.uk   £54.00 - £80.00
Open: all year   Map ref no. 07

see p.340

Ann Howard
Tan Dinas Country House   Coed Cynhellier Road
Betws-Y-Coed LL24 0BL   Conwy
Tel: (01690) 710635

Near Rd: A.5
A Victorian country house, offering peace, seclusion & a
wonderful view. Surrounded by woodland yet only 500
yds from the village. Start your adventure with a delicious
breakfast, coming home to relax in the comfortable lounge
or retire with a video or book to an attractive, individually
furnished bedroom which is appointed for your comfort.
There are forest walks from house. Tan Dinas is an ideal
touring centre. Ample car-parking. A delightful home for
a relaxing break in Wales.

anntandinas@hotmail.com   www.tandinas.4t.com
£54.00 - £60.00   Open: all year
Map ref no. 07

Tan Dinas Country House

Coed Cynhellier Road Betws-Y-Coed LL24 0BL

Tel:(01690) 710635 email:anntandinas@hotmail.com www.tandinas.4t.com

see p.343

Mr & Mrs P.K. Pitman
Tan-Y-Foel Country House   Capel Garmon
Betws-Y-Coed LL26 0RE   Conwy
Tel: (01690) 710507   Fax 01690 710681

Near Rd: A.470, A.5
Tan-Y-Foel Country House is a personally run bijou house built of magnificent Welsh stone. Set away from traffic in secluded gardens with panoramic views of the rolling countryside to the majestic mountains of Snowdonia. It is elegant & luxurious, with the ultimate in comfort. This contemporary country house offers every 5-star amenity & has been awarded top accolades for its superior cuisine. Tan-Y-Foel is ideal for relaxing or exploring the many famous castles within the beautiful National Park. Children over 7 years are welcome.

enquiries@tyfhotel.co.uk   www.tyfhotel.co.uk
£99.00 - £160.00   Open: jan - nov
Map ref no. 08

Chris & Rosina Nichols
Hafod Country House   Trefriw   Llanrwst LL27 0RQ
Conwy
Tel: (01492) 640029   Fax 01492 641351

Near Rd: B.45106
Set in the lovely Conwy Valley, on the edge of Snowdonia, Yr Hafod (The Summer Dwelling) is a former 17th-century farmhouse, extensively furnished with antiques. The bedrooms each offer a highly individual sense of style & are extremely comfortable. Genuine, warm hospitality at this award-winning hotel is complemented by outstanding food, while drinks can be enjoyed in the oak-panelled bar or in front of a log fire on chilly evenings. Children over 12 years are welcome. Animals by arrangement. A delightful home from which to explore glorious Wales.

hafod@breathemail.net   www.hafodhouse.co.uk
£60.00 - £90.00   Open: mid feb - dec
Map ref no. 10

Michael & Wendy Vaughan
The Old Rectory Country House   Llanrwst Road
Llansanffraid Glan Conwy Conwy LL28 5LF Conwy
Tel: (01492) 580611   Fax 01492 584555

Near Rd: A.470
The Old Rectory country house is set amidst beautiful gardens, overlooking the grand sweep of the Conwy estuary, historic Conwy Castle & the Snowdonia Mountains. The award-winning accommodation includes exquisite guest rooms, furnished with antiques, fine paintings, porcelain & attention to detail. Yet a relaxed atmosphere prevails in this outstanding home. Enjoy a superb Welsh breakfast, before exploring the local area & beyond. Chester, Caernarfon & Betws-y-Coed within easy reach. 3 championship golf courses nearby. Children over 5.

info@oldrectorycountryhouse.co.uk
www.oldrectorycountryhouse.co.uk   £99.00 - £169.00
Open: mid jan - mid dec   Map ref no. 09

see p.342

Jen & Bert Spencer
Eyarth Station Llanfair D. C. Ruthin LL15 2EE
Denbighshire
Tel: (01824) 703643   Fax 01824 707464

Near Rd: A.525
A warm & friendly reception awaits the visitor to Eyarth Station. A super, converted, former railway station located in the beautiful countryside of the Vale of Clwyd. There are 6 comfortable en-suite bedrooms. T.V. lounge, & guests are welcome to use the garden, sun patio & outdoor heated pool. Conveniently located for the many historic towns in the region including Conwy, Caernarfon & Ruthin & their castles, with a medieval banquet 2 mins' drive away. Chester is also within driving distance. 1987 winner of Best Bed & Breakfast Award.

stay@eyarthstation.com   www.eyarthstation.co.uk
£62.00 - £62.00   Open: mar - dec
Map ref no. 11

Eyarth Station

Llanfair D.C. Ruthin LL15 2EE

Tel:(01824) 703643 Fax 01824 707464

email:stay@eyarthstation.com   www.eyarthstation.co.uk

Tan-Y-Foel Country House
Capel Garmon Betws-Y-Coed LL26 0RE
Tel:(01690) 710507 Fax 01690 710681 email:enquiries@tyfhotel.co.uk www.tyfhotel.co.uk

Abercelyn Country House

Llanycil Bala LL23 7YF

Tel:(01678) 521109 Fax 01678 520848

email:info@abercelyn.co.uk www.abercelyn.co.uk

see p.346

Elizabeth A. Parry
Llainwen Ucha   Pentre Celyn   Ruthin LL15 2HL
Denbighshire
Tel: (01978) 790253

Near Rd: A.525
Llainwen Ucha is a working farm set in 130 acres overlooking the very beautiful Vale of Clwyd. Offering 3 pleasantly decorated rooms with modern amenities, & accommodating up to 6 persons. All rooms are centrally heated. Delicious breakfasts made with fresh local produce; vegetarian options are available on request. The farm is conveniently situated for visiting Chester, Llangollen, beautiful Snowdonia & the coast. Offa's Dyke & fishing nearby. Medieval banquets are held at Ruthin Castle throughout the year.

www.bestbandb.co.uk
£40.00 - £44.00   Open: all year (excl. xmas)
Map ref no. 12

N. & M. Steele-Mortimer
Golden Grove   Llanasa   Nr. Holywell CH8 9NA
Flintshire
Tel: (01745) 854452   Fax 01745 854547

Near Rd: A.5151
Beautiful Elizabethan manor house set in 1,000 acres, close to Chester, Bodnant Gardens & Snowdonia, & en route to Holyhead. The Steele-Mortimer brothers & wives, having returned to the family home from Canada & Ireland, provide a warm welcome for their guests at Golden Grove. The menu features home produce, including lamb & game, together with interesting wines & home baking (24hrs advance notice is required.) The atmosphere is friendly & informal. Children over 12 years welcome. Dogs by arrangement. Licensed.

golden.grove@lineone.net   www.bestbandb.co.uk
£90.00 - £90.00   Open: mar - oct
Map ref no. 14

see p.344

Mrs Mary Jones
Greenhill Farm Guest House   Bryn Celyn
Holywell CH8 7QF   Flintshire
Tel: (01352) 713270

Near Rd: A.55
A 16th-century working dairy farm, overlooking the Dee Estuary, which retains its old-world charm, with a beamed & panelled interior. Bedrooms are tastefully furnished, all have either en-suite or private bathrooms. Relax & enjoy typical farmhouse food in the attractive dining room. (Dinner by prior arrangement.) Children's play area & utility/ games room also available. Greenhill Farm is a lovely home,. within easy reach of Chester, the coast & Snowdonia. No single supplement.

mary@greenhillfarm.fsnet.co.uk
www.greenhillfarm.co.uk   £52.00 - £52.00
Open: jan - nov   Map ref no. 13

Mrs Lindsay Hind
Abercelyn Country House   Llanycil   Bala LL23 7YF
Gwynedd
Tel: (01678) 521109   Fax 01678 520848

Near Rd: A.494
Set in award-winning landscaped gardens with its own mountain stream running alongside, this Grade II listed former rectory dates back to before 1729. Situated in the Snowdonia National Park, it is ideally located for walking or touring amongst the spectacular scenery. Bright & spacious en-suite bedrooms with views over Bala Lake, evenings relaxing before open log fires. Delicious breakfasts. Guided walking & outdoor activities available. Also, self-catering traditional cottages.

info@abercelyn.co.uk   www.abercelyn.co.uk
£50.00 - £70.00   Open: all year (excl. xmas)
Map ref no. 15

Golden Grove

Nr. Llanasa Holywell CH8 9NA

Tel:(01745) 854452 Fax 01745 854547 email:golden.grove@lineone.net www.bestbandb.co.uk

see p.348

Richard Bayles
The White House Llanfaglan Caernarfon LL54 5RA
Gwynedd
Tel: (01286) 673003

Near Rd: A.487
The White House is a large detached house set in its own grounds, overlooking Foryd Bay, & with the Snowdonia mountains behind. The accommodation includes 3 tastefully decorated & furnished bedrooms, all with bath or shower, tea/coffee-making facilities & colour T.V. Guests are welcome to relax in the comfortable residents' lounge & gardens & make use of the outdoor pool. The White House is ideally situated for birdwatching, walking, windsurfing, golf & visiting the historic Welsh castles. Animals by arrangement.

RWBAYLES@SJMS.CO.UK   www.bestbandb.co.uk
£51.00 - £51.00 Open: mar - nov
Map ref no. 16

Janet Anderson-Kaye
Plas Dolmelynllyn Hall Ganllwyd Dolgellau LL40 2HP
Gwynedd
Tel: (01341) 440273   Fax 01341 440640

Near Rd: A.470
Dolmelynllyn Hall is an ancient Welsh manor house standing in 3 1/2 acres of delightful gardens & superbly situated above the beautiful Mawddach Valley & Coed y Brenin forest. Offering 9 unique & elegantly decorated bedrooms, including a 4-poster room, with lovely views, & equipped with every comfort. You will be offered warm & gracious hospitality in this immaculate home. Menus feature delicious local ingredients & vegetables from the kitchen garden when in season. The perfect location for a relaxing break in Wales.

info@dolly-hotel.co.uk   www.dolly-hotel.co.uk
£70.00 - £180.00 Open: mar - dec
Map ref no. 18

Sue Williamson
Min-Y-Gaer Hotel Porthmadog Road Criccieth
LL52 0HP   Gwynedd
Tel: (01766) 522151   Fax 01766 523540

Near Rd: A.497
A pleasant, licensed house in a quiet residential area, offering very good accommodation in 10 comfortable rooms, all of which have a bathroom en-suite. All of the bedrooms have colour T.V. & tea/coffee-making facilities. The hotel enjoys commanding views of Criccieth Castle & the scenic Cardigan Bay coastline, & is only 2 mins' walk from the safe, sandy beach. Car parking is available on the premises. A completely no-smoking hotel. This is an ideal base for touring Snowdonia.

info@minygaer.co.uk   www.minygaer.co.uk
£54.00 - £58.00 Open: mar - oct
Map ref no. 17

Bridge & Derek Stenberg
Maelgwyn House Ffordd Isaf   Harlech LL46 2SW
Gwynedd
Tel: (01766) 780087   Fax 01766 780835

Near Rd: A.496
Maelgwyn House, a former Edwardian manse built in 1907, is situated on a massive rock escarpment known as the 'Harlech Dome' 300ft above sea level. It enjoys magnificent views across Tremadog Bay to the Llyn peninsula & Mt Snowdon. The lovely bedrooms have recently been refurbished to a very high standard & are all en-suite. Ideally situated for touring. Maelgwyn House is also only a few minutes walk from the castle & town centre. Children over 14 years welocme.

maelgwyn.harlech@virgin.net
www.maelgwynharlech.co.uk £60.00 - £75.00
Open: all year Map ref no. 19

Plas Dolmelynllyn Hall

Ganllwyd Dolgellau LL40 2HP

Tel:(01341) 440273 Fax 01341 440640

email:info@dolly-hotel.co.uk www.dolly-hotel.co.uk

Deborah Williams
Gwrach Ynys Country Guest House   TalsarnauNr.
Harlech LL47 6TS Gwynedd
Tel: (01766) 780742   Fax 01766 781199

Near Rd: A.496
A warm Welsh welcome awaits you at Gwrach Ynys, a non-smoking, Edwardian country house set in 1 acre of garden, nestled between the sea & the mountains in the beautiful Snowdonia National Park. The accommodation includes 6 en-suite bedrooms, individually decorated & furnished to a high standard. 2 comfortable guest lounges & a separate dining room. Conveniently located for exploring North Wales & an excellent area for ramblers, walkers, birdwatchers & golfers. Close to Harlech Castle, Portmeirion, Ffestiniog Railway, Snowdon, the Royal St. David's golf course & many sandy beaches.

bestbandb@gwrachynys.co.uk www.gwrachynys.co.uk
£56.00 - £70.00 Open: all year (excl. xmas & new year)
Map ref no. 20

Stephanie & Watkin Morgan
Bulkeley Mill   Rowen LL32 8TS
Gwynedd
Tel: (01492) 651052

Near Rd: B.5106
Bulkeley Mill set in Snowdonia National Park combines old charm & modern facilities All of the guest bedrooms are spacious, well equipped & provide en-suite facilities. The double room with balcony overlooks the working waterwheel & historic gardens. The twin room looks onto the gardens & mountains beyond. Through the dining room window the waterwheel slowly rotates against the backdrop of azaleas & hydrangeas. The history, ambience & gently splashing waterwheel will leave you breathless standing still. Bulkeley Mill is an ideal location for a relaxing break amidst the beautiful Welsh countryside.

stephatthemill@bulkeley-mill.wanadoo.co.uk
www.bulkeley-mill.co.uk   £66.00 - £66.00
Open: all year (excl. xmas & new year) Map ref no. 22

Judith Davies
Coed Talon 1 Llwyn Ddu   Llwyrngwril LL37 2JH
Gwynedd
Tel: (01341) 251025

Near Rd: A.493
Coed Talon is situated in the delightful coastal village of Llwyngwril on the edge of the Snowdonia National Park, just minutes from the beach. The house is within easy walking distance of all local amenities which include tea rooms, a craft gallery & a pub. 3 beautifully furnished rooms, 2 en-suite doubles & 1 twin-bedded room with private facilities. All with T.V. , DVD player, hairdryer, clock radio & tea/coffee facilities. A guest lounge in which to relax & a pretty garden. Private parking. Garaging is also available by prior arrangement.

judyd@btinternet.com   www.coedtalon.co.uk
£56.00 - £60.00 Open: all year
Map ref no. 21

Pat Chadwick
Cefn-Coch Country Guest House Llanegryn
Tywyn LL36 9SD Gwynedd
Tel: (01654) 712193

Near Rd: A.493
Cefn Coch is an old coaching inn on the edge of Snowdonia National Park & is situated in over an acre of garden. It has been tastefully renovated throughout to provide quality accommodation. There are 3 attractively furnished period en-suite bedrooms, each room having exceptional mountain views. Also included in the rooms are a range of beverage-making facilities. Only a short distance from some of the most beautiful mountains, beaches & coastline in mid/north Wales. Cefn Coch is a perfect base for exploring the Snowdonia National Park.

pat@cefn-coch.co.uk www.cefn-coch.co.uk
£56.00 - £60.00 Open: all year
Map ref no. 23

The Wenallt

Gilwern Abergavenny NP7 0HP

Tel (01873) 830694

www.bestbandb.co.uk

see p.352

Mrs Jane Howkins
Tan-Y-Coed Isaf Bryncrug Tywyn LL36 9UP
Gwynedd
Tel: (01654) 782639   Fax 01654 782639

Near Rd: A.493
Tan-Y-Coed is a traditional Welsh farmhouse set amidst
stunning scenery in a steep verdant valley between the
mountains of Cader Idris & the beautiful sandy beaches of
Cardigan Bay. Guest enjoy exclusive use of the beamed
dining & sitting room with inglenook fireplace & log fires
on cooler evenings. The south facing en-suite bedrooms,
have every amenity & mountain views overlooking the
terraced garden. Excellent dinners are served by
arrangement prepared by your host - a Cordon Bleu chef.
Children over 12 years.

tanhow@supanet.com   www.tanycoedisaf.co.uk
£50.00 - £60.00   Open: all year
Map ref no. 24

Peter Vrettos
Parva Farmhouse Hotel & Restaurant   Tintern Nr.
Chepstow NP16 6SQ   Monmouthshire
Tel: (01291) 689411   Fax 01291 689557

Near Rd: A.466, M.48
A delightful 17th-century stone farmhouse situated 50 yards
from the River Wye. The quaint en-suite bedrooms, with
their designer fabrics, are gorgeous, & some offer
breathtaking views over the River Wye & woodland. The
beamed lounge, with log fires, leather Chesterfields &
'Honesty Bar', is a tranquil haven in which to unwind.
Mouth-watering dishes, served in the intimate, candlelit
Inglenook Restaurant, reflect the owner's love of cooking.
Parva is a super home, perfect for a relaxing break or for
exploring beautiful Wales.

parva_hoteltintern@hotmail.com
www.hoteltintern.co.uk   £68.00 - £90.00
Open: all year Map ref no. 26

see p.350

B. L. Harris
The Wenallt Gilwern Abergavenny NP7 0HP
Monmouthshire
Tel: (01873) 830694

Near Rd: A.465
The Wenallt is a 16th-century Welsh longhouse set in 50
acres of farmland in the Brecon Beacons National Park &
commanding magnificent views over the beautiful Usk
Valley. Retaining all its old charm, with oak beams &
inglenook fireplace, yet offering a high standard of
accommodation, with attractive en-suite bedrooms, good
food & a warm welcome. The Wenallt is an ideal base
from which to see beautiful Wales & the surrounding areas.
Animals by arrangement.

www.bestbandb.co.uk
£48.00 - £56.00   Open: all year
Map ref no. 25

Mrs Dinah Price
Great House Isca Road Old Village Caerleon
Nr. Newport NP18 1QG Monmouthshire
Tel: (01633) 420216   Fax 01633 423492

Near Rd: A.48
A pretty 16th-century Grade II listed home on the banks of
the River Usk, with clematis garden. Excellent night
stopover for those travelling to Wales & Ireland. Retaining
much of its original character (including beams & inglenook
fireplaces), offering 3 bedrooms with T.V. & tea/coffee. A
drawing room with T.V. & woodburner. Within easy reach
of superb golf course, fishing & forest trails. The ancient
village of Caerleon is very near with its amphitheatre,
museums & Roman Baths. Good pubs. Children over 6.

dinah.price@amserve.net www.visitgreathouse.co.uk
£65.00 - £70.00 Open: all year
Map ref no. 27

Parva Farmhouse Hotel & Restaurant

Tintern Nr. Chepstow NP16 6SQ

Tel:(01291) 689411Fax 01291 689557

email:parva_hoteltintern@hotmail.com www.hoteltintern.co.uk

Diana Vickers
Ailgynnau Abercych Boncath SA37 0HD
Pembrokeshire
Tel: (01239) 842065   Fax 01239 842066

Near Rd: B.4332
Ailgynnau, our family home was built to take advantage of the fabulous views towards the Cych and Teifi valleys. Ailgynnau offers a warm welcome, scrummy traditional Welsh breakfast and other tasty treats. Each of the 3 bedrooms has television, tea and coffee making facilities, an en-suite or private bathroom and the little extras just to make your stay truly memorable. You can also relax on the sun deck & enjoy afternoon tea or a drink in the evening & you may even catch a glimpse of a buzzard or red kite, or one of the many other birds, which frequent the garden. Children over 12 years welcome.

diana@ailgynnau.co.uk   www.ailgynnau.co.uk
£62.00 - £69.00   Open: feb - dec
Map ref no. 28

Joyce Fielder
Old Stable Cottage Picton Terrace Carew
Tenby SA70 8SL   Pembrokeshire
Tel: (01646) 651889

Near Rd: A.4075
The Cottage (Grade II listed), with inglenook fireplace & original bread oven, was once a stable & carthouse to 13th-century Carew Castle situated near the entrance & the creek of Carew River with its Tidal Mill. A spiral staircase leads to 2 charming, oak beamed en-suite bedrooms with colour T.V., home-baked Welsh cakes & tea/coffee-making facilities. Delicious breakfasts are prepared in the lovely farmhouse kitchen on the Aga. A conservatory overlooks the pretty garden. Children over 10 years welcome. There is a good local pub & restaurant offering evening meals, within walking distance.

www.bestbandb.co.uk
£50.00 - £65.00   Open: feb - nov
Map ref no. 30

Mrs Virginia Lort Phillips
Knowles Farm   Lawrenny SA68 0PX
Pembrokeshire
Tel: (01834) 891221

Near Rd: A.4075
A lovely old farmhouse which faces south & overlooks organic farmland & ancient hanging woods. The boundary is the Cleddau Estuary & is a delight to discover. Your hosts can arrange river trips; you can leave the car & walk to castles, pubs, woodland or enjoy the birds & wild flowers. Gardens, galleries, beaches, riding, fishing & ancient monuments nearby. Many good pubs or restaurants offering food, or if you prefer, then enjoy a home-cooked organic meal in front of the fire or in the garden when the weather is fine (by arrangement). Children over 12.

ginilp@lawrenny.org.uk www.lawrenny.org.uk
£54.00 - £65.00 Open: mar - oct
Map ref no. 29

Marion Meredith
Lodge Farm Talgarth Brecon LD3 0DP
Powys
Tel: (01874) 711244   Fax 01874 711244

Near Rd: A.479
The Merediths welcome you to their 18th-century home, sharing its comfort, old family treasures & warm hospitality. Freshly prepared, interesting meals using home & local produce are a speciality & are served in the attractive dining room with original inglenook fireplace & flagstone floor. Cosy en-suite bedrooms. A lounge with T.V., literature & local maps etc to help you make the most of your stay. A large garden in which to relax with mountain views; quietly situated 1 1/2 miles from Talgarth within the Brecon Beacons National Park. Animals by arrangement.

marionlodgefarm@fwi.co.uk www.bestbandb.co.uk
£54.00 - £58.00 Open: all year
Map ref no. 31

Glangrwyney Court

Glangrwyney Crickhowell NP8 1ES

Tel:(01873) 811288 Fax 01873 810317 email:info@glancourt.co.uk www.glancourt.co.uk

Peter & Barbara Jackson
Canal Bank   Ty Gardd   Brecon LD3 7HG
Powys
Tel: (01874) 623464

Near Rd: A.40, A.470
One of a new breed of small, luxury B&B's. Once a row of canal workers' cottages now converted into a stunning home offering 3 stylish bedrooms with relaxing hydrotherapy bathrooms. Peaceful, canal side location just 300 metres to Brecon's historic centre and canal marina. Out of the garden gate you can stroll across the field to the River Usk – famous for it's brown trout and salmon. The emphasis at Canal Bank is definitely on quality, with it's air-spa baths, big comfy beds, goose down duvets and hosts who offer a genuine welcome!

enquiries@accommodation-breconbeacons.co.uk
www.accommodation-breconbeacons.co.uk
£70.00 - £75.00 Open: all year   Map ref no. 32

Sue Newall & Jon Field
The Bear   2 Bear Street   Hay-on-Wye HR3 5AN
Powys
Tel: (01497) 821302

Near Rd: A.438
The Bear is a 16th-century former coaching inn, in the centre of Hay, the famous book town. Attractive & comfortable bedrooms combine ancient beams & panelling with newly refurbished bathrooms. Ideal for book & antique browsers, Hay is also on Offa's Dyke footpath & the Wye Valley Walk; other outdoor activities are offered in this lovely area. Private parking. Luggage transfers & packed lunches available, if booked in advance. There is an excellent choice of restaurants nearby. Children over 9 years by arrangement.

jon@thebear-hay-on-wye.co.uk
www.thebear-hay-on-wye.co.uk   £54.00 - £66.00
Open: all year   Map ref no. 34

see p.354

Mrs Christina Jackson
Glangrwyney Court   Glangrwyney   Crickhowell
NP8 1ES   Powys
Tel: (01873) 811288   Fax 01873 810317

Near Rd: A.40
Glangrwyney Court is a Georgian mansion set in 4 acres of established gardens & surrounded by parkland. All rooms are comfortably furnished with antiques, fine porcelain & paintings, & there is a welcoming & homely atmosphere. Accommodation is in 5 attractive & well-appointed bedrooms, each with a private or en-suite bathroom. During the winter, log fires burn in all the sitting rooms, & in the summer guests are able to relax with a drink in the gardens. Evening meals by arrangement.

info@glancourt.co.uk   www.glancourt.co.uk
£65.00 - £90.00 Open: all year
Map ref no. 33

see p.356

Tony & Anne Millan
Guidfa House   Crossgates   Llandrindod Wells
LD1 6RF   Powys
Tel: (01597) 851241   Fax 01597 851875

Near Rd: A.483, A.44
Stylish Georgian house, with an enviable reputation for it's comfort, award-winning food & service. Excellently located for touring both Wales & the Borders. The individually furnished en-suite bedrooms are all spacious & bright & include many thoughtful extras. A ground floor room is also available. Imaginative meals are prepared by Cordon Bleu trained Anne, accompanied by an excellent wine list. Children over 10. Behind the main house is the Coach House which contains a self-catering unit, ideal for 2 adults.

guidfa@globalnet.co.uk   www.guidfahouse.co.uk
£64.00 - £72.00 Open: all year
Map ref no. 35

Guidfa House

Crossgates Llandrindod Wells LD1 6RF

Tel:(01597) 851241 Fax 01597 851875 email:guidfa@globalnet.co.uk www.guidfahouse.co.uk

see p.358

Gaynor Bright
Little Brompton Farm   Montgomery SY15 6HY
Powys
Tel: (01686) 668371   Fax 01686 668371

Near Rd: A.489
Robert & Gaynor welcome you to this charming 17th-century farmhouse, situated on this working farm. The house has much original character, with beautiful old oak beams. The pretty, comfortable en-suite bedrooms, are enhanced by quality antiques. T.V.. Offa's Dyke runs through the farm. Situated on the B.4385, just 2 miles east of the beautiful Georgian town of Montgomery. Come & be cosseted in old-fashioned comfort with value for money in this peaceful, stress-free countryside. A haven from the hectic life.

gaynor.brompton@virgin.net
www.littlebromptonfarm.co.uk £56.00 - £60.00
Open: all year   Map ref no. 36

Mrs Sue Jones
Lower Trelydan   Guilsfield   Welshpool SY21 9PH
Powys
Tel: (01938) 553105   Fax 01938 553105

Near Rd: A.490
Graham & Sue welcome you to their wonderful, award-winning black-&-white farmhouse, set on their working farm & listed for its history & beauty. The attractive bedrooms are en-suite, tastefully furnished & have colour T.V.. There is an oak-beamed lounge & a dining room where evening meals are served by arrangement. Home cooking is a speciality here. Licensed bar. Powis Castle & many beauty spots are nearby, as well as various leisure activities & walks. Capture the atmosphere of 4 centuries of history in this outstanding house.

stay@lowertrelydan.com   www.lowertrelydan.com
£58.00 - £58.00   Open: all year (excl. xmas & new year)
Map ref no. 37

Lower Trelydan
Guilsfield Welshpool SY21 9PH
Tel:(01938) 553105 Fax 01938 553105 email:stay@lowertrelydan.com www.lowertrelydan.com

Towns & Counties

TOWNS	COUNTY	COUNTRY
Aberfoyle	Stirlingshire	Scotland
Abergavenny	Monmouthshire	Wales
Aboyne	Aberdeenshire	Scotland
Airdrie	Lanarkshire	Scotland
Alnwick	Northumberland	England
Ambleside	Cumbria	England
Ampleforth	Yorkshire	England
Andover	Hampshire	England
Appin	Argyll	Scotland
Arbroath	Angus	Scotland
Arundel	Sussex	England
Ascog	Isle of Bute	Scotland
Ashbourne	Derbyshire	England
Ashford	Kent	England
Aston Cantlow	Warwickshire	England
Axminster	Devon	England
Aylmerton	Norfolk	England
Aylsham	Norfolk	England
Ayr	Ayrshire	Scotland
Bala	Gwynedd	Wales
Bampton	Northumberland	England
Banbury	Oxfordshire	England
Banff	Aberdeenshire	Scotland
Barnstaple	Devon	England
Bath	Somerset	England
Bath	Wiltshire	England
Bedale	Yorkshire	England
Bedford	Bedfordshire	England
Berkhamsted	Hertfordshire	England
Betws-y-Coed	Conwy	Wales
Beverley	Yorkshire	England
Bideford	Devon	England
Bishop Auckland	Durham	England
Bishop's Stortford	Essex	England
Bolney	Sussex	England
Boncath	Pembrokeshire	Wales
Boston	Lincolnshire	England
Bourne	Lincolnshire	England
Bourton-on-the-Water	Glos	England
Bowness	Cumbria	England
Bradford-on-Avon	Wiltshire	England
Brampton	Cumbria	England
Brecon	Powys	Wales
Bridgwater	Somerset	England
Bridlington	Yorkshire	England
Bridport	Dorset	England
Brighton	Sussex	England
Bristol	Gloucestershire	England
Broadford	Isle of Skye	Scotland
Bude	Cornwall	England
Bungay	Suffolk	England
Buntingford	Hertfordshire	England
Burford	Oxfordshire	England
Burley	Hampshire	England
Burrowbridge	Somerset	England
Buttermere	Cumbria	England
Buxton	Derbyshire	England
Caerleon	Monmouthshire	Wales
Caernarfon	Gwynedd	Wales
Callington	Cornwall	England
Cambridge	Cambridgeshire	England
Canterbury	Kent	England

Towns & Counties

TOWN	COUNTY	COUNTRY
Carlisle	Cumbria	England
Carmarthen	Carmarthenshire	Wales
Carnforth	Lancashire	England
Carrbridge	Inverness-shire	Scotland
Castle Douglas	Dumfriesshire	Scotland
Chagford	Devon	England
Cheltenham	Gloucestershire	England
Chelwood Gate	Sussex	England
Chepstow	Monmouthshire	Wales
Chester	Cheshire	England
Chichester	Sussex	England
Chippenham	Wiltshire	England
Chipping Campden	Glos	England
Christchurch	Hampshire	England
Cirencester	Gloucestershire	England
Clitheroe	Lancashire	England
Coalville	Leicestershire	England
Cockermouth	Cumbria	England
Colyton	Devon	England
Conwy	Conwy	Wales
Corfe Castle	Dorset	England
Corsham	Wiltshire	England
Crackington Haven	Cornwall	England
Cranbrook	Kent	England
Cranleigh	Surrey	England
Craven Arms	Shropshire	England
Crediton	Devon	England
Crianlarich	Perthshire	Scotland
Criccieth	Gwynedd	Wales
Crickhowell	Powys	Wales
Cricklade	Wiltshire	England

TOWNS	COUNTY	COUNTRY
Dartmoor	Devon	England
Dartmouth	Devon	England
Daventry	Northants	England
Diss	Norfolk	England
Dolgellau	Gwynedd	Wales
Dorchester	Dorset	England
Dorking	Surrey	England
Dover	Kent	England
Dulverton	Somerset	England
Dumbarton	Dunbartonshire	Scotland
Dumfries	Dumfriesshire	Scotland
Dundonald	Ayrshire	Scotland
Dunkeld	Perthshire	Scotland
Dunster	Somerset	England
Durham	Durham	England
Dursley	Gloucestershire	England
Eastbourne	Sussex	England
Edinburgh	Edinburgh	Scotland
Elgin	Morayshire	Scotland
Ely	Cambridgeshire	England
Ennerdale Bridge	Cumbria	England
Exeter	Devon	England
Exmoor	Somerset	England
Eyam	Derbyshire	England
Fairford	Gloucestershire	England
Falmouth	Cornwall	England
Faringdon	Oxfordshire	England
Faversham	Kent	England
Fintry	Stirlingshire	Scotland
Folkestone	Kent	England
Fordham	Cambridgeshire	England

Towns & Counties

TOWNS	COUNTY	COUNTRY
Fordingbridge	Hampshire	England
Fortwilliam	Inverness-shire	Scotland
Frampton-on-Severn	Glos	England
Gatwick	Surrey/Sussex	England
Girvan	Ayrshire	Scotland
Glastonbury	Somerset	England
Glossop	Derbyshire	England
Gloucester	Gloucestershire	England
Grantham	Lincolnshire	England
Grantown on Spey	Morayshire	Scotland
Grasmere	Cumbria	England
Grimsby	Lincolnshire	England
Haddington	Lothian	Scotland
Hadleigh	Suffolk	England
Hailsham	Sussex	England
Harlech	Gwynedd	Wales
Harrogate	Yorkshire	England
Hartfield	Sussex	England
Haslemere	Surrey	England
Hastings	Sussex	England
Haverfordwest	Pembrokeshire	Wales
Haverhill	Suffolk	England
Hawkhurst	Kent	England
Hawkshead	Cumbria	England
Hay-on-Wye	Powys	Wales
Haywards Heath	Sussex	England
Helmsley	Yorkshire	England
Henley	Oxfordshire	England
Hereford	Herefordshire	England
Hexham	Northumberland	England
Hitchin	Hertfordshire	England
Holsworthy	Devon	England
Holywell	Flintshire	Wales
Hope Valley	Derbyshire	England
Horsham	Sussex	England
Hungerford	Berkshire	England
Hurstpierpoint	Sussex	England
Ilsington	Devon	England
Inverness	Inverness-shire	Scotland
Ipswich	Suffolk	England
Isle of Anglesey	Anglesey	Wales
Isle of Wight	Hampshire	England
Kelso	Roxburghshire	Scotland
Kendal	Cumbria	England
Kentallen of Appin	Argyll	Scotland
Keswick	Cumbria	England
Kettering	Northants	England
Kings Lynn	Norfolk	England
Kingussie	Inverness-shire	Scotland
Kinross	Perthshire	Scotland
Knutsford	Cheshire	England
Launceston	Cornwall	England
Lavenham	Suffolk	England
Lawrenny	Pembrokeshire	Wales
Leamington Spa	Warwickshire	England
Ledbury	Herefordshire	England
Leek	Staffordshire	England
Leominster	Herefordshire	England
Lewes	Sussex	England
Lincoln	Lincolnshire	England
Liskeard	Cornwall	England
Llandrindod Wells	Powys	Wales

Towns & Counties

TOWN	COUNTY	COUNTRY
Llandysul	Ceredigion	Wales
Llanrwst	Conwy	Wales
Llwyrngwril	Gwynedd	Wales
Loch Awe	Argyll	Scotland
Lochgilphead	Argyll	Scotland
Lochwinnoch	Glasgow	Scotland
London	London	England
Longhope	Gloucestershire	England
Looe	Cornwall	England
Ludlow	Shropshire	England
Lydney	Gloucestershire	England
Lyme Regis	Dorset	England
Lymington	Hampshire	England
Lyndhurst	Hampshire	England
Lynton	Devon	England
Maidenhead	Berkshire	England
Maidstone	Kent	England
Malmesbury	Wiltshire	England
Malpas	Cheshire	England
Malton	Yorkshire	England
Malvern	Worcestershire	England
Mansfield	Nottinghamshire	England
Mayfield	Sussex	England
Melton Mowbray	Leicestershire	England
Melton Mowbray	Notts	England
Midhurst	Sussex	England
Minchinhampton	Glos	England
Mitcheldean	Gloucestershire	England
Moffat	Dumfriesshire	Scotland
Mold	Denbighshire	Wales
Montgomery	Powys	Wales
Moreton-in-Marsh	Glos	England
Moretonhampstead	Devon	England
Morpeth	Northumberland	England

TOWNS	COUNTY	COUNTRY
Newark	Nottinghamshire	England
Newbury	Berkshire	England
Newquay	Cornwall	England
Newton Abbot	Devon	England
North Walsham	Norfolk	England
Northallerton	Yorkshire	England
Northleach	Gloucestershire	England
Norwich	Norfolk	England
Nottingham	Nottinghamshire	England
Nuneaton	Warwickshire	England
Oakham	Rutland	England
Oban	Argyll	Scotland
Okehampton	Devon	England
Oswestry	Shropshire	England
Oxford	Oxfordshire	England
Penrith	Cumbria	England
Penzance	Cornwall	England
Petersfield	Hampshire	England
Pewsey	Wiltshire	England
Pickering	Yorkshire	England
Pitlochry	Perthshire	Scotland
Plymouth	Devon	England
Polperro	Cornwall	England
Portree	Isle of Skye	Scotland
Reading	Berkshire	England
Redhill	Surrey	England
Redruth	Cornwall	England
Retford	Nottinghamshire	England
Ripon	Yorkshire	England
Romsey	Hampshire	England
Romsey	Hampshire	England
Ross-on-Wye	Herefordshire	England
Rowen	Gwynedd	Wales
Royal Forest of Dean	Glos	England

Towns & Counties

TOWNS	COUNTY	COUNTRY
Royston	Cambridgeshire	England
Ruthin	Denbighshire	Wales
Rye	Sussex	England
Saffron Walden	Essex	England
Salisbury	Wiltshire	England
Sandy	Bedfordshire	England
Scarborough	Yorkshire	England
Sedbergh	Cumbria	England
Sevenoaks	Kent	England
Sherborne	Dorset	England
Shipton-under-Wychwood	Oxfordshire	
Shrewsbury	Shropshire	England
Sinnington	Yorkshire	England
Solihull	Warwickshire	England
Somerton	Somerset	England
South Brent	Devon	England
South Molton	Devon	England
St. Andrews	Fife	Scotland
St. Austell	Cornwall	England
St. Briavels	Gloucestershire	England
St. Ives	Cornwall	England
Stevenage	Hertfordshire	England
Stirling	Clackmannanshire	Scotland
Stoke Lacy	Herefordshire	England
Stoke-on-Trent	Staffordshire	England
Stow-on-the-Wold	Glos	England
Stratford-upon-Avon	Warks	England
Stroud	Gloucestershire	England
Sturminster Newton	Dorset	England
Tarporley	Cheshire	England
Taunton	Somerset	England
Tavistock	Devon	England
Teignmouth	Devon	England
Tenby	Pembrokeshire	Wales

TOWNS	COUNTY	COUNTRY
Thetford	Norfolk	England
Thornton-le-Dale	Yorkshire	England
Tintern	Monmouthshire	Wales
Tiverton	Devon	England
Tonbridge	Kent	England
Torpoint	Cornwall	England
Torquay	Devon	England
Totnes	Devon	England
Truro	Cornwall	England
Tunbridge Wells	Kent	England
Tywyn	Gwynedd	Wales
Uttoxeter	Staffordshire	England
Wadebridge	Cornwall	England
Wallingford	Oxfordshire	England
Wareham	Dorset	England
Warminster	Wiltshire	England
Wells	Somerset	England
Welshpool	Powys	Wales
Weston-Super-Mare	Somerset	England
Wetherby	Yorkshire	England
Weymouth	Dorset	England
Wheddon Cross	Somerset	England
Whitby	Yorkshire	England
Whitehaven	Cumbria	England
Wimborne	Dorset	England
Winchester	Hampshire	England
Windermere	Cumbria	England
Witney	Oxfordshire	England
Woking	Surrey	England
Woodbridge	Suffolk	England
Worcester	Worcestershire	England
Wrexham	Cheshire	England
Yelverton	Devon	England
York	Yorkshire	England

Recommendations & Complaints

Thank you for taking the time to supply this information. We value your comments & will take appropriate action. We regret we are unable to reply to you individually.

Proproprietors name

Establishment

Address

Please be specific with your comments. State exactly what was right or wrong with your stay e.g. the room, food, house keeping etc.

Date of stay;

Reply to; Best Bed & Breakfast. P.O. Box 31655 London. W11 4WR

Recommendations & Complaints

Thank you for taking the time to supply this information. We value your comments & will take appropriate action. We regret we are unable to reply to you individually.

Propropprietors name
Establishment
Address

Please be specific with your comments. State exactly what was right or wrong with your stay. e.g. the room. food, house keeping etc.

Date of stay;

Reply to; Best Bed & Breakfast. P.O. Box 31655 London. W11 4WR

Recommendations & Complaints

Thank you for taking the time to supply this information. We value your comments & will take appropriate action. We regret we are unable to reply to you individually.

Proproprietors name

Establishment

Address

Please be specific with your comments. State exactly what was right or wrong with your stay e.g. the room, food, house keeping etc.

Date of stay;

Reply to; Best Bed & Breakfast. P.O. Box 31655 London. W11 4WR

Recommendations & Complaints

Thank you for taking the time to supply this information. We value your comments & will take appropriate action. We regret we are unable to reply to you individually.

Propropriertors name
Establishment
Address

Please be specific with your comments. State exactly what was right or wrong with your stay. e.g. the room. food, house keeping etc.

Date of stay;

Reply to; Best Bed & Breakfast. P.O. Box 31655 London. W11 4WR

Recommendations & Complaints

Thank you for taking the time to supply this information. We value your comments & will take appropriate action. We regret we are unable to reply to you individually.

Proproprietors name

Establishment

Address

Please be specific with your comments. State exactly what was right or wrong with your stay e.g. the room, food, house keeping etc.

Date of stay;

Reply to; Best Bed & Breakfast. P.O. Box 31655 London. W11 4WR